Faith in Politics

No account of contemporary politics can ignore religion. The liberal democratic tradition in political thought has long treated religion with some suspicion, regarding it as a source of division and instability. *Faith in Politics* shows how such arguments are unpersuasive and dependent on questionable empirical claims: rather than being a serious threat to democracies' legitimacy, stability, and freedom, religion can be democratically constructive. Using historical cases of important religious political movements to add empirical weight, Bryan McGraw suggests that religion will remain a significant political force for the foreseeable future and that pluralist democracies would do well to welcome rather than marginalize it.

BRYAN T. MCGRAW is Assistant Professor of Politics and International Relations in the Department of Politics and International Relations at Wheaton College.

Faith in Politics

Religion and Liberal Democracy

Bryan T. McGraw

Wheaton College

CAMBRIDGE
UNIVERSITY PRESS

CAMBRIDGE UNIVERSITY PRESS

Cambridge, New York, Melbourne, Madrid, Cape Town, Singapore,
São Paulo, Delhi, Dubai, Tokyo

Cambridge University Press
The Edinburgh Building, Cambridge CB2 8RU, UK

Published in the United States of America by
Cambridge University Press, New York

www.cambridge.org
Information on this title: www.cambridge.org/9780521130424

First published 2010

Printed in the United Kingdom at the University Press, Cambridge

A catalogue record for this publication is available from the British Library

Library of Congress Cataloguing in Publication data
McGraw, Bryan T.
    Faith in politics : religion and liberal democracy / Bryan T. McGraw.
        p.   cm.
    Includes bibliographical references and index.
    ISBN 978-0-521-11333-5 – ISBN 978-0-521-13042-4 (pbk.)
    1. Christianity and politics.   2. Liberalism.   I. Title.
    BR115.P7M318 2010
    322'.1–dc22
    2010011224

ISBN 978-0-521-11333-5 Hardback
ISBN 978-0-521-13042-4 Paperback

To Martha

Contents

Acknowledgements

I first began to conceive of this project nearly a decade ago while sitting in a café in central Krakow, Poland, watching the crowds spill out of the cathedral after a mid-week Mass. It occurred to me that I was in the midst of what many political theorists would consider a tremendous contradiction: a thriving democratic transition coupled with high levels of religious participation. It has been quite a while since then, and I have incurred any number of debts along the way as the project has developed into the book before you.

I owe a great deal to friends and colleagues who had the patience and kindness to discuss my sometimes unorthodox views and offer their critiques, suggestions, and encouragement. Edward Song, Patrick Frierson, Kyla Ebels Duggan, John Michael Parrish, Joseph Coleman, Lucas Swaine, Carla Marie, Ioannis Evrigennis, Ian MacMullen, Sarah Olack, Randy Beck, Philip Munoz, Michael Boda, Kimberly Conger, Micah Watson, Jesse Covington, Paul Brink, Eric Gregory, Randy Boyagoda, and Kevin den Dulk all had a hand in what appears below, even if, of course, they still find it misguided.

The horror stories associated with graduate school and the first few years of the academic career are legion. No one, I think, has less reason to complain than I do, as I have been blessed immeasurably with institutions and faculty who helped shape me (whether they would like to admit it or not) into something approaching a real scholar. Nicholas Wolterstorff first planted the seeds of the book in our discussions during a hot summer in Austin. Grzegorz Ekiert and Dennis Thompson showed tremendous grace in being willing to sit on my dissertation committee and provide great guidance (and critiques). John Tomasi has had a deep and lasting influence on my work and I treasure his kind, yet incisive, questions. Notre Dame's Erasmus Institute was a great place to reconsider where the project was heading, and John Witte offered me a temporary home at Emory's Center for the Study of Law and Religion, without which I doubt I would have finished it as I have. To my former colleagues at Pepperdine and my current ones at Wheaton, my thanks for your support and encouragement.

But my greatest intellectual and academic debt is undoubtedly to Nancy Rosenblum. She took on a graduate student with very little background in political theory and showed me what it meant to be a true scholar. She is the embodiment of what an advisor ought to be, probing and critiquing yet never failing to let me make my own argument. I hope this book does justice to what she has taught me.

Finally, I owe so much to my wife, Martha. She has endured the frustrations of graduate school, dissertation, and book-writing with a kindness and support I do not deserve. It is to her that I dedicate this book.

Introduction

The liberal democratic tradition of political thought has long made religion an important, even central, subject of study and debate. Constructed in part as a means of avoiding the sorts of destructive religious wars that plagued post-Reformation Europe, liberalism[1] has both relied on religious ideals to buttress its claims about human freedom and equality, and treated it as a threatening force, ready to upend political peace for the demands of faith.[2] Among contemporary theorists, recourse to supportive religious doctrines has largely dissipated while the view of religion as incipient threat remains and has even intensified – and perhaps with good reason. Religion may not be alone as a cause, but the deadly conflicts in the Middle East, the former Yugoslavia, Nigeria, and the Indian subcontinent, to take a few examples, are all profoundly tied up with religion. Closer to home, the most contentious issues in American politics – abortion, euthanasia, homosexuality, and so on – all have important religious connections, and liberals and politically organized religious

---

[1] Throughout this work, I use the terms "liberal," "liberal democratic," and "democratic" more or less interchangeably, despite the fact that at least the first and last represent two arguably distinct traditions. I do so since in the contemporary world the traditions have largely merged in defense of a political system that is characterized by the rule of law, defense of individual liberties, representative institutions, and the like. Different theorists will obviously emphasize different elements of the tradition, but it is difficult to find a political theorist who denies the importance of protecting rights or thinks that democratic institutions are not important or salutary. Even theorists who are quite critical of the tradition nonetheless affirm many of its central attributes, though they may do so on distinctly non-liberal grounds. See, for example, John Finnis, *Natural Law and Natural Rights* (New York: Oxford University Press, 1980); Robert P. George, "The Concept of Public Morality," *American Journal of Jurisprudence* 45, no. 17 (2000); Robert P. George, ed., *Natural Law, Liberalism, and Morality: Contemporary Essays* (New York: Oxford University Press, 1996); John Kekes, *Against Liberalism* (Ithaca, NY: Cornell University Press, 1997); John Kekes, *A Case for Conservatism* (Ithaca, NY: Cornell University Press, 1998).

[2] For an example of the former, see Jeremy Waldron, *God, Locke, and Equality: Christian Foundations in Locke's Political Thought* (Cambridge: Cambridge University Press, 2002). He makes the case that Locke's arguments for human equality are inextricably tied to Christian theological claims. This is not to say that claims like human freedom and equality necessarily depend on religious claims, but merely that for some liberal thinkers religious

1

believers almost always seem to find themselves opposed to one another. As Jeff Spinner-Halev has noted, "The religious conservative haunts liberalism today."[3]

In this context liberal political theorists have coalesced around a rough consensus regarding the dangers posed by religion and their possible remedies. Liberals are, of course, often accused of falling decisively short of consensus on pretty much everything, but there is little exaggeration in saying that most liberal thinkers have concluded that constitutional democracies, especially under the kinds of wide moral and religious pluralism evident in modern societies, are made more legitimate, stable, and free when religion is largely excluded from and reshaped to be made more compatible with a just political order. This is nothing entirely new to liberalism and does not, on its own, even indicate hostility to religion per se.[4] Rather, if we think of religion as a "distinctive way of life of communities of followers shaped by their particular system of beliefs and practices that are oriented toward the supernatural,"[5] it is easy to see why liberal theorists might see it as such an especially disruptive force. The supernatural's capacity to inspire (and perhaps even direct) political action with claims of divine sanction and eternal reward and punishment, can quite plausibly be thought to uniquely disturb and destroy

---

beliefs were part and parcel of their intellectual toolkit. For contemporary examples of believers making religious claims for liberal democratic government, see Daniel A. Dombrowski, *Rawls and Religion: The Case for Political Liberalism* (Albany: State University of New York Press, 2001); Nicholas Wolterstorff, "Do Christians Have Good Reasons for Supporting Liberal Democracy?" *Modern Schoolman* 78 (2001). For quite the opposite claim, that Christianity is in particular incompatible with at least one understanding of liberal democratic government, see Robert P. Kraynak, *Christian Faith and Modern Democracy: God and Politics in the Fallen World* (Notre Dame, IN: University of Notre Dame Press, 2001). The examples of the latter, especially in the context of American politics, are legion. See Michelle Goldberg, *Kingdom Coming: The Rise of Christian Nationalism*, 1st. edn. (New York: W.W. Norton & Co., 2006); Damon Linker, *The Theocons: Secular America under Siege*, 1st. edn. (New York: Doubleday, 2006); Kevin P. Phillips, *American Theocracy: The Peril and Politics of Radical Religion, Oil, and Borrowed Money in the 21st Century* (New York: Viking, 2006); Andrew Sullivan, *The Conservative Soul: How We Lost It, How to Get It Back*, 1st. edn. (New York: HarperCollins Publishers, 2006).

[3] Jeff Spinner-Halev, *Surviving Diversity: Religion and Democratic Citizenship* (Baltimore, MD: Johns Hopkins University Press, 2000), 24.

[4] For a distinctly different view, see Stephen L. Carter, *The Culture of Disbelief: How American Law and Politics Trivialize Religious Devotion* (New York: Basic Books, 1993). Even Tocqueville, clearly not hostile to religion, largely fits into this consensus. This does not mean, of course, that hostility to religion plays *no* role in liberal democratic thought. Voltaire's *écrasez l'infâme!* still echoes through a great deal of contemporary thought. See Richard Rorty, "Religion as a Conversation-Stopper," in *Philosophy and Social Hope*, ed. Richard Rorty (New York: Penguin Books, 1999). But this kind of instinctive hostility is not necessary for generating the consensus's arguments.

[5] Christian Smith, ed., *The Secular Revolution: Power, Interests, and Conflict in the Secularization of American Public Life* (Berkeley: University of California Press, 2003), vii.

even well-ordered societies.[6] Religion often has something to say about the sorts of clothes we wear, the food we eat, how we work and rest and play. It makes claims about sex, the nature of reality, and – crucially for our purposes here – about how we are to live together, about our politics. When one group's clear assurance that God has spoken regarding the whole society's common life looks like nonsense or heresy to another group, it is certainly not unreasonable to think that bad things can occur, especially in a world where it has happened (and happens) all too often.

The liberal consensus does more than merely issue jeremiads about the dangers of religion; it offers remedies as well. These remedies appear as a pair of strategies: (1) the construction of a public political order independent of any direct or significant involvement on the part of ecclesial authorities or religiously rooted normative claims; and (2) the reconstruction or reshaping of religious faith and practice to meet the requirements of such an order. The first is the most famous and obvious one. It stands at the very heart of liberal political thought, perhaps best exemplified by Locke's *Letter Concerning Toleration*, where he says, "I esteem it above all things necessary to distinguish exactly the business of civil government from that of religion, and to settle the just bounds that lie between the one and the other."[7] Religion has the "business ... [of] the regulating of men's lives according to the rules of virtue and piety"[8] but without the threat of force. Physical coercion (or the threat of it) lies solely within the purview of the magistrate, who rules over "life, liberty, health, and indolency of body; and the possession of outward things, such as money, lands, houses, furniture, and the like."[9] This is perhaps not quite the "naked public square,"[10] but it is a step in that direction. It is at the very least a claim that political life has ends and purposes separate from religious life and that the latter cannot comprehensively govern the former.[11]

---

[6] See, for example, Rodney Stark, *For the Glory of God: How Monotheism Led to Reformations, Science, Witch-Hunts, and the End of Slavery* (Princeton, NJ: Princeton University Press, 2003). He argues that monotheism has been responsible for enormous wrongs (and enormous progress).

[7] John Locke, *A Letter Concerning Toleration* (Amherst, NY: Prometheus Books, 1990 [1689]), 18.

[8] Ibid., 13.   [9] Ibid., 18.

[10] The phrase is from Richard John Neuhaus, *The Naked Public Square: Religion and Democracy in America* (Grand Rapids, MI: Eerdmans Publishing, 1984).

[11] Though this does not seem to require, as an empirical matter, the "high wall of separation" evidenced in some First Amendment jurisprudence, it does require that religion and politics give each other what Alfred Stepan has called "freedom of movement." See Alfred Stepan, "Religion, Democracy, and the 'Twin Tolerations'," *Journal of Democracy* 11, no. 4 (2000). He points out the seeming compatibility of relaxed religious establishments and democratic regimes, such as the kind found in Great Britain.

The converse, that politics cannot govern religion, is not held quite so comprehensively, or at least it is not as widely and clearly acknowledged. The consensus's second strategy, that religion needs (or might need) some reshaping in order to be compatible with a liberal democratic polity, is what Nancy Rosenblum has called the argument for "congruence."[12] Again, Locke's *Letter*:

[Those] who attribute unto the faithful, religious, and orthodox, that is, in plain terms, unto themselves, any peculiar privilege or power above other mortals, in civil concernments; or who, upon pretense of religion, do challenge any manner of authority over such as are not associated with them in their ecclesiastical communion; I say these have no right to be tolerated by the magistrate; as neither those that will not own and teach the duty of tolerating all men in matters of mere religion.[13]

Stephen Macedo takes this to mean that "Liberal politics cannot leave religion to one side: it cannot altogether leave the soul alone and care only for the body, for the soul and religion need to be shaped in accordance with political imperatives."[14] Liberal democratic societies populated by people with diverse and potentially conflicting ways of life must ensure that citizens have the habits and virtues necessary to sustain such a society. Most obviously, those with theocratic ambitions have to be thwarted. Less obviously, but perhaps just as importantly, so do those whose religious views make them intolerant or "ethically servile."[15] Of course, liberals disagree a great deal on the degree to which religious traditions need to be remade. Macedo's liberal "hegemony" is to be as "gentle" as possible. Others have looked for sweeping transformations in religion, even the replacement of supernatural faiths with a "Religion of Humanity," to use Mill's phrase.[16]

Even though Mill's humanistic religion (or Dewey's common faith, for that matter) has hardly swept all before it, both strategies have been remarkably successful in their own way. Though religion continues to be a contentious part of public political life in the United States and elsewhere, the contentiousness is for the most part far removed from the religious conflicts of Europe's sixteenth and seventeenth centuries.

[12] Nancy L. Rosenblum, *Membership and Morals: The Personal Uses of Pluralism in America* (Princeton, NJ: Princeton University Press, 1998).

[13] Locke, *A Letter Concerning Toleration*, 63.

[14] Stephen Macedo, "Transformative Constitutionalism and the Case of Religion: Defending the Moderate Hegemony of Liberalism," *Political Theory* 26, no. 1 (1998): 64.

[15] The phrase is from Eamonn Callan, "Political Liberalism and Political Education," *Review of Politics* 58, no. 1 (1998). See chapter 5 for a discussion.

[16] Cf. John Stuart Mill, *Three Essays on Religion* (Amherst, NY: Prometheus Books, 1998). See also John Dewey, *A Common Faith* (New Haven: Yale University Press, 1991 [1934]).

Religious liberty is a cornerstone of global human rights movements and religion itself has changed, especially with respect to its political commitments. The Catholic Church, as Macedo has pointed out, officially embraced the idea of religious liberty only in the 1960s as it came to understand the benefits of having such liberty and the drawbacks of its absence.[17] If Alan Wolfe is even halfway correct in his descriptions of American religion, then liberalism has been really quite successful.[18] Whatever the inadequacies of the liberal consensus – and the rest of this work will repeatedly press on these points – its successes cannot and should not be blithely disregarded.

And yet. Despite those successes, or perhaps because of them, the consensus's philosophical, moral, and sociological underpinnings have shifted of late, and the question of religion's place in public political life and the accommodation owed to it have once again become live questions. Philosophically, we have witnessed over the past half century or so a real loss of confidence in Reason and especially in its ability to secure a universal or near-universal agreement about the nature of morality or justice (or pretty much anything else, for that matter). We need not even venture into the fever swamps of postmodern thought to see this. In his well-regarded book *Patterns of Moral Complexity*, Charles Larmore argues that we should recognize morality as "a motley of ultimate commitments" and acknowledge that "moral conflict can be ineliminable."[19] The upshot is that morality's heterogeneous status means that many of our conflicts will prove "morally irresoluble" and that the best we can do is to develop, he suggests, neo-Aristotelian practices of judgment that can help us sift through their complexities.[20] My point here is not that Larmore is necessarily right (though I think he is right enough in many respects), but just that he is emblematic of a much broader philosophical trend toward recognizing that even the full and free exercise of reasoned

---

[17] See Stephen Macedo, *Diversity and Distrust* (Cambridge, MA: Harvard University Press, 2001). He rightly emphasizes the importance of the American experience and especially the work of John Courtney Murray to the embrace of religious liberty at Vatican II. It is also true, however, that sufferings of Catholics under communism were just as instructive.

[18] Alan Wolfe, *Moral Freedom: The Impossible Idea That Defines the Way We Live Now*, 1st. edn. (New York: W.W. Norton, 2001); Alan Wolfe, *One Nation, after All: What Middle-Class Americans Really Think About, God, Country, Family, Racism, Welfare, Immigration, Homosexuality, Work, the Right, the Left, and Each Other* (New York: Viking, 1998); Alan Wolfe, *The Transformation of American Religion: How We Actually Live Our Faith* (New York: Free Press, 2003).

[19] Charles E. Larmore, *Patterns of Moral Complexity* (New York: Cambridge University Press, 1987), xi. As an aside, the "can" here is puzzling, since much of the rest of the book is dedicated to the proposition that moral conflict *is* ineliminable.

[20] Ibid., 145.

argument does not lead us to secure and universal agreements about the good, justice, and the like. Locke could rather confidently make "toleration to be the chief characteristical mark of the true church"[21] (an audacious statement when you reflect on the intolerance that has often marked Christianity throughout its history) in large part because he had such confidence in Reason that he was sure that not only could it provide the answers to our most pressing political questions, but that it could even compellingly tell us what to believe in matters of faith as well.[22] We lack that confidence, and with that loss has gone some portion of our capacity to say something persuasively definitive about religion and its relation to modern political life.[23]

On the flip side, moreover, religion has proven itself a vital and sometimes vitally dangerous competitor to liberal democratic government across the globe. Those whom Mark Juergensmeyer has called "religious nationalists" have explicitly denied the consensus's claims and have instead embarked on efforts to establish (or re-establish) religion as the axiological basis for political life.[24] In India, Hindu nationalists loudly proclaim that to be Indian just *is* to be Hindu, with obviously pernicious consequences for India's religious minorities. Nigeria finds its tentatively consolidated democracy buffeted by efforts to impose Islamic *sharia* law in its northern (mostly Muslim) states, and it nearly goes without saying that the radical vision behind al Qaeda and similar Islamist movements does not comport well with liberal democratic government.

In much of the developed democratic world, however, as Jean Bethke Elshtain has noted, genuine theocrats are few and far between, and the

---

[21] Locke, *A Letter Concerning Toleration*, 13.

[22] See John Locke, *The Reasonableness of Christianity: As Delivered in the Scriptures* (New York: Clarendon Press, 1999 [1695]). Jürgen Habermas has, of late, done a great deal of reflection on what it might mean for philosophy to recognize that it operates within a "post-secular" and "post-metaphysical" world. See Jürgen Habermas, "A Conversation about God and the World," in *Time of Transitions*, ed. Ciaran Cronin and Max Pensky (Malden, MA: Polity, 2006); Jürgen Habermas, "On the Relations between the Secular Liberal State and Religion," in *Political Theologies: Public Religions in a Post-Secular World*, ed. Hent De Vries and Lawrence Sullivan (New York: Fordham University Press, 2006); Jürgen Habermas, "Religion in the Public Sphere," *European Journal of Philosophy* 14, no. 1 (2006). I take his claims up in chapter 3.

[23] Judd Owen has penned a thoughtful argument about the dangers that this development poses to liberalism. See J. Judd Owen, *Religion and the Demise of Liberal Rationalism: The Foundational Crisis of the Separation of Church and State* (Chicago: University of Chicago Press, 2001). The fact that he spends chapters attempting to combat it merely serves to prove my point.

[24] Mark Juergensmeyer, *The New Cold War? Religious Nationalism Confronts the Secular State* (Berkeley: University of California Press, 1993); Mark Juergensmeyer, *Terror in the Mind of God: The Global Rise of Religious Violence* (Berkeley: University of California Press, 2000).

likelihood of religious war seems so remote as to be nearly nonexistent.[25] Instead, what we have seen in established democracies is a resurgence of traditionalist religious movements that have eschewed the consensus's emphasis on separation without obviously falling into the theocratic or religious nationalist category. Most prominent, of course, have been conservative Protestants in the United States, whose organizing skills and enthusiasm have translated into real political influence.[26] But they are hardly alone. The Catholic bishops' sharp criticism of Catholic politicians' support of abortion rights (including, of course, the 2004 Democratic presidential nominee) is but a continuation of the bishops' earlier formal statements on nuclear weapons and economic justice in the 1980s. A recent poll showed that only 37 percent of Americans in general were "uncomfortable" with candidates discussing their religious faith, that 68 percent thought that the president ought to have a strong religious faith, and that 53 percent agreed that organized religious groups had a place in politics.[27] What's more, this is not limited to the United States; to the contrary, it truly is a global phenomenon.[28] Rather than quietly accept its

---

[25] Jean Bethke Elshtain, "The Bright Line: Liberalism and Religion," *New Criterion* 17, no. 7 (1999). It is worth noting that Juergensmeyer's cases come almost exclusively from the developing world. There are, perhaps, two exceptions to this observation: radicalized Muslim immigrants and Christian reconstructionists. The former, perhaps more often in Europe than in the United States, are often accused of desiring to implement Islamic states under *sharia* law. For a good consideration of the place of Muslims within European politics see Joel S. Fetzer and J. Christopher Soper, *Muslims and the State in Britain, France, and Germany* (New York: Cambridge University Press, 2005). Within the United States, the "theocratic" accusation is leveled more often at conservative Christian political organizations, and in its more serious forms accuses them of having organizational and intellectual links to self-professed theocrats such as R.J. Rushdoony and Gary North. Such claims seem only marginally persuasive and often turn policy disagreements into something much more fundamental, a mirror, ironically enough, of a significant chunk of Christian Right rhetoric. See the concluding chapter for a relatively short discussion of political Islam and the Christian Right.

[26] Cf. John C. Green *et al.*, eds., *Religion and the Culture Wars: Dispatches from the Front* (Lanham, MD: Rowman & Littlefield, 1996); John C. Green, Mark J. Rozell, and Clyde Wilcox, *The Christian Right in American Politics: Marching toward the Millennium* (Washington, D.C.: Georgetown University Press, 2003); John C. Green, Mark J. Rozell, and Clyde Wilcox, *Prayers in the Precincts: The Christian Right in the 1998 Elections* (Washington, D.C.: Georgetown University Press, 2000); James L. Guth *et al.*, "American Fifty/Fifty," *First Things* 116 (2001); Mark J. Rozell and Clyde Wilcox, *God at the Grass Roots: The Christian Right in the American Elections* (Lanham, MD: Rowman & Littlefield, 1997); Kenneth Wald, Silverman Adam, and Kevin Fridy, "Making Sense of Religion in Public Life," *Annual Review of Political Science* 8 (2005); Clyde Wilcox, *Onward Christian Soldiers? The Religious Right in American Politics* (Boulder, CO: Westview Press, 1996).

[27] Fourth National Survey of Religion and Politics, Bliss Institute University of Akron, March–May 2004. Available at http://pewforum.org (accessed December 2004).

[28] Cf. Paul Freston, *Evangelicals and Politics in Asia, Africa and Latin America* (New York: Cambridge University Press, 2001); Jeffrey Haynes, *Religion in Global Politics* (New York: Longman, 1998); Jeffrey Haynes, *Religion in Third World Politics* (Boulder, CO: Lynne

place in private or social life, religion has re-emerged, for good and ill, as a political force in democratic life.

Political theorists have hardly stood pat while things have changed around them. Taking account of the growing and growingly assertive cultural particularism in modern societies, scholars have warmed to arguments for multiculturalism and greater degrees of political accommodation with pluralism.[29] Consider Rawls' shift from *A Theory of Justice* to *Political Liberalism*, one clearly motivated by an acknowledgement that the claims put forth in *Theory* were "unrealistic" as they unreasonably assumed that every rational person would or could affirm justice as fairness simply on the basis of their common human reason.[30] To the contrary, modern society seems to include a fair number of "reasonable romantics," many affirming some form of religious belief, for whom justice as fairness (as laid out in *Theory*) was in principle unpalatable.[31] Rawls' conclusion was that such principled opposition meant that a society governed by justice as fairness could be open to problems of stability. No *moral* claim could be adduced to persuade the reasonable romantics that they were definitively mistaken in their rejection of comprehensive liberalism. So as with Larmore earlier, Rawls embraced the idea of irresoluble moral conflict, and – again in tandem with Larmore and others – shifted the ground of argumentation into

Rienner Publishers, 1994); Philip Jenkins, *The Next Christendom: The Coming of Global Christianity* (New York: Oxford University Press, 2002).

[29] On multiculturalism and pluralism, see (among many, many others) Monique Deveaux, *Cultural Pluralism and Dilemmas of Justice* (Ithaca, NY: Cornell University Press, 2000); Will Kymlicka, *Multicultural Citizenship: A Liberal Theory of Minority Rights* (New York: Clarendon Press, 1995); Jacob T. Levy, *The Multiculturalism of Fear* (New York: Oxford University Press, 2000); Charles Taylor and Amy Gutmann, *Multiculturalism: Examining the Politics of Recognition* (Princeton, NJ: Princeton University Press, 1994); William A. Galston, *Liberal Pluralism* (Cambridge: Cambridge University Press, 2002); William A. Galston, "Two Concepts of Liberalism," *Ethics* 105, no. 3 (1995); William A. Galston, "Value Pluralism and Liberal Political Theory," *American Political Science Review* 93, no. 4 (1999). Even Brian Barry's quite skillful polemic against multiculturalism ends up, as Jacob Levy has pointed out, conceding in the particulars that political accommodation with demands for legal exemptions on the basis of cultural and religious identity is often a good idea. See Brian M. Barry, *Culture and Equality: An Egalitarian Critique of Multiculturalism* (Cambridge, MA: Harvard University Press, 2001); Jacob T. Levy, "Liberal Jacobinism," *Ethics* 114 (2004).

[30] John Rawls, *Political Liberalism*, 2nd. edn. (New York: Columbia University Press, 1996), xix.

[31] For a pretty clear explanation of the basis for a shift to a "political" liberalism, see Charles Larmore, "Political Liberalism," *Political Theory* 18, no. 3 (1990). The phrase "reasonable romantics" is his. By it he means those people who live lives bounded in some fashion by tradition, culture, or the like, meaning that their non-political lives are illiberal in some fashion, but who are also politically liberal, or at least plausibly so. Alasdair MacIntyre or Charles Taylor would be representative here.

a *political* mode, eventually articulating a political, as opposed to his earlier comprehensive, liberalism.[32]

Though some scholars have rejected the idea, it seems clear to me that Rawlsian political liberalism is a genuine attempt to plumb the capaciousness of liberal democratic political thought, especially in regard to religious believers.[33] The introduction to *Political Liberalism* is shot through with references to religion,[34] and in restating the argument for public reason, he focuses especially on the question of religion:

How is it possible for those holding religious doctrines, some based on religious authority, for example, the Church or the Bible, to hold at the same time a reasonable political conception that supports a reasonable constitutional democratic regime? Can these doctrines still be compatible for the right reasons with a liberal political conception? To attain this compatibility, it is not sufficient that these doctrines accept a democratic government merely as a modus vivendi. Referring to citizens holding religious doctrines as citizens of faith we ask: How is it possible for citizens of faith to be wholehearted members of a democratic society who endorse society's intrinsic political ideals and values and do not simply acquiesce in the balance of political and social forces? Expressed more sharply: How is it possible – or is it – for those of faith, as well as the nonreligious (secular), to endorse a constitutional regime even when their comprehensive doctrines may not prosper under it, and indeed may decline?[35]

Though I shall argue in chapter 4 that his arguments are insufficient to tackling this conundrum, it is clear that a significant motivation for the development of political liberalism is the desire to make more room within the liberal democratic settlement for certain kinds of religious believers, especially those whose faith tends in a "totalistic" or comprehensive direction. The "desecularization of the world"[36] poses a real challenge to the liberal consensus, and whether and how liberalism meets that challenge has important consequences, both practical and theoretical.

---

[32] Ibid.; John Rawls, "Justice as Fairness: Political Not Metaphysical," in *John Rawls: Collected Papers*, ed. Samuel Freeman (Cambridge, MA: Harvard University Press, 1999); Rawls, *Political Liberalism*. For a wholehearted critique, see Brian M. Barry, "John Rawls and the Search for Stability," *Ethics* 105 (1995).

[33] Both Amy Gutmann and Eamonn Callan reject the idea that political liberalism is actually more capacious than comprehensive liberalism, positions that I criticize in chapters 5 and 6. See Eamonn Callan, *Creating Citizens: Political Education and Liberal Democracy* (New York: Clarendon Press, 1997); Amy Gutmann, "Civic Education and Social Diversity," *Ethics* 105 (1995).

[34] See pp. xxv–xxxi, xlv, li.

[35] John Rawls, "The Idea of Public Reason Revisited," *University of Chicago Law Review* 64, no. 3 (1997): 780–81.

[36] Peter L. Berger, *The Desecularization of the World: Resurgent Religion and World Politics* (Washington, D.C.: Ethics and Public Policy Center, 1999).

Practically speaking, for those interested in seeing liberal democratic governments continue to spread across the globe (and stick once they get there), having a clear sense as to the possibilities and limits of religion's place in public life looks quite important. I noted earlier that those whom Juergensmeyer calls "religious nationalists" think of themselves already as viable competitors to liberal democracy. Part of the nationalists' appeal lies in the perception (perhaps quite unfair) that to embrace liberalism is to embrace a kind of atheism or agnosticism. Or, worse yet, it is to embrace a kind of Christianity, since especially in many parts of the Muslim world the separation of religion and state is seen not as the triumph of "secular humanism" (as some religious conservatives in our part of the world might have it) but as a consequence of the Christian heresy.[37] In either case, getting a clearer sense of liberalism's relation to religion ought in turn give us a better grasp on democracy's possibilities and limits.

Less explosively, but contentious nonetheless, it is clear as well that some of the most divisive political issues in the United States owe a large part of their divisiveness to their religious connections. Consider the dissenting opinions of Justices Stevens and Souter in the narrowly decided case *Zelman* v. *Simmons-Harris*.[38] The case involved a publicly funded voucher program for poor children in Cleveland, which critics charged violated the First Amendment's establishment clause because most of the participating students used those vouchers at religious schools. The court, in a 5–4 ruling written by Chief Justice Rehnquist, affirmed the program's constitutionality, largely because the parents and not the state decided where the vouchers would be spent. Justice Stevens objected to the public funding of "religious indoctrination," noting that his views had been affected by "the impact of religious strife on the decisions of our forebears to migrate to this continent, and on the decisions of neighbors in the Balkans, Northern Ireland, and the Middle East to mistrust one another. Whenever we remove a brick from the wall that was designed to separate religion and government, we increase the risk of religious strife and weaken the foundation of our democracy." Justice Souter likewise worried that the voucher program would end up stoking "religious disagreement" that could only threaten the nation's social fabric.[39] Or consider further the reaction to George W. Bush's re-election in November 2004. Garry Wills, an esteemed historian and practicing

---

[37] Mark Juergensmeyer, "Holy Orders," *Harvard International Review* 25, no. 4 (2004); Mark Juergensmeyer, "The New Religious State," *Comparative Politics* 27, no. 4 (1995).

[38] 536 US 639 (2002).

[39] For a quite persuasive critique of this sort of argument, see Richard W. Garnett, *Religion, Division, and the First Amendment* (Notre Dame Law School Legal Studies Research Paper 05–23) (Notre Dame, IN: Notre Dame Law School, 2004).

Catholic, penned what can only be called a rather intemperate essay in *The New York Times* entitled, "The Day the Enlightenment Went Out." Claiming that President Bush's victory depended on the votes of conservative Protestants (alternately described as "fundamentalists" and "evangelicals"), Wills suggested that their religious influence is no less baleful than those that motivated the terrorist attacks on Washington and New York City in September 2001:

> The secular states of modern Europe do not understand the fundamentalism of the American electorate. It is not what they had experienced from this country in the past. In fact, we now resemble those nations less than we do our putative enemies.
>
> Where else do we find fundamentalist zeal, a rage at secularity, religious intolerance, fear of and hatred for modernity? Not in France or Britain or Germany or Italy or Spain. We find it in the Muslim world, in al Qaeda, in Saddam Hussein's Sunni loyalists. Americans wonder that the rest of the world thinks us so dangerous, so single-minded, so impervious to international appeals. They fear jihad, no matter whose zeal is being expressed.[40]

Even taking into account the freshness of the election and granting to Wills (and others) a sincere disappointment over its outcome, such remarks clearly show what a volatile political issue religion and its relation to politics can be. People often overstate the dangers posed by heated rhetoric, but when our public "deliberations" (to use the term loosely) are filled with charges and countercharges across religious divides that accuse one another of infidelity to basic political commitments (as opposed to mere policy disputes), we have good reason to think carefully about the liberal consensus on religion and whether or how it might be revised, both morally and practically.

One way to do this – and it is consistent with what most liberal theorists have done – is to ask: what is it that a liberal political order should reasonably expect of its religious citizens? On the face of it, the question admits of a relatively straightforward answer (and one quite compatible with the consensus): a liberal political order committed to religious freedom, political equality, and the rule of law, among other things, should expect no more and no less than it does of its other citizens. It should expect them to live within properly constituted laws, commit themselves to exercising their civic rights and obligations responsibly, and treat their fellow citizens with reasonableness and respect. This is all, in its way, quite compelling and its wide acceptance a very real political achievement, especially for religious believers. However clever or

---

[40] Garry Wills, "The Day the Enlightenment Went Out," *The New York Times*, November 4, 2001.

sophisticated or profound some might find critiques of liberal orders for their "disciplinary regimes" or "hollow" liberties,[41] and however much believers might declaim the "naked public square,"[42] it is undeniable that liberal democratic polities protect and defend a wider scope of religious liberty than has ever been known to human civilization. No one is in danger of going to the gallows or burning at the stake in Western democracies for having the wrong theological convictions or for refusing to participate in religious worship of a particular type. Religious believers have gained a great deal from the democratic order and should contest its claims with a great deal of care.

But if we think more carefully about the question above – what is it that a liberal political order should reasonably expect of its religious citizens – then things quickly get much more complex and the answers adduced by the consensus much less persuasive. To ask what we might *reasonably* expect of religious citizens contains an important ambiguity, one that engages both moral and empirical criteria. To ask what we may reasonably expect of another is to ask both what we think constitute her moral obligations *and* to implicitly surmise what we take to be her *actual* capabilities. If we think that "ought implies can," then we should be careful to tailor our moral expectations regarding our fellow citizens – religious and otherwise – to empirically reasonable views about how those same citizens might be able to fulfill them. Though a social and political order filled with perfectly altruistic persons would doubtlessly be a better one than any we could nearly imagine, it would be utopian in the worst sense of the word to try and construct an order on the expectation that others would actually *be* consistently altruistic. To consider what we should reasonably expect of religious citizens within liberal democratic orders requires, then, a practice not unlike Rawls' "reflective equilibrium,"[43] considered deliberations that move back and forth between understanding what democracies require philosophically and how those requirements can be reconciled with citizens as they actually are. To perhaps be a bit quick about things, we might say that to understand what we may reasonably expect of religious citizens we just need to follow Rawls' lead and especially his move from *A Theory of Justice* to *Political Liberalism.*

---

[41] See, for example, John Milbank, *Theology and Social Theory beyond Secular Reason* (Oxford and Cambridge, MA: B. Blackwell, 1991). Milbank engages in a rather Foucault-like genealogical expedition as a critique of modern, secular social science, and, by extension, modern liberal society.

[42] Neuhaus, *The Naked Public Square.*

[43] John Rawls, *A Theory of Justice*, rev. edn. (Cambridge, MA: Harvard University Press, 1999), 42–45. See also T.M. Scanlon, "Rawls on Justification," in *The Cambridge Companion to Rawls*, ed. Samuel Freeman (Cambridge: Cambridge University Press, 2002).

There, as I have already mentioned, Rawls shifts at least the basis for the argument in large part, it seems, because the former can no longer secure (if it ever could) the allegiance of a significant number of citizens who appear politically quite reasonable. And this creates, he argues, problems of "stability" that can only on his terms be remedied in reconceptualizing the grounds of our moral, and thus political, obligations. In this work, I follow Rawls' lead and suggest that combining our moral and philosophical reflections regarding religion's relationship to liberal democratic orders with observations drawn from some pertinent empirical investigations on the same gives us good reasons to think carefully about and adjust what we take to be citizens' moral obligations and our concurrent expectations therein. That is, once we consider what we take to be morally and philosophically reasonable about citizens' obligations and get a clearer picture of how it is that religious citizens actually *do* engage politically in liberal democratic orders, we might reconsider what it is that we may reasonably expect of them in the first place.

How to do this? Though Rawls lays out for us a general framework, or perhaps procedure, that suggests means for integrating moral and empirical reflection, in the particulars he turns out to be not all that much help to us. There seems to be little in his published work that directs the reader to the sort of evidence he might have found persuasive in reformulating his political theory, and, indeed, he even seems to boast a bit about the "ideal" nature of his work, refusing in the introduction to the paperback edition of *Political Liberalism* to "apologize" for the "abstract and [unworldly] nature of [*Political Liberalism* and *A Theory of Justice*]."[44] Others are similarly unhelpful. Macedo, for example, in the course of an argument for allowing the state to interfere with the transmission of religious beliefs from parent to child for civic education purposes, deigns to dig too deeply into what John Tomasi calls the "sandy empirical terrain" of the intersection of theoretical reflection and empirical observations.[45] Ian Shapiro has famously (and sharply) castigated political theorists for *not* engaging empirical evidence enough.[46]

But a great deal of other work *does* combine empirical and moral reflection, often to real effect. Amy Gutmann's claim that the Supreme Court

---

[44] Rawls, *Political Liberalism*, lxii. The text actually says "unwordly" but I assume that is simply a misprint, since Rawls' texts are anything but "un-wordy." He makes this sort of claim in spite of the fact that *Political Liberalism* is itself, he says, a product of precisely the sort of "reflective equilibrium" I noted above.

[45] Stephen Macedo, "Liberal Civic Education and Religious Fundamentalism: The Case of God v. John Rawls?" *Ethics* 105, no. 3 (1995): 485; John Tomasi, *Liberalism Beyond Justice* (Princeton, NJ: Princeton University Press, 2001), 16.

[46] Ian Shapiro, *The State of Democratic Theory* (Princeton, NJ: Princeton University Press, 2003).

was wrong to allow the Wisconsin Amish to withdraw their children from school at age fourteen largely hangs on whether another two years of high school makes someone significantly more tolerant or not.[47] Eamonn Callan suggests that the psychological and moral capacities necessary to living in a liberal political society powerfully incline individuals – as an empirical, not moral matter – toward a comprehensive morally autonomous perspective.[48] Jeff Spinner-Halev's premises his attempt to carve out a more generous space for conservative religious groups on the sociologically grounded idea that simply living in a pluralistic society is sufficient for developing the proper civic capacities a liberal polity demands.[49] In criticizing what he calls the "argument from Bosnia," Christopher Eberle points out that of the numerous philosophers and political theorists who darkly warn of religion's incendiary political effects, none has to date done any serious empirical work to back up such claims.[50] Though it seems reasonably clear that religion's entrance into political life does have such potential in some societies – say, in Israel and Palestine or perhaps India – that does not then mean that religion has such potential everywhere and to suggest otherwise is simply "dystopian."[51] Similarly, Paul Weithman employs empirical studies to suggest that the view of citizenship that the liberal consensus offers (e.g. that we view our role as citizens separate from our other, including religious, selves) is not just implausible philosophically, but an inaccurate picture of how many good and reasonable citizens actually do think about their citizenship.[52]

Usually, though, works in political theory and political philosophy do not employ empirical evidence, and when they do, do so without a great deal of systematization. They might *illustrate* their arguments with empirical cases, but all too rarely do theorists actually seem to build their arguments *out of* such evidence. There are good reasons for this

---

[47] Gutmann, "Civic Education and Social Diversity," 567. Gutmann adduces a number of quite strong moral reasons as well, of course.

[48] Callan, *Creating Citizens*; Callan, "Political Liberalism and Political Education."

[49] Spinner-Halev, *Surviving Diversity: Religion and Democratic Citizenship*. Someone living in a more homogeneous society would have fewer opportunities for being exposed to different cultural and moral orientations and would, it seems, be a less plausible candidate for the kind of accommodations he recommends.

[50] Christopher J. Eberle, *Religious Conviction in Liberal Politics* (New York: Cambridge University Press, 2002), 160.

[51] Ibid., 163.

[52] Paul J. Weithman, *Religion and the Obligations of Citizenship* (Cambridge: Cambridge University Press, 2002). As a side-note, this work represents a shift for Weithman, who just a few years ago defended Rawls' claims against many of these same sorts of critiques. See Paul J. Weithman, "Religion and the Liberalism of Reasoned Respect," in *Religion and Contemporary Liberalism*, ed. Paul J. Weithman (Notre Dame, IN: University of Notre Dame Press, 1997).

reluctance. First, and perhaps most importantly, it is quite difficult to match up concepts used by normative theorists and empirically minded social scientists. For example, when Rawls talks about "stability" he has a great deal more in mind than merely the absence of civil strife. He means something along the lines of a political order consistently endorsed by the vast majority of citizens on the basis of a certain class of moral reasons. A lack of civil strife is partially indicative of "stability," but is certainly not the whole of it, nor does such a concept subject itself easily to empirical operationalization. Additionally, while social science can do a great deal to illuminate how things are and even how they came to be, it is much less effective in ascertaining where things will go, at prediction. Normative theorizing inevitably involves pointing at where things *should* go, and while all but the most idealist thinkers will recognize that such theorizing ought to remain in the realm of the possible, the limits of the possible are, of course, much disputed and only partly illuminated by empirical work – precisely because social science can see only darkly what might lie ahead. Even if we agree that "ought implies can" and thus that the "can" limits the "ought," getting widespread agreement on what constitutes our proper empirical expectations seems unlikely, or at the very least open to serious reasonable disagreement.

Nonetheless, as I show in the subsequent chapters, the arguments for the liberal consensus compel an entrée into empirical observation, if for no other reason than these arguments are themselves inextricably suffused with empirical claims. We will only be able to know if it is *true* that pluralist liberal democracies are made more stable, legitimate, and free under the terms of the consensus if we engage its moral and philosophical arguments in the context of a solid understanding of the role religion has played in some actually existing democratic (or, as the case may be, democratizing) orders. The historical record cannot simply tell us *normatively* what is reasonable to expect of religious citizens, but in illuminating how religion has impacted those polities it may help provide evidence in favor of or against any particular normative claim.

A generation ago, perhaps, we would have had scant recourse to much reliable empirical evidence regarding religion's impact on democratic politics. The truth of the matter seems to be that most scholars did not think of religion as all that important politically. Or at least, they thought that whatever importance it once possessed had faded along with its followers. Whatever sorts of challenges would be presenting themselves to late modern, postindustrial democracies, the continued pace of modernization and secularization assured that religion would not be among them. The last thirty years have witnessed a "return" of religion to public life, and the quite profound reorientation of scholarship that it has provoked has enlightened us enormously regarding how religion impacts voting behavior, economic choices, normative orientations, and the like. The change has been so great as to produce what we might think of as an embarrassment of riches: religion seems to have a political impact in so many ways and in so many different contexts that its study can prove rather unwieldy, especially when what we are interested in is how such evidence might inform our more central normative arguments. To do that we need some more focused cases hopefully consistent with the wider evidence that will produce the theoretical leverage we need for our more broadly normative arguments.

John Tomasi's *Liberalism beyond Justice* explores the ways in which political liberalism could take account of how political institutions affect citizens' non-political lives, suggesting, a bit whimsically, that we might divide people according to their relationship to the most thoroughgoing sort of liberalism, say one rooted in the thought of Mill or Kant.[53] A-people are comprehensive liberals for whom autonomy and individualism stand at the center of their moral and practical universe. D-people, alternatively, are those committed to an illiberal private life *and* are opposed to even the most basic sorts of liberal democratic claims. Theocrats, I suggest, perhaps most clearly illustrate this category (though those who deny the political equality of women or racial minorities would just as clearly qualify as well). C-people, by contrast, are those who affirm non-public views that liberals (especially "A-people" liberals) find noxious, but whose political views qualify them as citizens in good standing.[54] Even if (and this is Tomasi's example) they think that women should be submissive within the family, they nonetheless think that women should be treated equally politically. Tomasi's work largely focuses on this last category of people, as they might seem to have the most to worry about if liberalism's political ethos "spills over" into private life and threatens to reconstruct that ethos in liberalism's image.

But suppose we push things a bit further and ask about those whom we might call "C-minus"-people. These individuals do not obviously qualify as bad citizens: they accept the rule of law, affirm other citizens as free and equal like themselves, embrace the protections of individual liberties, and the like. But unlike their marginally more liberal cousins, they challenge the liberal consensus's view regarding the political role that their non-public, especially religious, views might play. They are what I

---

[53] Tomasi, *Liberalism beyond Justice*, 17–26.

[54] B-people, who Tomasi supposes make up the majority of Americans, are those who mostly "muddle along" and often find themselves torn between the sorts of things the A-people and C-people believe.

shall call here _religious integrationists_. For these sorts of religious believers, the obligations incurred by their religious faith include the idea that all the spheres of one's life – work, family, community, and so on – should be tied together by and interwoven with one's faith. When deciding what sorts of economic views they ought to hold, how they ought to educate their children, for whom to vote in an upcoming election, or whether they should buy the expensive free-range chicken, these believers feel compelled to make these decisions in the context of, not apart from, their faith. Nicholas Wolterstorff describes them well:

> It belongs to the _religious convictions_ of a good many religious people in our society that _they ought to base_ their decisions concerning fundamental issues of justice _on_ their religious convictions. They do not view it as an option whether or not to do so. It is their conviction that they ought to strive for wholeness, integrity, integration, in their lives: that they ought to allow the Word of God, the teachings of the Torah, the command and example of Jesus, or whatever, to shape their existence as a whole, including, then, their social and political existence. Their religion is not, for them, about _something other_ than their social and political existence; it is _also_ about their social and political existence.[55]

Tomasi is careful to circumscribe his C-people within the contours of those who respect as a matter of course the strictures of political liberalism and especially the divisions it asks them to draw between their public and private views. In the contemporary world, of course, it is often _that_ claim – that those who consciously employ their religious convictions politically do so contrary to their civic obligations – that is at issue in debates surrounding religion's proper role in democratic life. Proponents of "Intelligent Design" and Creationism are pilloried as much for the religious roots of their claims as for the claims themselves; similar criticisms flood public critiques vis-à-vis religiously influenced arguments regarding abortion, embryonic stem cell research, and the like. It is enough on these accounts that religion seems to play some sort of role in their fellow citizens' policy views to brand them "theocrats" and thus rule them (and their arguments) out of bounds morally and politically. If we were to take that to be true and accept that Tomasi's C-people represent the outer limits of reasonable conceptions of democratic citizenship, then much

[55] Robert Audi and Nicholas Wolterstorff, _Religion in the Public Square: The Place of Religious Convictions in Political Debate_ (Lanham, MD: Rowman & Littlefield, 1997), 105. See also Eberle, _Religious Conviction in Liberal Politics_, 140–50. Wolterstorff actually uses the term "integralist." I use the term "integrationist" as I think it captures the phenomena as well as "integralist" and avoids conflation with the late nineteenth- and early twentieth-century use of the "integralist" label, which connoted someone who was profoundly opposed to the whole of liberal institutions. As I try to illustrate, the integrationist is not opposed to liberal institutions, though many liberals will not much like the integrationist's interpretations of what those institutions should be about.

of our inquiry here would be unnecessary. The "C-minus"-people would simply be akin to, if not in fact, theocrats and since theocrats are almost by definition simply incompatible with even the most basic claims of the liberal democratic order, pressing the argument about their relation to the liberal consensus would seem hardly worth the time.[56] But thinking more carefully about things suggests that while it would certainly be right to say that theocrats are a sort of integrationist, they do not exhaust the category – and the liberal consensus is not so easily defended.

Suppose we think, as we should, that it is morally wrong for the state to coerce its citizens into the expression of a religious faith (or, as the case may be, not expressing any faith). The grounds of such a "theocratic mistake" lie in thinking that securing strictly religious goods (say, salvation) lies within the proper purview of political authority. However noble the theocrats' intentions might be, liberals are perfectly right to think them politically out of bounds and to find ways to thwart their political ambitions. As Rawls puts it, "that there are doctrines that reject one or more democratic freedoms is itself a permanent fact of life, or seems so. This gives us the practical task of containing them – like war and disease – so that they do not overturn political justice."[57] But the fact that one is an integrationist does not commit one to being a theocrat. It is perfectly plausible to think that all the spheres of one's life should be organized around the faith without also thinking that the state should employ its coercive force to secure strictly religious goods. Consider two cases from contemporary American politics of what I take to be paradigmatic (if a bit provocative) examples of non-theocratic religious integrationism.

First, consider the US Catholic bishops' argument in their recent statement regarding Catholic politicians who support abortion rights:

In the United States of America, abortion on demand has been made a constitutional right by a decision of the Supreme Court. Failing to protect the lives of innocent and defenseless members of the human race is to sin against justice. Those who formulate law therefore have an obligation in conscience to work toward correcting morally defective laws, lest they be guilty of cooperating in evil and in sinning against the common good ... Catholics who bring their moral convictions into public life do not threaten democracy or pluralism but enrich them and the nation. The separation of church and state does not

---

[56] Though, as Lucas Swaine points out, it might still be the case that liberal orders owe theocrats *reasons*. Lucas Swaine, *The Liberal Conscience: Politics and Principle in a World of Religious Pluralism* (New York: Columbia University Press, 2006). My point is merely that defenders of liberal democratic orders do not need to worry much about the fact that self-professed theocrats find such orders less than amenable to their claims.

[57] Rawls, *Political Liberalism*, 64 fn. 19.

require division between belief and public action, between moral principles and political choices, but protects the right of believers and religious groups to practice their faith and act on their values in public life.[58]

Clearly, there are elements here very much at odds with the liberal consensus, but just as clearly there is nothing here that would suggest the bishops are guilty of making the theocratic mistake. Politics, they claim, should be oriented toward "justice" and the "common good," and there is no suggestion that the bishops wish to secure for themselves any sort of political authority. Rather, they deem themselves "teachers of the Catholic faith and of the moral law" which should be binding on Catholics, both those in and outside of public life, but only as a matter of conscience and without the threat of coercive force.[59] On this account, Catholics ought to be integrationists (of a sort) but there is no claim here that could be deemed theocratic.

Similarly, when the National Association of Evangelicals (NAE) released a manifesto recently attempting to detail what it is that evangelicals actually believe about politics, they too affirmed a responsibility to employ their faith publicly *within* the political context of a liberal democracy:

We engage in public life because God created our first parents in his image and gave them dominion over the earth (Gen. 1:27–28). The responsibilities that emerge from that mandate are many, and in a modern society those responsibilities rightly flow to many different institutions, including governments, families, churches, schools, businesses, and labor unions. Just governance is part of our calling in creation.

We also engage in public life because Jesus is Lord over every area of life. Through him all things were created (Col. 1:16–17), and by him all things will be brought to fullness (Rom. 8:19–21). To restrict our stewardship to the private sphere would be to deny an important part of his dominion and to functionally abandon it to the Evil One. To restrict our political concerns to

---

[58] US Conference of Catholic Bishops, "Catholics in Political Life" (accessed February 2005 at www.usccb.org/bishops/catholicsinpoliticallife.htm).

[59] Ibid. Even the threat to withhold communion or even excommunicate pro-choice public officials does not, I think, make this sort of integrationism theocratic. Any sort of expressive association that organizes itself around a set of moral claims – and religious associations certainly qualify – must, if associational liberty and integrity is to mean anything, be able to set moral standards for membership, and to the degree that such standards include claims that overlap on issues of public concern, these associations seem perfectly within their rights to enforce those standards. As Locke notes in his *Letter*, "no church is bound by the duty of toleration to keep [offenders of ecclesial law] in her bosom" so long as such excommunication does not "deprive the excommunicated person of any of these civil goods that he formerly possessed" (Locke, *A Letter Concerning Toleration*, 26–27). Since no one can be thought to have the "right" to be considered a Catholic in good standing, even if the loss of such recognition means diminished electoral prospects, bishops executing such discipline cannot be thought to have made the theocratic mistake.

matters that touch only on the private and the domestic spheres is to deny the all-encompassing Lordship of Jesus (Rev. 19:16) …

We thank God for the blessings of representative democracy, which allow all citizens to participate in government by electing their representatives, helping to set the priorities for government, and by sharing publicly the insights derived from their experience. We are grateful that we live in a society in which citizens can hold government responsible for fulfilling its responsibilities to God and abiding by the norms of justice.

We support the democratic process in part because people continue to be sufficiently blessed by God's common grace that they can seek not only their own betterment, but also the welfare of others. We also support democracy because we know that since the Fall, people often abuse power for selfish purposes. As Lord Acton noted, power tends to corrupt and absolute power corrupts absolutely. Thus we thank God for a constitutional system that decentralizes power through the separation of powers, fair elections, limited terms of office, and division among national, state, and local authorities.[60]

Clearly, the NAE means to advance an integrationist sort of politics. They claim that "Jesus is Lord over every area of life" and that to pursue ends in the public sphere considered apart from that sovereignty would be to in part deny that faith. But just as clearly they are not advancing a political program that could plausibly be deemed theocratic. Rather, the view on display is that their faith gives them a particular (and particularly good) insight into what the proper political ends are. Now, of course, I have pointed to two thoughtful and relatively considered integrationist arguments, and no doubt others could point to others whose non-theocratic character would be less sure. But as Nancy Rosenblum has noted, in the course of an argument critiquing this approach to politics, these days "[b]elievers seldom advocate the political rule of clergy or the subordination of secular to religious authority … Religious challengers do not necessarily see themselves as antidemocratic."[61] Perhaps more importantly, even if there *are* those religious believers who claim to be organized around non-theocratic ends, but in fact just *are* theocrats (or may be reasonably thought so), this does not at all affect my point. The two examples above speak to the empirical and conceptual *possibility*, even the likelihood given their contemporary political prominence, of a non-theocratic, but robustly religious integrationist politics.

So we can imagine at least as a thought experiment (with some real-world correlatives) non-theocratic integrationists who can plausibly avoid

[60] National Association of Evangelicals, "For the Health of the Nation: An Evangelical Call to Civic Responsibility" (accessed at www.nae.net/images/civic_responsibility2.pdf November 2004).

[61] Nancy L. Rosenblum, ed., *Obligations of Citizenship and the Demands of Faith* (Princeton, NJ: Princeton University Press, 2000), 15.

the theocratic mistake by refusing to conflate the worlds of faith and politics without entirely separating them either. They accept and are willing
to work within established political avenues and eschew the idea that
the state should be in the business of securing strictly religious goods.
In the democratic context, non-theocratic integrationism would accept
"the requirements of constitutional democracy ... defined as a set of
political institutions and practices embodying the principles of popular,
representative, and limited government under the rule of law."[62] But they
would reject the idea that such institutions and practices require a concomitant embrace of the consensus's views on religion and its relation to
public life.

The non-theocratic integrationist may indeed *be* a bad citizen and integrationism threatening to democratic politics, but that needs arguing, for
unlike the theocrat, the non-theocratic integrationist has, it seems, at
least a prima facie claim to qualifying as a reasonable citizen. He then
stands as a potentially sharp and principled challenge to the consensus's
claims and on that score seems to invite especially careful study. If we
want to understand whether the liberal consensus on religion and public
life is well grounded and think that part of how we might come to that
understanding is a careful examination of the empirical evidence regarding religion's *actual* impact on democratic life, then considering how
non-theocratic integrationists relate to democratic political orders would
seem a nearly ideal opportunity. Unlike their theocratic cousins, they do
not obviously run afoul of the strictures of democratic life, but they also
do not fit within the constraints of the consensus. In short, getting empirical evidence regarding how non-theocratic integrationists have actually
impacted democratic life will help greatly in understanding what we may
reasonably expect of religious citizens and whether and how the liberal
consensus might be modified or reconstructed.[63]

---

[62] Jonathan Chaplin, "Can Liberal Democracy Accommodate Religious 'Integralism': A
Dialogue with Nancy Rosenblum," paper presented at American Political Science
Association Meeting, Philadelphia, PA, 2006, 11.

[63] We might think of this as an exercise in what Archon Fung has recently called practical
reasoning regarding a "pragmatic equilibrium." See Archon Fung, "Democratic Theory
and Political Science: A Pragmatic Method of Constructive Engagement," *American
Political Science Review* 101, no. 3 (2007). In this sort of effort (one related to Rawls'
"reflective equilibrium"), we consider how the empirical outcomes of certain institutional arrangements show how those arrangements themselves are effective in reflecting
the normative claims according to which they are purportedly effecting. Fung suggests a
number of ways of evaluating such value-effectiveness, among them expanding the range
of cases or contexts in which they might (or might not) work. In this work, I (loosely)
follow this model, suggesting that by testing the consensus's claims in the context of
some interesting integrationist cases, we discover that the consensus is less persuasive
than many suppose. See the discussion in chapter 1 for more.

Our contemporary world suffers from no lack of possible examples for this sort of integrationist politics, and it might seem natural, even inexorable, to turn our inquiry toward considering cases related to, say, the Catholic Church in America or NAE. But to inquire after the political effects on the American democratic order of Catholic ecclesial mobilization or conservative Protestant political movements poses a number of important problems. First, it is hard to see at this point in time precisely what sorts of effects they might produce. Though Catholic ecclesial organizations have been politically engaged in the United States at least since the middle of the nineteenth century,[64] conservative Protestant groups like the Moral Majority or the Christian Coalition have been active only since the late 1970s. It is simply too early to tell with any assurance what sorts of impacts they might have, though at points we might be able to draw some provisional conclusions. Moreover, it would be difficult to draw any solid conclusions on their impact if for no other reason than we lack any similar cases with which to compare them. America's constitutional order, particularly its federal electoral system, and comparatively broad religious diversity, among other things, make it quite different from its democratic counterparts. This is not to say that there is nothing to be learned from the American experience, but just that thinking we can say something in general about religion's relation to democratic politics on the basis of investigating a small slice of *American* political history should strike us as a mistake. Also problematic would be trying to draw any broad lessons out of investigations into religious political movements in India, Israel, or Turkey, or any number of other contemporary examples. Again, we might be able to make some quite fruitful observations on those particular cases, but the disparities in their political systems, economic development, historical experiences, and constituent religious traditions make empirically grounded inferences difficult to near impossible.

I suggest instead that we can learn a great deal more about religious integrationism's impact on democratic politics by studying a series of case studies of which neither political scientists nor philosophers have much availed themselves. Though many have returned time and time again to Europe's religious wars in the sixteenth and seventeenth centuries as a way of warning about religion's baleful political effects, few have seemingly thought very much about the conclusions we might draw from studying how politically mobilized religion impacted the liberalizing and democratizing polities in much the same portions of Europe

[64] See John T. McGreevy, *Catholicism and American Freedom: A History*, 1st. edn. (New York: W.W. Norton, 2003).

in the late nineteenth and early twentieth centuries. Spurred on by a nineteenth-century brand of (mostly liberal) anti-clerical politics, religious communities in a number of European countries organized socially and politically to build a very successful network of unions, newspapers, farmers' cooperatives, and political parties united by a common religious identity, creating what amounted to an alternative set of civil societies.[65] These were religious integrationists *par excellence*: no area of social, political, or economic life was immune from consideration rooted in religious claims. As Abraham Kuyper, the leader of the Dutch Calvinists' Anti-Revolutionary Party proclaimed, "There is not a square inch in the whole domain of human existence over which Christ, who is sovereign over all, does not cry: 'Mine!'"[66] But they were also not theocrats; Kuyper's newspaper *De Standaard* had as its motto "A Free Church in a Free State." From roughly 1870 to 1930, the most powerful political parties in Belgium, the Netherlands, Germany, and Austria were the ones organized around a particular religious belief and identity. Whether it was Belgium's Catholic Party holding a parliamentary majority from 1884 until after World War I or Germany's (Catholic) Center Party regularly winning a plurality in national elections in the face of a sometimes vicious anti-Catholic campaign, these parties and their affiliated networks of institutions and associations exercised a powerful influence on their respective national political orders and played in particular important roles in those orders' democratic successes and failures.

I will have more to say in chapter 1 about why I think these cases especially useful, but for now simply note that to the degree that these integrationists and their political activity turn out to be compatible with or even beneficial to liberal polities that are legitimate, stable, and free, we will have some quite interesting evidence to count against the consensus. Political parties are ubiquitous in democracies,[67] and remain the primary means through which citizens organize themselves for the acquisition and exercise of democratic political power. They are especially important for consolidating new democracies and sustaining them over the medium

---

[65] Thomas Ertman, "Liberalization, Democratization, and the Origins of a 'Pillarized' Civil Society in Nineteenth-Century Belgium and the Netherlands," in *Civil Society before Democracy: Lessons from Nineteenth-Century Europe*, ed. Nancy Bermeo and Philip Nord (Lanham, MD: Rowman & Littlefield, 2000); Stathis N. Kalyvas, *The Rise of Christian Democracy in Europe* (Ithaca, NY: Cornell University Press, 1996). I will develop out the criteria for what counts as a religious party rather more in chapter 1.

[66] Abraham Kuyper, *Lectures on Calvinism* (Grand Rapids, MI: Eerdmans Publishing, 2000 [1906]).

[67] Seymour Martin Lipset, "The Indispensability of Political Parties," *Journal of Democracy* 11, no. 1 (2000); Elmer Eric Schattschneider, *The Semi-Sovereign People* (New York: Holt, Rinehart, and Winston, 1960).

to long term.[68] *Religious* political parties represent an attempt by religious citizens to organize on the basis of religious belief and identity in order to achieve political goals in large part shaped by those beliefs and identities. No other manifestation of organized religion short of a coercive state church so closely connects religion to the exercise of political power and no other manifestation should therefore stand as so politically dangerous in the eyes of the liberal consensus.

What the evidence gleaned from a comparison of these histories will suggest is that though politically mobilized religion does sometimes pose a very real threat to the establishment and maintenance of democratic politics, it more often does not, and that democratic prospects can actually be improved when religious believers organize themselves socially and politically and press their publicly oriented concerns within institutions of electoral contestation and political deliberation. The very things that (quite reasonably) most worry liberal theorists actually can do the most to promote democratic consolidation, namely: the integrationists' intense (and exclusivist) religious identity and the robust organization and socio-political mobilization of that identity. In other words, these histories show that socially and politically mobilized *sectarianism* can work powerfully to solidify and entrench, not upend and destroy, free and stable democratic institutions. Let me indicate briefly the grounds for such a counterintuitive view.

It seems right to say that being an integrationist in any modern pluralist society does not come easily, even absent any overt anti-integrationist political strategies on the part of the liberal state. The experience of moral and religious pluralism, though it does not itself necessarily compel one to embrace a kind of skepticism or latitudinarianism, does certainly seem to give a psychological shove in that direction.[69] Resisting such a drift requires a concomitant series of supporting institutional structures – schools, media, labor associations, political organizations and the like – all of which go some distance toward insulating the believer and creating what Peter Berger has termed "plausibility structures" of belief.[70] Nothing can guarantee religious belief (or disbelief, for that matter), but it is reasonable to think that people tend to adopt the views that permeate and orient the institutions in which they live, work, play, and worship.

---

[68] Scott Mainwaring, "Party Systems in the Third Wave," *Journal of Democracy* 9, no. 3 (1998); Scott Mainwaring, *Rethinking Parties in the Third Wave of Democratization: The Case of Brazil* (Stanford, CA: Stanford University Press, 1999).

[69] See Christian Smith and Michael Emerson, *American Evangelicalism: Embattled and Thriving* (Chicago: University of Chicago Press, 1998).

[70] Peter L. Berger, *The Sacred Canopy: Elements of a Sociological Theory of Religion* (New York: Anchor Books, 1969).

We might think here of the Amish as an extreme example of what might be required, though with an important caveat. Unlike the Amish, most religious integrationists, especially the sort that concern proponents of the liberal consensus, are not looking to withdraw from modern society as such. Quite the opposite. They wish, in general, to engage the modern world and help shape it in ways compatible with their faith, though, as we will see, this does not commit them to imposing the sort of monistic social and political order incompatible with the fundamental guarantees of liberal democratic politics. Integrationists seem to require both institutions *internal* to their communities as a means of maintaining the faith within a broader pluralist society (schools, media, and so on) and efforts *external* to those communities as a means of making those internal efforts available. To illustrate with education, integrationists seem to need schools that reflect their particular worldview in order to educate their children in the faith *and* political organizations to protect their schools' relative ideological autonomy from the state and perhaps even secure public funding for them.

Generally speaking, when these integrationist institutions and strategies of mobilization worked to democracy's advantage (and they did not always do so), their corresponding *internal* and *external* effects on the prospects for democratic consolidation took certain shapes.[71] Externally, to the degree that that their political mobilization was successful – i.e. they won majorities or pluralities in parliamentary elections – they effectively stymied politically illiberal actions aimed especially at constructing a more nationally cohesive and unified citizenry whose particularist religious beliefs were modulated in favor of a "greater" national identity.[72] This tended, to different degrees, to reshape the developing democratic political system in a structurally pluralist direction, one that reflected reasonably well the respective countries' cultural divisions within the context of a single political order. That is, their political mobilization helped produce stable democracies in which social life was at least partially segmented according to religious or ideological affiliation, and the state accorded its respective subcultures maximally feasible space in which those subcultures could organize themselves largely as they saw fit. The strong institutional linkages within the religious subcultures and common religious identity also tied believers quite tightly to their respective parties, making those parties reliable and reasonable partners

---

[71] My thinking here has been influenced by the discussion in Mark Warren, *Democracy and Association* (Princeton, NJ: Princeton University Press, 2001).

[72] See Charles Glenn, *The Myth of the Common School* (Amherst: University of Massachusetts Press, 1988), for a good discussion about how public schooling was designed precisely with these sorts of goals in mind.

for their opponents, an especially important factor early in the consolidation process (when "commitment problems" are at their greatest) and when these democracies were under threat from radical challengers in the 1920s and 1930s.[73]

These linkages and the religious communities' subcultural organization also had important effects internally, shaping their members' attitudes and civic capacities. One especially interesting feature of the integrationists' institutional arrangements was how they combined strong linkages with a fair degree of tactical autonomy for political elites. The parties themselves were not so much "kings" of their subcultures but instead were tightly integrated into them while also being free to exercise a great deal of prudential judgment regarding how best to pursue the communities' political objectives. Citizens "schooled" in this kind of institutional framework learned to appreciate the distinctiveness of political life, even as their actions insisted that politics was not entirely divorced from their religious concerns. Moreover, the mere fact that these integrationist communities decided to pursue their public objectives via political organization and mobilization in the context of democratic (or at least electoral) politics meant that their members imbibed, as it were, the sense that doing politics just meant contesting elections, petitioning government, debating in parliament, and so on. Finally, to the degree that the integrationists' subcultural communities stretched across other social cleavages like class or ethnicity, what Nancy Rosenblum has called the "experience of pluralism"[74] provided opportunities to appreciate political differences and learn how to cooperate across those differences, even if at the same time they were mobilized politically by what appears to be a quite intense sectarian view.

The upshot is that in ways not all that dissimilar to the evolution of once-revolutionary socialist parties in Europe,[75] these religious integrationists largely found ways to mitigate their own worst temptations and participate in the often contentious and uncertain construction and consolidation of liberal democratic regimes. They made for the most part positive rather than negative contributions to the region's democratizing orders, and while they were far from democratic heroes, the evidence quite strongly suggests that the respective countries' orders would have been less legitimate, less stable, and less free had the religious

---

[73] Subcultural identity went so far in guiding voting behavior that some scholars have likened the voting to censuses as opposed to "real" elections.

[74] Rosenblum, *Membership and Morals*.

[75] Sheri Berman, "Taming Extremist Parties: Lessons from Europe," *Journal of Democracy* 19, no. 1 (2008); Adam Przeworski and John Sprague, *Paper Stones: A History of Electoral Socialism* (Chicago: Chicago University Press, 1986).

communities eschewed social and political mobilization. This suggests, in turn, that to the degree that the liberal consensus rests on the quite plausible supposition that religion poses a dangerous threat to a just and stable democratic political order, we will need to rethink that consensus, perhaps even modifying some of liberalism's most basic philosophical and moral claims along the way.

In chapters 2–6, I explore how this evidence, when combined with philosophical reflection on some of liberalism's most important moral claims, ought to reshape our thinking in just this manner. After explaining in chapter 1 in more detail why I think empirical evidence in general and these cases in particular are helpful for thinking about the consensus, I then take up its claims in two separate parts. In chapters 2, 3, and 4 I focus especially on contemporary liberal arguments regarding political legitimacy and their implications for religious participation in public deliberation. Perhaps no single liberal claim has been as powerful as the one that suggests that political orders must be *justified* to those whom they govern, an idea that means citizens have a set of moral obligations governing the kinds of coercive laws they might propose to their fellow citizens. Some have suggested of late that integral to these obligations are ones concerning the sorts of reasons we might offer for our proposed laws, the idea being that a particular political order could only be justified to its citizens provided that those citizens could affirm for themselves the reasons behind it. What I call *the argument for deliberative restraint* requires that religious citizens avoid (or severely minimize) employing their religious views when deliberating about or participating in political life, since religious views are among the class of views about which we quite reasonably disagree and therefore could not be expected to serve that justificatory role.

Chapter 2 develops the historical and moral claims behind the restraint argument and how it means to rescue political legitimacy from the dangers posed by what Rawls calls "the fact of reasonable pluralism." In chapter 3, I examine the two most important versions of the claim that citizens need to employ secular reasons in public debate, taking up the arguments of Robert Audi and Jürgen Habermas in turn. For Audi, secular reasons are simply more reliable epistemologically than religious ones, and religion's entrance into political life has the effect of being so politically divisive as to risk plunging a polity into civil war, a claim that Christopher Eberle calls the "argument from Bosnia."[76] Audi's arguments suffer on account of epistemological problems, while Habermas' works only to the degree that his rather clear expectations

---

[76] Eberle, *Religious Conviction in Liberal Politics*.

regarding the secularization of the modern world actually hold. Though there is no doubt that the modern world is more secular than medieval Christendom, my European cases serve to reinforce the much broader evidence now generally adduced against the sort of wholesale secularization he seems to depend upon. I argue in contrast that the "desecularization of the modern world"[77] opens up political possibilities heretofore closed off by the expectation that the modern world requires as a matter of course that religion be curtained off from public political life. While it seems correct to say that religion can no longer serve as an axiological basis for political community, it need not resign itself, even in the context of pluralist democracies, to merely being one participant among many within the distinctively non-political civil sphere. Rather, it can – and indeed does – do something rather more robust, undermining the sociological basis for Habermas' normative claims.

The argument for deliberative restraint is, I think, indelibly marked by the interleaving of moral and empirical considerations. Chapter 4 presses this claim further in the context of discussing its most prominent American exponent, John Rawls. Rawls does not entirely rule out religious reasons as such, but instead suggests that conditions of moral and religious pluralism require that citizens *prioritize* public ones. Since citizens may reasonably differ with regard to their religious beliefs (including having no religious beliefs), laws that are ultimately or perhaps even partially dependent on particular religious claims can only be seen by those who do not share those claims to be unjust impositions. Religious believers who respect their fellow citizens properly will then abstain from relying solely or primarily on their religious views and will instead deliberate about political matters on the basis of reasons that citizens may hold in common. Rawls' powerful moral claims depend, I show, on empirically grounded expectations regarding the sort of political order we can reasonably expect, expectations he hopes to be "realistically utopian."[78] In sketching out a comparative history of how Europe's integrationists impacted their respective countries' democratic prospects, I undercut expectations of inevitable religious warfare and show empirically how political legitimacy can coexist with and even be energized by politically mobilized religious movements.

What the integrationists' histories suggest is that the political organization of religion can invest believers in the broader political system while at the same time moderating their political demands. When democratic (or democratizing) societies have significant groups of religious believers

---

[77] Berger, *The Desecularization of the World.*
[78] See his introduction to John Rawls, *Lectures on the History of Political Philosophy* (Cambridge, MA: Harvard University Press, 2007).

whose faith includes a public component (i.e. it has something to say about how social and political institutions ought to be arranged) democratic legitimacy is often better served by integrating those demands within political institutions. More broadly, I suggest here that what finally divides those who think religious reasons may be employed and those who do not is a differing set of expectations about what may be reasonably hoped for regarding political legitimacy. For Rawls and other proponents of deliberative restraint, thinking about our moral obligations as citizens begins with a rather too idealized view of the possibilities of liberal democratic societies, namely, that they can achieve what he terms an "overlapping consensus" of the varied and several worldviews that inhabit any modern democratic order. Though such possibilities are certainly in principle available, we are better off, I think, structuring our political life in ways that take account of the fact that many democratic (and democratizing) societies have significant groups of integrationist-like believers within them, and that to announce and persistently demand that others submit themselves to the obligations of deliberative restraint does little to secure political legitimacy and may do a great deal to undermine it. We are better off with something like what Rawls calls (and thinks insufficient) a constitutional, rather than an overlapping, consensus, and consequently religious believers should not be expected to abide by the putative norms of deliberative restraint.

In chapters 5 and 6, I shift my focus to another pair of arguments, this time about whether religion has pernicious effects on the sorts of capacities and attitudes citizens need in order to make pluralist democracies work. As I noted above, sustaining integrationist communities in pluralist societies is no easy task and seems to require a whole set of institutions and social practices. To this end, the religious communities in these case studies constructed what amounted to an alternative civil society organized around a common religious identity, replete with schools, newspapers, trade unions, employers' associations, and political parties. This was a rather exaggerated institutionalized form of what Christian Smith has dubbed, in describing the strategies of conservative Protestants in the United States, "subcultural distinctiveness."[79] It found its fullest expression in the Netherlands, where for much of the twentieth century Dutch citizens lived largely encapsulated within vertically organized social "pillars."[80] This was integrationism *par excellence*.

---

[79] Smith and Emerson, *American Evangelicalism*. Smith's argument is meant to apply specifically to American evangelicals and explain why it is they do so well in comparison with other religious groups.

[80] The classic American work on this is, of course, Arend Lijphart, *Politics of Accommodation* (New Haven: Yale University Press, 1967). For more detail, see chapter 1.

Liberal theorists have concerns about these sorts of institutional arrangements along two broad lines. In chapter 5, I take up the claim that they damage the prospects for individuals acquiring both personal and political autonomy. The protection and cultivation of individual autonomy has long been seen to be a central liberal value, at least since John Stuart Mill's famous defense, if not before. With the development of political liberalism, however, autonomy's status is less clear, since *political* liberals (as opposed to their "comprehensive" cousins) try to take seriously the notion that it is reasonable for people to live lives that do not embrace Millian individualism. I do three things in chapter 5. I argue, first, that political liberals are largely right to eschew the comprehensive liberal claim that autonomy, strongly understood, constitutes a necessary part of the good life for human beings, and, second, that political liberalism does not itself entail an embrace of comprehensive, as opposed to simply political, autonomy. I then, third, show how the integrationists' social and political institutions are compatible with this understanding of political autonomy, largely absolving the integrationists of the autonomy critique.

In chapter 6, I consider the final major critique leveled at religious believers: that their tendency toward moral absolutism inclines them toward intolerance and, when mobilized politically, such intolerance can and often does create a politics of oppression. Liberals are correct to say, I think, that religious beliefs do incline toward what is perceived as intolerance. Believing in a divine being whose moral law is supreme does make it easier to think that the state ought to enforce things that any liberal regime rightly avoids, such as religious worship. Even if it is the case that skepticism does not necessarily lead you to toleration (since a thoroughgoing skeptic would also have to be skeptical of the value of toleration), there is a kind of psychological affinity between the two and tension between religious belief and toleration. But before condemning the believer as intolerant, we need to understand just what we mean by toleration in general, political toleration in particular, and just how the former is related to the latter. I develop an argument in chapter 6, then, that conceives of toleration as the practice of judgment that we take up when confronted by competing and irreconcilable goods, a practice inevitably marked by imprecision and a profound reliance on experience and historical knowledge.

I then turn to political toleration and argue that political neutrality, conceived as "substantive neutrality," best makes sense of what it is we should expect political toleration to do, namely, provide the maximal feasible space to allow people to live their lives as they see fit. I finally then suggest that though religious integrationists may (and often are) privately intolerant on any number of issues, the European integrationists' histories suggest that their political mobilization may in fact be quite helpful to constructing just such a system of political toleration. In particular, the integrationists' encapsulation and pillarization reduces the demand for having the political system instantiate their particular view of the good – a key factor in producing political oppression – while at the same time giving their political elites the freedom to use their judgment to negotiate with their political opponents. Finally, even to the degree that religion's political mobilization does threaten political oppression, it may simply be an unavoidable risk, one mitigated by the fact that sometimes religion turns out to be crucial in relieving injustice and in making political toleration possible in the first place. The parties in at least the Netherlands and Germany were not organized as an effort to dominate others; rather, they were organized as an effort to protect their respective communities against what they saw as unjust attempts to reconstruct their communities in the image of a particular (political) orthodoxy. If they had not organized, things would have gone much more poorly for those believers, and unjustly so. If toleration is a practice of adjudicating among irreconcilable and competing goods, then constructing a system of political toleration means constructing a system in which politics remains the primary avenue by which societies weigh and judge those goods. Politically organized religion is compatible with this sort of political toleration and at times even productive of it.

I then conclude with some reflections on what a positive alternative to the current liberal consensus might look like. Much of the work here is necessarily negative, criticisms of what I see as the consensus's shortcomings. But as it should be clear from this introduction, the discussion here goes far beyond the particular question of religion's role in public political life. It goes to the heart of some of liberalism's most important claims about legitimate government and the nature of citizenship. That should not be surprising, of course, since liberalism itself was first forged as a distinctive set of claims in the afterglow of Europe's devastating religious conflicts. Liberal thinkers were eager to demonstrate that political life could hold together in the absence of a common confession, and so they made politics an emphatically terrestrial affair, clearly distinguishing between the kingdoms of God and man. For this, we should be sincerely grateful, for the benefits of liberal democratic government are enormous and obvious to anyone with eyes to see.

But this is not the seventeenth century, and most of our religious political activists are not prepared, as Calvin did, to burn Servetus at the stake. Though we should be most unwilling to countenance those who would attempt to fuse the two kingdoms, we should also look with some skepticism at those who say they must be entirely unrelated. A good many religious believers in a good many democratic – and democratizing – countries reject both the theocratic and separationist claims, and in my concluding chapter I suggest how a form of what scholars have termed "structural pluralism" could go some distance in better reconciling those believers to the liberal project without fatally undermining it.

1   Europe's religious parties and
       the liberal consensus

Here miracles and ecstasy, there Kant with a cudgel.

Klaus-Michael Mallmann[1]

In drawing on the cases of Europe's nineteenth-century religious integrationists, the argument here stands at some distance from the main body
of political theory. Political theorists do not spend a great deal of time
engaging the sorts of empirical observations produced by political scientists, sociologists, and economists.[2] Among those that do, even fewer
attempt to develop and apply conclusions drawn from their own set of
comparative case studies. Why this sort of empirical evidence is important and why these cases in particular can prove so helpful needs some
elaboration. So in this chapter I do four things. First, I explain why certain sorts of empirical evidence help us to reflect on what I have called
the liberal consensus on religion. I then discuss why religious integrationists pose an interesting challenge to the liberal consensus and why the
European integrationists are especially helpful exemplars in that regard.
Finally, I sketch their histories, focusing on their political activities as a
prelude to the normative arguments that follow on.

Political theory, social science, and the
   liberal consensus

One of the (many) peculiarities of modern academic life is the uneasy
status of political theory. Though housed within political science depart-
ments, political theorists often have as much, if not more, in common
with moral, legal, and political philosophers as they do with the social
scientists down the hall. Indeed, it is no secret that political theory,

[1] Helmut Walser Smith, *German Nationalism and Religious Conflict: Culture, Ideology,
Politics, 1870–1914*, 109.
[2] Ian Shapiro, *The Flight from Reality in the Human Sciences* (Princeton, NJ: Princeton
University Press, 2005); Ian Shapiro, "Problems, Methods, and Theories in the Study
of Politics, or What's Wrong with Political Science and What to Do About It," *Political
Theory* 30, no. 4 (2002).

ostensibly one of the discipline's four main subfields, stands as something of an unwanted stepchild, tolerated but often little loved. For many, the reason is rather straightforward: political theorists just do not do social science. They do not, as a rule, undertake empirically oriented studies, employ qualitative or quantitative methods, and are more committed to the "ought" of articulating generalized moral principles than the "is" of explaining the causes of social and political phenomena. One comparative political scientist, for example, counseled me that political theory was "as far as one could get" from the discipline of political science (and I do not think he meant that as a compliment).

Though surely a caricature, such disdain does capture something real about much of contemporary political thought. Political theorists do not pursue or even much attend to empirically minded studies any more than their philosopher counterparts. Even if works of political theory do tend to be less abstract than their self-consciously philosophical peers, it is often the moral or legal claims doing the heavy lifting in any particular argument; empirical cases tend to illustrate more than guide conclusions. Of course, theorists have good reasons to steer clear of too much empirical work. For one thing, a division of labor within the disciplines frees them up to think more broadly and normatively than perhaps might otherwise be the case if they spent their time doing archival or statistical work. No one can research or think about everything. More importantly, perhaps, the focus on moral and legal questions makes a great deal of sense on its own terms. Law is the most direct vehicle through which the sorts of claims political principles theorists articulate get put into political practice (to the degree that they do). Disputants' contentions and the resulting decisions, especially at the appellate and Supreme Court level, often invoke both constitutional and moral principles. Sorting through these kinds of claims and picking out where they make sense and where they do not is both useful and important.

Perhaps most critically, making the worlds of social science and philosophical argument mesh well turns out to be a conceptually difficult task. This is, of course, nothing new. The attempt to make sense of the distinction (or connection) between "fact" and "value" or "ought" and "is" has always been a central feature of political thought. Ian Shapiro and Ruth Grant have recently tried to make some headway here, at least as they apply to political theory's role in the wider discipline(s). Shapiro suggests that political theorists should stand ready to produce critiques – and if his are any guide, they should be pungent, full-bodied ones – of theoretical approaches where assumptions or presuppositions are ill considered or just untrue.[3] In this way, he hopes, the gap between normative and

---

[3] Shapiro, "Problems, Methods, and Theories."

empirical political theorists can be narrowed or even eliminated. For her part, Grant emphasizes political theory's philosophical tendencies but connects that to a larger project, one that it shares with political science, of "understanding" politics.[4] What makes theorists distinctive is that at their best they plumb the "meaning" and "significance" of social and political phenomena, while empirical social science looks to uncover phenomena's causes and effects.

Neither of these arguments seems to me especially wrong, but neither seems quite complete either. Political theory stands at that muddy intersection of what Weber distinguished as "fact" and "value," and if it wanders too far in one direction or another, it runs the danger of falling into the error of being what Dennis Thompson has called "prescriptive" or "descriptive."[5] That is, if it abandons the lessons drawn from empirical observation and becomes solely philosophical (what he means by prescriptiveness) it runs the danger of being made irrelevant to our actually lived political life. As Thompson rightly notes, we commonly think that if the best empirical evidence shows some moral claims impossible, we are less inclined to think it has real purchase on us.[6] More to the point, if political theories are constructed on claims that can be shown empirically to be false, why would we take those theories seriously? No one in their right minds, after all, would consider a theory of politics to be true or even reasonable if it started with the assumption that human beings were wholly altruistic and incapable of selfish acts. It would be like designing a bridge for a world where the laws of physics were nonexistent (or perhaps fundamentally different from our own).

That said, political theorists are also wise to steer away from the prescriptivist's opposite, the tendency to accept what "is" as being fundamentally unchangeable. Theorists, as Grant accentuates, provide real value to the understanding of politics in that their work is "obstinately philosophical."[7] It may not be quite right to say, to borrow loosely from Marx, that the point of the theorist's enterprise is to change the world rather than know it, but it does seem right to say that to *know* (or understand) the world around us inevitably entails understanding how we might and should change it. Political theory is "obstinately philosophical" and normative because we as human beings are obstinately philosophical and normative, driven to inquire after and understand things and inclined to try and make whole what is broken (even if we are equally inclined

---

[4] Ruth W. Grant, "Political Theory, Political Science, and Politics," *Political Theory* 30, no. 4 (2002).

[5] Dennis F. Thompson, *The Democratic Citizen: Social Science and Democratic Theory in the Twentieth Century* (London: Cambridge University Press, 1970).

[6] Ibid., 36.   [7] The term is Isaiah Berlin's.

toward breaking it in the first place).[8] Fashioning our inquiries in ways that abandon or neglect that philosophical and normative impulse would be to ignore or discount as unimportant a central feature of human life, i.e. the impulse to think normatively and attempt to act accordingly. We might say, then, that an attempt to become too "empirical" would be essentially self-defeating.

We thus cannot avoid integrating empirical observations into our theoretical arguments, nor can we simply be at those observations' mercy. So how to proceed? There are a number of ways theorists have fruitfully navigated this muddy intersection. At their most narrow, empirical cases or studies can serve illustrative purposes, fleshing out rather than driving or even framing the argument.[9] This is, as I have noted, often quite useful and productive, but does have its limitations. Illustrations can be like hypotheticals. At their best, they help uncover our deepest intuitions and challenge sloppy thinking. At their worst, they can merely serve to reinforce our intuitions and blind us to our argument's weak spots. Perhaps more importantly, recourse to legal cases – a quite common strategy, especially in dealing with religion in the American context – can do as much to distort as to illuminate. Arguments made in legal disputes are arguments, after all, made to win cases, not to prove a moral or philosophical point, and the distance between the two is not always particularly helpful. More to the point, using cases or studies as illustrations may help a reader better understand the argument or flesh it out in some details but insofar as they are *mere* illustrations, they really are not doing any work. The argument would be the same whether the cases were there or not.[10]

At perhaps the opposite end of the spectrum lies the sort of work we find in George Klosko's *Democratic Procedures and Liberal Consensus*.[11] Though Klosko retains a measure of normative prescriptiveness in his argument, he suggests that the shape of contemporary liberal democracies – a shape he largely defines by citing public opinion surveys – should point

---

[8] See Christian Smith, *Moral, Believing Animals: Human Personhood and Culture* (New York: Oxford University Press, 2003).

[9] For two (of the many examples) of political theorists focusing on court cases to make their claims plausible see Shelley Burtt, "In Defense of *Yoder*: Parental Authority and the Public Schools," in *Political Order: Nomos XXXVIII*, ed. Ian Shapiro and Russell Hardin (New York: New York University Press, 1996); Callan, "Political Liberalism and Political Education."

[10] The employment of empirical cases in this way may serve a kind of limiting function, in that the author may decide to revise the argument if no plausible cases can be found to illustrate it. But that seems like a pretty narrow use, and I suspect that few authors cannot conceive of cases that they think illustrate their arguments.

[11] George Klosko, *Democratic Procedures and Liberal Consensus* (New York: Oxford University Press, 2000).

us to acknowledging that the more robust moral hopes of someone like Rawls look unrealistic. I confess a great deal of sympathy with this sort of approach. A portion of the argument in chapters 3 and 4 leans on a similar sort of analysis. Any work of political theory necessarily starts with some basic assumptions, a framework within which the argument can be made intelligible. We all work within what MacIntyre calls a "tradition" of philosophical thought, and likewise we all take certain facets of social and political life to be givens, things we cannot imagine changing.[12] In the tradition of liberal democratic thought, our focus is not so much *whether* we should have liberal democracies as what liberal democracies we do have should look like. No one who identifies with this tradition – and many who are openly critical of it – questions whether we should elect our representatives at regular intervals, have religious liberty protected in law, or any other of a number of fundamental democratic principles. We disagree about what these mean in the particular, of course, but not whether we should have them or whether they are important. But sometimes – and Klosko's work edges close to this line – we can be too sanguine about what it is that we should accept as given politically and fall into an quiescent affirmation of the status quo. In the next section, I criticize José Casanova on just this sort of point, arguing that his heavy indebtedness to a particular historical path – Europe's secularization – blinds him unnecessarily to the possibilities of what he calls public religion. We all have to assume something, but taking too much for granted can leave our arguments stunted and insufficiently normative.

In between these two poles lies a practice not dissimilar to what Rawls has described as a "reflective equilibrium."[13] According to Rawls' description we ought not tie ourselves too tightly to any particular moral principle (though we will inevitably always have to start from somewhere and thus leave something unquestioned) or, certainly, accept the observed social and political phenomena as inevitable givens. Instead, we start with our "considered" (if still provisional and no doubt mistaken in some sense) moral claims and move back and forth between those claims and whatever sorts of counterexamples or counterarguments we might encounter. As we find places where these counterarguments point to inconsistencies or obvious flaws in our more basic moral claims, we might adjust those claims to take better account of

---

[12] Alasdair C. MacIntyre, *After Virtue: A Study in Moral Theory*, 2nd. edn. (Notre Dame, IN: University of Notre Dame Press, 1984); Alasdair C. MacIntyre, *Whose Justice? Which Rationality?* (Notre Dame, IN: University of Notre Dame Press, 1988).

[13] See, for example, John Rawls, *Collected Papers*, ed. Freeman, 288–91; John Rawls, "Outline of a Procedure for Ethics," *Philosophical Review* 60 (1951); Rawls, *A Theory of Justice*, 42–45.

the critiques. What remains unclear in Rawls' formulation is what role he thinks empirical observations ought to play in the equilibrium. On the one hand, Rawls tends to characterize his equilibrium in terms of competing moral considerations.[14] But in reflecting on the shift from *A Theory of Justice* to *Political Liberalism*, he is frustratingly elusive in parsing out exactly what motivated him to conclude that the system articulated in the former had a problem of "stability." What seems clear is that he came to recognize that some reasonably large number of people had good reasons to reject the Kantian individualism at the heart of *Theory* and so, as I will discuss later on, could reject its moral and political legitimacy. But this "fact of reasonable pluralism," as he calls it, has both moral and empirical elements. It is a moral claim in that it recognizes some objections to *Theory*'s Kantianism as reasonable, and it is an empirical claim in that it suggests that such rejections are part and parcel of free societies as we see them around us. It is not at all clear, however, what sort of work each part is doing or, more broadly, how Rawls thinks we *ought* to combine our moral reflections and empirical observation.

Archon Fung has recently articulated a means to overcoming that lacuna, describing how what he calls his "pragmatic equilibrium" can help political theorists engage with observations drawn from social science to better understand, compare, and reconsider the competing contemporary conceptions of democratic rule.[15] To simplify somewhat, Fung suggests that one way to evaluate, for example, deliberative or aggregative models of democracy is to first consider what sorts of institutions each model occasions and then see whether the empirical outcomes of those sorts of institutional arrangements actually conform to the basic moral claims behind the model itself. Disappointing empirical outcomes – say Cass Sunstein's study that suggests deliberation might induce more political polarization rather than less[16] – would require reconsideration either of the recommended institutional arrangements or of the model's basic moral premises. Paul Weithman's book *Religion and the Obligations of Citizenship* offers a nice example of this, as it moves back and forth between reflecting on Rawls' moral claims about citizenship and some empirical evidence about how some Americans actually

---

[14] See the discussions in Samuel Richard Freeman, *Justice and the Social Contract: Essays on Rawlsian Political Philosophy* (New York: Oxford University Press, 2007); Fung, "Democratic Theory and Political Science"; Paul J. Weithman, "Review of Samuel Freeman, *Justice and the Social Contract: Essays on Rawlsian Political Philosophy*," *Notre Dame Philosophical Reviews* (2007).

[15] Fung, "Democratic Theory and Political Science."

[16] Cass Sunstein, "The Law of Group Polarization," *Journal of Political Philosophy* 10 (2002).

conceive of their roles as citizens.[17] This certainly does not excise all ambiguity in the intersection between philosophical reflection and empirical observation – I suspect that is a permanent condition – but it does seem to do a reasonably good job in taking account of both without overly impugning either. In what follows, I put this conception into practice by reflecting on the basic moral premises informing the liberal consensus on religion's place in liberal democratic politics and bring those reflections into close conversation with a particular, and highly interesting, set of empirical cases.

I described in the introductory chapter how liberal democratic political thought has come to a rough consensus that under conditions of religious and moral pluralism, liberal democracies are made more legitimate, stable, and free when religion is largely excluded from public political life and reshaped in conformity with liberal political ends. In large part, the consensus is formed around moral claims regarding the requirements of political legitimacy, the importance of autonomy for human flourishing, and the demands of democratic citizenship. But it is also formed around a number of propositions and expectations that are quite empirical, even if they are not always clearly spelled out as such. That is, the consensus depends in important ways not just on some quite strong moral claims about the human person and the nature of democratic politics, but also on claims whose validity depends ultimately on the observations and conclusions of historians and social scientists. The conclusions I draw from my comparison of the European cases engages the consensus in two ways. First, and most broadly, they serve to ground an alternative set of expectations about the possible shapes of liberal democratic polities. By showing that liberal democratic regimes develop and are sustained in the presence of significant religious political mobilization, these histories help show that the empirical presumptions built into the consensus are vulnerable and that an alternative is at the least empirically plausible. Second, the evidence compiled here contradicts a number of more specific claims advanced about religion's allegedly pernicious effects on political stability and citizens' attitudes and civic habits. Of course in any case, a few – even quite interesting – cases do not on their own give us reason to discard entirely the consensus's powerful moral claims. But in complicating its empirical component, I hope to go some way toward showing the consensus as a whole to be mistaken and making its alternatives plausible, both empirically and morally.

---

[17] Weithman, *Religion and the Obligations of Citizenship.* He relies mainly on Sidney Verba, Kay Lehman Schlozman, and Henry E. Brady, *Voice and Equality: Civic Voluntarism in American Politics* (Cambridge, MA: Harvard University Press, 1995).

Public religion and religious integrationism

One of the difficulties in developing the sort of empirical evidence that might make such a claim persuasive to the skeptical reader is that the ways in which religion both directly and indirectly affects politics makes any sort of comprehensive investigation well-nigh impossible. Just for starters, religion as a value system influences voting patterns,[18] ecclesial bodies make public pronouncements or intervene directly in political bargaining,[19] religious social movements press for particular policy changes,[20] and religion most broadly even perhaps structures the cultural ethos of "civilizations."[21] What's more, we are not even able to quite conceive of religion as an entirely independent variable, for inasmuch as it affects the surrounding political order, it too is influenced and at least partially shaped by the order itself.[22] It is difficult, in other words, to get a clear reading on religion's political effects.

One way to focus our inquiry is with what José Casanova has called public religion, or religion that "abandons its assigned place in the private sphere and enters the undifferentiated public sphere of civil society to take part in the ongoing process of contestation, discursive legitimation, and redrawing of boundaries."[23] Public religion is not the private, individualist faith concerned only with a person's spiritual condition or eternal salvation, but rather is that part of the faith that extends itself beyond the strictly spiritual and beyond its own particular communities. Religion here is *public* precisely in that it impacts those beyond itself through its pursuit of social and political ends. In *Public Religions in the Modern World*, Casanova presents five case studies (Spain, Brazil, Poland, and Catholics

---

[18] Louis Bolce and Gerald De Maio, "Our Secularist Democratic Party," *Public Interest*, no. 142 (2002); Michael Gehler, Wolfram Kaiser, and Helmut Wohnout, eds., *Christian Democracy in 20th Century Europe* (Cologne: Routledge, 2002); Guth *et al.*, "American Fifty/Fifty."; Haynes, *Religion in Third World Politics*; Kalyvas, *The Rise of Christian Democracy in Europe*; W.E. Miller and P.C. Stouthard, "Confessional Attachment and Electoral Behavior," *European Journal of Political Research* 3 (1975); Mark J. Rozell and Clyde Wilcox, eds., *God at the Grassroots* (Lanham, MD: Rowman & Littlefield, 1996).

[19] Timothy A. Byrnes, *Catholic Bishops in American Politics* (Princeton, NJ: Princeton University Press, 1991); Timothy A. Byrnes, *Transnational Catholicism in Postcommunist Europe* (Lanham, MD: Rowman & Littlefield, 2001).

[20] Christian Smith, ed., *Disruptive Religion: The Force of Faith in Social-Movement Activism* (New York: Routledge, 1996).

[21] Samuel P. Huntington, *The Clash of Civilizations and the Remaking of World Order* (New York: Simon & Schuster, 1996). Each of the clashing civilizations is defined mostly by religion.

[22] See Nathan O. Hatch, *The Democratization of American Christianity* (New Haven: Yale University Press, 1989).

[23] José Casanova, *Public Religions in the Modern World* (Chicago: University of Chicago Press, 1994), 66.

and conservative Protestants in the US) where religion has played some significant political role in order to draw some broader conclusions about religion's public limits within modern democracies. Though his primary concern, as a sociologist, is with the theories of secularization and not with liberal democratic political theories per se,[24] his findings – and their limits – help show why it is that *religious integrationists* are so important for thinking through the consensus's normative claims.

Secularization theories, he notes, have wrongly asserted that under modernity's advance religion would either disappear entirely or, at the very least, become privatized, relegated to the domestic, "feminine" sphere of life, irrelevant to politics. What those theories got right, however, was how social differentiation would continue apace and in particular how religious authority would become increasingly and irreversibly distinct from temporal, political authority. This differentiation cannot be reversed, because the surrounding social structures have irrevocably changed, as has religion. Not only are the obviously anti-clerical and anti-religious political movements largely a thing of the past, but also for most citizens in advanced democratic societies, religious claims just do not hold the sort of social or political authority they once had. Religions themselves have largely imbibed the Enlightenment's critique and those that have survived have reconstructed themselves as "free religious institutions of civil society."[25]

This means, among other things, that churches can no longer hope to guide political life simply on the basis of their religious ideals; religion can no longer serve as the "axiological" basis for modern democratic societies. Even though religion may indeed pursue political objectives, it may only do so as one of many institutions of civil society and in defense of universalized human rights. More concretely, this means for Casanova that churches have (at their democratic best) generally become what Tocqueville described them as being in 1830s America: voluntary associations of individuals joined together for worship and mutual assistance that are themselves not directly political but among whose political effects was the nurture and sustenance of democratic political life.[26] Religion may have a public role to play (mostly depending on religion's

---

[24] See chapter 2, where his arguments about secularization figure in my discussion of Habermas.

[25] Casanova, *Public Religions in the Modern World*, 220.

[26] Ibid., 220–21. For an example of Tocqueville's argument: "I have said that American priests pronounce themselves in a general manner to be in favor of civil freedom without excepting even those who do not accept religious freedom; however one does not see them lend their support to any political system in particular. They take care to keep themselves outside affairs and do not mix in the schemes of the parties. Therefore one cannot say that in the United States religion exerts an influence on the laws or on the details of political opinions, but it directs mores, and it is in regulating the family that it

strength and its own inclination to public activity), but that role subsists within the sphere of civil society and cannot involve any long-term, institutionalized activity within what he terms "political society."[27]

There is much that seems right about Casanova's account, but the analysis leaves some important questions unanswered. It seems entirely right to say that religion cannot serve as the "axiological basis" for free societies, if for no other reason than the wide and deep religious pluralism extant in any democratic society makes such efforts simply inconceivable.[28] But if it is true, as he says, that the widespread disappearance of religious belief in Western and Northern Europe was a historical "option" and not a historical necessity, why is the presence or effectiveness of organized religious *political movements* any less "optional" for modern democracies? Casanova argues that such movements run counter to the fundamental, structural, currents of modern society, that there is something basic to democratic government or modernity more generally that precludes organizing politically on the basis of religious faith or identity. It seems unclear, though, just what that something actually is and whether it is quite as fundamental as Casanova suggests. In increasingly pluralist societies, such appeals may be fragmenting and unhelpful electorally, but that is a pragmatic objection dependent on the sociological or political makeup of a particular society, not on a view of how democratic societies are structured more generally. Even if it is the case that modern democratic societies have developed in such a manner as to make political religious appeals pragmatically ineffective, it does not follow that there is anything essential about democracy that would preclude such organizing, nor is it clear that changes in modern society (say, a widespread return to organized religion in Western Europe) would not make it a live option once again. Or, rather, if there is something in a constitutional democracy that precludes such organizing, Casanova does not tell us what it is.

More importantly, it is not clear that Casanova can sustain the clear sociological distinction he wants to draw between civil and political society. (In his argument religion may freely organize and participate in the former but not in the latter.) Consider political parties. Though

works to regulate the state" (Alexis de Tocqueville, *Democracy in America*, trans. Harvey C Mansfield and Delba Winthrop [Chicago: University of Chicago Press, 2000], 278.)

[27] He borrows this phrase from Alfred Stepan, who distinguished three elements within modern societies: civil society, economic society, and political society. See Alfred Stepan, *Arguing Comparative Politics* (New York: Oxford University Press, 2001).

[28] See, for example, the argument in Steve Bruce, *Conservative Protestant Politics* (New York: Oxford University Press, 1998). Bruce argues that conservative Protestants in the US never stood much of a chance of winning serious political power precisely because they were and are too divided internally.

seemingly a constitutive element of political society, parties also act and are rooted in civil society.[29] Parties link citizen demands to policy decisions, mobilize voters to effect political goals, and serve as incubators of civic identity. They are the primary (though by no means the only) means in democracies through which public opinion is developed and translated into public policy.[30] In mass parties especially, party organizations involve citizens in all sorts of ancillary organizations that attempt to immerse them within partial political communities that could then be mobilized on behalf of candidates or issues. On a smaller, more focused scale, social movements would seem to do similar things – they organize a set of disparate individuals on the basis of some identity or issue and seek to effect political change. Both clearly cross the line between civil and political society, and Casanova would seemingly be hard pressed to think either incompatible with modern democracies. What's more, given his willingness to countenance religion's intermittent political engagement in defense of human rights or against the colonization of the "lifeworld" (i.e. civil society) by either the market or the state,[31] he would seem to be equally hard pressed to explain how public religion could do so effectively without an organized political presence? Preachers on street corners usually do not on their own persuade many people that the end of the world is actually near, and though large social movements like the civil rights movement can change the course of politics, they can only do so (in a democracy, at least) to the degree that elected officials pass and enforce new laws. If religion can "help modernity save itself"[32] only by disdaining any real means of effecting political goals, it is hard to see what is so interesting about this supposedly "public" religion.

Stepan, from whom Casanova borrows his distinctions between civil and political society, apparently agrees. He suggests,

A democracy should not be considered consolidated in a country unless, among other things, there is the opportunity for the development of a robust and critical civil society that helps check the state and constantly generates alternatives ... For such civil society alternatives to be aggregated and implemented, political society, especially parties, should be allowed unfettered relations with civil society.[33]

---

[29] Nancy L. Rosenblum, "Political Parties as Membership Groups," *Columbia Law Review* 100, no. 3 (2000).

[30] R.J. Dalton and M.P. Wattenberg, eds., *Parties without Partisans: Political Change in Advanced Industrial Democracies* (Oxford: Oxford University Press, 2000); Larry Diamond and Richard Gunther, eds., *Political Parties and Democracy* (Baltimore, MD: Johns Hopkins University Press, 2001); Rosenblum, "Political Parties as Membership Groups."

[31] Casanova, *Public Religions in the Modern World*, 228–29.

[32] Ibid., 234.   [33] Stepan, *Arguing Comparative Politics*, 216.

In other words, if elements of civil society (including religion) are to be able to effectively defend their rights and interests, they must be able to organize, pursue, and in some sense exercise political power. His conclusion is straightforward: "[individuals and religious communities] should also be able to publicly advance their values in civil society, and to sponsor organizations and movements in political society, as long as their public advancement of these beliefs does not impinge negatively on the liberties of other citizens, or violate democracy and the law, by violence."[34] There is no empirical evidence, Stepan thinks, to support the claim that politically organized religion ought not pursue its political goals on the same basis as everyone else, insofar as those goals do not impinge on basic rights and liberties (just like everyone else).[35] Casanova has made, in the end, what amounts to a category mistake, failing to recognize that there is conceptual space between religion serving as the axiological basis of a social order (as it does in a theocracy, for example) and serving *only* as a free association in the context of a civil society divorced in some reasonably strict manner from political life. Religious political movements certainly *can* (and do) tip over into the former and thus delegitimize themselves democratically, but they need not do so, at least not any more than perhaps similarly situated political movements organized on the basis of class, race, or any other sort of identity.

The point here, I should emphasize, is not that differentiation in some fashion has not occurred or that it is possible for religious movements to "turn back the clock" and re-establish some mythical, fully integrated social order. My view is much more modest. However much social and political authority religion has lost in modernity, it still has a nearly unparalleled power to inspire and order people's lives, including their collective sense of how to order their politics. Given a particular set of circumstances, that power may quite plausibly develop into formal political organization. Suppose, for example, that the US operated under a more parliamentary-style system. It seems quite reasonable to think that the emergence of politically active conservative Protestants after World War II would have led to a religious political party advancing their interests. If that is right, then Casanova's claim that religion may not – normatively and sociologically – organize within political society looks to be arbitrary to some degree and as "optional" as the old secularization theories he targets so successfully. I suggest that if we want to engage seriously the liberal consensus's empirical claims, we should focus precisely on *those* sorts of efforts and see where that leads us.

---

[34] Ibid., 217.
[35] This is, of course, a rather big "insofar" and I take it up in chapter 6.

So if we take it as given that democracies cannot be theocracies (and vice versa) *and* if it is right to say that the sociological strictures of modern society do not necessarily limit religion to civil society (as Casanova would have it), then what I have described as religious integrationism would seem to be excellent fodder for thinking about the consensus's empirical claims. Unlike Casanova's public religion, religious integrationism eschews the strict divisions between political and civil society (though as will be clear later, it does not necessarily make the theocratic mistake of fusing them, either) and retains the view that the public political sphere can be an object of religious judgment and mobilization. What makes it even *especially* promising for our purposes is that it seems to represent religion's "high-water mark," politically speaking. That is, religious integrationism is the most robustly public sort of religion plausibly compatible with liberal democratic politics. A coercive religious establishment clearly runs afoul of guarantees of religious liberty, and while religion making "public" claims in the sphere of civil society is worrisome to some,[36] it seems historically naïve and normatively silly to suggest that making such claims in any sense endangers the democratic order. A politically engaged integrationism seems much more plausibly dangerous than religion in civil society, since it is seeking to wield political power toward a particular set of ends. But it is also much more plausibly compatible with democracy than the straightforward theocrats, at least to the degree that it eschews the theocratic aim of reorganizing the social and political order toward a religious end like, say, the salvation of souls. Of course, religious integrationism may turn out not to be compatible as such, but that is not obviously the case, and that strategic ambiguity makes it a compellingly attractive sort of religious phenomenon, at least for purposes of thinking through the claims of the liberal consensus.

Europe's religious integrationists and religious political parties

So the next question is *which* integrationists would be especially helpful? Since no one so far as I can tell actually goes around calling themselves "integrationists," this is not such an easy process. One option would be to focus on the spiritual descendants of the Radical Reformation – the Mennonites, Amish, Huttites – or similar groups in other religious traditions. To varying degrees, these religious communities clearly qualify as

---

[36] Consider, for example, the furor sparked over rebukes given by Catholic bishops to pro-choice Catholic politicians and voters.

integrationists in that they attempt to organize themselves entirely around a particular religious identity. Usually, however, these groups are fairly insular and removed from the rest of society. Though there are some interesting questions surrounding the degree of autonomy they ought to possess vis-à-vis the larger political community, they mostly just want to be left alone to structure their lives and their communities as they see fit. They do not seek to exercise political power over others and as a matter of practical politics seem to represent a fairly marginal problem.[37]

I suggest instead that we train our attention on the very people Casanova would suggest have had their day and are now gone forever,[38] a set of religious believers in late nineteenth- and early twentieth-century Europe who, responding to the challenge of modernizing social structures and secularizing politics, constructed powerfully integrated subcultural communities, replete with their own schools, newspapers, trade unions, employers' associations, and the like – "alternative civil societies" organized entirely around religious identity and belief.[39] In Belgium, the Netherlands, Germany, and Austria,[40] these subcultural communities went some distance toward "encapsulating" their members within networks of like-minded organizations, and organized political parties (or their functional equivalents) to represent their interests and pursue their political goals. By the turn of the century, religious parties controlled governments in Belgium and the Netherlands and were regularly winning pluralities in national elections in Germany and Austria. These parties were the vehicles through which religious communities organized and mobilized themselves as a means to achieving political goals defined in part by those beliefs and identities.[41] As I mentioned above, no other manifestation of politically organized religion, save a coercive state church, so closely connects religion to the exercise of political power, and no other set of cases offers such a rich, interesting, and fruitful set

---

[37] For these groups, of course, the question of their autonomy vis-à-vis the state is anything but minor.

[38] "It is one of the central theses of the present work that, at least in Western Europe, this historical epoch, the 'age' of reactive organicism, of secular-religious and clerical-anti-clerical cultural and political warfare, of Catholic Action, of religious pillarization, and of Christian Democracy has come to an end" (Casanova, *Public Religions in the Modern World*, 61.)

[39] Bermeo and Nord, eds., *Civil Society before Democracy*.

[40] I was first alerted to these parties' histories by the excellent discussion in Kalyvas, *The Rise of Christian Democracy in Europe*.

[41] So far as I know, there is no generally accepted definition of what counts as an authentically religious political party. To be a religious party, it seems to me that it is not enough to simply draw on religious communities for votes, the way the Republican Party in the US now draws on conservative Protestants. Rather, a religious party should fulfill the following criteria: (1) it must self-identify as a religious party (and have that self-identity confirmed by its political opponents); (2) its members and supporters must support it in

of observations as these. Focusing on the integrationists and how their movements and especially parties affected political outcomes in Belgium, the Netherlands, Germany, and Austria (and not on similar parties in Italy, Israel, India, or Turkey, for example) has a number of important advantages: we know the historical outcomes; the parties were especially powerful over a reasonably extended period of time; they acted in the context of rapidly changing political systems and were important factors in those systems' democratic transitions and consolidations (or failures therein); and, finally, they acted in roughly contemporaneous times and under roughly similar circumstances.

First, these are closed historical cases whose outcomes are known to us. Each of the communities began to organize themselves in the early to mid nineteenth century and founded their parties in the 1860s and 1870s, continuing to operate politically well into the inter-war period. Unlike, say, with Turkey's Justice and Development Party or India's BJP, we know that though all four countries became democracies after World War I, Belgian and Dutch democracies survived the 1930s at least in part *because* of their respective religious parties, while Austria's Christian Social Party overthrew the First Republic in 1934 and Germany's Center Party voted for Hitler's Enabling Act and for its own dissolution just the year before. Knowing how things turned out and knowing that they turned out differently gives us a more reliable basis for making comparative judgments than if all the cases had been successful or if the outcome were still uncertain.[42]

Second, of religious communities who organized parties or similar political organizations in democratic or proto-democratic orders, these parties and their communities were, in my judgment, the most powerful examples of religious integrationism we know anything about, both in terms of political influence and social comprehensiveness. This was

large part because of its religious identity; (3) its political goals must have some religious ends, even if that means merely defending particular religiously defined communities or institutions; and (4) it must use religion as an organizing and mobilizing tool. All four of the integrationist communities I study here had parties that qualify, though as we will see their *degree* of religiousness makes an important difference in their political effects (and not one the liberal consensus would predict).

[42] An early reader of my work here suggested that I was making the mistake of "selecting on the dependent variable" since my cases' outcomes vary as they do. See Gary King, Robert O. Keohane, and Sidney Verba, *Designing Social Inquiry: Scientific Inference in Qualitative Research* (Princeton, NJ: Princeton University Press, 1994). Perhaps that is so, but with small-N studies, it is implausible to do otherwise, especially if we are interested in saying something about when it is that religious integrationism is compatible with democratic life and when it is not. This might mean that whatever inferences I draw from my comparisons are that much weaker, but it seems to me that is a function not of selecting cases that vary on the dependent variable (e.g. democratic outcomes) but rather of the relatively small number of cases I consider.

especially true in the Belgian and Dutch cases, where the religious "pillars" were extremely influential even long after World War II. Belgium's Catholic Party held a parliamentary majority from 1884 until World War I, and the Netherlands had at least one religious party in every government from the turn of the century until 1994. Germany's Center Party routinely captured over two-thirds of the Catholic vote, and its leaders were often more influential over German Catholics than even the national bishops. Austria's Christian Socials were even powerful enough, alas, to overthrow the country's democratic republic and replace it with a corporatist dictatorship. These movements and political parties made a significant political impact (for good and ill).

Third, these communities organized in the context of a rapidly changing political environment, one in which political systems were moving, however haltingly, toward liberal democracy. Examining whether and the ways in which integrationism is compatible with democratic government when it is at its *most vulnerable* – that is, during its (long) transition and consolidation period – would seem to be an especially helpful exercise. Unconsolidated democracies evince "commitment problems" where various parties, themselves not fully committed to democratic rule, have to decide whether to submit their political fates to the uncertainty of electoral outcomes and legislative deliberation.[43] Political parties tied to robust religious communities might quite plausibly be thought to present an insuperable barrier to opponents' commitment. When they are not, and when they are not under the most trying political conditions, we would have some powerful evidence regarding the plausibility of the consensus's empirical claims, especially in places, like the United States, where the democratic order is quite well consolidated.[44]

Fourth, these countries have a very interesting mix of similarities and differences that will prove quite useful in ferreting out how and why integrationism affects democratic life. Belgium and Austria were almost entirely Catholic, while Germany's Catholics were a distinct minority, about a third of the population. Dutch Catholics, too, were

---

[43] Adam Przeworski, *Democracy and the Market: Political and Economic Reforms in Eastern Europe and Latin America* (Cambridge: Cambridge University Press, 1991).

[44] For an interesting discussion of how Algeria's 1989 elections were derailed precisely because the Islamists' political opponents were not convinced that they were reliable, see Stathis N. Kalyvas, "Commitment Problems in Emerging Democracies: The Case of Religious Parties," *Comparative Politics* 32, no. 4 (2000). They could not be assured, as it were, that the Islamists would not follow the mantra of "one man, one vote, one time." He contrasts that Belgium's 1884 elections, where the newly emergent Catholic Party faced the same skepticism and only overcame it when the church quashed the more radical elements of Belgian political Catholicism.

a minority, as were the orthodox Calvinists that organized in the late 1870s (though together they could sometimes cobble together a slim electoral majority). The parties organized and were especially influential at roughly the same times, meaning that the international environment was similar for all, though of course being in Germany and Austria after World War I differed a good deal from being in Belgium or the Netherlands.

Finally, focusing on these cases seems quite helpful given the degree to which much of our thinking about religion and politics is shaped by a different European history, that of Europe's post-Reformation religious wars in the sixteenth and seventeenth centuries. The brutality and fruitlessness of those wars powerfully shaped liberalism's thinking about religion, even in the United States, where our religious conflicts have been relatively non-violent, certainly at least by the standards of the Thirty Years War. Those wars, as awful as they were and as much as we should keep them in mind, do not tell us the whole story, even in Europe. To the degree that these cases tell a much more positive story, we can perhaps begin to refashion our thinking about religion's place in democratic politics away from a context in which the first thing that comes to mind is religious war. That rather apocalyptic tendency is neither accurate in describing religion's political effects nor helpful in grounding our normative deliberations.

A few explanations and caveats are in order at this point, though. Some might wonder why these cases and not others, even contemporaries in Europe? Italy had a quite robust Christian Democratic movement and Spain's history is closely wrapped up in its religious-political conflicts.[45] I decided not to include Italy largely on account of the presence of the Vatican in Rome and the way in which its involvement in Italian politics makes the country difficult to compare to its neighbors. I doubt, in any case, that Italy's experience would much alter my conclusions.[46] Spain is rather tougher, as it is clear that the Catholic Church was persistently opposed to Spain's liberalization and democratization, and that the horrible violence of the Spanish Civil War had a central religious

---

[45] France, as will become evident, does appear, though as a kind of background case.

[46] For a description and analysis of events in Italy, see Nicholas Atkin and Frank Tallett, *Priests, Prelates and People: A History of European Catholicism since 1750* (New York: Oxford University Press, 2003); Claus von Beyme, *Political Parties in Western Democracies* (Aldershot: Gower, 1985); Mario Caciagli, *DC, Christian Democracy in Europe: Barcelona 1992* (Barcelona: ICPS, 1992); Mario Einaudi and François Goguel, *Christian Democracy in Italy and France* (Hamden, CT: Archon Books, 1969); Michael Patrick Fogarty, *Christian Democracy in Western Europe, 1820–1953* (Notre Dame, IN: University of Notre Dame Press, 1957); Ronald Eckford Mill Irving, *The Christian*

component.[47] It is not at all unreasonable for partisans of the liberal consensus to point to Spain's experience as an example of religion's political dangers. But to the degree that Spanish Catholics opposed wholeheartedly the Second Republic and were mainstays of the Francoist regime, they are not so interesting to our questions here. I do not at all question the notion that religion can be and is dangerous politically. But to say that we should be concerned about religious political movements because some religious political movements oppose democratic politics conflates two plausibly distinct sorts of religious political movements. If Franco's Catholic supporters were simply opposed to democratic rule, that teaches us very little about religious believers whose political orientations are not obviously anti-democratic. Spain is not included in the study not because it does not tell us anything about religion's political effects (it does) but because it does not illuminate especially well the sorts of politically motivated believers who provide the best test for the liberal consensus. No one, I suspect, thinks that virulently anti-democratic religious movements (say, Aryan Christians or radical Islamists) are a boon to democratic life, but religious integrationists run afoul of the liberal consensus, yet do so for what seem to me unfair reasons. Spain gives us a picture of the former anti-democratic movements but not the latter ones.

Europe's religious integrationists in Belgium, the Netherlands, Germany, and Austria provide a good basis, then, from which to draw some interesting and hopefully fruitful comparative inferences about how religion relates to democratic politics and the liberal consensus. Though whatever conclusions I draw can hardly be definitive on the basis of four comparative cases, they can be quite suggestive and suggestive enough, I think, to make us reconsider how much stock we want to put in the consensus. Given that most know little about these parties and their affiliated communities, let me sketch out each of their histories before I turn to that consensus in the next chapter.

Democratic Parties of Western Europe (London: Allen and Unwin, 1979); Kalyvas, *The Rise of Christian Democracy in Europe*; Richard A. Webster, *Christian Democracy in Italy, 1860–1960* (London: Hollis & Carter, 1961); Richard A. Webster, *The Cross and the Fasces: Christian Democracy and Fascism in Italy* (Stanford, CA: Stanford University Press, 1960).

[47] See Margaret Lavinia Anderson, "The Divisions of the Pope: The Catholic Revival and Europe's Transition to Democracy," in *The Politics of Religion in an Age of Revival: Studies in Nineteenth-Century Europe and Latin America*, ed. Austen Ivereigh (London: Institute of Latin American Studies, 2000); Atkin and Tallett, *Priests, Prelates and People*; José Casanova, "Church, State, Nation and Civil Society in Spain and Poland," in *The Political Dimensions of Religion*, ed. Saïd Amir Arjomand (New York: State University of New York Press, 1993).

Party histories

Belgium

The religious parties in both Belgium and Holland emerged in the second half of the nineteenth century as liberal governments pushing legislation designed to curtail churches' role in public life, especially in regard to education and marriage, ran into a revitalized and resurgent set of religious communities.[48] Belgian Catholics and liberals had generally cooperated with one another after the 1830 revolt that formed the country out of the most heavily Catholic Dutch provinces. The new government did not officially establish the church, but they did provide public support.[49] However, Catholics and liberals soon found themselves at odds as liberal governments began, gently at first, to wrest control of education away from the church. The big break came in 1878, when the newly minted liberal government proposed and passed several bills that made civil servants, not priests, responsible for school inspections, limited religious instruction, and mandated primary school attendance.[50] Alarmed at these (and other) anti-clerical measures, church officials mobilized Catholic voters and politicians alike in support of what was called the "school war."[51] The church's responses ranged from letters to the king urging him to block implementation of the law (which he declined) to denying the sacraments to Catholic parents who either sent their children to public schools or taught in the schools themselves. This response on the part of Catholics more generally was, however, far from monolithic, as the more moderately minded Catholic parliamentarians and the more militant ultramontanes fought each other bitterly for the church's official support. The ultramontanes were mostly upper bourgeoisie or noble Catholics deeply committed to the church and, in some manner, "the restoration of the social reign of Jesus Christ."[52] They were deeply opposed to Belgium's relatively liberal constitution and thought that the

[48] For a good description of this resurgence of religious belief and practice, a resurgence that also occurred in other European countries, see Anderson, "The Divisions of the Pope."

[49] Val Lorwin, "Belgium: Religion, Class, and Language in National Politics," in *Political Oppositions in Western Democracies*, ed. Robert A. Dahl (New Haven: Yale University Press, 1966), 130.

[50] Stathis N. Kalyvas, "Democracy and Religious Politics: Evidence from Belgium," *Comparative Political Studies* 31, no. 3 (1998). The law in question was called the van Humbeck law, which the Catholics dubbed the *loi de malheur* (law of misfortune).

[51] For a more detailed description of these conflicts, see Charles Glenn, *The Myth of the Common School*. Michael Fogarty quotes an unnamed liberal as saying, in the context of the political struggles over the schools, "A corpse lies across the world barring the road to progress ... let us call it squarely by its name – Catholicism" (Fogarty, *Christian Democracy in Western Europe, 1820–1953*, 172.)

[52] See Kalyvas, "Democracy and Religious Politics."

church's political goals should be the creation of a confessional state. The Catholic parliamentarians, on the other hand, thought that such goals were not just counterproductive, but potentially disastrous. The two sides attacked each other in print and petitioned the bishops and Rome for some definitive resolution. At first, the Vatican and the national episcopate equivocated.

The ultramontanes had on their side the mass of the Catholic press, many of the lower clergy, about half of Belgium's bishops, and, perhaps most importantly, the sympathy of the Vatican, especially Pope Pius IX.[53] Further, they were more in line with official Catholic theology than were the conservatives, since, as Pius IX had clearly spelled out in the Syllabus of Errors, the Catholic ideal was fundamentally opposed to liberal constitutional regimes. What the ultramontanes did not have was a political organization that could actually win elections, and even though the conservatives had been rather mild in their defense of the church (the ultramontanes might have said "weak-kneed"), they were at least capable of accomplishing that defense within Belgium's constitutional structures. So when Leo XIII became pope, he made it clear in 1879 that the Belgian Catholics should appreciate their constitutional order, which though not ideal (a "hypothesis" as opposed to the Catholic confessional state "thesis"), was worth defending. Belgium's bishops quickly fell into line and quashed the ultramontane movement, forcing its newspapers to cease attacking Catholic parliamentarians and removing some of its more outspoken leaders.[54] The church threw its support behind the (renamed) Catholic Party in the 1884 elections, and the party won an outright majority in parliament, a majority that it would not lose until World War I. It proceeded to restore to the church some of the privileges it had lost under liberal governments, but maintained Belgium's liberal constitutionalism and refrained from making Belgium a confessional state.

Though the party retained its parliamentary majority into World War I, it struggled electorally, largely because of the way that Belgium's linguistic and regional differences reproduced themselves inside the party. To accommodate (and in some sense combat) these divisions – and reinforce a common Catholic identity – the party strengthened its ties to secondary associations, even making membership in the party only an "indirect" function of membership in those associations. Such efforts probably went some distance toward stanching the electoral fall-off, and the party did not see its vote totals drop below 30 percent until 1936.[55]

[53] Ibid.   [54] Ibid.
[55] Martin Conway, "Introduction," in *Political Catholicism in Europe, 1918–1965*, ed. Tom Buchanan and Martin Conway (Oxford: Clarendon Press, 1996).

In the end, 1936 turned out to be quite a watershed year for Belgium's democracy. Under the pressure of economic dislocation and the political instability that had gripped much of Europe, Belgium faced the rise of a radical protest party, Leon Degrelle's Rex Party.[56] The Rexists were, in some sense, heirs of the earlier ultramontanes, except that they were now infused with that radical enthusiasm that would eventually turn them into a rather fascistic movement. Faced with the Rexists and the country's economic troubles, the Catholics, socialists, and liberals joined together in the Van Zeeland cabinet in 1935. In 1937, with his party at the height of its popularity (it had twenty-one seats in parliament), Degrelle forced a by-election in which he ran against the Catholic Prime Minister, Paul van Zeeland. The bishops in the person of Archbishop of Malines condemned Degrelle and van Zeeland won 80 percent of the vote, setting the stage for Rex's disappearance (at least until the German occupation).

The Netherlands

The Netherlands' political history had long been characterized by "a tradition of compromise and an acceptance of disagreement and diversity."[57] Under pressure after the 1848 revolutions, William II installed a relatively liberal constitution, guaranteeing many personal liberties, providing for the direct election of parliament (under limited male suffrage rights), and made the government responsible to parliament, not the king. The new constitution also separated church and state, disestablishing the Dutch Reformed Church and, formally at least, freeing the Catholic Church from restrictions on public worship and ecclesial government. Catholic deputies entered the parliament as liberals and helped them pass a wide range of legislation. Over the next twenty years, as public schools became progressively more secularized, both Catholics and Calvinists began to develop networks of alternative schools and to organize themselves politically. Frustrated by parliament's continued intransigence toward the confessional schools and what he saw as the political timidity of orthodox Protestant legislators to make it a significant issue, Groen van Prinsterer called on orthodox Calvinists to vote out incumbent legislators in 1871 and vote instead for his "*anti-revolutionaire*" candidates, who ran a national program of equalizing the status of state and confessional schools. Most

---

[56] This account is based on Lorwin, "Belgium: Religion, Class, and Language in National Politics" and Martin Conway, "Belgium," in *Political Catholicism in Europe, 1918–1965*, ed. Buchanan and Conway.

[57] Hans Daalder, "The Netherlands: Opposition in a Segmented Society," in *Political Oppositions in Western Democracies*, ed. Dahl, 189.

prominent among these candidates was a polymath cleric named Abraham Kuyper. Though the campaign was a failure, it represented the beginning of Kuyper's political career, as he quickly founded the "Anti-School Law League" and the national daily newspaper *De Standaard*, both geared towards organizing orthodox Calvinists politically. By 1874, the League had 144 branches and over 10,000 members, and in 1875 it was super-seded by a national *anti-revolutionaire* campaign organization and eventually by the Anti-Revolutionary Party (ARP) in 1879.[58]

Catholics, influenced by a growing ultramontanism and taking their cues from a revitalized (and intransigent) Vatican, began to found their own religious schools in earnest after 1868, when the Dutch bishops issued a *Mandement* expressing a clear preference for Catholic, as opposed to "neutral," schooling.[59] Politically, though, Catholics did not organize as fervently as the orthodox Protestants, suffering from internal divisions on issues beyond education and from electoral laws that gerry-mandered districts and restricted suffrage in ways that hurt the generally poorer Catholics. The priest and journalist H.J.A.M. Schaepman's calls for the creation of a Center-like Catholic party as early as 1877 went generally unheeded, however, as Catholic notables (especially in the south, where they were in the majority) saw little need for political organization, and many conservative Catholic elites were suspicious of Schaepman's "democratic" tendencies.[60] Perhaps most crucially, the church hierarchy declined to commit itself to such a project.

The dispute over education reached a crucial point in the late 1870s, as liberals passed a new school bill after winning the 1877 elections. Over the vehement objections of both Catholics and orthodox Calvinists (who managed to collect 400,000 signatures on petitions out of a population of only 4 million), the liberal Prime Minister Kappeyne van de Coppello's education bill mandated a set of improvements that all schools (public and alternative) would have to meet (lower student–teacher ratios, better facilities, higher teacher salaries, and so forth), and increased central state subsidies to public schools, while still withholding such subsidies from the alternative ones. The intent was clear: "to provide just the first steps toward a single, secular, national school system for all children."[61] The Calvinist and Catholic deputies in response formed a "monstrous

---

[58] Stanley Carlson-Thies, "Democracy in the Netherlands: Consociational or Pluriform?" (unpublished dissertation, University of Toronto, 1993), 127–30; Daalder, "The Netherlands: Opposition in a Segmented Society," 201.

[59] Carlson-Thies, "Democracy in the Netherlands", 113.

[60] Herman Bakvis, *Catholic Power in the Netherlands* (Kingston: McGill-Queen's University Press, 1981), 62; Carlson-Thies, "Democracy in the Netherlands", 166.

[61] Carlson-Thies, "Democracy in the Netherlands", 143.

alliance" and won a combined parliamentary majority in 1888 (the first elections held under the expanded suffrage law). The new cabinet's first act was to amend the school law, extending subsidies to confessional schools and reducing the inequalities between public and private schools. Dutch politics continued to be deeply divided, however, as disputes over suffrage and religious education in particular continued and the newly emergent socialist party began to flex its electoral muscles.

These divisions came to a head with the "Pacification" of 1917, as the socialists, liberals, and confessionals were at loggerheads over the questions of suffrage and education. Socialists and some liberals had pushed for the expansion of suffrage, and though the ARP and its Catholic allies were not opposed per se (though the more elite and conservative Calvinist Christian Historical Union was), they refused to go along until the state's support for public and private (religious) schools was equalized. Their intransigence on the matter forced the liberal-led government to accept equalization and thus was consolidated the Dutch method for reconciling public purposes and pluralism: whenever state action would touch on society's diverse communities (say, in the public financing of health care, allocation of radio or television licenses, and so on), the presumption would be that funds would be allocated in proportion to those community's share of the population and that control would remain in the hands of that community (with a reasonable dose of central state regulation). The Netherlands had become a "consociational" democracy,[62] and Dutch society's pillarization (*verzuiling*) accelerated, reaching its heights in the 1950s.[63]

Austria

After the failures of the 1848 revolutions, the Catholic Church in Austria found itself in a quite favorable position, and it used that favor to negotiate the concordat of 1855, which not only guaranteed the church full autonomy from state control, but also put it in charge of nearly all public elementary education and gave it control over Catholic marriages.[64] The concordat would prove, however, to be a rather hollow victory, as

---

[62] Lijphart, *Politics of Accommodation*.

[63] Joseph J. Houska, *Influencing Mass Political Behavior: Elites and Political Subcultures in the Netherlands and Austria* (Berkeley: Institute of International Studies, University of California, 1985).

[64] This paragraph on pre-Christian Social political Catholicism is heavily indebted to Ellen Lovell Evans, *The Cross and the Ballot: Catholic Political Parties in Germany, Switzerland, Austria, Belgium and the Netherlands, 1785–1985* (Boston: Humanities Press, 1999), 123–28.

it incited non-Catholics (and those indifferent to their Catholicism or opposed to the church's politics) to embrace wholeheartedly a highly successful anti-clerical politics. After Austria's defeats in 1866, anti-clerical liberals passed a new constitution (1867), which contained guarantees of religious freedom and confessional parity, both of which contravened the 1855 concordat. In 1868, the Reichsrat passed the anti-clerical "May Laws," which provided for civil marriage and lay inspect-ors for public schools. This "mild *Kulturkampf*" was for the most part unopposed, except among a few Catholic aristocrats. Some Catholics began to organize political clubs and even found some representation in the Reichsrat, but for the most part, political Catholicism lay quiescent until the early 1890s.[65]

The Christian Social Party got its start as an odd conglomeration of artisans, lower clergy, radical democrats, and anti-Semites who were united mostly by their disdain, perhaps hatred, of the reigning liberal elites. The architect of the party's development and eventual success was Karl Lueger, a rather religiously indifferent Viennese radi-cal. Lueger had been a fixture on the Viennese political scene, but had been mostly unsuccessful politically. By 1886, he had begun to develop tactical alliances between anti-Semites and democrats; political anti-Semitism had been a part of Austrian politics at least since the 1870s, but it had remained rather ineffective and riven by personal and ideo-logical conflicts.[66] Lueger's politically astute innovation was to marry the economic anti-Semitism of Vienna's artisans and the respectability of the lower clergy to create a viable basis for an anti-liberal political coalition.[67]

---

[65] Political Catholicism was ineffective, it seems, for at least two reasons. First, anti-clericalism was a dominant and dominantly successful political strategy on the part of Austria's liberal elites. See John W. Boyer, *Political Radicalism in Late Imperial Vienna: Origins of the Christian Social Movement 1848–1897* (Chicago: University of Chicago Press, 1981), 28–31. Second, the church itself was not predisposed to fight the regime: its hierarchy benefited from the church's privileged status and their training in Josephist church–state relations made them unwilling to challenge the effective state supremacy under which they worked. It was only when the lower clergy, concerned with their position within Viennese society, joined forces with Lueger that political Catholicism really found any voice at all in Austria. Boyer notes that the May Laws, which hardly affected the episcopate at all, threatened to seriously undermine the lower clergy's position in Austrian society. Without their supervision of schools and control of marriage, their influence and social standing were in serious jeopardy. See Boyer, *Political Radicalism in Late Imperial Vienna*, 122–23. See also William D. Bowman, "Religious Associations and the Formation of Political Catholicism in Vienna, 1848 to the 1870s," *Austrian History Yearbook* 27 (1996).

[66] Boyer, *Political Radicalism in Late Imperial Vienna*, 90–98.

[67] See also Carl Schorske, "Politics in a New Key: An Austrian Triptych," *Journal of Modern History* 39, no. 4 (1967).

Through a series of elections and political maneuvers, Lueger won election as mayor of Vienna in 1895, and though the emperor at first would not accept him, the Christian Socials leveraged a papal endorsement to force his hand.[68] Christian Socialism finally displaced liberalism as the dominant political power in Vienna, if not in Austria. The "new key" of Viennese and Austrian politics created what was essentially a three-way contest for electoral power among the Christian Socials, the newly emergent socialists, and the coalition of liberals and German nationalists.[69] Though not as well organized as, say, the Dutch pillars, both the socialists and Christian Socials developed their own *Lager* and created two nations within one, including mass parties (the Christian Socials and Social Democrats) that represented "absolutist cultural visions and appeals to the whole of society,"[70] which could not, it seemed, be broached without one or the other losing everything.[71] On the socialist side, the Social Democrats were increasingly successful in recruiting workers and embraced wholeheartedly an Austro-Marxism that was both radical and anti-clerical.[72] On the Christian Social side, the party made itself a *Reichspartei* by allying with Alpine Catholics, and a new generation of leaders began to make more of an issue of the party's heretofore rather nominal Catholic identity.[73] In 1911, on the crest of Lueger's death and implementation of universal suffrage, the socialists finally won Vienna and division between the parties was complete: the socialists represented workers and "Red Vienna," while the Christian Socials represented the rural peasants, Alpine Catholics, and middle-class burghers. The stage was set for their fateful clash in the First Republic.

Austria's defeat in World War I and the subsequent loss of its empire meant that what had been one of Europe's great powers was relegated to the category of small countries, its very existence a matter of continuing controversy.[74] The Christian Socials, led by Monsignor Ignaz Seipel, joined with the Social Democrats (led by the moderate Karl Renner)

---

[68] Boyer, *Political Radicalism in Late Imperial Vienna*, 340–6.

[69] Schorske, "Politics in a New Key."

[70] John W. Boyer, "Religion and Political Development in Central Europe around 1900: A View from Vienna," *Austrian History Yearbook* 25 (1994): 32.

[71] Evans, *The Cross and the Ballot*, 185. The socialists were much more adept at this than the Christian Socials, who only got serious about building affiliated organizations in the 1920s. See also Houska, *Influencing Mass Political Behavior*.

[72] Indeed, Boyer suggests that the SDs played up their anti-clericalism as a way of cementing the otherwise tenuous ties among the different national groups. See John W. Boyer, *Culture and Political Crisis in Vienna: Christian Socialism in Power* (Chicago: University of Chicago Press, 1995), 170–74 and Alfred Diamant, *Austrian Catholics and the First Republic: Democracy, Capitalism, and the Social Order, 1918–1934* (Princeton, NJ: Princeton University Press, 1960), 73–80.

[73] Boyer, *Culture and Political Crisis in Vienna*, 320–33.

[74] Even the Social Democrats wanted to join Weimar Germany, until, of course, Hitler came to power.

in a coalition government until 1920, when the threat of communist revolution had passed and the parties felt it safe to oppose one another again.[75] Crucially, their respective commitment to democratic rule – and this is especially true of the Christian Socials – became overwhelmed by political conflicts that were increasingly bitter, uncompromising, and violent.[76] In 1926, the Social Democrats, now under Otto Bauer's more intransigent and orthodox Marxist leadership, formulated the Linz program, which though it did not call directly for revolutionary violence, also did not emphatically endorse democratic ideals, either.[77] In response, and out of a growing intransigence on its part, the Christian Socials assembled a "Unity List" for the 1927 elections, a list that collected every anti-Marxist party available, including the National Socialists. The radicals' electoral emergence began to eat away at the Christian Socials' vote totals at the same time that they were losing more and more ground to the Social Democrats (who had won over 42 percent of the vote in the elections). As a result, they were forced to rely on the nationalist parties – and their paramilitaries – to keep control of the government.

On July 15, 1927, rioting workers angry over the acquittal of three right-wing paramilitaries clashed with the police in Vienna and burned down the *Justizpalast*. The police responded with brutal force, killing hundreds and effectively radicalizing the Social Democrats for good.[78] After the collapse of the Credit-Anstalt bank in 1931, Seipel and Christian Socials offered the Social Democrats a place in government, but Bauer and Renner spurned the offer, correctly thinking that it was little more than an attempt to co-opt them in unpopular policies. Engelbert Dollfuss replaced Seipel as chancellor in 1932, and since the Social Democrats still refused to cooperate with his party in government, he was forced to ask, for the first time, for members of the *Heimwehr* to join the government.[79]

---

[75] Evans, *The Cross and the Ballot*, 188–89.
[76] Alfred Diamant, "Austria: The Three *Lager* and the First Republic," in *Consociational Democracy: Political Accommodation in Segmented Societies*, ed. Kenneth D. McRae (Toronto: McClellan and Stewart, 1974); Diamant, *Austrian Catholics and the First Republic*; Peter Gerlich and David F.J. Campbell, "Austria: From Compromise to Authoritarianism," in *Conditions of Democracy in Europe, 1919–39: Systematic Case Studies*, ed. Dirk Berg-Schlosser and Jeremy Mitchell (New York: St. Martin's Press, 2000); Klemens von Klemperer, *Ignaz Seipel: Christian Statesman in a Time of Crisis* (Princeton, NJ: Princeton University Press, 1972); Ekkart Zimmerman, "Political Breakdown and the Process of National Consensus Formation: On the Collapse of the Weimar Republic in Comparative Perspective," in *Research on Democracy and Society: Democratization in Eastern and Western Europe*, ed. Frederick Weil (Greenwich, CT: JAI Press, 1993).
[77] Klemperer, *Ignaz Seipel*, 252–4.
[78] R. John Rath, "The Deterioration of Democracy in Austria, 1927–1932," *Austrian History Yearbook* 27 (1996): 214–20.
[79] R. John Rath, "The Dollfuss Ministry: The Democratic Prelude," *Austrian History Yearbook* 39 (1998): 161–5.

Dollfuss struggled to keep himself independent of the *Heimwehr*, who increasingly agitated either for a putsch or *Anschluss* with Germany. In the end, it was this association with the *Heimwehr* and the associated pressure from the fascist parties that persuaded Dollfuss – once a convinced democrat – that an authoritarian solution is all that could be expected to protect Austria from the National Socialists.[80] In March, 1933, acting on the basis of a rather technical issue in the Nationalrat, Dollfuss declared the parliament dissolved and Austria's experiment with democracy was effectively ended.[81]

Building on romantic Catholic social thought (and explicitly on the papal encyclical *Quadragesimo Anno*), Dollfuss and the Christian Socials then set about constructing a corporatist authoritarian state. Socialist and Nazi paramilitary forces were outlawed, and the Christian Social Party itself was folded into a Fatherland Front, as was the *Heimwehr*.[82] In February 1934, a short civil war erupted between the socialists and the Dollfuss regime, leading to the outlawing and destruction of the socialist organizations. Dollfuss officially promulgated the corporatist constitution in May 1934, but was assassinated two months later. His successor, Kurt Schuschnigg, attempted without avail to avoid incorporation into Hitler's Reich.

Germany

Germany obviously has a long history of religious politics, dating back at least to Martin Luther's Reformation and the religious wars that followed. For much of the nineteenth century, however, political Catholicism was mostly intermittent, disorganized, and dispersed across the political spectrum (though weighted toward its liberal end).[83] Over the course of the century, however, religious revival and political realignments would work to make political Catholicism in many ways the dominant force in German politics.

German Catholics experienced a religious revival in the middle third of the nineteenth century, one that emphasized theological orthodoxy, emotional expressions of religious devotion, and the construction of a "*counter-world* ... within which Catholics would remain

---

[80] R. John Rath, "The Dollfuss Ministry: The Intensification of Animosities and the Drift toward Authoritarianism," *Austrian History Yearbook* 30 (1999): 83.
[81] For an extremely detailed account of the events directly preceding this, see R. John Rath, "The Dollfuss Ministry: The Demise of the Nationalrat," *Austrian History Yearbook* 32 (2001).
[82] Evans, *The Cross and the Ballot*, 190–91.
[83] Margaret Lavinia Anderson, "The Kulturkampf and the Course of German History," *Central European History* 19, no. 1 (1986): 84–85.

together, depend upon each other – and keep apart from those with different commitments."[84] Politically, this meant a resistance to a sort of all-encompassing nationalism, a resistance most pointed in its opposition to "the presumptions of the Erastian state to a say in church affairs (*Staatskirchentum*)."[85] Socially, priests and lay Catholics organized networks of social clubs, workingmen's associations, and the like both to combat the ill effects of rapid industrialization and to revitalize Catholic communities.

Nonetheless, as Evans notes, "there is very little evidence, before 1848, of the existence of an active political Catholicism in any part of Germany except Prussia," where Catholics felt "threatened by state domination which was both Protestant and authoritarian."[86] Beginning in 1868, however, with the elections to the German *Zollparlament*,[87] Catholic deputies re-entered German parliaments *as Catholics*, that is, as representatives of constituents defined above all by their Catholic identity. Catholic notables re-formed the defunct Center Party (persuading a few Protestant "particularists" to sit with them as well) to run in the 1871 Reichstag elections, winning about a third of the Catholic vote and fifty-four seats. In the 1874 elections, the party doubled its votes and increased its share of the Catholic vote to 83 percent, making it the second largest party in both the Prussian Landtag and the German Reichstag.[88] The Center was firmly established as *the* party

---

[84] Margaret Lavinia Anderson, "The Divisions of the Pope," 32. See also Helmut Walser Smith, *German Nationalism and Religious Conflict: Culture, Ideology, Politics, 1870–1914* (Princeton, NJ: Princeton University Press, 1995); Jonathan Sperber, *Popular Catholicism in Nineteenth-Century Germany* (Princeton, NJ: Princeton University Press, 1984).

[85] Margaret Lavinia Anderson, "The Limits of Secularization: On the Problem of the Catholic Revival in Nineteenth-Century Germany," *Historical Journal* 38, no. 3 (1995): 666. Anderson argues that this opposition eventually developed "into a critical, independent stance towards state authority itself" and "thus inevitably took on populist and ultimately even democratic elements" (666). The first stirrings of this opposition can be seen in the "*Kölner Wirren.*" In 1837 Clemens August von Droste-Vischering took up the position of Archbishop of Cologne. Unlike his predecessor, he refused to sanction mixed marriages (i.e. Catholic–Protestant) except (in conformity with Canon Law) when the couple agreed to raise all of their children in the Catholic faith. This contravened Prussian civil law, which mandated that sons would be raised in their father's faith and daughters in their mother's. He was promptly jailed, setting off huge protests among the Catholic population and giving a taste of the *Kulturkampf* to come. Similar protests occurred in the Polish-speaking province of Posen-Gnesen, where the archbishop also refused to sanction mixed marriages under Prussian law. See Ellen Lovell Evans, *The German Center Party, 1870–1933: A Study in Political Catholicism* (Carbondale, IL: Southern Illinois University Press, 1981), 4–6.

[86] Evans, *The German Center Party*, 10.

[87] These elections were conducted, it should be noted, under a universal male franchise and secret direct ballot for the first time.

[88] Kalyvas, *The Rise of Christian Democracy in Europe*, 214 n. 22.

at the head of a Catholic voting bloc that would persist for sixty years or longer.[89] What had changed? The difference lies in one word: *Kulturkampf*.

Bismarck, hoping to forestall parliamentary government and achieve his political goals, needed to bring the Liberals into his government camp while holding on to the Protestant nationalists, a trick he pulled off rather neatly by appealing to one value they held in common: anti-Catholicism.[90] Through a series of legislative and administrative measures, Bismarck increasingly asserted the state's control of church matters, interfering in clerical education, diocesan administration, and the selection of bishops.[91] Large majorities in the Reichstag approved bill after bill, proving to Bismarck that he could put working majorities together without moving toward parliamentary government, all by raising the "Roman Menace." As Smith notes, the *Kulturkampf* was a "progressive" political strategy, one that – even for self-proclaimed liberals – "urged the repression of ultramontanism, not in opposition to, but rather in consonance with, their basic principles."[92] For the government, the *Kulturkampf* measures proved extremely popular.

For Germany's Catholic citizens, the state had become a despised oppressor. By 1876, all of Prussia's bishops were either in jail or in exile,

---

[89] Anderson notes that even in 1994, "the most important predictor of voting behavior in the Federal Republic" was confessional identity. See Margaret Lavinia Anderson, *Practicing Democracy: Elections and Political Culture in Imperial Germany* (Princeton, NJ: Princeton University Press, 2000), 105.

[90] Sperber, *Popular Catholicism*, 207–9.

[91] In July 1871, Bismarck reorganized the Ministry of Religion, liquidating its separate Catholic division. That December, he pushed through the "pulpit law," forbidding clerics from speaking on political subjects from the pulpit in the (vain) hope of hobbling their political influence. The Reichstag voted to expel the Jesuits in 1872, and in May 1873, the Prussian legislature passed the four "May Laws." Priests could no longer study in Rome or in diocesan seminaries (except those under state authority) and they had to receive a degree from a German gymnasium and pass a state examination in German culture to be eligible to serve. The state asserted the right to review bishops' ecclesiastical authority over priests and limited their ability to execute excommunications. Finally, the fourth May Law allowed church members to withdraw their membership by simple statement (a law the Center did not oppose).

The following May (1874), citing continued Catholic noncompliance, the government forced the issue further, passing a new series of laws that gave local administrators even more control over parishes, allocating to them the livings of empty parishes and requiring cathedral chapters to elect new bishops if the seat was empty as a result of a bishop's exile or imprisonment. Priests who defied state orders to abstain from their duties or to remain in one area were, under the Imperial Expatriation Law, to be deported and stripped of their citizenship. In May 1875, Catholics were purged from the higher levels of the civil service, the Prussian Constitution was amended to remove guarantees of church autonomy, and all religious orders (except the Sisters of Mercy) were dissolved and their property expropriated. Finally, the Prussian Landtag passed the Breadbasket Law, which stipulated that only those priests who positively proved their obedience to the *Kulturkampf* laws would receive their salaries.

[92] Smith, *German Nationalism and Religious Conflict*, 40.

almost a quarter of its parishes pulpits were unfilled,[93] and 241 priests, 136 editors, 210 Center members, and 55 other persons had been arrested.[94] Nonetheless, Bismarck's *Kulturkampf* proved a failure. By 1878, the Center had become the largest party in the Reichstag,[95] and its parliamentary leader, Ludwig von Windthorst, was a celebrated hero.[96] More broadly, the *Kulturkampf* provoked the growth of mass Catholic organizations whose origin was in a merely defensive crouch against state persecution but whose ultimate destiny was the deepening and sustaining of Catholic mobilization. Bishop Ketteler's Mainz Association (or Association of German Catholics) had branches in nearly every German city where Catholics resided in any significant numbers, holding mass rallies and mobilizing Catholic voters.[97] The Catholic press, organized under the St. Augustine association, exploded in popularity, eventually reaching over 2.5 million readers by 1912.[98] The *Volksverein*, formed as a mass organizational vehicle, grew from 108,000 members in 1891 to 805,000 in 1914 – over 13 percent of the male Catholic population.[99] The vigorous Catholic opposition forced Bismarck to seek an end to the conflict.

As the *Kulturkampf* passed and German politics became, for Catholics at least, "normalized," the party struggled a little. Rates of religious observance declined, intermarriage increased and Catholic "identity" became, for the Center at least, dangerously diluted. Catholic turnout dropped in the 1880s and 1890s,[100] as the Catholic "milieu," the tight-knit communities that provided much of the Center's support, began to erode under the pressures of urbanization and industrialization.[101] The ties of religious sentiment, which had so powerfully bound together communities otherwise divided by class, profession, region, or nationality, weakened and threatened the party's very existence.

The Weimar Republic presented the Center with a new set of challenges. Germany was no longer a monarchy coupled with some parliamentary representation; rather, it was a democratic republic, guaranteeing to its

---

[93] Margaret Lavinia Anderson, *Windthorst: A Political Biography* (New York: Oxford University Press, 1981), 178.

[94] Evans, *The German Center Party*, 67.

[95] Noel D. Cary, *The Path to Christian Democracy: German Catholics and the Party System from Windthorst to Adenauer* (Cambridge, MA: Harvard University Press, 1996), 17.

[96] The annual Catholic congresses became, at times, little more than fetes in honor of Windthorst.

[97] Sperber, *Popular Catholicism*, 211.

[98] Evans, *The German Center Party*, 106.

[99] Kalyvas, *The Rise of Christian Democracy in Europe*, 215.

[100] Jonathan Sperber, *The Kaiser's Voters: Electors and Elections in Imperial Germany* (Cambridge and New York: Cambridge University Press, 1997), 20.

[101] Smith, *German Nationalism and Religious Conflict*, 82–93.

citizens a wide range of rights and liberties. Germany's Catholics bene-fited from this change as much as anyone, as the new constitution gave them nearly everything they had been asking for since the 1870s: free-dom for religious orders, no state interference in religious appointments, fiscal support for churches via tax lists, and so on. Though Catholics were more of a minority than ever before, they were no longer, it seemed, cultural or political strangers. The party struggled to maintain electoral support. Though it was in nearly every Weimar government, the Center saw its total vote share and its share of the Catholic vote decline with every election until 1932, as Catholic men especially deserted the party in favor of both the left and the right.[102] With the constitutional guarantees contained in the new constitution, the party's various factions had little incentive to mitigate their often contradictory demands. Compounding the problem, the Center's affiliated organizations began to atrophy and disappear. The *Volksverein*, which had at one time had over 800,000 members, saw its membership drop continuously throughout Weimar, and it ceased to function entirely by 1930.[103] Priests dropped their affili-ations with the party and stopped working as organizers, forcing it to construct new electoral organizations and find new spaces for their meet-ings. Catholic congresses ceased being stand-ins for Center rallies, and its Bavarian wing split off in 1920 to form its own, independent party, the BVP. The party itself began to suffer organizationally as its top leadership became isolated from the regional branches.

As Weimar's crises burgeoned, the Center emphasized even more strongly its *Kulturpolitik*, with fateful consequences. From about 1926 to 1928 the Center was in a coalition government with the conservative parties. Ignoring warnings that its standing with workers was in danger unless it took steps toward providing social relief, the Center focused its attention on the denominational school issue. In the end, the party rejected a compromise measure that would have allowed parents to petition for denominational schools and allowed clerics to teach reli-gion in mixed schools. It was, Evans argues, an ominous development for German democracy because the deal on offer was the best that was realistically possible under Weimar's constitutional democracy.[104] The Center's unwillingness to go along with such a compromise spoke vol-umes about its commitment to democratic government.

Over the next five years, the Center would assume a more and more central role in the Weimar government, participating in every government

---

[102] This was made up in part by the votes of Catholic women, who comprised about 59 percent of its electorate. See Evans, *The German Center Party*, 242.
[103] Ibid., 257.   [104] Ibid., 329.

and providing four of its chancellors. The Center's Chancellor Brüning initiated the use of the infamous Article 48, and party leader Monsignor Kaas helped to elevate Papen to the chancellorship in 1932. In March 1933, the Bishops' Conference withdrew their prohibition against membership in the Nazi Party, and the Center provided the final votes necessary for Hitler's Enabling Act. The party was dissolved on July 5, at least partly in response to instructions from the Roman curia, whose conclusion of the *Reichskonkordat* (agreed to on July 22 with the National Socialist government) was probably dependent on a cessation of Catholic political activity. The Center finally – and ignominiously – folded.

Conclusion

When Anglo-American political theorists working in the liberal democratic tradition think about the history of religious political mobilization in Europe, they almost inevitably seem to jump to the sixteenth and seventeenth centuries, when brutal wars ravaged the continent following the Reformation. Those wars are important to keep in mind, but they do not form the whole of the European experience with religion's political mobilization. As parts of Europe, however fitfully, moved toward democratic rule in the second half of the nineteenth century, religious communities, especially in Belgium, the Netherlands, Germany, and Austria, organized powerful networks as a means both of protecting their members against the corrosive acids of modernity and of pursuing their social and political goals via electoral contests and parliamentary debate. I will leave more detailed analysis of what this might mean for the liberal consensus to the next five chapters, but as a preliminary thought it seems clear that consolidated democracies and religious political mobilization are not mutually incompatible, though, as at least the case of Austria shows, neither are they *always* compatible. Much of the following chapters' discussion of these cases centers around distinguishing between these two outcomes and seeing what they tell us about the consensus's philosophical and moral claims.

2 The argument for deliberative restraint

The liberal consensus regarding religion and democratic life has any number of components: views emphasizing the importance of separating church and state, concerns about religion's ambiguous relationship to the political virtue, a tendency to view religion as especially prone to fits of irrational passion, and so on. These overlapping concerns form the basis for the consensus's efforts to develop ways of constructing and maintaining political orders relatively free of public religious influence. Within the context of democratic politics, it has been religion's involvement in everyday political life, especially elections and public policy debates, that has made one concern in particular the subject of wide and vigorous debate. That concern centers on whether citizens may employ (or how they may employ) their religious views politically, whether they should propose and justify laws with rationales that depend on particular theological claims for their persuasiveness. Our arguments over any number of highly contentious public policy questions – abortion, euthanasia, cloning, and so on – run along two levels: we have arguments over the policy question in particular (e.g. should abortion be legal?); and we have arguments over how we ought to be arguing (e.g. what sorts of reasons should we bring to bear on those questions?). Digging into the arguments concerning any one of these sorts of questions almost always reveals a claim about how this or that sort of argument should be out of bounds precisely *because* it is religious (or maybe anti-religious) and that its employment violates in some central way the moral and civic obligations attendant on democracies.[1] Though there are, as we will see, any number of variations on this theme, what I call the Argument for Deliberative

---

[1] Consider as an example Judith Jarvis Thomson, "Abortion," *Boston Review: A Political and Literary Forum* (2005). If we think of this essay as something of an update to her famous 1972 *Philosophy and Public Affairs* argument, it is striking how much ground she concedes to abortion opponents, only to claim that the law should still guarantee a woman's right to an abortion because the arguments against abortion rights are largely, perhaps inherently, religious in nature. Similar examples abound in debates over homosexual rights, cloning, embryonic stem cell research, euthanasia, and the like.

Restraint[2] broadly claims that citizens must engage one another politically on grounds that all (or nearly all) could endorse. Religious believers
who propose or support laws on the basis of theological claims that other
citizens might reasonably (and do) reject do so at the cost of violating
what should be fundamental political commitments regarding the nature
of the democratic polity and the freedom and equality of all. Those who
employ religious reasons politically do so at the cost of those democratic
commitments and endanger, in turn, the democratic order itself.

It might seem puzzling to some that this debate over the sorts of reasons
citizens may use politically, especially over their use of religious reasons,
would figure so prominently among political theorists over the past fifteen years or so.[3] There is nothing more natural, at least in the American
context, than the use of religious imagery, rhetoric, and reasons in the
pursuit of some political end.[4] Nearly every American president has
made religious references in his most important speeches, and most have
made official proclamations declaring days of thanksgiving or mourning
with explicit reference to the divine. It is probably impossible to account
adequately for any period of American history without making reference

---

[2] I borrow the term "restraint" from Eberle, *Religious Conviction in Liberal Politics*.

[3] Indeed, when I offered a very early version of my argument to a number of political
scientists who are more empirically minded, one of the first questions they posed was
why would anyone be concerned about this question? A partial slice of the literature on
the debate over "religious reasons" would include Robert Audi, "The Place of Religious
Argument in a Free and Democratic Society," *San Diego Law Review* 30 (1993); Robert
Audi, *Religious Commitment and Secular Reason* (Cambridge and New York: Cambridge
University Press, 2000); Stephen L. Carter, *God's Name in Vain: The Wrongs and Rights of
Religion in Politics*, 1st. edn. (New York: Basic Books, 2000); Jonathan Chaplin, "Beyond
Liberal Restraint: Defending Religiously Based Arguments in Law and Public Policy,"
University of British Columbia Law Review 33, no. 3 (2000); Eberle, *Religious Conviction
in Liberal Politics*; Jean Bethke Elshtain, "State-Imposed Secularism as a Potential
Pitfall of Liberal Democracy" (paper presented at the Religious Liberty Conference,
Prague, Czech Republic, 2000); Kent Greenawalt, *Private Consciences and Public Reasons*
(New York: Oxford University Press, 1995); Amy Gutmann and Dennis F. Thompson,
Democracy and Disagreement (Cambridge, MA: Belknap Press, 1996); Habermas, "On
the Relations between the Secular Liberal State and Religion"; Jürgen Habermas,
"'Reasonable' Versus 'True,' Or the Morality of Worldviews," in *The Inclusion of the
Other: Studies in Political Theory*, ed. Ciaran Cronin and Pablo de Greiff (Cambridge,
MA: MIT Press, 1999); Jürgen Habermas, "Reconciliation through the Use of Public
Reason," in Cronin and de Greiff, eds., *The Inclusion of the Other*; Habermas, "Religion
in the Public Sphere"; Charles Larmore, "The Moral Basis of Political Liberalism,"
Journal of Philosophy 96, no. 12 (1999); Larmore, "Political Liberalism"; Macedo,
"Transformative Constitutionalism"; Michael J. Perry, *Religion in Politics: Constitutional
and Moral Perspectives* (New York: Oxford University Press, 1997); Rawls, "The Idea of
Public Reason Revisited"; Weithman, *Religion and the Obligations of Citizenship*; Paul J.
Weithman, ed., *Religion and Contemporary Liberalism* (Notre Dame, IN: University of
Notre Dame Press, 1997).

[4] See James A. Morone, *Hellfire Nation: The Politics of Sin in American History* (New Haven:
Yale University Press, 2003). This is much less true of contemporary Europe.

to how religion played some important role, and as Michael Burleigh has recently pointed out, the same is likely true of modern Europe as well.[5] Finally, while political theorists have largely settled on a view that religious reasons are more or less out of bounds politically, the broad swathe of the American public has fewer such compunctions.[6]

We might rather cynically think there is no mystery here at all. Perhaps the most striking feature of American politics over the past thirty years or so has been the emergence and consolidation of potent social and political movements populated by religious conservatives, what many tend to call the "Christian Right" or, more generically, the "Religious Right." Beginning with what *Time* magazine called the "Year of the Evangelical" in 1976 followed by the founding of Jerry Falwell's Moral Majority in the run-up to the 1980 presidential election, religious conservatives have had a great deal of influence on American politics and perhaps even more on its academic critics, who tend to view it and its associated religious communities with some suspicion, fear, and even contempt.[7] It is tempting, then, when thinking about why this question of religious reasons has attracted so much attention from political theorists to see little more than partisan posturing. What better way, a cynic might suggest, of silencing one's opponents than by claiming not just that their views are incorrect or even noxious, but also that they are essentially undemocratic to boot?[8] Consider, for example, that it is well-nigh impossible to find in the voluminous literature on religious reasons any critiques of the

---

[5] Michael Burleigh, *Earthly Powers: The Clash of Religion and Politics in Europe from the French Revolution to the Great War*, 1st. edn. (New York: HarperCollins Publishers, 2005); Michael Burleigh, *Sacred Causes: The Clash of Religion and Politics, from the Great War to the War on Terror*, 1st. edn. (New York: HarperCollins, 2007).

[6] According to a 2003 Pew Forum on Religion and Public Life survey, 52 percent of Americans think churches should express views on political matters and 41 percent think that politicians make expressions of faith too rarely. Only 44 percent and 21 percent think otherwise, respectively. See http://pewforum.org/docs/index.php?DocID=26. An August 2008 Pew Forum Poll switched those numbers, with 52 percent of Americans saying churches should "keep out" of political debates and 45 percent saying they should express their views. See http://pewforum.org/docs/?DocID=334. For a compilation of similar studies that suggest that something similar to what I am calling "deliberative restraint" does not comport well with most Americans' views, see Klosko, *Democratic Procedures and Liberal Consensus*.

[7] According to a recent survey, 71 percent of American university faculty agreed that the country would be better off if "Christian fundamentalists kept their religious beliefs out of politics," and evangelicals were the *only* group that a majority non-evangelical professors said they felt "cool" or "unfavorable" toward. See www.jewishresearch.org/PDFs2/FacultyReligion07.pdf, accessed September 2007.

[8] See Rawls, *Political Liberalism*, li–lii. While presenting an earlier version of my argument, I was repeatedly pressed by a senior scholar who said that she was quite "worried" about its main claims, not because of any concerns she had about legitimacy and the like, but because allowing religion "back into" politics might reopen political questions that "we have already decided."

US Conference of Catholic Bishops' statements in the 1980s criticizing nuclear weapons or less regulated market economies or of the very close ties of African-American Protestant churches to Democratic Party politics. We might just well conclude that the whole matter is little more than partisan politics and leave it at that.

While this partisan interpretation no doubt partly explains both the attention paid to religious reasons and the restraint argument's success,[9] it would be a mistake to see this as merely another instance of "liberal" academics seeking to delegitimize their most favored bogeymen. To do that would be to slight the ways in which the argument is a serious attempt to respond, however imperfectly, to the explosion of wide moral and religious pluralism now inhabiting modern democratic societies and to the ways in which such pluralism threatens to undermine what is perhaps the liberal democratic order's most central moral claim, namely that political authority's legitimacy depends on the free consent of those over whom that authority is to be exercised. Ascribing the various claims in favor of deliberative restraint to mere partisan sentiment is to miss the more important story at work here. It is to miss in particular the way in which moral and religious pluralism threatens central claims in the liberal tradition, how restraint attempts to defend against that threat, and, ultimately, how the restraint argument's failure suggests that we should make some serious reconsideration of those same central liberal claims. It is *these* sorts of issues that make the questions surrounding religious reasons so central to the consensus and the ones to which I will attend over the next few chapters. For the rest of this chapter, I will sketch out what has made the question of religious reasons such a pressing one for political theorists and how most of them have responded in turn.

The moral and historical sources of the argument for deliberative restraint

What then accounts for the veritable explosion of interest in these questions? Until the late 1980s, no one seemed to care much at all about the sorts of reasons that citizens employed politically and certainly no one was focused on the question of *religious* reasons. Rawls' famous 1971 work *A Theory of Justice* does focus on the sorts of reasons participants in the Original Position might offer one another, but his focus is on how the "veil of ignorance" precludes its participants from offering self-interested reasons, the same sort of claim repeated in Bruce Ackerman's *Social Justice*

---

[9] It seems to me that this is especially true in works on the more popular level. See Linker, *The Theocons*; Sullivan, *The Conservative Soul*.

in the Liberal State.[10] It is only in the mid-1980s, as Rawls began to revise his argument for "justice as fairness" and work out the idea of "public reason," that other scholars in turn began to pay more attention.[11] So part of the story is clearly the influence that Rawls in particular wielded in political theory debates in the last third of the twentieth century. But the focus on reason-giving, deliberation, and deliberative restraint emerges more broadly, I think, out of a much deeper conundrum within the liberal democratic political tradition itself, one whose parameters became more clear as that tradition grappled with the increased pluralization of free societies in the post-World War II era.

As I suggested above, at the core of the liberal democratic political tradition lies a view that ties political legitimacy to the consent of the governed. This in itself may seem a rather unexceptional claim and one that many might pass over with nary a quibble; indeed it is almost a cliché. We are, after all, a society dedicated (in aspiration, if not in fact) to the proposition that "Governments are instituted among Men, deriving their just powers from the consent of the governed." But peering more closely at the claimed linkages between consent and legitimacy inevitably reveals a relationship much less clear and straightforward, as any number of critics within and outside of the tradition have long argued. What does it mean to give one's consent? Can you take it back? Must *everyone actually* consent, or may some majority speak for the rest? Can one be held to have consented tacitly simply by living in a society? Do you have to consent to everything the government does or just its constitutional framework?

The problem is that, construed strictly, making actual consent the legitimating keystone of political authority is plainly implausible; or, at the least, it makes every plausible government almost by definition illegitimate. Even if we could devise a system by which citizens could render (or withhold) their consent, it is hard to see how that consent could be permanently binding or even how it could be "free and fair."[12] More plausible, but still ambiguous in its political salience, is the Lockean claim for

---

[10] See John Rawls, *A Theory of Justice* (Cambridge, MA: Belknap Press of Harvard University Press, 1971), especially chapter III, and Bruce A. Ackerman, *Social Justice in the Liberal State* (New Haven: Yale University Press, 1980). Both are examples of a broader effort to articulate what Nagel has called the "view from nowhere," a view that would (it seems) preclude religious reasons but more importantly self-interested reasons as well.

[11] See his article "Justice as Fairness: Political Not Metaphysical" (first published in 1985) in Rawls, *Collected Papers*, ed. Freeman 388–414.

[12] The place of immigrants in a modern democracy helps make this clear. Even if an immigrant explicitly comes to endorse a particular political order – through an oath of citizenship, say – if he comes to regret that commitment or finds later that he no longer thinks of the government as legitimate, it is no simple thing to pick up and head "home." The complications are just as great, if not more so, for native-born citizens.

tacit consent, the idea that citizens might be said to have implicitly given their consent to the broad cast of political authority to the degree that they have benefited from that authority. There is something to this claim, at least in the sense that to the degree we acquiesce in a certain construction of political authority, we can plausibly be thought to have affirmed in practice our approval of that construction. But even this claims too much, since people sometimes acquiesce in a certain political authority out of fear or because of effective propaganda techniques (think contemporary North Korea), and it has the rather dubious effect of inoculating governments precisely against what the legitimacy–consent linkage was meant to do in the first place. Whatever else Locke and the rest of the social contract tradition means to do by linking the idea of consent to political legitimacy, they clearly mean to establish some principled grounds from which actual governments could be critiqued and perhaps improved. Rawls' Original Position device, like Locke's state of nature, was not meant to describe some "actual" historical or even psychological event but to help articulate what an "ideal" government might look like and on that basis criticize and improve current practices. The idea of consent in this respect matters at least because it provides a way of generating principled critiques of political authority. So *even if* as a practical (and philosophical) matter it is hard to see how consent *actually* serves to legitimate (or delegitimate, as the case may be) a particular political order, it still remains a powerful moral ideal and helps us think seriously about how our politics ought to be organized (or reformed).

The key contemporary problem in making consent "work" in terms of liberal political legitimacy is, perhaps ironically, the very sort of thing that made (and makes) liberalism so necessary and so successful: moral and religious pluralism. It is a commonplace of course that liberalism largely got its start as a response to Europe's wars of religion in the sixteenth and seventeenth centuries. That seems right so far as it goes, but the problem that Locke and liberalism more generally have tried to solve goes far beyond merely trying to figure out how to construct a social and political order such that citizens of different and deeply opposed religious persuasions will desist from trying to kill one another. The more basic problem is constructing a political order which those same citizens – and others of no religious persuasion, as well – can endorse or give their consent to. That is, the central historical problem liberalism means to answer is one of moral and religious pluralism, the sociological reality that as societies have become more open they have also become places where citizens come to disagree more widely with one another in their basic moral claims, in how they see the world and their place in it.[13] When all of a territory's citizens ascribe to a particular religious confession, it seems fairly straightforward to make the claim that such-and-such political authority is justified on account of that confession. When those confessions pluralize, such claims become either implausible or can only be imposed via coercion, a problem that only grows with secularization, when even the most anodyne and generic religious references cannot, seemingly, function as justifications of political order.

Locke attempted to solve this problem of pluralism by reaching "beyond" religious confession to reason and, in particular, to the state of nature, where he hoped that each of us might be able to imagine ourselves as pre-political creatures who shared a common set of concerns and, ultimately, could develop a common set of solutions. The trick, of course, is to show that there are some sorts of political institutions that do in fact work as a common set of solutions and that correspond to something – perhaps reason or nature – that we all do in fact share. Whatever else Rousseau meant to suggest with his often perplexing invocation of the "General Will," he seemed to point at just this sort of claim, namely how can the social contract *actually* be binding for a particular political community when individual members of that community will likely differ on just what the substantive conclusion of the social contract should look like. That is, to the degree that consent is meant to mark out not just the sorts of political institutions and practices to which we *should* be able to subscribe but also help make it possible for us to *actually* subscribe (if only by pointing out the ways a particular government falls short), the moral and religious pluralism that makes the liberal social contract necessary also threatens to make it implausible – or worse. If we disagree not just about God and a hundred other things but also about the nature of justice and the shape of the good political order, then it is hard to see how we can give our consent in any intelligible sense of the word. Or perhaps more to the point, it is hard to see how any particular political order could be *justified* without recourse to notions that many would (reasonably) dispute. Rousseau's answer was famously to endow a founder (i.e. the "legislator") with almost God-like powers to reshape

---

[13] It is quite possible to write the history of liberalism and emphasize different elements: the emphasis on the rule of law, the circumscription of political authority, the protection of individual liberties, the promotion of social and political equality, etc. My point here is merely to suggest that as a practical matter, the strand of liberal political thought that reaches back to Locke – the social contract tradition – finds its historical origins primarily in the attempt to grapple with the moral and religious pluralism that emerges after the Protestant Reformation.

citizens so that they might be able to form a coherent General Will, one reinforced by a civil religion that would tie those citizens all the more tightly to the community by investing it with a kind of divine aura.[14] Needless to say, such options are hardly on the table for the contemporary liberal political theorist, though as I discuss in chapter 5 some are certainly tempted in that direction.

I noted previously that I have chosen to employ the terms "liberal," "liberal democratic," and "democratic" more or less interchangeably, notwithstanding the fact that at least the terms "liberal" and "democratic" represent two quite distinctive strands of political thought, historically speaking. Indeed, even today those who describe themselves as "democratic" theorists often frame their arguments in ways to accentuate their differences with "liberal" alternatives.[15] There is good reason, though, to think that at least today such differences are fairly minimal and the two traditions have largely merged. No democratic theorist I know of is willing to do away with the constitutional protections of individual liberties, and self-styled liberal theorists are hardly eager to do away with democratically elected representatives. Rawls' and Habermas' celebrated exchange over their competing views was striking more for how similar these purportedly distinct "liberal" and "deliberative democratic" theories looked.[16] But inasmuch as those traditions have merged or at least are now a "family" of similarly focused arguments, such convergence brings with it an interesting philosophical challenge with respect to consent, legitimacy, and moral pluralism.

Liberal theories of politics, at least those in the social contract strand of liberalism, have long emphasized the importance of articulating a set of pre-political principles that should govern or animate our political institutions. As I noted above, both Locke's state of nature and Rawls' Original Position fit this mold, as do any number of other similar

---

[14] See Jean Jacques Rousseau, *On the Social Contract*, trans. Donald Cress (Indianapolis: Hackett Publishing, 1987 [1762]), bk. II, ch. VII and bk. IV, ch. VIII.

[15] One particularly clear example of this is in Benjamin R. Barber, *Strong Democracy: Participatory Politics for a New Age* (Berkeley: University of California Press, 1984).

[16] See Jürgen Habermas, "Reconciliation through the Public Use of Reason: Remarks on John Rawls's Political Liberalism," *Journal of Political Philosophy* 92, no. 3 (1995) and John Rawls, "Political Liberalism: Reply to Habermas," *Journal of Political Philosophy* 92, no. 3 (1995). Habermas has taken of late to calling his deliberative theories a sort of "political liberalism" while Rawls' last published article described his political liberalism as a kind of "deliberative democracy." See Habermas, "On the Relations between the Secular Liberal State and Religion" and Rawls, "The Idea of Public Reason Revisited." For an early review that emphasized Rawls' democratic turn see Joshua Cohen, "A More Democratic Liberalism: Political Liberalism," *Michigan Law Review* 92, no. 6 (1994).

devices.[17] Democratic theories, as with Rousseau's noted above, emphasize instead the importance of having political authority actually invested in and exercised by all citizens acting together as a single community. Benjamin Barber's "strong democracy" criticizes liberal theories precisely on this point, claiming that they tend to posit (and inflame, in his view) divisions within the body politic and underplay its collective potential.[18] Though something quite powerful is achieved by the traditions' convergence, real tensions are evinced as well. Most importantly for our purposes, by bringing the liberal and democratic traditions together, theorists have suggested the promise not just of articulating principles of justice that *ought* to govern our political communities and thus offer us a critical platform from which to examine our current practices but also of finding ways to make it such that we *actually do* (or *actually can*) endorse those principles and thus actually govern ourselves. Or, at the very least, such convergence gets us *closer* to actual endorsement.[19] It is one thing, after all, to suggest that there is a set of governing principles to which all rational persons should subscribe (the "liberal" view). Even if no government actually reaches the bar set by those principles, at least we gain some insight into what justice requires and, perhaps less obviously, where things need to be changed. It is quite another, on the other hand, to begin at the other end of things and make a government's justness and legitimacy hang on how well it reflects a population's collective will (the "democratic" view). To do *both*, to find a way to match up popular will and disinterested justice, is both the promise and challenge posed by the convergence of the two traditions.

The convergence of the two traditions offers the *promise* of reconciling what seem to be two quite different things, rational principles of justice and popular will, but in doing so it brings into sharp relief the actual distance between the two, a distance that seems ever wider and perhaps ever more unbridgeable. At the same time as the two traditions have largely merged and suggested to us (if often only implicitly) the promise that we might inhabit a social and political order that both reflects our will and is just, we have come to recognize that the social and political order that we *actually* inhabit subsists in a wide pluralism that belies such promise. And to the degree we think that democratic legitimacy depends on the

---

[17] See Ackerman, *Social Justice in the Liberal State*. There he uses the device of asking his readers to imagine themselves on a spaceship on their way to a new colony, free to establish any sort of social and political order they wish. Rawls' Original Position is only partly pre-political, as its participants know the general sociological and economic contours of how modern societies work.

[18] Barber, *Strong Democracy*.

[19] See Paul J. Weithman, "Deliberative Character," *Journal of Political Philosophy* 13, no. 3 (2005).

promise of such a convergence, we might find ourselves sorely – and dangerously – disappointed. Moral and religious pluralism makes the effort to articulate principles of political legitimacy crucial, but it also threatens to make such efforts philosophically and practically implausible, perhaps undermining a core liberal democratic claim in the process.

We could just avoid the problem altogether by not concerning ourselves about moralistic norms of legitimacy in the first place. A quite robust strain of democratic thought denies that such claims about legitimacy and the like have much to do with how democracies actually function. These thinkers suggest instead that in reality democracies succeed simply by arranging their political institutions in ways that reasonably balance out competing interests, something akin to what Schumpeter or, more recently, Przeworski defended as the only plausible kind of democratic politics.[20] As long as political institutions do a decently good job at being responsive to a society's varied interests, individuals and groups will resolve their differences within the established institutions and procedures. Democracy will be the "only game in town."[21] Moral claims about legitimacy and obligation need not figure at all; we need nothing more than a well-designed modus vivendi.

Most liberal theorists argue that this sort of "minimalist" theory, though it does capture in part how democracies actually do work, fails to take seriously enough the practical importance of self-generated moral obligations. Even if it seemed true that modus vivendi democracies were relatively stable and functioned reasonably fairly, they would still find such democracies wanting morally and be convinced that their moral deficit has important practical consequences. The social contract liberals are not just interested in stability per se, but in what Rawls calls "stability for the right reasons" or what I will call, following Klosko, "moral stability."[22] This is the sort of stability that consists in having citizens' basic and enduring moral commitments include those principles underpinning political institutions, thus connecting our views about what makes for human flourishing and meaning to our political loyalties more or less seamlessly. We identify with and are committed to a particular

[20] Adam Przeworski, "Minimalist Conception of Democracy: A Defense," in *Democracy's Value*, ed. Ian Shapiro and Casiano Hacker-Cordon (Cambridge: Cambridge University Press, 1999); Joseph A. Schumpeter, *Capitalism, Socialism and Democracy* (New York: Harper and Brothers, 1942). See also Ian Shapiro, "Enough of Deliberation: Politics Is about Interests and Power," in *Deliberative Politics: Essays on Democracy and Disagreement*, ed. Stephen Macedo (New York: Oxford University Press, 1999).

[21] Giuseppe Di Palma, *To Craft Democracies: An Essay on Democratic Transitions* (Berkeley: University of California Press, 1990).

[22] George Klosko, "Rawls's Argument from Political Stability," *Columbia Law Review* 94, no. 6 (1994); Rawls, *Political Liberalism*, 390.

democratic political order on this account not because it happens to meet our needs or to protect our interests – though it certainly must do those things – but because that system is, in some important sense, "ours."[23] In a morally stable regime, we would no more easily set our political commitments aside than we would our moral or religious ones. This sort of political order – if workable – would be quite stable in the ordinary sense of the word, but for reasons much more substantial than a modus vivendi.

This emphasis on "moral stability" is expressed most clearly in Rawls' discussion of stability in *A Theory of Justice*. In chapters VIII–IX, he describes how it is that he thinks a society governed by justice as fairness can maintain itself over time, especially focusing on the way in which individuals come to develop a "sense of justice" that provides them the inclination and motivation to act in conformity with those principles of justice. Rawls' hope is that justice as fairness's moral psychology is such that it accurately describes ways in which its social and political institutions cultivate in normal adults a desire (or "moral sentiment") that generally overcomes any impulse to act unjustly, encouraging them to adjust their life-plans such that they are effectively "regulated" by justice as fairness. The basic idea here for Rawls is that we can best develop as individuals in the context of a community in which each is committed to treating the other justly. In such a (liberal) community, we conform our life-plans to principles that express most clearly what it means to treat each other justly and thus internalize these principles as an expression of our own, highest ends. In a well-ordered society, then, there is no (or very little) conflict between our individual life-plans and the collective common good; they are mutually supportive and perhaps even interdependent. It is easy to see why such an order would be stable, at least so long as its moral psychology accurately described human development. If growing up under just institutions helped shape individuals committed to the maintenance and development of those institutions as an integral part of their own plans for human flourishing, then it seems quite reasonable to expect that those individuals would, under most circumstances, be quite resistant to attempts at undermining them.[24]

---

[23] So in this case, Claudia Mills and Bernard Dauenhauer are at least somewhat misguided in their different claims that a modus vivendi democracy could be stable and morally satisfying. See Bernard P. Dauenhauer, "A Good Word for a Modus Vivendi," in *The Idea of a Political Liberalism: Essays on Rawls*, ed. Victoria Davion and Clark Wolf (Lanham, MD: Rowman & Littlefield, 2000); Claudia Mills, "Not a Mere Modus Vivendi," in Davion and Wolf, eds., *The Idea of a Political Liberalism*.

[24] For more on this, see Freeman, *Justice and the Social Contract*, 143–45; Weithman, "Review of Samuel Freeman, *Justice and the Social Contract*."

Modus vivendi democracies lack that sort of moral depth. They hold our loyalty to the degree that they serve as useful instruments for the pursuit of our private (and diverse) ends and thus might plausibly be thought to be more vulnerable to instability and failure. If there is no deep connection between our individual sense for what makes for a good life and our plans to achieve it and the social and political institutions in which we find ourselves, then if our life-plans change or we find those institutions to be obstacles for our life-plans, we might very well decide that the institutions need changing – or overthrow. Moral stability is an important characteristic of the just society because it both expresses our commitments to the maintenance of a just political order on into the future and does a better job of securing that order than the available alternatives (i.e. the modus vivendi).

But if liberal theorists find modus vivendi accounts of democracies unsatisfying because of their moral poverty, those who emphasize more the other (democratic) end of things have a raft of complaints as well. For inasmuch as this "realist" view purports to describe how democracies "actually" function it misses what makes democracy so powerful and enticing: its vision of a political community governed by a popular and collective will that secures the interest of all along with the interest of each. Balancing out interests is not the same thing as finding what is in the common interest; by comparison, modus vivendi accounts look downright pedestrian. What's more, modus vivendi democratic theories have problems even on their own terms, as balancing the competing claims of interest is fraught with all sorts of difficulties, empirical and theoretical. "Expressed" interest may not be the same thing as "true" interest. Preference formation may be deeply conditioned by pre-existing conditions.[25] These modus vivendi models also find it difficult to avoid creating perpetual minorities and plausibly leave basic liberties poorly protected against democratic majorities. And, finally, such minimalist democracies must still be *justified*, even if only in the sense that they claim to represent fairly a society's diverse interests and so still make claims of moral obligation about which citizens must deliberate.[26]

The minimalist view of democracy does help illuminate, however, the ways in which contemporary liberal democracies do not rely solely on the quality of animating principles for their legitimacy but also on their claims to reflect the popular will. If you were to ask even a reasonably well-informed and well-educated democratic citizen whether she thought

---

[25] For the classic account of this critique, see Jon Elster, *Sour Grapes: Studies in the Subversion of Rationality* (New York: Cambridge University Press, 1983).
[26] My thanks to Dennis Thompson for this last point.

that her government was "legitimate," her answer would, of course, have an obviously moral component consisting of reflections on whether she agreed with the kinds of principles guiding the extant political order. You would also, I suspect, get in her answer some reflection of whether she thought the actually existing government was doing the things she thought a government should be doing – and doing them well or poorly.[27] The two sorts of legitimacy are obviously related. However magnificently constructed a set of political institutions might be, malign or inept public officials can, through repeated policy failures, damage not only their own legitimacy but the whole system's as well.[28] And even if a political system can make the "trains run on time," it remains vulnerable to failure if its basic principles run afoul of citizens' basic moral commitments. We can call this first view of legitimacy, one that tends toward to what I have been calling the liberal view of things, *moral legitimacy*, as it reflects the ways in which principles animating political institutions are (or can be) endorsed by citizens on their own terms. We can call the second view of legitimacy *popular legitimacy*, denoting the ways in which citizens' views of their government depend in part on how well that government takes account of their actual interests and pursues policies reflective of them. *Political legitimacy* in liberal democracies is best understood as combining these two interrelated components: a moral legitimacy that concerns the ties between political institutions' underlying principles and citizens' basic normative commitments; and a popular legitimacy that concerns the political institutions' performance and their responsiveness to citizens' actual political interests and desires. In a landscape where our democratic and liberal traditions have largely merged, any successful view of political legitimacy will need to account for both of these components.

I suggested above that the tradition's claims regarding legitimacy were in part a response to the moral and religious pluralism emerging in post-Reformation Europe. The hope, characteristic especially of Hobbes' and Locke's social contract theories, was that we could articulate a set of

---

[27] For a discussion of how many Western democracies are having some difficulties on this point, see Susan J. Pharr and Robert D. Putnam, *Disaffected Democracies: What's Troubling the Trilateral Countries?* (Princeton, NJ: Princeton University Press, 2000).

[28] For a rather robust defense of the relationship between modernization and democratic politics, see Adam Przeworski and Fernando Limongi, "Modernization: Theories and Facts," *World Politics* 49, no. 2 (1997). What is particularly striking is how once a democracy achieves a certain level of wealth, it seems invulnerable to failure. What lies behind that relationship is not altogether clear, but I suspect that part of the answer is that being wealthier cushions poor policy choices and constrains whatever erosion of legitimacy stems from this to the particular public officials responsible for those choices. Poorer countries have much less margin for error, and as such bad policy choices are much more likely to make citizens think the system as a whole is at fault rather than a particular party or official.

principles to which all rational individuals could subscribe and which could then serve as the basis for a stable, legitimate, and just political order. That hope courses through the post-World War II era's most influential work of political philosophy, *A Theory of Justice*. Strikingly, though, it was but a few years later that Rawls had already begun to revise significant elements of his argument, a revision occasioned largely out of his concern that parts of *Theory* were "unrealistic." Rawls' shift by 1993 from *Theory* to *Political Liberalism* was emblematic of a broader shift among political theorists, as they began to recognize and grapple with the difficulties emergent in what he has called the "fact of reasonable pluralism." In tracing briefly Rawls' adjustments to the argument for "justice as fairness," we will see more clearly just how it is that the challenges moral and religious pluralism posed for constitutional democracy's political legitimacy occasion the recourse to the claims of deliberation and, by extension, deliberative restraint.

Rawls' argument for justice as fairness in *Theory* centers on his claim that its two principles of justice are the most rationally defensible ones available and that a just social and political order will both reflect and attempt to put them into practice. As I noted above, the oft-neglected third part of the book describes the ways in which the social and political order envisioned by justice as fairness could maintain itself over time and thus show itself to be reasonably stable. The crux of this argument in *Theory* was that individuals who grew up under just institutions would develop a "sense of justice" such that their moral inclinations and the extant political institutions would be mutually reinforcing precisely because those individuals would organize (and reorganize) their life-plans in conjunction with the publicly affirmed principle of justice. We might say that in *Theory* Rawls thought justice as fairness was realistic in that it argued (not implausibly) that a well-ordered society would help produce and would be produced in turn by well-ordered individuals whose life-plans, though diverse, conduced toward and were compatible with justice as fairness.

Rawls became convinced that *Theory*'s version of justice as fairness could not serve as the basis for a well-ordered democratic society, in particular because the comprehensive moral views likely to persist within such a society would inevitably include some whose premises were indelibly at odds with *Theory*'s Kantian individualism. These "reasonable romantics," as Charles Larmore described them,[29] eschewed *Theory*'s presumptions regarding the importance of comprehensive moral autonomy

---

[29] See also Larmore, "Political Liberalism." Larmore seems to have people like Michael Sandel and Alasdair MacIntyre in mind. Rawls explicitly dismissed the notion that the shift from *Theory* to *Political Liberalism* was in any way related to their sorts of critiques (often described as "communitarian"), but it seems clear that at the least their sort

while at the same time genuinely endorsing basic democratic essentials. Rawls came to conclude that this "fact of reasonable pluralism" is not a remediable product of economic conditions or cultural desuetude, but rather is the *natural* outcome of a society in which men and women are left free to seek and develop their own views on the good:

> The diversity of reasonable comprehensive religious, philosophical, and moral doctrines found in modern democratic societies is not a mere historical condition that may soon pass away; it is a permanent feature of the public culture of democracy. Under the political and social conditions secured by the basic rights and liberties of free institutions, a diversity of conflicting and irreconcilable – and what's more, reasonable – comprehensive doctrines will come about and persist if such diversity does not already obtain.[30]

We are simply quite unlikely to overcome very many of our disagreements on substantive moral matters, including, it seems, on what constitutes justice.

Even under ideal conditions, it appeared that the institutions and practices of a well-ordered constitutional democracy could not be expected to produce individuals whose life-plans cohered well with justice as fairness, at least as Rawls articulated it in *Theory*. They could reasonably reject *Theory* as being premised on a view of human flourishing incompatible with their own understanding, meaning that they could also reasonably refuse to endorse its consequent political orders. Or at the least, their endorsement of such orders would be on grounds other than those found in justice as fairness, meaning that the "sense of justice" Rawls hoped would develop under such institutions would be uneven at best. If the conception of justice as articulated in *Theory* could not be endorsed by all reasonable citizens, then it would appear that the hope for a pluralist democratic order's legitimacy and stability could be put at risk. In the absence of those kinds of reliable moral commitments, a democracy's legitimacy would, inevitably perhaps, come to rest on majority will, the satisfaction of interests, or simply coercive force, all of which Rawls seemed to think conduced to ordinary instability and perhaps political failure. If individuals may reasonably disagree about justice, then what justifies our political institutions to those whom they govern? If there is no reasonable expectation that the laws passed will be "our" laws, then why think that we have even a prima facie obligation to obey them? The

---

of obduracy regarding the Kantian individualism in *Theory* served as an illustrative exemplar for the reasonableness of such claims. That is, there seemed to be plenty of citizens who, like Sandel and MacIntyre, were "reasonable" in the sense of embracing democratic essentials but who rejected Kantian views of autonomy. *Political Liberalism* is Rawls' attempt to account for these sorts of citizens.

[30] Rawls, *Political Liberalism*, 36.

upshot for Rawls was that justice as fairness had a "stability" problem in that it could not expect even under fairly ideal conditions to secure to itself the free and full commitment of citizens whose democratic bona fides were not in question.[31] As a persuasive explication and justification of constitutional democracy, *Theory* seemed to fall short, then, even on its own terms, as wide moral pluralism threatened to make political legitimacy – at least its moral component – a dead letter.

Whatever we might think of Rawls' arguments in *A Theory of Justice* or *Political Liberalism*, it seems nearly undeniable to say that in his reconsideration of the argument in *Theory*, he has put his finger on something quite true. Namely, he has rightly pointed out how "reasonable pluralism" is indeed a "fact" of life in free societies. It is simply implausible to suggest that the many and vast disagreements we have regarding not just the nature of the good life but also the nature of justice, beauty, and the like is but a product of economic structures, psychological deformities, or what have you. These factors no doubt play a role, but to presume that they can explain in some reductionist matter the wide disagreement with which free societies seem inundated beggars belief. And that suggests that Rawls is also right in being concerned about pluralism's effect on our ability to justify our political institutions and thus on democratic political legitimacy.

Rawls asks what I take to be his central guiding question in the introduction to *Political Liberalism*: "How is it possible that there may exist over time a stable and just society of free and equal citizens [defined as a constitutional democracy] profoundly divided by reasonable religious, philosophical and moral doctrines?"[32] His response was to affirm that it was indeed possible, and to reconstruct justice as fairness on political grounds, suggesting that a political (rather than comprehensive) conception of justice could secure democratic legitimacy by appealing to a wider variety of citizens, including those "reasonable romantics." His gambit in particular is to argue that legitimate and stable constitutional democracies are compatible with "reasonable pluralism" by showing how those who are "reasonable," meaning (in broad terms) those who accept basic democratic claims, have good *political* reasons to think such a government legitimate, whatever their more basic moral disagreements. I will talk a good bit more about Rawls' particular response in chapter 4; for now we should just note that his arguments in *Political Liberalism* are by and large merely the best-known instance of the broader effort among political

---

[31] Samuel Freeman makes this point as well. See Freeman, *Justice and the Social Contract*, 217–18.
[32] Rawls, *Political Liberalism*, xxvii.

theorists to deal with moral and religious pluralism and its effects on political legitimacy. This effort, as I have described above, has responded to pluralism's challenge vis-à-vis political legitimacy along two lines: the challenge pluralism poses to the likelihood of finding some normative agreements even among reasonable, reflective adults about the nature of justice and how it ought to animate political institutions; and the challenge that such disagreement poses to citizens' *actual* sense that their government deserves their loyalty. For Rawls and many others, meeting those challenges meant having recourse to a relatively new (or a newly redescribed) way of thinking about democratic politics, deliberation.[33]

Proponents of deliberation[34] unite around the conviction that institutions and practices that embody and promote rational deliberation on matters of common interest best show how a reasonable respect for moral pluralism can be squared with the kinds of obligations that ground democratic legitimacy and produce moral and practical stability. Though of course such proponents disagree among themselves regarding precisely how deliberation matters (or should matter) politically and what a more deliberative democratic order would look like in its institutional particulars, they generally endorse two related claims. First, they endorse the idea that deliberation will produce outcomes that better correspond to the common interest or the demands of justice. And, second, they accept the claim that promoting political deliberation will reduce disagreement among citizens and maybe even produce a rough consensus on some issues.[35] Deliberation as a set of normative and empirical claims about *how* democratic institutions ought to be organized rests fundamentally on the sense that *consensus* best expresses democracy's normative impulse. Democracy on this account means, at some basic level, that citizens hold political authority collectively and equally and that political decisions in an ideal world would be the product of consensual decision making. In its most ideal form, such a democratic order would maximize political legitimacy, since such decisions would be ones in which,

---

[33] He explicitly makes political liberalism out to be a species of deliberative democracy in Rawls, "The Idea of Public Reason Revisited."

[34] Some of the more important works on deliberative democracy would include Seyla Benhabib, *Democracy and Difference: Contesting the Boundaries of the Political* (Princeton, NJ: Princeton University Press, 1996); James Bohman, "Public Reason and Cultural Pluralism: Political Liberalism and the Problem of Moral Conflict," *Political Theory* 23, no. 2 (1995); James Bohman and William Rehg, eds., *Deliberative Democracy: Essays on Reason and Politics* (Cambridge, MA: MIT Press, 1997); Cohen, "A More Democratic Liberalism"; John S. Dryzek, *Deliberative Democracy and Beyond: Liberals, Critics, Contestations* (New York: Oxford University Press, 2000); Gutmann and Thompson, *Democracy and Disagreement*; Habermas, *The Inclusion of the Other*; John Haldane, "The Individual, the State and the Common Good," *Social Philosophy and Policy* 13 (1996).

[35] For claims on both counts see Gutmann and Thompson, *Democracy and Disagreement*.

to borrow from Rousseau, each would be obeying just himself and the whole at the same time. Deliberation thus aims at a political order in which we can truly be both author and subject of the law and where consensus and persuasion is the order of the day, not power and coercion.

Of course, we do not live in such an ideal world and consensus is unlikely, to understate the matter just a bit. But for deliberation's proponents, the hope is that political practices and institutions that promote deliberation will move things *toward* consensus, even if there is little practical expectation of actually getting there, and by moving things closer to that ideal, it will secure for particular political outcomes and the system as a whole a greater degree of legitimacy. This corresponds to some commonsensical views most have regarding deliberation on even everyday sorts of matters. Many times we find that what we take to be wide or even unbridgeable differences with others turn out to be quite manageable or even nonexistent once we take the time and effort to discuss them. Moreover, it seems quite reasonable to think that getting more input rather than less improves the quality of a final decision and that if we feel that our concerns have been taken into consideration and that we have had a fair chance to influence that final decision we are certainly less likely to feel aggrieved if we think it mistaken or wrongheaded. Deliberation works, its proponents claim, on both sides of political legitimacy's pluralism problem by showing how it is that deliberative institutions and practices can shape outcomes and the processes producing those outcomes so that they come closer to reflecting popular will and normative principles of justice. Not only does deliberation improve our chances of doing what is right politically, but it also makes its participants more likely to accept it as a legitimate and binding decision. Deliberation, we might say, goes some distance toward solving legitimacy's problem with pluralism by providing means for that pluralism to be morally reconciled and politically effaced.

But the legitimacy that flows from deliberation does so only if the deliberation itself is conducted in a manner that allows decisions to be in principle affirmed by all concerned. That is, deliberation *works* with respect to political legitimacy only in that the content and procedures in place proceed and produce outcomes that we find to be at least reasonable and acceptable. Just as most have had the experience of finding that our differences with others can be reconciled once we talk things out, most have also experienced the opposite, where we discover that our differences are in fact greater than we imagined or are stubbornly resistant to reconciliation.[36] Imagine, for example, a group of citizens who

---

[36] See Sunstein, "The Law of Group Polarization."

have been tasked with reviewing a local school district's sexual education policies. Given the wide range of views in our society about what sorts of sexual behavior should be deemed proper, it is easy to see how such a group – if they represented that wide range – might find it quite difficult to come to anything resembling consensus, outside perhaps of the most narrow and anodyne kinds of claims.[37] What's more, it is quite hard, given the ways in which the views on appropriate sexual behavior in particular seem intimately connected to broader views about human flourishing, to see how more discussion on its own could bridge those differences. If the group were to endorse, say, a curriculum designed to free students from the conceits of what might be considered "old-fashioned" views (i.e. sex as morally proper only within the context of marriage), we would not be surprised if those who held the "old-fashioned" views were less than thrilled with the outcome and even thought it unfair or illegitimate, especially if they thought the process weighed against their sorts of views. (The same frustration would no doubt hold for the non-traditionalists if the circumstances were reversed). To the degree that the decision reflects, even indirectly, a view of human flourishing all do not share, it would be entirely unsurprising if such decisions were seen by some as entirely unacceptable. Deliberation on its own might "go some distance" in solving the problem of pluralism, as I noted above, but it has its limits, especially when it is operating in a context where participants do not share basic moral views.

So deliberation can "work" vis-à-vis moral and religious pluralism to the degree that the participants in the deliberation can engage one another within a shared moral and practical framework. If the participants in my sexual education hypothetical all shared, for example, the idea that, whatever else such a program might want to do, it should work to preserve the physical health and well-being of teenagers, then we could imagine that the participants, divided as they are on notions of sexuality and its relation to human flourishing, could come to some agreement on what such a program ought to look like. Indeed, it seems quite plausible to think, then, that even if a particular group were to lose out in the particulars, provided that they were convinced that the outcome reflected a good-faith effort to promote ends with which they agreed and in ways they found reasonable (even if they thought them mistaken), they would

---

[37] For a parallel story about textbooks in American secondary education, see Diane Ravitch, *The Language Police: How Pressure Groups Restrict What Students Learn* (New York: Vintage Books, 2004). Here the significant disagreement within American society over any number of historical themes has translated into political pressure on boards of education to avoid controversial claims in textbooks, leading to books that are boring and contain only the most basic and uncontroversial sorts of particulars.

be likely to find the outcomes acceptable and therefore legitimate. The crucial difference here is that their mutually acceptable ends – physical health and well-being – give rise to mutually acceptable reasons. If, say, one participant were to suggest that the program include material on sexual liberation with the idea that it held the key to a particular form of human flourishing, others could rightfully resist his suggestions by pointing to the way it exceeds their agreed-upon framework. If the sex liberation proponent persisted in pressing his point, the other participants would then have to choose whether to give up on the prospect of finding consensus and to impose the majority view. Deliberation "works" when its participants share enough in the way of basic moral and practical claims to make for effective outcomes.

We can see how this highlights deliberation's limits, as it requires participants to engage one another on grounds common to all.[38] Deliberation cannot then "work" vis-à-vis pluralism *simpliciter*, but rather only pluralism circumscribed by some limiting value. Most obviously, this means that deliberation works only to the degree that participants rely upon and can offer to one another reasons that everyone else could accept. Participants in the sexual education group might find agreement if everyone in the group is willing to engage in discussions using reasons rooted in commonly held suppositions about physical health and well-being, while such agreement is quite unlikely if some portion of the group insists on offering reasons rooted in views about human flourishing that not everyone else accepts. Deliberation's success as a strategy for mitigating or overcoming the problem of pluralism depends above all on whether the group in question shares enough in the way of common values or beliefs to generate mutually persuasive reasons rooted in those values or beliefs.

Politically speaking, then, we might say that deliberation can work to secure a democracy's political legitimacy even under conditions of wide pluralism provided that most or all citizens are willing and able to offer one another reasons that other citizens could plausibly accept. The deliberative theorists hope that even if citizens cannot fully agree with one another, even on some constitutional issues, they will accept political outcomes as legitimate and binding because they are based on reasons that are in principle not foreign to them. They are reasons they *could* accept in general, even if they do not in any particular case. If we are concerned to preserve and strengthen our democratic political orders

---

[38] For a critique of this element of deliberation, see Gerald F. Gaus and Kevin Vallier, "The Roles of Religious Conviction in a Publicly Justified Polity: The Implications of Convergence, Asymmetry and Political Institutions," *Philosophy and Social Criticism* 35, no. 1–2 (2009).

and especially to secure them against the challenges of moral pluralism, then under the deliberative scheme we have a moral obligation to engage our fellow citizens politically on grounds common to us all. More to the point of the discussion here, we have a moral obligation to rely upon and employ reasons politically that other citizens might reasonably be expected to accept. Recourse to arguments rooted in sectarian or particularistic views of the world ought to be set aside in favor of ones that can properly be held in common by all citizens similarly committed.

This call for *deliberative restraint* argues, then, that the legitimacy and stability of pluralist constitutional democracies require that we be able to develop some distance from our more comprehensive and basic beliefs and engage one another politically on grounds common to all (or most all). This means that reasons whose persuasive force depends on views we reasonably disagree about ought to be considered out of bounds and should not be invoked or relied upon to justify acts of political coercion. This plausibly includes philosophical views like Kantianism or utilitarianism, as well as distinctly religious views. Reasonable people may (and do) disagree about those views, and coercing others on their basis would make political legitimacy seemingly impossible. Just as Rawls came to recognize that his argument for justice as fairness could not secure the sort of legitimacy and stability necessary because there seemed to be plenty of "reasonable" individuals who rejected *Theory*'s Kantian individualism, so too should others recognize that they cannot expect to persuade their fellow citizens if they employ arguments rooted in hedonistic utilitarianism or some sort of Christian reconstructionism.[39] Even if consensus as a standard is impractical (and of course it is), if we wish to find ways of reconciling what it is we *should want* (i.e. what is morally proper and normatively binding) with what we actually *do want* (i.e. our interests and desires), deliberation can move us in that direction and secure our democratic orders provided that we abide by deliberative restraint. To ignore these obligations is to ignore a central duty of citizenship and to invite mutual suspicion, civic mistrust, and even political failure.

A prologue to the rest of the argument

As I have emphasized, the restraint norm means to say that any of us who hold basic beliefs that others might reasonably reject (and that would be most everyone, it seems) must be able to put those beliefs at some

---

[39] The latter is a set of Christian political views propounded in the US most famously by R.J. Rushdoony which more or less argue that modern political orders should be "reconstructed" on the basis of the moral and legal codes found in the Old Testament.

distance when deliberating about or engaging in political life. Note here first of all that this is an argument about the conditions under which pluralist democracies might be able to secure their legitimacy and the moral obligations regarding politics that flow from such conditionals. It is not an argument about rights per se and should not, for example, affect at all free speech rights.[40] Nor is it an argument about our non-political life, where we are free – indeed, perhaps encouraged – to think and argue in ways that reflect those basic, comprehensive views. The norm of restraint is only about what makes for legitimate and stable democratic societies and, correspondingly, what makes for good citizens within such societies.

Not only do these obligations extend to all citizens, but they also extend to all sorts of basic comprehensive belief systems. As I noted above, the argument for restraint makes invocations of Kant or Mill as problematic as Deuteronomy, though of course it is the latter sort of argument that has attracted nearly all the attention, a fact we should not find at all surprising. Not only has American politics (the context for most of the debate) been roiled over the past few decades by conservative religious activists, but the focus on religion offers theorists a philosophically strategic opportunity as well. If the argument for deliberative restraint works on religious reasons, then it will, the thinking seems to go, also surely work elsewhere. After all, we pay enormous deference to religious belief and practice and (quite rightly, in my view) go out of our way to protect religious institutions from political pressure or manipulation.[41] And, finally, religion "works" politically in ways quite unlike other basic views. It has a capacity to inspire action that clearly overawes its competitors. No one, after all, has yet organized a Kantian Coalition and those movements that do compare themselves really look quite "religious" in their rhetoric and methodology.[42] So the focus on religion is not itself a sign of deliberative restraint's hostility toward religion per se (though

---

[40] Even though deliberative restraint's proponents sincerely argue that these moral obligations do not connect directly to speech rights, it may be the case, but as I show in chapter 5, they do make a difference in other rights. For an argument that those who fall outside the circumscribed range of pluralism dictated by the requirements of deliberation need not have their "unreasonable" views tolerated, see Erin Kelley and Lionel McPherson, "On Tolerating the Unreasonable," *Journal of Political Philosophy* 9, no. 1 (2001).

[41] In recent years, this circumspection has come under increased scrutiny, as the expansion of anti-discrimination laws and the concerns regarding religion's political effects – ranging from the shaping of civic virtue and vice to being seedbeds of civic strife and violence – have combined to suggest to some that such deference is unwise.

[42] Consider communism, for example. As a "political" movement, it has all the hallmarks of a kind of secularized Christianity. It has its holy texts, its saints, even an eschatology. More to the point, it has shown an ability to motivate a fervent following, albeit one that, unlike religion, has had almost entirely negative results in the twentieth century.

there is plenty of that in the debates[43]) but instead a reasonable concern regarding one of society's most potent and important ways of organizing our lives. Religion matters a great deal to a great number of people, and attending to it as a kind of focal case for the broader question of deliberative restraint, at its best, merely reflects that fact.

As I have noted (perhaps rather repetitively) most theorists working in the liberal tradition – and some outside of it[44] – generally agree that believers ought to put their religious beliefs at some distance from their political activities, both when deliberating about political matters and when making political proposals to others. Scholars disagree over the exact nature of the obligation, arguing about whether it should apply only to very basic political questions or to the whole of political life, whether special obligations attend to legislators and judges, and so on.[45] In the following two chapters, I focus on what I take to be the modal case here and ask to what extent ordinary citizens in pluralist liberal democracies should accept as binding the sometimes quite strongly articulated obligation to restrain in significant fashion the political employment of their religious views. My answer is mostly critical, arguing that the strongest arguments for deliberative restraint rest on mistaken moral, epistemological, and empirical claims and that given a society in which some portion of its citizens have religious views with public import, the obligations attendant on those believers are much more attenuated than the restraint argument suggests. What emerges, if only in outline form, is a view of liberal democratic life both more passionate, perhaps, in its engagement with our basic moral and religious commitments and more modest in its expectations of consensus and political agreement. Indeed, I argue toward the end of chapter 4 that under conditions of modern pluralism constitutional democracies are ill served by lofty claims regarding political legitimacy and that more modest goals regarding how we engage one another politically do better to undergird political orders that are decent, durable, and democratic.

---

[43] See the embrace of Voltaire's *écrasez l'infâme* in Richard Rorty, "The Moral Purposes of the University: An Exchange," *Hedgehog Review* 2, no. 3 (2000).

[44] See Robert P. George and Christopher Wolfe, eds., *Natural Law and Public Reason* (Washington, D.C.: Georgetown University, 2000). George, no fan of liberal political thought, argues in favor of the need to engage politically on the basis of commonly accepted reasons. It may be worth noting, though, that he thinks natural law arguments should count as being among those sorts of reasons, while Rawls and most other proponents of deliberative restraint do not.

[45] For a nicely detailed exploration of these issues, see Greenawalt, *Private Consciences and Public Reasons*.

3   The problem with secular reasons

As I noted in chapter 2, even though most scholars who have exam-
ined the issue coalesce around a broad consensus that argues against
the use of religious reasons in political life, there persists a good deal
of disagreement over the particulars.[1] A few suggest that religion ought
never intrude into political deliberations, while others think it may play
some role depending on the sort of political question at hand, the particular office someone may hold, or the venue in which the deliberation
occurs. I do not mean, in this chapter and the next, to engage the whole
range of arguments included in what I have called deliberative restraint;
that would be a book unto itself. Instead, I mean to examine what I
take to be the most persuasive arguments available within the consensus
and show why they are mistaken on both moral and empirical grounds.

---

[1] For just an introduction to the debates over religious reasons, you would need to consult
the following works: Audi, "The Place of Religious Argument in a Free and Democratic
Society."; Audi, *Religious Commitment and Secular Reason*; Peter Berkowitz, "John Rawls and
the Liberal Faith," *Wilson Quarterly* 26, no. 2 (2002); Carter, *God's Name in Vain*; Chaplin,
"Beyond Liberal Restraint: Defending Religiously Based Arguments in Law and Public
Policy"; Dombrowski, *Rawls and Religion*; Christopher J. Eberle, "Basic Human Worth
and Religious Restraint," *Philosophy and Social Criticism* 35, no. 1–2 (2009); Christopher
J. Eberle, "Religion, Pacifism and the Doctrine of Restraint," *Journal of Religious Ethics*
34, no. 2 (2006); Eberle, *Religious Conviction in Liberal Politics*; Elshtain, "State-Imposed
Secularism as a Potential Pitfall of Liberal Democracy"; Greenawalt, *Private Consciences
and Public Reasons*; Gutmann and Thompson, *Democracy and Disagreement*; Habermas,
"On the Relations between the Secular Liberal State and Religion"; Habermas, "Religion
in the Public Sphere"; Jeff Jordan, "Religious Reasons and Public Reasons," *Public Affairs
Quarterly* 11, no. 3 (1997); Sharon R. Krause, *Civil Passions: Moral Sentiment and Democratic
Deliberation* (Princeton, NJ: Princeton University Press, 2008); Larmore, "The Moral
Basis of Political Liberalism"; Larmore, "Political Liberalism"; Macedo, "Transformative
Constitutionalism"; John Parkinson, *Deliberating in the Real World* (Oxford: Oxford
University Press, 2006); Perry, *Religion in Politics*; John Rawls, "The Idea of Public Reason
Revisited," here cited from *The Law of Peoples*, ed. John Rawls (Cambridge, MA: Harvard
University Press, 1999); Rosenblum, ed., *Obligations of Citizenship and the Demands of Faith*;
Lucas Swaine, "Deliberate and Free: Heteronomy in the Public Square," *Philosophy and
Social Criticism* 35, no. 1–2 (2009); Robert Talisse, "Dilemmas of Public Reason: Pluralism,
Polarization, and Instability," in *The Legacy of John Rawls*, ed. Thom Brooks and Fabian
Freyenhagen (New York: Continuum, 2005); Weithman, *Religion and the Obligations of
Citizenship*; Weithman, ed., *Religion and Contemporary Liberalism*.

The broad consensus in favor of deliberative restraint makes mistakes both moral and empirical in that it overestimates both the plausibility and attractiveness of a "restrained" political order and the threat of a religiously "engaged" one. Proponents of deliberative restraint weave together a seemingly compelling set of claims making restraint a linchpin of the democratic social and political order, but these do not stand up to closer examination, especially one that disentangles their moral and empirical threads. I focus first on deliberative restraint's moral claims, in particular those that argue for the priority of secular and then "public" reasons. I suggest that scholars like Robert Audi, Jürgen Habermas, and John Rawls too quickly dismiss religious reasons as epistemologically and morally suspect and that they also make unwarranted empirical claims about the near-inevitability of religion's political privatization or its potential for sparking political conflict. The upshot here is that to the degree that deliberative restraint is an effort to secure political legitimacy in a constitutional democratic order distinguished by a wide and deep moral pluralism, it simply cannot be sustained. It is overly ambitious with regard to the degree of moral and political consensus we can reasonably expect under such pluralist conditions and oblivious to the potential that efforts to push forward in any case may turn out to be deeply counterproductive.

Audi's secular principles

While some sort of Rawlsian public reason argument usually occupies the high ground within the academic debates over religious reasons (and I will take up that set of claims in the next chapter), within the broader public debate it is the claim in favor of *secular* reasons that has the most currency. Religion has always been an important element in American political life, but in the wake of terrorist attacks motivated largely by religious ideology and a highly polarized polity where religious belief and practice seems to sort citizens politically, we have seen a groundswell of support for the view that religion is dangerous or unreliable politically and so should be at the least privatized and made politically irrelevant, if not done away with entirely.[2]

Scholars have typically been a bit more circumspect. Very few followed the late Richard Rorty, who at one time suggested that the use of

---

[2] Some clear examples of this line of thinking in more popular books can be found in Sam Harris, *The End of Faith: Religion, Terror, and the Future of Reason* (New York: W.W. Norton & Co., 2004); Sam Harris, *Letter to a Christian Nation* (New York: Knopf, 2006); Linker, *The Theocons*; Phillips, *American Theocracy*; Sullivan, *The Conservative Soul*.

religious reasons was a "conversation-stopper" and that those committed to democratic government should make it seem like "bad taste" for citizens to bring their religious views to bear politically (and especially voice them in public debates).[3] Rorty himself came to abandon such claims, acknowledging that such a putative obligation simply relied on an implausible construction of how it is that individuals come to their political views.[4] The view that religious citizens should reason and act politically in ways entirely divorced from their religious views posits an entirely unrealistic model of human psychology, as if religious believers (or anyone else, for that matter) could neatly wall off their beliefs about the ultimate nature of the universe and our place in it from their beliefs regarding what ends their political communities should be pursuing.[5] It might make for good political sloganeering when your partisan opponents have controversial religious connections to say that citizens should keep their religious views entirely out of politics, but as a claim about how politics actually can work and our moral obligations therein, it looks quite implausible.

But it can make for good political sloganeering precisely because one of the things – perhaps *the* thing, as Charles Taylor argues[6] – that makes modernity in general and modern democratic societies in particular so distinctive is their undeniably *secular* character. It is not just that large swathes of the population in Europe and parts of North America claim no religious affiliation; it is, more importantly, that whole spheres of social and political life that had been once at least nominally under the tutelage of religious authorities now stand independent, or "differentiated," to use Weberian terminology. And so it is no wonder that in thinking about what sorts of reasons might be able to justify a democratic order under the sort of pluralism currently in play, scholars (and the public) would naturally point to reasons that are emphatically secular in nature.

No one has offered more serious considerations in the American context in favor of the importance of secular reasons than Robert Audi, who has been thinking through these questions for well over a decade. In a series of articles and books, Audi argues that citizens should *prioritize* secular reasons over religious ones in their political deliberations because secular reasons are precisely the kinds of reasons other citizens can find intelligible and plausibly persuasive. On his account reasons that do not

---

[3] Rorty, "Religion as a Conversation-Stopper."
[4] See Richard Rorty, "Religion in the Public Square: A Reconsideration," *Journal of Religious Ethics* 31, no. 1 (2003). Greenawalt makes a similar claim in Greenawalt, *Private Consciences and Public Reasons.*
[5] See Krause, *Civil Passions*, especially chapter 2.
[6] Charles Taylor, *A Secular Age* (Cambridge, MA: Harvard University Press, 2007).

depend for their persuasiveness on any particular view of God are the sorts of reasons we all in fact do hold in common, thus making them reasonable grounds for political coercion in a democratic polity. That is, Audi constructs a largely epistemological case meant to show why religious reasons, as a class of reasons, cannot serve such a justificatory role. Though intuitively plausible, the claim for the prioritization of secular reasons mischaracterizes how people typically employ religious reasons politically, meaning that such reasons are not, as Audi claims, categorically unintelligible or unreliable. Moreover, a consistent application of Audi's principles, depending on how we understand them, would end up either leaving politics largely denuded of moral arguments altogether or would affect things so slightly as to be irrelevant politically. Finally, since even what counts as "secular" reason can change and reasonably be contested in ways not dissimilar to religiously rooted claims, relying on secularity as a standard for framing our moral obligations vis-à-vis one another politically turns out to be quite problematic. In short, Audi's argument for secular reasons fails because it misconceives how we tend to use religious reasons, fails to articulate a plausible argument for the role of moral convictions in politics, and shows political naïveté in the faith it places in secular views over against religious ones.

Audi's argument for secular reasons in politics addresses both a citizen's stated rationale for supporting a particular law and what motivates such support. His *principle of secular rationale* says that "One has a prima facie obligation not to advocate or support any law or public policy that restricts human conduct unless one has, and is willing to offer, adequate secular reason for this advocacy or support."[7] His *principle of secular motivation* in turn asserts that "One also has a prima facie obligation to abstain from such advocacy or support unless one is sufficiently motivated by adequate secular reason."[8] An individual must not only be willing to offer a nonreligious rationale for her preferred policy positions, but she must also find that rationale motivationally sufficient independent of her religious beliefs. She may *also* offer and rely upon religious reasons, but to rely solely on them commits her to coercing others absent a sufficient justification. Since it might very well be the case that our secular and religiously rooted justifications could conflict, we might fairly characterize Audi's position as one favoring the *prioritization* of secular reasons. There is no need here for citizens to try and cut themselves off from

---

[7] Secular reasons are those reasons "whose normative force [do] not evidentially depend on the existence of God or on theological considerations, or on the pronouncements of a person or institution qua religious authority" (Audi, "The Place of Religious Argument in a Free and Democratic Society," 691–2.)

[8] Ibid., 692.

their religious views politically, but they must be able to set them aside in some sense so as to be able to reflect on what proposals they think best, absent those beliefs. If their religious and secular beliefs come into conflict, it is the secular ones that ought to win out, primarily because they are the sorts of reasons that can legitimately justify political coercion.

Generally speaking, Audi suggests, since "the best rationales for liberal democracy forbid restricting freedom except where it is required to prevent serious harm or to preserve equal basic liberties or equal basic political power,"[9] a politically adequate reason justifying such restrictions is one that "any adult rational citizen will find persuasive and can identify with."[10] We can see here how Audi's argumentation lines up nicely within a deliberative framework, even if he never (so far as I know) makes himself out to be a proponent of deliberative democracy. In order for a reason to be plausibly persuasive it must, he argues, possess an "intelligibility of a certain kind" which in turn requires "secularity."[11] Secular reasons are the sorts of reasons that all rational adults can find intelligible and plausibly persuasive while religious ones are not. Since religious reasons are "ultimately grounded in God's nature or commands"[12] (or, more accurately, in our perception of God's nature or commands), they are not simply intelligible in the same way secular reasons are. In particular, he suggests, religious reasons are "directly or indirectly viewed as representing an infallible authority, in a sense taken to imply that the propositions expressing them *must* be true."[13] This infallibility means, to the believer at least, that a position taken to be reflective of God's nature or command cannot be critiqued rationally and, to the degree that laws are based on religious reasons, makes the justification of coercive political acts by religious reasons impermissible. We cannot be persuaded by that which we cannot critique, and so, Audi concludes, a politically adequate reason must be secular.

Audi's argument looks plausible. We generally do think of secular reasons as being among the class of reasons that any rational person should generally be able to grasp and think about whether he is persuaded or not.[14] The same is not at all obviously true of religious reasons. Quite the opposite, actually, as we tend to think of reasons rooted particular theological claims ("Mohammed is God's Prophet" or "Jesus has a divine nature", for example) as being in some sense opaque to rational critique. Either you accept them or you don't, and it is not at all clear

---

[9] Audi, *Religious Commitment and Secular Reason*, 30.
[10] Audi and Wolterstorff, *Religion in the Public Square*, 16.   [11] Ibid., 17.
[12] Audi, *Religious Commitment and Secular Reason*, 100.   [13] Ibid.
[14] Galston, *Liberal Pluralism*, 45. The only exceptions might be reasons that require highly specialized expertise, such as scientific knowledge or the like.

that reason or some common human rationality plays a decisive role in that "choice." Indeed, even though liberal states treat religious belief and practice as something that we "choose" (or "un-choose," as the case may be), the sociological reality seems to be that for most of us, our religious views are not chosen at all. They are either handed down to us by family and community or they seem to just come upon us (or leave us) in ways quite beyond our rational control.[15] And if it is true that justifications for coercion should be rooted in "concepts we share (or can readily share)," they will necessarily be intelligible and amenable to rational critique for each of us. I cannot plausibly offer you a reason for doing something that is rooted in some esoteric, inexplicable concept and expect you to be capable of actually consenting. You might agree to cooperate in any case, but if you do not as a epistemic matter truly understand the reasons behind my proposal, then whatever consent you might give will reflect either a kind of modus vivendi or mere acquiescence. That is, if as a matter of your own knowledge, experience, and rational considerations you are *incapable* of understanding, interrogating, and eventually *choosing* whether you can buy into the reasons I am offering, whatever consent you might give to my proposition will at best be strictly limited. More likely, it will simply be nonexistent.

An example might help make Audi's point clearer and explicate a little how it is that so many of us suppose that religious reasons fall into the category of reasons that are "unshared" and thus should be out of bounds politically. Suppose Jill is a firmly committed Christian who accepts the claim that "The fear of the Lord is the beginning of wisdom"[16] and so develops a proposal for her local school system that makes studying the Bible as a source of unerring moral guidance obligatory for all students. We might readily object to such a proposal on the grounds that it violates religious liberty protections for students who (or whose parents) do not share Jill's views, but Audi's argument in favor of secular reasons points us to deeper claims that work to undergird the constitutional one. If pressed by others who do not share her beliefs as to why students should be so instructed, Jill would likely simply point to scripture and, especially as a Christian, perhaps even sketch out how the New Testament and Jesus in

---

[15] This is a point addressed in Michael J. Sandel, *Democracy's Discontent: America in Search of a Public Philosophy* (Cambridge, MA: Harvard University Press, 1996). Of course there are very good reasons for the liberal state to treat religious beliefs as choices, since doing so provides a powerful buttress for the protection of religious liberty. This way of thinking about religious beliefs as being not quite within the orbit of rational control fits well, moreover, with some of the most famous conversion experiences known to Christianity, including the Apostle Paul, Augustine, Wesley, and so on.

[16] Proverbs 1:7.

particular rely on Old Testament law as a sure source of moral guidance. If pressed further regarding why this particular religious work or early Christians' use of it should be persuasive to those who do not share her religious views, Jill might respond by developing historical or exegetical arguments regarding the Bible's historicity or moral coherence, but it seems likely, perhaps inevitable, that eventually the discussion would terminate in something of a fundamental standoff. Jill *believes* that the Bible offers an especially reliable source of moral guidance, inerrant even, one that transcends particular religious traditions on account of its status as divinely inspired; her critics do not.

Now consider an alternative scenario. Jack too thinks that the local school district should have students study the Bible as a source of moral guidance, but unlike Jill he does not himself have any relevant beliefs regarding whether to think of it as divinely inspired or not. He does, however, believe that the moral codes he thinks are in the Bible are the ones most appropriate for human flourishing, both individual and collective. Following biblical moral codes will produce, he supposes, greater feelings of individual fulfillment, more harmonious communities, happier and more secure families, and so on. Whatever Jack's fellow citizens might think of his proposal and the moral claims behind it, it seems clear why Audi (and most others) would suppose that his proposal, even if in its execution it looked quite similar to Jill's, strikes a very different cord from hers. To the degree that those other citizens share the individual and collective outcomes Jack inscribes into his proposal, the fact that it involves the study of religious texts is likely to be controversial only in it may strike others as something of a "stalking horse" for Jill's. Religion's *instrumental* use is not itself all that controversial precisely because it does not rely on any claims of divine inspiration or inerrancy; if someone could convince Jack that studying John Stuart Mill was a better path to individual and collective human flourishing, then he would have no reason, presumably, for not switching. Not so with Jill, as her commitment to the Bible as a reliable moral code looks like it *precedes* her rational deliberation on the matter, and so it seems reasonable to think that she would be much more resistant (perhaps entirely resistant) to rethinking its utility. Perhaps more to the point, to the degree that Audi's characterization that laws can be justified only by reasons that any rational, well-informed adult "will find persuasive" is the correct one, it is clear why he (and many others) would suggest secular as over against religious reasons. If you do not already believe that the Bible (and its moral code) is divinely inspired, it is hard to see why you would agree to Jill's proposal, unless you were convinced by something like Jack's. But then it would be Jack's claims about the *secular* outcomes that would be doing the justificatory work, not any sort of *religious* reasons, and so Audi's point remains.

Thus Audi's claims certainly have a kind of intuitive plausibility. But since his argument relies on the claim that secular reasons, as opposed to religious ones, are the sorts of reasons that anyone can find persuasive and belong to (or contain) the class of concepts that we "readily share," thus making them "intelligible" to all, we should ask how it is we know which concepts we share, or – and this is even more tenuous – we can *readily* share? After all, to recognize that we live in societies marked by a quite wide sort of pluralism is to recognize that, in fact, there is a great deal we do not share and that our moral conflicts (conceptual or otherwise) go "all the way down." It certainly is not an uncommon experience within academia (mostly in the humanities and, to a lesser degree, social sciences) to discover that disputants over a particular research question are talking past one another on account of their quite divergent moral or theoretical commitments. Similar circumstances obtain in broader public debates, as well. Perhaps the most implausible part of my example with Jack above is the supposition I made (for argumentative purposes) that Jack's fellow citizens would share enough of his moral conceptualizations and goals concerning human flourishing to give his proposal a reasonable likelihood of success. The truth is that citizens in free societies share only the most banal descriptions of moral claims (e.g. "the freedom and equality of all") while disagreeing wildly over their substantive meanings.[17] If we need to focus on the reasons justifying political coercion precisely because of an increased awareness of just how much we disagree, an *intuitively* plausible claim about how secular reasons are ones we all readily share is insufficient.

Audi, I think, recognizes this and suggests that we can know what concepts we share by seeing if they could be held by a kind of idealized "surrogate," some person who is "fully rational" and "adequately informed," but who does not hold our religious or other basic moral beliefs.[18] Redolent of Nagel's "view from nowhere" and Rawls' "Original Position," this criterion attempts to ensure that we are rigorously checking

---

[17] There is certainly a case to be made that the American "culture wars" thesis is overblown, especially the "war" rhetoric. For all of the invective hurled in American politics, there is precious little actual violence. But there are serious differences in the moral visions animating Americans' political goals. For debates surrounding this question, see Morris P. Fiorina, Samuel J. Abrams, and Jeremy Pope, *Culture War? The Myth of a Polarized America*, 2nd. edn. (New York: Pearson Education, 2006); James Davison Hunter, *Culture Wars: The Struggle to Define America* (New York: Basic Books, 1991); James Davison Hunter and Alan Wolfe, *Is There a Culture War? A Dialogue on Values and American Public Life* (Washington, D.C.: Pew Research Center and Brookings Institution Press, 2006).

[18] Audi, *Religious Commitment and Secular Reason*, 115.

to check that we do not smuggle in, even inadvertently, some of our own religious or similar sorts of views when judging whether our reasons for supporting or making political proposal are properly grounded. But what constitutes "fully rational" and "adequately informed" is certainly not obvious or uncontroversial; indeed, we might think that it is fully a part of the moral and religious pluralism that makes reflecting on the *kinds* of reasons we give politically necessary in the first place. I would guess that all of Audi's departmental colleagues, for example, would think of themselves as both rational and more than adequately informed about a whole host of things and would still find themselves in quite strong disagreement, both with him and each other. More to the point, Paul Weithman (one of Audi's current colleagues, as it turns out) seems right when he suggests that Audi's justification principle is too demanding philosophically and largely irrelevant politically. This theoretical "surrogate" would be so different from who *we* actually are that using the surrogate as an adequacy standard would result in "norms of rationality and informational adequacy" which would have little natural or even reasonable appeal for us.[19] The question at hand is not whether some ideal surrogate could share our views, but whether other actual citizens, who themselves have varied and diverse foundational moral and religious commitments themselves, might be able to share our views – and, more importantly, whether the "secular reasons" argument on offer from Audi can actually describe a set of concepts or reasons that all rational adults in modern democracies could actually accept. George Klosko's very helpful compilation of surveys on the matter suggests very strongly we have good reason to be skeptical as to whether "secular" describes a category of reasons all rational adults could share.[20]

Moreover, depending on how we take Audi's arguments, they may exclude so much as to make politics practically impossible or so little as to make his strictures largely irrelevant. Audi himself admits that some "secular" philosophies – like revolutionary Marxism – would also fail his intelligibility test. They are like religious claims, he supposes, in that they accept certain propositions as necessarily true, making them seemingly invulnerable to rational critique.[21] But if that is right, then Audi is not really talking about "secular" reasons, he is talking about any set

---

[19] Weithman, *Religion and the Obligations of Citizenship*, 177. For a similar worry, even if this sort of rationale can justify principles like Audi's, it is hard to see how it can impose duties on us unless, perhaps, it connects more closely to our actually lived lives, see Philip Quinn, "Religious Citizens and the Limits of Public Reason," *Modern Schoolman* 78 (2001).

[20] See Klosko, *Democratic Procedures and Liberal Consensus*.

[21] Audi, *Religious Commitment and Secular Reason*, 103.

of reasons whose premises cannot be shared across pluralistic divides. Consider what other sorts of views might get excluded if we should not use reasons in political debates that have premises that are in principle "unintelligible" to other citizens. Hedonistic utilitarianism should be out, given its preference for elevating the moral status of physical pleasure and pain over every other value. So ought Kantianism, various kinds of materialism (Marxist and otherwise), environmentalist philosophies, and so on. I do not mean here to endorse entirely some sort of Humean non-cognitivist moral theory, but as a practical political matter the widespread acceptance of Audi's principles would demand the exclusion of a great deal, if not most, of our common political discourse. Nearly *every* kind of political reason relies at some point on premises or arguments that its proponents deem reasonably self-evident and that their opponents deem nonsensical. This is what Rawls means by "reasonable pluralism."[22] Political reasons, moreover, often involve moral commitments tied up with personal identities not easily explicable or persuasive to others who do not share that identity or commitment.[23] Any consistent political application of his principles would rule so much of our political discourse out of bounds as to make democratic deliberation itself practically impossible, or it would simply reduce the democratic order to a mere modus vivendi, with all the problems the deliberation model is meant to avoid.

Taken in another way, however, it is not clear that his principles exclude enough to make them at all interesting. Consider, for example, the continuing disputes in American public schools over the teaching of evolution. I assume that Audi would be committed to saying that its Creationist competitor ought not to be taught in science classes because at least certain forms of Creationism rely fundamentally on Scriptural resources whose evidentiary value are themselves premised on an 'infallible' religious faith. Perhaps that is right, but perhaps it is also rather beside the point. There are, I think, at least two kinds of "religious views": *basic* religious views, those basic points of theology that constitute the core of a faith (i.e. Christ as Incarnation, Mohammed as God's true prophet); and *applied* religious views, which are views about how the basic views relate to the social and political world (i.e. Creationism should be taught in public schools, *sharia* should be the basis for civil law). It might be

---

[22] He says: "The fact of reasonable pluralism … means that the differences between citizens arising from their comprehensive doctrines, religious and nonreligious, are irreconcilable and contain transcendent elements" (Rawls, *Political Liberalism*, xlvi.). It is these transcendent elements that largely defy commensuration.

[23] For a thoughtful argument about the impossibility of distinguishing "secular" and "religious," see Steven D. Smith, "The 'Secular,' the 'Religious,' and the 'Moral': What Are We Talking About?," *Wake Forest Law Review* 36 (2001).

the case that religious believers' basic religious views have the quality of infallibility, but the real question ought to be about believers' applied religious views, since these are the ones doing the justificatory work in political arguments. Do believers hold *these* views in ways that are infallible or unintelligible?

The Creationist's arguments are not basic views, or at least they need not be. Rather, the argument for teaching Creationism in public schools is developed on the basis of certain premises – the authority and reliability of scripture, among others – and applied to matters of public policy. At each step of the argument, the believer inevitably relies on some non-religious reasons to reach his conclusions (e.g. arguments that public schools should reflect biblical teachings), and it seems rather unlikely that someone will hold *these* reasons to be infallible in the same way that he holds his basic religious beliefs to be (if he does). The fact that Creationists offer a "creation science" implies that even they think that their applied religious beliefs need scientific validation (i.e. non-religious reasons) to make them persuasive, perhaps even to themselves. Christopher Eberle points out, for instance, that it is "obviously and straightforwardly indefensible" for anyone to claim that biblical inerrancy means that no extra-biblical information is involved in interpreting and applying scripture.[24] Regardless of the fact that the Bible seems to say (in poetic language) that the sun revolves around the earth, no one believes that – and certainly no one suggests it ought to be a part of a school's science curriculum. That suggests that everyone (or pretty close to everyone) takes on board a variety of kinds of information when developing their applied beliefs, even if do they hold their basic beliefs as infallible. In this respect at least, applied religious views are quite amenable to rational criticism and do not obviously fail the intelligibility test, at least not any more than with most anyone else's political views.[25] A non-believer could easily critique the interpretative method of the Creationist or reflect on the viability of his creation science, or even dispute his account of the purpose of public schools. None of these is beyond the non-believer's ken.

But here is the real kicker: why should we accept the proposition that religious beliefs are somehow inevitably held in a way that makes them immune to rational deliberation and critique? Earlier, I acknowledged

[24] Eberle, *Religious Conviction in Liberal Politics*, 274.
[25] There is one interesting exception to my objection – the theocratic command. The religious believer who thinks that God's commands include religious political rule might plausibly hold that view as infallible and thus be disqualified in this interpretation. For an interesting argument for including even straightforward theocrats into the deliberative process see Swaine, *The Liberal Conscience*.

that purely rational arguments have their limits when it comes to our religious views, and I do not mean to throw that claim over after only a few pages. But saying that our religious views are themselves not predicated fully on rational arguments is *not* the same thing as saying that religious beliefs are by definition immune to rational critique. How people come to their religious beliefs (or lack thereof) is something of a mystery and no doubt differs from person to person (and from society to society). But to say as a general proposition that religious views are held in such a way as to make them immune to rational critique and deliberation – and thus make them poor candidates for justifying political coercion – is to do real injustice to the actual lived experience of religious belief and practice. One need only peruse the religion section of any decent bookstore to recognize quickly that interspersed among the piles of treacly devotions are a fair number of works dedicated to serious intellectual engagement on a whole range of theological issues. Whether it is a dispute over the reliability of scripture, the nature of God, or the moral and political implications of theological claims, any fair skim of those works would compel one, I think, to acknowledge that rationality and human reason have a great deal to say about the shape and direction of religious belief and practice. And perhaps more importantly, such a perusal might suggest to the non-believer that understanding the religious claims, making them intelligible, is not so far out of reach as might be expected. While the choice of whether to accept some basic religious claims is probably not itself dependent on some strictly rational criteria, there are rationally defensible claims that believers can (and do) hold and that others can (and do) grasp, even if at the end of the day they find them unpersuasive. Chris Eberle seems right when he notes that religion "is a conversation *stopper* only for those who don't want to do what it takes to enter into the conversation in a productive manner."[26] If we take Audi's concern mainly to be that religious beliefs are held in such a way as to make them immune to rational critique and thus unintelligible to other citizens, it looks like his principles are really not all that interesting – they would catch such a narrow slice of political discourse as to be irrelevant politically.

Even if these critiques are correct, Audi might still have grounds for his claims in favor of secular reasons. He suggests that any mature religious believer ought to abide by what he calls a *theo-ethical equilibrium*, which argues that "where religious considerations appropriately bear on matters of public morality or of public choice, religious believers – at least insofar as they have civic virtue – [should] seek an equilibrium between

---

[26] Eberle, *Religious Conviction in Liberal Politics*, 272. The phrase "conversation stopper" is, of course, from Rorty, "Religion as a Conversation-Stopper."

those considerations and relevant secular standards of ethics and political responsibility."[27] For the religious believer, Audi avers, God is the
author of all truth. The believer might then "expect God to structure us
and the world so that there is a (humanly accessible) secular path to the
discovery of moral truths, at least to those far-reaching ones needed for
civilized life."[28] Thus, a "mature, conscientious theist who cannot reach
[an equilibrium] should be reluctant or unwilling to support laws or public policies that cannot be placed in that equilibrium."[29]

What is crucial to recognize about this theo-ethical equilibrium principle, however, is that it is not exactly an equilibrium. Audi says that
mature religious believers will recognize the need to *reconcile* religious
and secular truth claims and that his principles are not meant to elevate secular over religious rationale: they should have a "special kind of
cooperation."[30] In some respects, this seems correct. Consider, if you will,
my endorsement of Eberle's point above that no one takes the Psalms'
invocations of the sun circling the earth to be an accurate description of
the physical phenomenon. To the degree that some once thought this to
be the case, accepting a geocentric view of the universe because it com-
ported with the biblical text and then embracing a heliocentric one in
large part because of the relevant scientific evidence, we might very well
understand such a shift in terms of Audi's equilibrium. But this "special
kind of cooperation" turns out to seem much less like cooperation and
much more like subordination. It is impossible to read his arguments
and come to any other conclusion but that what he actually thinks is that
believers should adjust their religious truth claims so that they are in conformity with secular reasons. How else would this principle sit easily – in
equilibrium, we might say – with his other two? If we are to offer secular
reasons that we find sufficiently persuasive on their own, then it seems
clear that in the equilibrium calculus, it is the secular side that intrinsically has the upper hand.

Audi clearly thinks that secular claims are more *reliable* than religious
ones, suggesting "one may sometimes be better off trying to understand
God through ethics than ethics through theology" while never suggesting that the converse might also be true.[31] What distinguishes the two
on this account is that, unlike religious views that can persist even in the
face of overwhelming evidence regarding their falseness, secular views
have almost intrinsic self-correcting mechanisms to them. Because they

[27] Robert Audi, "The State, the Church, and the Citizen," in *Religion and Contemporary
Liberalism*, ed. Paul J. Weithman (Notre Dame, IN: University of Notre Dame Press,
1997), 62.
[28] Ibid., 49.   [29] Ibid., 53.
[30] Audi, *Religious Commitment and Secular Reason*, 112.   [31] Ibid., 130.

are views presumably held on the basis of some rationally intelligible evidence, Audi believes, they can be shown to be false much more easily than the religious ones. Religious believers should have their theological and secular views "cooperate" in the sense of giving their secular views *priority* over at least their applied religious beliefs (and perhaps the basic ones as well) because the secular arguments intrinsically have self-correcting mechanisms, and so ought to be more reliable in the long run than comparably situated religious arguments.

There are a number of problems with this equilibrium claim. Even if it were the case that secular grounds were more reliable in the long run, citizens deciding whether to support or oppose a particular proposal have to decide whether *that* proposal is proper. In any particular case, "secular" grounds need not be more reliable than religious ones, especially when we are dealing with moral questions as opposed to strictly scientific or empirical ones, as we so often are when thinking about religion's political engagement. Moreover, what counts as "secular grounds" in these sorts of cases are often in fact "cultural grounds, grounds we find plausible, in large part, because we have been socialized into one culture and not another."[32] This presents two problems for Audi's argument. First, since all cultures change, what counts as secular will also change and the direction that change takes will itself be part of any society's moral and political conflicts. Consider Philip Hamburger's historical description of the evolution of legal language as it applies to First Amendment jurisprudence.[33] What was considered "neutral" or held in common became, in part because of a set of concerted legal strategies and in part because of the increasing pluralism of American culture, secular or whatever was not religious. In turn, the term "sectarian" migrated from describing small minority Christian sects (or Catholics) to meaning any sort of religious claim or group. Repairing to *secular* reasons to solve the political problems of pluralism cannot work if the idea of secularism is itself part of the conflict.

Second, "secular" cultural grounds are sometimes deeply corrupted themselves – or at the least not any more reliable than religious ones. A Christian in the American South prior to the Civil War might be tempted to think that God's commands forbid him from participating in the atrocity that was chattel slavery, but if he considered the best "secular" evidence available to him, how should he decide?[34] Or consider further the deeply disreputable participation of mainline Protestant clergy in the

---

[32] Eberle, *Religious Conviction in Liberal Politics*, 314.
[33] Philip Hamburger, *Separation of Church and State* (Cambridge, MA: Harvard University Press, 2002).
[34] Eugene Genovese has a fascinating study on post-Civil War white preachers in the American South and their attitudes toward blacks. In this book, he documents how it

American eugenics movement in the first half of the twentieth century.[35] Their reconceptualization of religious claims, especially those regarding the ideas of progress and eschatology, were driven almost entirely by a desire to bring their religious views into conformity with the prevailing (secular) cultural ideas. The problem is not that secular ideas are somehow intrinsically deficient morally or that religious ones carry with them an inevitable divine spark that always illumines things clearly and without error. One need only reflect on religious support for slavery or, in our day, for terrorism and the like to recognize that appending religion to some claim does not on its own make it reliable in any sense of the word. But that ought not to lead us into the opposite error of thinking that secular claims are thereby always *more* reliable.

The difficulty here is that the sorts of questions that religious reasons almost always come to bear upon politically are qualitatively different from, say, those like the question of whether to defend a geocentric view of the universe in the face of evidence to the contrary. For the most part, when religion speaks politically, it does so in the context of moral questions whose resolution does not depend in any direct sense – or at all – on what science or some other sort of putatively secular sort of evidence might have to say on the matter. Consider, if you will, the question of abortion rights. For some, the question seems to hinge on certain biological claims – the likelihood a fetus can survive outside the womb, the point at which it becomes sensitive to pain or aware of its surroundings, and so on. But quite clearly, individuals can hold to the same set of secular empirical views and still come to quite different conclusions regarding whether and when abortion is morally licit. There just is no slam-dunk batch of evidence available to all that will drive any reasonable person to a particular conclusion; there are simply too many other, non-empirical moral claims that get in the way, so to speak. Secular reasons just cannot – or maybe better, just do not – do the job alone in providing us definitive answers.

So it seems to me that Audi's claims in favor of secular reasons suffer on at least two counts: they distinguish inadequately between religious and secular reasons, unfairly making the former out to be immune to rational deliberation; and they make religious arguments out to be especially unreliable guides for political decisions, ignoring similar problems

---

was, in many cases, the more liberal (theologically speaking) Protestant preachers who took on the pseudo-scientific racism of their era and proclaimed the natural inferiority of the former slaves. See Eugene Genovese, *A Consuming Fire* (Athens: University of Georgia Press, 1999).

[35] Christine Rosen, *Preaching Eugenics: Religious Leaders and the American Eugenics Movement* (New York: Oxford University Press, 2004).

with secular reasons. None of this is to say that religious believers ought simply to take their basic theological claims and apply them willy-nilly to all sorts of political situations. There are enough examples of how this can go wrong to nearly fill a library, and though I eschew Audi's faith in secular reasons, I hardly mean to suggest that rational deliberation on political matters is misguided. After all, I do suggest that one reason we should not be so suspicious of religious reasons is that they are not as irrational or immune to rational deliberation as Audi and others make them out to be. But at least on the sorts of epistemological grounds that Audi advances, there seems to be little reason for citizens to think they have an obligation to employ secular as over religious reasons in their political deliberations.

Habermas and secularization

Consider, though, what seems to me an interesting and potentially acute critique of the argument so far. I suggested that we need not accept Audi's claims largely because there are good reasons to be skeptical of his rather neat distinction between secular and religious reasons. Either the distinctions are so broad that they catch almost every sort of moral-political argument or they are so narrow that they catch only the smallest slice of the sorts of religious arguments citizens typically make. Religious reasons are not as such inimical to rational deliberation and critique and so, I claim, ought not to be suspect on Audi's epistemological grounds. Still, Audi's arguments have a great deal of intuitive plausibility precisely because we do feel as though there is something distinct about claims made on the basis of one's religious faith and that to coerce someone on such a basis is deeply troubling. Such a view reflects the sense that something quite important has shifted in the modern world such that the credence we might have once almost instinctually given to religiously rooted claims has been, perhaps permanently, displaced. In a word, we have become – religious believers included – secularized, at least in the sense that we all acknowledge the distinctiveness of religious claims and (this is probably less universally held) the reasonableness of our disagreement over them. Therefore, when searching for good reasons to justify political coercion, it seems natural that we shy away from claims widely held in serious dispute, whatever might be said about the epistemological merit of such a move in the end. Audi's claims (and ones like them) are so plausible because we do live in what Charles Taylor has called a "secular age."[36]

[36] Taylor, *A Secular Age*.

Now why might this matter for my critique of deliberative restraint? Recall how I earlier suggested that deliberative restraint (and deliberation more broadly) is meant to reconcile our plural and varied interests in a way that we can all (or most all) find reasonably legitimate. Part of the concern here is clearly with our subjective sense of the political order. Political outcomes should not just reflect (as best they can) what is *actually* in our collective interest; we should also be able to *recognize* them as such. Part of the problem with religious reasons is that to the degree that a particular outcome reflects a particular religious claim, it may be impossible to expect citizens who do not endorse the religious claim to recognize the outcome as legitimate. Even if the sorts of epistemological arguments on offer from Audi and others do not quite pass muster philosophically, it still might be the case that citizens should offer one another reasons that do not depend on religious claims precisely because most generally *do* expect that those other citizens – whatever their religious affiliations – will make secular arguments in public debates. The undeniable sociological changes over the past five or six centuries have shifted the ground on which political arguments can be constructed, and as a significant component of those changes, secularization has made religiously rooted justifications for political coercion both practically and morally problematic. Or so we largely think.

In what follows, I want to suggest that this sense of things – that secularization has more or less permanently made recourse to religious reasons politically problematic – is itself contestable not just as an epistemological matter (as I showed with respect to Audi's arguments) but as a sociological one as well. That is, to the degree that the "secular" version of the argument for deliberative restraint relies on a sociological claim about the broader phenomenon of secularization, a closer look into what secularization actually is and what it is not will make us more skeptical of its utility in grounding a claim in favor of secular over religious reasons in political deliberation. I propose to substantiate that view in something of a roundabout way, namely by tracing some of the arguments offered by Jürgen Habermas, who early on in his considerations of these sorts of questions comes across as very much in favor of decidedly secular reasons but whose recent considerations seem to be pressing toward what he calls "post-secular" formulations. The critical examination offered below helps show how recent shifts in understanding the substantial changes in the modern social order, especially in understanding secularization, make the claims in favor of secular reasons much less tenable, if not implausible.

Jürgen Habermas has probably done more than any other scholar to place deliberation at the center of democratic theory, and his arguments exert a wide influence in debates over the sorts of reasons we may properly employ politically. Much of Habermas' political theory work in the 1990s does not reflect the sense that contemporary conditions of moral pluralism make a comprehensive theory of justice unrealistic. Criticizing Rawls' arguments as too generous toward contextualist critics, he argues that in *Political Liberalism*, "practical reason is robbed of its moral core and is deflated to a reasonableness that becomes dependent on moral truths justified otherwise. The moral validity of conceptions of justice is now no longer grounded in a universally binding practical reason but in the lucky convergence of reasonable worldviews whose moral components overlap to a significant degree."[37] That is, those who start off by abandoning any hope of constructing a theory of justice that is universally plausible do so at the cost of nearly abandoning the very idea of justice itself – or at least its "moral validity."

Instead, he suggests that the very idea of moral obligation under conditions of moral pluralism (he calls it the "post-metaphysical condition") "presupposes the intersubjective recognition of moral norms or customary practices that lay down for a community *in a convincing manner* what actors are obliged to do and what they can expect from one another."[38] We cannot talk about moral obligation out of one side of our mouth and then embrace its impossibility out the other; laws which we are morally obligated to follow – that have legitimacy, that is – must be justified to us. This means that moral obligation follows from the degree to which positive coercive law reflects *impartial* and *objective* truths grounded in practical reason. Now, for Habermas, these truths do not emerge from a transcendental consciousness or even something like Rawls' Original Position. Rather, they emerge from "disagreements that can be resolved convincingly from the perspective of participants on the basis of potential justifications that are equally accessible to all."[39] They emerge, that is, when participants in disagreement engage one another on common grounds. Achieving this cashes out, among other things, in a requirement for institutionalized rational discourse that takes into account only *"generalizable* value orientations" that "only [deserve] consideration from a moral point of view once ... stripped of [their] intrinsic relation to a first person perspective."[40] Under conditions of modern pluralism, only impartial deliberation generates moral obligation.

---

[37] Habermas, "'Reasonable' Versus 'True,' Or the Morality of Worldviews," 83.
[38] Jürgen Habermas, "A Genealogical Analysis of the Cognitive Content of Morality," in *The Inclusion of the Other*, 3.
[39] Ibid., 4.
[40] Habermas, "'Reasonable' Versus 'True,' Or the Morality of Worldviews," 81.

Armed with his theory of communicative action[41] and the confidence that in the modern world moral philosophy depends on a "post-metaphysical level of justification,"[42] Habermas relocates the derivation of moral norms from Kant's transcendental consciousness to the intersubjective discourse of free and equal persons deliberating on what is of interest to all. Note that Habermas thinks that morality has a cognitive content; otherwise, "it would have no advantage over other, more costly forms of coordination."[43] Construed in that way, "moral obligations recommend themselves by their internal relations to the gentle, persuasive force of reasons as an alternative to strategic, that is, coercive or manipulative, forms of conflict resolution."[44] We may be bound either by the results of our own reason or by the sword, Habermas suggests, and it is self-evident that the former is preferable to the latter.

But we find ourselves in a peculiar and difficult age for determining the cognitive content of moral (and hence, legal) laws: "with the transition to pluralism of worldviews in modern society, religion and the ethos rooted in it disintegrate as a *public* basis of a morality shared for all."[45] If the moral law is the law that could be true for all, then our lack of common religious or metaphysical beliefs undermines the natural epistemic authority that such a law might have under different social conditions. Instead, under "post-metaphysical" conditions, "the cognitive content of the moral language game can henceforth be reconstructed only on the basis of the reason and will of its participants."[46] Discovering the moral law requires a deliberative procedure "in which each participant is compelled to adopt the perspective of all others in order to examine whether a norm could be willed by all *from the perspective of each person*. This is the situation of a *rational discourse* oriented to reaching understanding in which all those concerned participate."[47] This procedure operates under two principles: the Discourse Principle (D) and the Universalization Principle (U). D stipulates that "only those norms can claim validity that could meet with the agreement of all those concerned in their capacity as participants in a practical discourse,"[48] while U says, "A norm is valid when the foreseeable consequences and side effects of its general observance for the interests and value-orientations of *each individual* could be *jointly* accepted by all concerned without coercion."[49] Under conditions of modern pluralism, democratic self-government only possesses moral legitimacy to the degree that it reflects an ideal deliberative procedure in

---

[41] Jürgen Habermas, *The Theory of Communicative Action*, vols. I–II, trans. Thomas McCarthy (Boston: Beacon Press, 1984–7).

[42] Habermas, "A Genealogical Analysis of the Cognitive Content of Morality," 11.

[43] Ibid., 4.   [44] Ibid.   [45] Ibid., 11.   [46] Ibid., 12.

[47] Ibid., 33.   [48] Ibid., 34.   [49] Ibid., 42.

which every citizen participates equally in the construction of laws in the interest of all. More fully:

A law is valid in the moral sense when it could be accepted by everybody from the perspective of each individual. Because only "general" laws fulfill the condition that they regulate matters in the equal interest of all, practical reason finds expression in the generalizability or universalizability of the interests expressed in the law. Thus a person takes the moral point of view when he deliberates *like* a democratic legislator on whether the practice that would result from the general observance of a hypothetically proposed norm could be accepted by all those possibly affected viewed as potential co-legislators.[50]

Immediately, our skeptical antennae ought to go up: if the rationale for a deliberative procedure stems from the condition of moral pluralism that constitutes the modern world, then how does resorting to a deliberative procedure, ideal or not, resolve the issue? Or, as McCarthy asks, "On what grounds should we suppose that everyone would, even under ideal conditions agree in a judgment" about the moral law?[51] Surely Habermas is not just some naïf who thinks that the world's problems could be solved if we just sat down and talked them out? Well, he is certainly not a naïf, but he does "expect that moral questions and questions of political justice admit in principle of universally valid answers."[52] Habermas draws his confidence from his theory of communicative action, where the presuppositions of discourse implicitly commit participants to the idea that the norm over which they may be arguing is necessarily amenable to rational and, thus, universal consensus. We simply do not get involved in political discussions over proposed norms unless we think that such discussions can result in some sort of agreement; an argument rejecting that conclusion is a performative contradiction in that it itself is an attempt to persuade us to agree with the norm that agreement on norms is impossible. The very structures of communication, Habermas argues, are shot through with validity claims and "the social integration of everyday life depends largely on communicative practices oriented toward mutual understanding and based on the recognition of fallible claims to validity."[53]

Not all validity claims, however, are universally binding. Claims about the particular practices of religious traditions and other sorts of ethically charged communities do not in themselves point toward universal validity claims. Habermas distinguishes between the universal moral discourses

---

[50] Ibid., 31.
[51] Thomas McCarthy, "Practical Discourse: On the Relation of Morality to Politics," in *Habermas and the Public Sphere*, ed. Craig J. Calhoun (Cambridge, MA: MIT Press, 1992), 61.
[52] Habermas, "'Reasonable' Versus 'True,' Or the Morality of Worldviews," 99.
[53] Ibid., 80.

that, within a political system, eventually come to be embodied in positive coercive law and "ethical disputes over the value of competing lifestyles and forms of life."[54] The latter, he argues, do not admit of universal rationalization and we cannot expect them "to lead to anything other than reasonable disagreements."[55] These latter sets of disputes, though they too are amenable to adjudication within rationalized discourses, are embedded in the presuppositions of particular ways of life and as such ought not to impinge on political or moral disputes about the necessarily universal laws that a political system imposes.[56]

How are we to distinguish between the moral and ethical? What if that distinction itself is at the heart of the dispute? For Habermas, the question is unproblematic, for the priority of political values expressed in the universal moral point of view written into law is a "requirement of practical reason ... to which comprehensive doctrines must *submit*" on the basis of "an epistemic authority that is itself independent of worldviews."[57] That is, in a conflict over what counts as ethical or political, between the particular claims of an ethical community and the universal claims of moral law, the impartiality of practical reason and its embodiment in deliberative procedures takes precedence and can be justified with reference to the presuppositions intrinsic to the very practice of deliberation itself.

Not just any sort of communicative practices count as practical discourse; there are rules for the kinds of reasons one may offer in the course of deliberation over moral norms, rules that Habermas roots in the deliberation's very presuppositions. He argues that, "the reasons that bear on the outcome must carry an epistemic weight and may not simply express what it is rational for a particular person to do in light of her existing preferences."[58] This means that:

Under the pragmatic presuppositions of an inclusive and noncoercive rational discourse between free and equal participants, everyone is required to take the perspective of everyone else and thus to project herself into the understandings of self and world of all others; from this interlocking of perspectives there emerges an ideally extended "we-perspective" from which all can test in common whether they wish to make a controversial norm the basis of their shared practice; and this should include mutual criticism of the appropriateness of the languages in terms of which situations and needs are interpreted. In the course of *successively* undertaken abstractions, the core of generalizable interests can then emerge step by step.[59]

---

[54] Ibid., 99.   [55] Ibid.
[56] These ethical sorts of discourses are the ones that take place within churches, civil associations, professional organizations, families, and so on.
[57] Habermas, "'Reasonable' Versus 'True,' Or the Morality of Worldviews," 93.
[58] Ibid., 81.
[59] Habermas, "Reconciliation through the Use of Public Reason," 58.

Two things become a bit clearer here. First, participants in a rational discourse committed to finding mutually persuasive norms to govern them all can expect their interests to broaden in the course of the deliberation. Deliberative democrats often attempt to distinguish themselves sharply from liberals precisely on this point: preferences, they argue, are not something pre-given but are shaped through our socialization with others.[60] The hope then is that preferences in regard to issues of "universal" concern will become universalized through a deliberative procedure that puts us in dialogue on an equal footing with all others.

But such universalization does not come naturally or easily in any sense. Though it may be rational, and thus moral, for us to conduct deliberation in this manner, it is clearly not a common practice, and Habermas wants to establish some "ground rules" or "pragmatic presuppositions" that anyone who accepts their fellow citizens as free and equal partners in a democratic government ought to accept.[61] Most crucially for our purposes, participants must provide "reasons that give equal weight to the interests and evaluative orientations of everybody [that] can influence the outcome of practical discourses."[62] This means that:

In practical discourses, only those interests "count" for the outcome that are presented as intersubjectively recognized values and hence are *candidates* for inclusion in the semantic content of valid norms. Only *generalizable* value orientations, which all participants (and all those affected) can accept with good reasons as appropriate for regulating the subject matter at hand, and which can thereby acquire binding normative force, pass this threshold. An "interest" can be described as a "value-orientation" when it is shared by other members of a community in similar situations. Thus an interest only deserves consideration from a moral point of view once it is stripped of its intrinsic relation to a first person perspective.[63]

Habermas here makes impartiality the keystone to a legitimately constructed deliberative democracy. If moral pluralism and democratic self-government are to be reconciled, democratic political institutions must be arranged so that citizens may engage in an deliberative process of moral and political will-formation that promises at least the potential of consensus insofar as participants offer one another their rationale for the validity of particular norms in ways that reflect a universal and general concern for the interests of the other free and equal participants in

---

[60] See also Joshua Cohen, "Procedure and Substance in Deliberative Democracy," in *Democracy and Difference: Contesting the Boundaries of the Political*, ed. Seyla Benhabib (Princeton, NJ: Princeton University Press, 1996).

[61] Habermas, "A Genealogical Analysis of the Cognitive Content of Morality," 44.

[62] Ibid.

[63] Habermas, "'Reasonable' Versus 'True,' Or the Morality of Worldviews," 81.

the deliberation. Clearly, then, religious reasons ought not to be a part of any public political discourse. They cannot plausibly represent views that others – who do not share the particular religious views at hand – could take as good reasons for binding themselves with the force of moral obligation. They are, instead, bearers of "ethical" viewpoints that have validity only within particular communities that can give them meaning. Relying on religious reasons for political action would be tantamount to simply coercing citizens against their will and eviscerating the very possibility of moral obligation. Call this, then, Habermas' *exclusive* argument for deliberative restraint.

Habermas' views are (obviously) complex, and I have hardly done justice to the full argument here. But it seems to me that the exclusive argument simply does not take moral pluralism seriously enough and overestimates the potential for any sort of real agreement or consensus within our wildly pluralistic societies. That is, despite the fact that his argument begins in some fashion with an acceptance of moral, religious, and social pluralism, he too confidently discounts that pluralism and its relevance for public political deliberations. I am not alone, it turns out, in suggesting that Habermas' relatively early work on deliberative democracy does not take moral pluralism seriously enough. Thomas McCarthy also worries that Habermas' distinction between moral and ethical discourses fails to do justice to the way in which divergence in ethical perspectives will inevitably affect moral deliberation as well. Universal consensus, he says, "may not be possible when there are fundamental divergences in value orientations ... we cannot agree on what is just without achieving some measure of agreement on what is good."[64] The problem here is not that the structure of rational deliberation has somehow changed or that it is impossible to imagine substantive agreement even across our moral divides. The problem is that our divergent ethical lives seem repeatedly to work their ways into our moral and political deliberations, regardless of whether they must or should do so. What reason can we have for thinking differently and hoping that a Habermasian deliberative procedure could overcome that? After all, if its achievement is impossible or even highly implausible, we may have good reason for doubting the strength of a putative moral obligation.

There are a number of ways that a deliberative theorist like Habermas might respond. First, they suggest that citizens might simply continue the dialogue and hope that participants' perspectives are "enlarged" in some way. This is not an unfamiliar experience, where the different sides in a dispute, simply by virtue of communicating across a table over a long

---

[64] McCarthy, "Practical Discourse: On the Relation of Morality to Politics," 62.

period of time, come to enlarge their sympathies and reach some sort of resolution. But some conflicts simply do not seem to open themselves to amelioration, and often, as I noted earlier, it is about just those conflicts that religion has something important to say politically. The most obvious of these is the perennial and continuing dispute over abortion, but it is hardly alone.[65] Cloning ("therapeutic" or "reproductive"), genetic manipulation, embryonic stem cell research, and a host of other issues continue to divide the public not because one side misunderstands the other or because one side has malignant intentions and the other is on the side of the angels, but because the conflict between (or among, as there are often more than two sides to these disputes) the disputing parties comes out of different and conflicting moral premises that are, in some sense, pre-rational and not obviously amenable to resolution, deliberative or otherwise. Take, for instance, Ronald Dworkin's attempt to find common ground on abortion in his book *Life's Dominion*.[66] Arguing that both sides view life as "sacred," he goes on to suggest that a moderately pro-choice view best makes sense of how we all actually think of life's sacredness. Dworkin can only come to that view, however, by subtly mischaracterizing what it is that opponents of abortion rights mean when they say life is sacred. To think of life as sacred in their sense means to think it inviolable, and that means they think it impermissible to trade off what they see as a life for another's use.[67] Sometimes, as Gutmann and Thompson remind us, the best that we can expect is to narrow our differences and try to minimize their impact on the community as a whole.[68]

Another response might be to suggest that deliberative democracy and its correlative rule of impartial, public discourse may act as an "ideal"

[65] Religion's role in making abortion and other similar issues a live political issue can clearly be seen in the contrast with Europe, where, though abortion rights are more constricted, its legality remains mostly unchallenged, largely, it seems, because the opposition to abortion rights is closely connected to religious commitment. For more on this, see Mary Ann Glendon, *Abortion and Divorce in Western Law* (Cambridge, MA: Harvard University Press, 1987); Michael Minkenberg, "Religion and Public Policy: Institutional, Cultural, and Political Impact on the Shaping of Abortion Policies in Western Europe," *Comparative Political Studies* 35, no. 2 (2002).

[66] Ronald Dworkin, *Life's Dominion: An Argument about Abortion, Euthanasia, and Individual Freedom*, 1st. edn. (New York: Knopf, 1993).

[67] See Robert P. George, *The Clash of Orthodoxies: Law, Religion, and Morality in Crisis* (Wilmington, DE: ISI Books, 2001), 40–42. Dworkin trades on a real ambiguity in the position of many opponents of abortion, namely their willingness to countenance abortion in the cases of rape or incest. In these cases, abortion opponents seem to evince an acceptance of life's "sacredness" as meaning life has value along some continuum, varying depending on our age, health, and other factors.

[68] Gutmann and Thompson, *Democracy and Disagreement*, 84–94. They suggest that participants in deliberative forums attempt to construct their arguments in such a way as to achieve an "economy of moral disagreement."

against which real political institutions ought to be measured. "The suggestion is, since we accept the intuitive ideal of a fair system of cooperation, we should want out political institutions themselves to conform, *insofar as it is feasible*, to the requirement that terms of association be worked out under fair conditions."[69] The fact that our discourses are imperfect and perhaps are always likely to be so does not undermine the "ideal" of deliberative democracy any more than the fact of obvious difference in natural talent among individuals undermines the moral equality of all human beings. But then we are faced with a real puzzle: how exactly should the unachievable "ideal" be used to judge the "real"? If the "ideal" means that moral legitimacy depends on a particular kind of rational-moral discourse and the "real" always includes something else, does that make moral legitimacy impossible? This response seems hardly satisfying.

Brian Shaw suggests that Habermas' rather exclusive view on display here is, in fact, more exclusive than it needs to be. He laments the exclusion of religious reasons as inconsistent with the Kantian thrust of Habermas' project and thinks that little would be lost (and much gained) by including religious claims within the discourse setting.[70] Perhaps that is true, but what Shaw perhaps misses and what makes the "ideal mirror" response not so persuasive is the degree to which Habermas' claims actually look to be premised on a *sociological* reading of modern life that is fundamentally indebted to claims of modernization and – crucially – secularization. As José Casanova notes, Habermas' "secularist theory of modernity" presumes that religion is "only an anachronism or a residue without much relevance or future," one that "ought to be superseded by postconventional secular morality."[71] The Habermasian exclusive argument cannot be interested in including religion in rational discourses, and the ideal deliberative position can act as a mirror to our own practices because they presume that modernity points toward a future where religion has all but disappeared (or at least been thoroughly privatized) and where it will be possible to engage in mutual deliberation simply as rational beings.

Inasmuch as many of our seemingly ineliminable moral-political conflicts persist on account of their religious connections, Habermas' exclusive view can posit the plausibility of a merely rational-moral discourse

---

[69] Joshua Cohen, "Deliberation and Democratic Legitimacy," in *Deliberative Democracy: Essays on Reason and Politics*, ed. James Bohman and William Rehg (Cambridge: MIT Press, 1999), 168.

[70] Brian J. Shaw, "Habermas and Religious Inclusion," *Political Theory* 27, no. 5 (1999).

[71] Casanova, *Public Religions in the Modern World*, 231.

theory only to the degree, then, that its sociological premise regarding secularization is true. It seems clear that the stubborn persistence of any number of political conflicts over what are often called "social issues" – abortion, issues dealing with sexuality, euthanasia, and so forth – get their political salience via their connection to religiously rooted moral views. It is not that disputes over those views are tied in any essential way to religion; they would be difficult moral and political issues in any case. But they have become and remain important and vital political issues in the American context and not so much in the European one, to draw no doubt an overly broad comparison, largely on account of the presence of religious political movements devoted precisely to those issues. Abortion, euthanasia, and such issues would continue to matter politically, but those sorts of issues would likely not have the salience they do in the US absent the religiously rooted groups that focus on them. So we might reasonably expect that they will continue to be serious and ineliminable conflicts so long as those groups remain influential, and those groups will remain influential, we might also suppose, just so long as a significant portion of the population not only remains religious but also religious in a way that moves beyond the strictly private realm. Habermas' exclusive version of deliberative restraint hangs together precisely to the degree, then, that his concomitant views on secularization also hold up. To put things a bit too simply, no secularization, no Habermasian-style deliberative restraint.

Secularization theories have long been perhaps the central part of the sociological discipline, beginning with Comte and Durkheim and extending through Weber, Berger, and a number of others. In its most straightforward form, the theory argued that as societies underwent processes of modernization and its attendant industrialization and urbanization, religion would become increasingly marginalized, perhaps to the point of nonexistence. In the European context (the context in which Habermas is writing, of course), it is hard not to think that the theory basically rings true. What was once called *Christendom* is, for the most part, among the most secularized of societies.[72] Even though most of the European democracies provide subsidies for or have outright establishments of particular Christian churches, only small percentages of Europeans attend religious services regularly or think of religion as having a high priority in their lives. And there certainly is no social or political equivalent to

---

[72] Cf. Steve Bruce, *God Is Dead: Secularization in the West* (Malden, MA: Blackwell Publishers, 2002); Hugh McLeod, *Secularisation in Western Europe, 1848–1914* (New York: St. Martin's Press, 2000); Hugh McLeod and Werner Ustorf, *The Decline of Christendom in Western Europe, 1750–2000* (New York: Cambridge University Press, 2003).

America's conservative Protestants. If Europe were to be your dataset for testing this sort of theory of secularization, you would be hard pressed to deny its validity.

Europe does not, though, constitute the whole of the modern world, and a number of sociologists have recently challenged this traditional paradigm of secularization, suggesting not only that Europe's secularization is the exception rather than the rule but also that what secularization we do see is more apparent than real. Chief among these secularization skeptics has been Rodney Stark, whose articles and books have applied the tools of economic analysis to the study of religion and shown, he argues, that the pre-modern world was not as religious as we imagine and that the modern world is becoming *more* religious, not less.[73] Steve Bruce and others have emphatically denied these claims, disputing both Stark's methodologies and evidence.[74] It is hard to say who exactly has the better part of the argument, especially since in at least one respect, it hangs on trying to discern empirically how religiously observant ordinary people were a couple of centuries ago as compared to today. Contemporary scholars often have a hard time figuring out how to "measure" religious observance with all of today's powerful survey tools, so it should not be surprising that making comparisons across such a length of time would be difficult or contentious. In any case, there does seem to be good reason to doubt the traditional secularization paradigm, at least insofar as it equated modernization with religion's disappearance; America is the most "modern" society in any number of respects and seems quite religious, and the developing world seems at times to suggest that modernization and increased religiosity can go together rather than be at odds.[75]

But it is a mistake, as Casanova points out, to think of the claims for secularization as a unified theory; they are, in fact, "three different propositions: secularization as religious decline, secularization as differentiation, and secularization as privatization."[76] The first, as he says, is likely untrue, and the longevity of its standing within sociological theory is a

[73] Roger Finke and Rodney Stark, *The Churching of America: 1776–1990* (New Brunswick, NJ: Rutgers University Press, 1992); Rodney Stark, *Exploring the Religious Life* (Baltimore, MD: Johns Hopkins University Press, 2004); Rodney Stark and William Sims Bainbridge, *The Future of Religion: Secularization, Revival, and Cult Formation* (Berkeley: University of California Press, 1985); Rodney Stark and Roger Finke, *Acts of Faith: Explaining the Human Side of Religion* (Berkeley: University of California Press, 2000). See also Berger, *The Desecularization of the World.*

[74] Steve Bruce, "Christianity in Britain, R.I.P.," *Sociology of Religion* 62, no. 2 (2001); Bruce, *God Is Dead*; Steve Bruce, ed., *Religion and Modernization: Sociologists and Historians Debate the Secularization Thesis* (Oxford: Oxford University Press, 1992).

[75] See Berger, *The Desecularization of the World*; Jenkins, *The Next Christendom.*

[76] Casanova, *Public Religions in the Modern World*, 7. See also Mark Chaves, "Religious Pluralism and Religious Participation," *Annual Review of Sociology* 27, no. 1 (2001);

testament to its centrality to the practice of sociology itself rather than any well-established body of evidence.[77] The last – privatization – had been largely true, but that trend seems to have reversed itself, as religious traditions have undergone a "deprivatization" of sorts. He suggests that the middle proposition, differentiation, "remains the valid core of the theory of secularization"[78] as it describes the processes by which the different functional spheres of life – the state, the economy, law, art, recreation, education and so on – have been "freed" from their relationship to religious institutions or dogma and have reorganized themselves according to their functional dictates. So the state evinces a "bureaucratic rationality" (à la Weber), the market pursues "efficiency" in the name of the productive allocation of scarce material resources, and, though religion need not be confined to the purely "private" sphere of individual devotion, neither can it move out of its location within the institutions of "civil society." To the degree that Casanova's argument is correct, it looks as if Habermas' normatively exclusive claims are only weakly supported sociologically. It is implausible to suppose as a matter of historical necessity that religion is but an "anachronism" waiting to be "superseded," and so we should not expect that the often contentious moral pluralism we see in contemporary democratic politics, especially in the United States, will go away anytime soon, if ever. It may be the case that religion will disappear, though there is precious little evidence of that in the United States or in the developing world.[79] But if differentiation – or something like it – is true, then the Habermasian emphasis on secular reasons may, in fact, be warranted.

In a series of publications and interviews since the September 2001 terrorist attacks, Habermas seems to have reconsidered his earlier suppositions regarding claims of secularization, acknowledging that the "political revitalization of religion" in the United States (and elsewhere) works to undermine the view that modernization and religion are fundamentally at odds with one another.[80] Instead, he suggests that we now actually inhabit not just a "post-metaphysical" society in which moral claims

---

Anthony Gill, "Religion and Comparative Politics," *Annual Review of Political Science* 4, no. 1 (2001); McLeod, *Secularisation in Western Europe, 1848–1914*; W.H. Swatos and K.J. Christiano, "Secularization Theory: The Course of a Concept," *Sociology of Religion* 60, no. 20 (2000); David Yamane, "Secularization on Trial: In Defense of a Neosecularization Paradigm," *Journal for the Scientific Study of Religion* 36, no. 1 (1997).

[77] Casanova, *Public Religions in the Modern World*, 26–35.

[78] Ibid., 212.

[79] Jenkins, *The Next Christendom*. If it does, I should note, then this whole discussion will be largely a moot point.

[80] Habermas, "Religion in the Public Sphere," 1. See also Habermas, "A Conversation about God and the World"; Jürgen Habermas, "Equal Treatment of Cultures and the Limits of Postmodern Liberalism," *Journal of Political Philosophy* 13, no. 1 (2005); Habermas, "On the Relations between the Secular Liberal State and Religion."

must be discursively deliberated upon, but also a "post-secular" one where non-believers must recognize that the "continued existence of religious communities first requires a change in mentality" that mirrors the one religious believers underwent in grappling with the religious critiques of the Enlightenment. Just as religious believers had to learn to accept that there were good reasons to doubt specific doctrinal claims and religious belief more generally, non-believers,[81] Habermas supposes, must now learn to refrain "from passing judgment on religious truths while insisting (in a non-polemical fashion) on drawing a strict line between faith and knowledge" as well as rejecting "a scientistically limited conception of reason and the exclusion of religious doctrines from the genealogy of reason."[82] The upshot here is that for Habermas, the failure of the traditional secularization paradigm, marked above all by the persistence of "religious communities," forces a shift in modernity's epistemological stance. No longer can religion be deemed merely an irrational leftover of earlier ages and no longer can what is "secular" be tied so closely to "universal" or "moral."

Moreover, no longer can a deliberative theory of democracy suppose that religious believers will or can entirely privatize their religious views in political matters. He suggests that believers have a "right ... to make contributions to public discussion in religious language"[83] and that to suppose that they should even make their political choices be guided "in the final instance ... by secular considerations is to ignore the realities of a devout life, an existence led in light of belief."[84] Clearly, by Habermas' lights, Audi's principles of secular motivation and theo-ethical equilibrium fall out, and the sociological reality of religion's persistence and its refusal to privatize means that religion will and may play a public, even political, role in modern pluralist democracies. At least to this degree, then, Habermas looks to have shed some of his earlier exclusivist claims, but not because he has given up on the idea of a deliberative democracy or the hope for rational-moral discourse.[85] So far as I can make out – and it seems as though Habermas is working

---

[81] He actually calls them "religiously-unattuned citizen[s]" (Habermas, "Equal Treatment of Cultures and the Limits of Postmodern Liberalism," 27.) "Non-believer" just seems to flow better.

[82] Habermas, "Religion in the Public Sphere," 15–16.

[83] Habermas, "Equal Treatment of Cultures and the Limits of Postmodern Liberalism," 27.

[84] Habermas, "Religion in the Public Sphere," 9.

[85] For some interesting commentaries along these lines see Simone Chambers, "How Religion Speaks to the Agnostic: Habermas on the Persistent Value of Religion," *Constellations* 14, no. 2 (2007); Maeve Cooke, "A Secular State for a Postsecular Society? Postmetaphysical Political Theory and the Place of Religion," *Constellations* 14, no. 2 (2007); Krause, *Civil Passions*; Christina Lafont, "Religion in the Public Sphere: Remarks on Habermas's Conception of Public Deliberation in Postsecular Societies," *Constellations* 14, no. 2 (2007).

some of these things out himself – he has shifted his arguments on the basis of continued sociological observation of the empirical status of religion in the modern world.

But it is important to note that while Habermas *shifted* his views and no doubt loosened the normative strictures regarding religion's participation in public life, he has not simply *upended* them. Indeed, he is still firmly committed to the idea that while religious citizens may deliberate on their own, with each other, or even in public forums employing their religious views, they must still find ways to translate those views into publicly accessible, *secular*, ones: "Every citizen must know and accept that only secular reasons count beyond the institutional threshold that divides the informal public sphere from parliaments, courts, ministries and administrations."[86] Indeed, he even suggests that there must be a kind of "institutional filter" that can screen out expressly religious claims, going so far as to recommend that parliaments have rules that would allow for "religious statements or justifications [to be] expunged from the minutes."[87] So citizens are perfectly justified in thinking about political proposals, discussing them with neighbors, and even making their arguments in "public" without running into any obligations to dissociate themselves from their religious views. They may even decide how to vote on the basis of those views. But beyond the hurly-burly of what Habermas calls the "informal public sphere," in the areas of life where laws are actually made, interpreted, and executed, they must learn the skill of "translation," of taking their religious views and making the same points, except this time in secular terms.[88]

Now this may seem at first blush an odd position, at least to the degree that it accepts the legitimacy of religious arguments in an "informal" public sphere and strictly rules them out within more "formal" contexts. But Habermas has some plausible grounds. The moral grounds for what we might call the translation obligation rests in a fairly traditional liberal argument about the need for the state to exercise its authority neutrally with respect to its citizens' diverse and often opposed worldviews.[89] The best way to do that, he supposes, is to ensure that such political authority is exercised only on the basis of reasons that could apply to all citizens, or secular reasons, even if, as he acknowledges, such limitations places

---

[86] Habermas, "Religion in the Public Sphere," 9–10.

[87] Ibid., 10.

[88] He does suggest at one point (ibid., 10) that if someone just cannot find a secular analogue to her religious argument then she should be allowed to make the religious argument. But I do not think there is any doubt that someone who must do that is being thereby a bad citizen (and presumably will have her remarks expunged in any case).

[89] See, generally, Habermas, "Religion in the Public Sphere."

asymmetrical obligations on religious believers.[90] I will deal with the requirements of fairness and neutrality in my discussion of Rawls below, so let me set this aside and focus instead on the much more interesting source of the argument, Habermas' sociological claims.

As I noted above, Habermas' exclusive claims "worked" insofar as his rather traditional secularization paradigm also "worked." But that paradigm now seems untenable, and Habermas has accordingly become much more open to religion's participation in public life, though with important normative limits. These limits seem to rely, perhaps unsurprisingly, on what Casanova has called secularization theory's "valid core," differentiation. Habermas accepts, *pace* the traditional secularization claim, that religious communities can and often do persist within modernity, and what's more, can actually make positive contributions toward the construction and understanding of a new, "post-secular" democratic society.[91] But these religious communities are distinctly modern in that they have imbibed in some fashion the critical arrows thrown their way via the Enlightenment and have become self-reflective regarding the tenability of their own dogmas, at least to the extent that they recognize that others might reasonably disagree with them regarding their religious commitments. In short, what at least makes a religious community *modern* and what makes it capable of surviving (even thriving) is that it is capable of fitting more or less well into the modern social order governed by a political authority – the state – that protects and practices religious toleration.[92] It need not give up its own truth claims, but it must give up its desire (if there) to impose those claims via violence (or political coercion). This, Habermas supposes, in turn necessitates a secular state and a secular (formal) public order. While those of us in the Anglo-American world tend to view the elements of the liberal state in largely normative terms, Habermas' argument builds just as much on the sense that there is a distinctive sociological shape to modernity, one that itself, in part independent of particular normative aspirations, imposes obligations on each. And for our purposes here, chief among those is the requirement to acknowledge the need for a secular state and formal public sphere as a means of making effective the very modern embrace

---

[90] To be clear, Habermas does not at all think his deliberative democracy requires anything like French-style *laïcité*, where public secularism is rather ruthlessly enforced. It does require a separation of church and state, but probably not even to the degree prevalent in the United States. Religious believers have asymmetric obligations vis-à-vis non-believers because they must do the translation work, while non-believers need only become reflexively self-aware of their participation in a "post-secular" culture.

[91] Habermas, "Equal Treatment of Cultures and the Limits of Postmodern Liberalism," 26.

[92] Habermas, "A Conversation about God and the World," 152.

of religious toleration. So in this way Habermas' implicit sociological claims track what Casanova takes to be the "valid core" of secularization, differentiation, and so in order to think about the degree to which we should accept his revised claims, we need to understand more fully how much we should accept the "validity" of differentiation.

As I pointed out earlier, Casanova suggests that the empirically valid core of a secularization theory is one that recognizes the ways in which various "spheres" of the modern social order have over time spun off on their own and now run more or less autonomously, especially with respect to religious authority. In the medieval world, of course, the church made claims on (sometimes effectively, sometimes not) almost every area of life: politics, economics, education, family life, and so on. Charles Taylor has quite nicely described how the modern "self" differs from its pre-modern predecessor precisely in that the pre-modern self was in large part defined by religious claims while the modern self can stand apart from them, can be "buffered" from them.[93] This buffered self, a self that understands itself as standing independently of any particular identity, emerges on account of a social order in which all the various institutions in which the self is tutored stand independently of any overarching or comprehensive identity. In some respects, of course, the "truth" of differentiation is undeniable. Businesses run according to the principles of profit maximization, for example, operating in ways that, say, Aquinas would have found quite distressing. Sundays are no longer set aside as days of rest and worship, but are more often set aside as a day of options – worship or recreation or shopping or some combination of all. Primary schooling has been largely secularized, and even a great number of the private religious colleges and universities have both formally and substantively separated themselves from their faith-based origins.

Most importantly, of course, politics in modern democracies does not run according to any particular religious dictates and certainly not according to any particular "church." The modern democratic state is universally secular, at least in the sense that it does not operate, in any case not explicitly, on the basis of any professed religious claims and does not have as one of its responsibilities the spiritual welfare of its citizens. Instead, it seeks goods – the rule of law, public safety, welfare, and so on – that are decidedly temporal, and so in that sense differentiation is obviously descriptively correct. But that does not quite settle the matter, for it is not enough that differentiation be an accurate description of the world we see around us; for Casanova, differentiation

---

[93] Taylor, *A Secular Age.*

is a "general modern structural trend," one that helps define modernity and, as such, it is not a "historical option" like privatization or religious decline. It is, in a sense, an inevitability built into the very fabric of the modern world.[94] Modern societies can have lots of religious believers and even have religion play a "public" role, but they cannot, indeed will not, extend that "public" role beyond the realm of "civil" and into "political" society. Or, to use Habermas' terms, modern societies necessarily wall religion off from participation in "formal" political life as a part of their differentiated social structures. Habermas can claim that religious believers have an obligation to translate their religiously rooted views into secular arguments when engaging in formal political life because to do otherwise would be to go against the very things that make modern democratic societies run, chief among them the differentiation of the "civil" and "political" orders. There is much to be said in favor of these sorts of claims and it would indeed be silly to pretend that there are not ways in which the modern world differs significantly from its pre-modern forebears. And it would be perhaps even sillier to deny that part of what makes the modern world *modern* is the crucial distinction we make between, broadly speaking, religion and politics. The state is not a church and the church is not a state; that much is, as I have said, obviously true. But there are two points, one broad and the other more specific, that need exploring before we take differentiation as perhaps both Habermas and Casanova understand it to be quite as empirically and normatively compelling as they suggest.

Broadly, Casanova argues that secularization as differentiation is a structural element of modern life, suggesting that we could no more dispense with it than we could with the other basic elements that make the modern world modern: assertions of basic civil and political liberties, rule of law, representative democratic government, and so on. These sorts of things are not inevitable in any strong sense of the word, but there is, Casanova seems to think, a rather strong natural impulse toward their instantiation, even if their particulars can be shaped by individual agency. In what I take to be a rather telling footnote, Casanova assigns a Tocquevillian quality to the process of differentiation in the sense that in just the same way that for Tocqueville democracy is a "providential" work of history, so too is differentiation.[95] Its particular characteristics can differ according to particular historical circumstances and the work of individual human agency, but its broad outlines are irresistible. To defy it is akin to defying God.

[94] Casanova, *Public Religions in the Modern World*, 212.
[95] Ibid., fn. 2, 298.

Now, it seems the better half of wisdom to avoid defying God, and I can see little reason to think that Casanova is wrong to suggest that there is something "structural" to the modern world's differentiation. Only a very few think that the state should have among its mandates the obligation to advance our spiritual, as opposed to temporal, welfare, and given the moral and religious pluralism extant in any free society it is near impossible to imagine a scenario in which at least that sort of differentiation could be reversed, even if it were desirable to do so (and it is most assuredly not). But in the particulars, Casanova's arguments seem less sure-footed. Most salient to the argument here is his claim, which I have noted before, that differentiation has worked itself out politically in such a way that even though religious communities can flourish, they can do so only within the sphere of civil society. The "deprivatization" of religion evident over the past three decades or so is one in which increasing numbers of religious believers have rejected the claim that religion belongs only to the private, intimate sphere of interior reflection, family devotion, and inwardly focused association. Whether it be America's religious conservatives, Communist Poland's Catholic-infused Solidarity trade union, or the like, no longer is the "privatization" of religion accepted as a necessary norm. Quite the opposite, of course. But Casanova is sure that this deprivatization has its structural boundary and that is at what he calls "political society." Religion can, quite legitimately, engage all sorts of public issues, influence public opinion, even seek decidedly political change. But what it cannot do is get engaged formally in the actual political contests that could eventually effect that change. That is, Casanova goes further than merely saying that a particular religion cannot be "axiological" in the sense of being a society's source of ordering legitimacy; it also cannot, on account of the structure of modern life, engage substantively in deliberative and electoral contestation at the level of political parties, legislatures, or other formal venues of political society.

To be sure, there are broad tendencies in support of this kind of differentiation. Consider how the American Catholic bishops' statement on Catholic politicians' responsibilities vis-à-vis abortion that I quoted in the Introduction occasioned all sorts of indignant claims about bishops exceeding their authority and "meddling" in politics. In May 2007 whilst on a trip to Mexico, Pope Benedict XVI suggested that the church might very well deny communion or even excommunicate politicians who supported abortion rights. In response, eighteen Catholic Representatives in the US Congress issued a statement defending their pro-choice views and suggested that threat of ecclesial sanction "directly conflicts with our fundamental beliefs about the role and responsibility of democratic representatives in a pluralistic America – it also clashes with freedoms guaranteed in our Constitution. Such notions offend the very nature of the American experiment and do a great disservice to the centuries of good work the church has done."[96] Here, it is the particular structure of (American) democratic life that is doing the work of patrolling religion's limits, and the pope should not threaten discipline *even within the church* over legislators' votes on account of "the very nature of the American experiment." This is, I think, precisely what Casanova (and, by extension, Habermas) has in mind. Religion can make claims about the morality or immorality of any particular law and it can urge political changes to meet its particular moral vision. But it cannot – on pain of running afoul of modernity's structural fundamentals – seek to flex its muscle politically and coerce others, even if that "coercion" is purely psychological or spiritual. Casanova concludes, "This study contends that the age of secular-religious cleavages, of struggles over the historical process of modern secularization, has basically come to an end in the historical area of Western Christendom."[97] Formal politics is secular and there is little to be gainsaid otherwise.

Except that there remains a great deal *still* to be said, to be argued over, regarding the precise nature of how the very real differentiation of politics and religion is to be worked out in the particulars. Casanova's rather too easy assurance about the end of secular–religious cleavages is only really obviously true in the sense that it is accepted by nearly all (and certainly all who are in any measure politically influential) that the democratic state cannot orient itself in favor of a particular religious confession on pain of forfeiting its status as a modern democratic state. There are not any significant political actors on the scene pressing for either a theocratic or anti-theistic state.[98] Beyond that, all sorts of disputes still rage.

But there is a broader analytical point to be made. The shape of differentiation at any one time may not simply be the product of a kind of "natural" process of modernization, but may also be the product of social and political struggles in which particular groups attempted – and largely succeeded – to reconstruct a wide array of social and political institutions to make them independent of any significant religious affiliation. Christian Smith has argued, in the course

---

[96] Available at www.house.gov/delauro/press/2007/May/Cath_Members_Pope_05_14_07. html (accessed November 2007). The pope later clarified his remarks to say that pro-choice politicians should consider excluding themselves from communion.

[97] Casanova, *Public Religions in the Modern World*, 220. This is meant to include, I think, the United States and other modern democracies as well.

[98] One exception might be certain forms of political Islam in Europe, though it seems difficult to say for sure.

of a volume considering the process of secularization within a series of late nineteenth- and early twentieth-century American institutions, that the sort of differentiation theory affirmed by Casanova misses how interests and human agency play a crucial role in making secularization happen.[99] Structural conditions create opportunities and provide resources in ways that may favor the secularizers, but they do not determine it by any means. Secularization "happens," he suggests, only when those committed to displacing religious authority (in Smith's cases, it is mainline Protestants and their control of American institutions) actually win control of particular institutions: the legal academy, universities, welfare agencies, and so on.[100] On this understanding of things, even secularization-as-differentiation is something of a historical option, at least in the sense that differentiation itself ought to be understood as a focus and product of *political* conflict.

Contemporary trends in the United States suggest that there is something to this. Consider the increasing rates of homeschooling and religious schooling (at the primary, secondary, and university levels), the sustained assertiveness of "religious" politics (even in the face of the demise of organizations like the Moral Majority and the Christian Coalition), and the efforts to influence even American foreign policy in the name of religious values.[101] These are not, I think, simply "fundamentalist" responses to a rapidly changing world; they actually look more like efforts to influence or even "capture" particular institutions and reorient them according to the presumptions of faith. They are distinctive attempts to reshape the particulars of differentiation in ways that run counter to one set of historical tendencies. The point here is not that we are likely to see, say, the public education system made into the arm of a particular religious group. Modern societies are much too diverse and religious communities much too fragmented for that to happen.[102] The point is, rather, that

---

[99] Smith, ed., *The Secular Revolution*. See especially 1–53.
[100] Mark Chaves, "Secularization as Declining Religious Authority," *Social Forces* 72, no. 3 (1994), makes a rather compelling case for understanding differentiation as "declining religious authority," and notes that this can happen even within religious institutions that hand authority over to professional managers. See Mark Chaves, "Intraorganizational Power and Internal Secularization in Protestant Denominations," *American Journal of Sociology* 99, no. 1 (1993).
[101] Allen D. Hertzke, *Freeing God's Children: The Unlikely Alliance for Global Human Rights* (Lanham, MD: Rowman & Littlefield, 2004).
[102] In this respect, Bruce, *Conservative Protestant Politics*, is entirely right in his pessimistic judgment on the possible successes of conservative Protestant political movements. They are too fragmented internally – and depend on that fragmentation as religious denominations – to sustain an effective political movement. On the other hand, given the decline of denominationalism and what some have called the "ecumenicism of the trenches," it is possible that Bruce's judgments are miscast.

differentiation – and secularization more broadly – is the product more of social and political agency than perhaps Casanova might suppose.

Consider in this regard the position of Dutch Catholics after the newly empowered liberals passed their school laws in 1857, making it harder for Catholics (and conservative Calvinists) to operate their own private schools and changing the public school curriculum to reflect a latitudinarian Protestantism.[103] The nation's public schools were meant to help construct a national citizenry, and they could only do that to the extent that they inculcated a common ethos, meaning that they could not be equally congenial to every community. Unable to win their putative allies in parliament over to their concerns, the Catholic bishops issued a *Mandement* in 1868 expressing their view that Catholic parents ought, if possible, to educate their children within Catholic schools. These bishops understood well that the cultivation of the "common ethos" necessarily meant that their own particular, Catholic, ethos would be at best ignored in the public schools and likely fare much worse. In 1917, Catholics (and their conservative Calvinist allies) secured public funding for their schools, and as late as 1960, over 80 percent of Catholic children attended Catholic primary and secondary schools.[104] This, along with other parts of the Catholic pillar, only collapsed once participation in organized churches collapsed in the mid-1960s. The religious integrationists in Belgium, the Netherlands, and Germany constructed the fairly insular institutions of their subcultural communities as an attempt to forestall the corrosive acids of secularization, and to a large degree they were quite successful.[105] If it is true that the decline of religious belief and practice is historically "optional" (as Casanova would have it) *and* that differentiation may be reshaped or even reversed in some respects, then why should we take it as a sociological and historical necessity that religion must, to borrow and no doubt mangle a phrase, stop at politics' edge?

Well, the short answer is that it need not, and just as the religious communities in Germany, the Netherlands, and Belgium formed political

---

[103] The historical elements here are based on Bakvis, *Catholic Power in the Netherlands* and Carlson-Thies, "Democracy in the Netherlands". A similar story could be told with respect to conservative Calvinists, though their decline was less abrupt and less severe.

[104] J.M.G. Thurlings, "Pluralism and Assimilation in the Netherlands," *International Journal of Comparative Sociology* 20, no. 1–2 (1979): 84.

[105] Karel Dobbelaere, "The Rationale of Pillarization: The Case of Minority Movements," *Journal of Contemporary Religion* 15, no. 2 (2000). The striking fact about the Netherlands – now considered among Europe's most secular countries – is that as of the early 1960s, a substantial part of the population was unaffiliated with any religious institution and a substantial part of the population very much affiliated. Almost two-thirds of Dutch Catholics, for example, attended Mass on a weekly basis in 1964. See Bakvis, *Catholic Power in the Netherlands*, 114. That all changed radically in the late 1960s.

parties as a way of representing their particular interests in parliamentary (though not quite democratic) elections, so too could religious movements do something similar even now without necessarily upending anything essential about modern democracies. While it seems true enough to say that the likelihood of religious communities forming such parties is much reduced since every democracy guarantees broad religious liberty protections, such efforts are not foreclosed in any fundamental way. They are, perhaps, more likely to be episodic, ad hoc, or less successful than in my European cases (especially in societies where religious pluralism is much wider and religious observance is much lower), but it seems dubious to claim that efforts in that direction are by their nature incompatible with the essentials of modern democratic life.

If that is right, then Habermas' sociological suppositions ought to be even narrower than he thinks. We might put it in this way: the structure of modern life is such that much of our social and political terrain is deeply contested, though with important limits. Chief among these limits is the mutual distinction between political and religious authority and the guarantees of equal liberties under law, which means (among many other things) that states are in some important sense secular entities. They are secular in the sense that they do not have and should not advance a particular set of religious or spiritual ends. Religious communities whose political goals would transgress these limits simply run afoul of both the normative and structural essentials of modern life and will find themselves moral and political failures. But religious communities whose goals do not transgress these limits may indeed engage politically, and while political success will likely be episodic and difficult to sustain (perhaps mostly because of religious pluralism), neither will it be impossible. That, in turn, suggests that even Habermas' relaxed version of deliberative restraint is not supported on sociological grounds. There are no necessary structural reasons why religious believers should have to translate their religious arguments into secular ones within even "formal" political institutions like legislatures. This suggests, further, that it is the moral or normative grounds for restraint that require attention, and it is to these, in the form of Rawls' arguments for public reason, that I turn next.

4 Public reason and religious conflict

> It is impossible to live in peace with those whom we believe damned.
>
> Jean Jacques Rousseau, *The Social Contract*

In chapter 3, I explored what I take to be the two most salient and powerful arguments in favor of the idea that citizens have a moral obligation to consult and employ *secular* as over religious reasons when deliberating about and deciding on political matters. I argued that Robert Audi's epistemological claims in favor of secular reasons failed to distinguish sufficiently between religious and secular reasons and provided only very weak, almost ad hoc, grounds for thinking religiously grounded claims were per se problematic. I then tried to show how Habermas' similar sorts of restrictions relied on untenable sociological claims about secularization that, even in their more nuanced, updated (i.e. "post-secular") form, failed to do justice to religion's political possibilities even within the context of our "secular age." Put more broadly, the previous chapter showed the weaknesses of both what we might call the moral-epistemological and the sociological case in favor of secular reasons. Neither does the job its proponents have hoped it would and so the argument in favor of deliberative restraint still needs substantiating.

Of course, Habermas and Audi are not the only scholars to have engaged this question – far from it – and their claims in favor of secular reasons, while redolent of the broader public debate, actually occupy a minority position within academic circles. Much more popular have been arguments in favor of something like Rawls' public reason, a set of claims suggesting that inhabiting the office of citizen in a pluralist constitutional democracy imposes deliberative obligations and that chief among these is the obligation to have at the ready – and hence prioritize – reasons in politics that other citizens *in their capacities as citizens* might be willing to endorse. Rawls' arguments are, of course, powerful, interesting, and philosophically sophisticated, especially in how they trade on a fairly intuitive sense of what it means for free and equal citizens to treat one another with the respect they deserve within a democratic polity.

But his arguments suffer, in the end, both from inflated expectations regarding what is reasonable for citizens to expect from one another and from dystopian views about the likely political effects of religion's political mobilization. That is, Rawls' arguments for citizens' moral obligation to prioritize public reasons over religious (and other non-public) ones articulates a sophisticated philosophical view about the reasonable expectations we ought to have of one another as free and equal citizens in a pluralist constitutional democracy. But such expectations turn out, I suggest, to be shot through with empirically tinged claims about citizens' reasonable expectations if public reason (and the other elements in his broader theory) were either fully in place *or* if it were widely ignored or discounted. To be rather too simple about it, Rawls' arguments for public reason hinge in part on empirical claims that suggest, first, that what he calls the "well-ordered society" is reasonably achievable, meaning for him that the norms inhabiting such an order impose themselves on us – who do not live in such a society – as well. Second, his arguments also suggest that we also run a quite serious risk of political failure along the lines of Europe's religious wars or Weimar Germany if citizens decide to ignore those norms. In short, Rawls' account of citizens' moral obligations in their political deliberations depends in part on his empirical claims about what we might reasonably expect to occur if we either fully embrace or ignore those obligations ourselves. If we embrace them, we can expect to achieve the well-ordered society; if we ignore them, we risk disaster.

In what follows I sketch out Rawls' argument for public reason and show just how it relies, if often only implicitly, on such empirical claims about the plausible outcomes of religion's entrée into political deliberations. I then consider some actual empirical evidence on that score by comparing the democratic political effects of the religious parties in my European cases, concluding that they show how religion's political mobilization, while it can indeed prove dangerous to the establishment and sustenance of democratic life, can also prove beneficial, even crucial for democracy's success. I finish up this section of the book by drawing the argument back to where we first began with deliberative restraint and consider again the question of political legitimacy. To somewhat anticipate the argument there, I suggest that a more modest set of expectations regarding legitimacy is the best we should expect given our conditions of moral and religious pluralism, but that rather than being disappointed by such a deflation we should recognize that this more modest conception is probably more durable and reasonable than its more ambitiously exacting competitors. That is, by tying our sense of legitimacy much more closely to something akin to what Rawls calls a "constitutional consensus," we are unlikely to set indelibly in our political firmament any

number of justice-claims that Rawls and others think essential to legitimate democratic government. Setting those aside is indeed deflationary
and makes the liberal democratic project less inspiring and dramatic, but
it also makes it more plausible and durable, and in an age where democracy's competitors (religious and non-religious alike) persist and perhaps
even thrive, that is nothing to discount.

Rawls and the argument for public reason

Like other deliberative theorists,[1] Rawls argues that the reconciliation of
moral pluralism and political legitimacy in constitutional democracies
requires that citizens engage one another on the basis of broadly shared
reasons. Unlike Audi, however, Rawls does not think this means we should
limit ourselves to or prioritize distinctly secular reasons. Rather, citizens,
by virtue of the obligations they take up as citizens, should *prioritize* what
he calls public reasons over non-public, and especially religious, ones.[2]
Otherwise, under conditions of moral and religious diversity, we will not
be able to make sure that political power is exercised in accordance with
the liberal principle of legitimacy.

As I noted earlier, Rawls laid out an intricate and comprehensive argument for justice as fairness in *A Theory of Justice*. He laid that argument
aside in part because it did not seem capable of dealing with the "fact of
reasonable pluralism." It was "unrealistic" to presume that all (reasonable) citizens could endorse justice as fairness "on the basis of ... a comprehensive philosophical doctrine."[3] If citizens could reasonably reject
justice as fairness (as a philosophical doctrine), that would produce a
problem of "stability."[4] This is not just the stability of ordinary political
language (e.g. the absence of civil disorder), though it does include that.
Stability in the sense that Rawls uses it means that the principles justifying a democratic society's political institutions – this he calls a political

---

[1] See Rawls, "The Idea of Public Reason Revisited," 773. Here he explicitly identifies
political liberalism as a species of deliberative democracy and public reason as a critical
element of deliberation.

[2] The precise claim is that citizens must have public reasons at the ready, even if they are
primarily motivated by religious reasons. As I point out below, this means that should
your "public" and "religious" reasons come into conflict, the public reasons must win
out, meaning that in practice citizens must give *priority* to them. Rawls declaims against
any attempt to apply the moral obligations of public reason to private deliberations and
suggests that such obligations are mandatory only when deliberating about "constitutional essentials and matters of basic justice." In everyday politics, it might be "highly
desirable" for citizens to invoke "the values of public reason" but that might not be possible (Rawls, *Political Liberalism*, 215–16.) Since I do not think that the distinctions make
much of a difference with respect to my argument, I ignore them here.

[3] Ibid., xviii.   [4] Ibid., xix.

conception of justice – are the object of an "overlapping consensus" of reasonable comprehensive views and as such are acceptable to reasonable citizens on their own terms.[5] So far as a political conception of justice can win this sort of commitment, then outside of those who reject the basic claims of a constitutional democracy outright, its authority will rest not on coercion (or the threat thereof) but on the free and settled consent of citizens. Public reason is integral to achieving both components of democratic political legitimacy, moral and popular.

Rawls claims that there already exists implicitly within the institutions and practices of modern democracies this overlapping consensus among reasonable comprehensive doctrines.[6] This overlapping consensus gives shape to a political conception of justice that itself marks out the sorts of justifications we may properly give for political coercion – "public reason." Instead of making the obviously implausible claim that laws and institutions are legitimate to the degree that they are in accordance with the will of each citizen, Rawls argues that "our exercise of political power is fully proper only when it is exercised in accordance with a constitution the essentials of which all citizens as free and equal may reasonably be expected to endorse in the light of principles and ideals acceptable to their common human reason."[7] Moral pluralism is compatible with democratic self-government insofar as citizens find that their reasonable comprehensive doctrines support a political conception of justice that can, in turn, provide a framework within which those same citizens can work out their political disputes. Key to Rawls' argument is, obviously, his view of what it means to be reasonable.

So what does "reasonable mean"? Rawls suggests:

Citizens are reasonable when, viewing one another as free and equal in a system of social cooperation over generations, they are prepared to offer one another fair terms of cooperation according to what they consider the most reasonable conceptions of political justice; and when they agree to act on those terms, even at the cost of their own interests in particular situations, provided that other citizens also accept those terms. The criterion of reciprocity requires that when those terms are proposed as the most reasonable terms of fair cooperation, those proposing them must also think it at least reasonable for others to accept them, as free and equal citizens, and not as dominated and manipulated, or under pressure of an inferior political or social position.[8]

---

[5] Ibid., 142ff. He says elsewhere, "Citizens affirm the ideal of public reason, not as a result of political compromise, as in a modus vivendi, but from within their own reasonable doctrines" (Rawls, *Political Liberalism*, 218.)

[6] Rawls defines a doctrine as comprehensive "when it includes conceptions of what is of value in human life, as well as ideals of personal virtue and character, that are to inform much of our nonpolitical conduct," Rawls, *Political Liberalism*, 175.

[7] Ibid., 137.   [8] Rawls, "The Idea of Public Reason Revisited," 770.

"Reasonable pluralism" means pluralism limited by a proviso, where citizens accept that it would be politically unfair and morally wrong to seek political ends on the basis of reasons that others could not reasonably be expected to endorse. Or, as Joshua Cohen rather more cogently puts it, citizens "are *reasonable* in that they aim to defend and criticize institutions and programs in terms of considerations that others, as free and equal, have *reason to accept*, given the fact of reasonable pluralism and on the assumption that those others are themselves concerned to provide suitable justifications."[9]

The idea of public reason picks out most clearly the sorts of reasons that are *not* acceptable. Most any kind of religious doctrine or argument whose persuasive force depends on an ethnic, sexual, or gender identity must be avoided. Even "secular philosophical doctrines," such as modern natural law or the liberalisms of Kant and Mill, do not qualify as public reason, for they "belong to first philosophy and moral doctrine, and fall outside of the domain of the political."[10] Individuals ought not present public political arguments whose force depends, for example, on a particular understanding of God or on an affirmation of ethical autonomy and reasonably expect that other citizens could agree to be bound therein without converting to that particular religious or philosophical view.

Being reasonable for Rawls has two "basic aspects": a willingness to propose fair terms of cooperation and an acknowledgement that such terms necessarily have substantive and epistemological limits, what he calls the "burdens of judgment." Those who affirm reasonable comprehensive doctrines must acknowledge the burdens of judgment, the view that, "It is unrealistic – or worse, it arouses mutual suspicion and hostility – to suppose that all our differences are rooted solely in ignorance and perversity, or else in the rivalries for power, status, or economic gain."[11] Even in optimal conditions of open and free inquiry, securing universal agreement about the good is not realistic, and it is unreasonable to think

---

[9] Joshua Cohen, "Democracy and Liberty," in *Deliberative Democracy*, ed. Jon Elster (Cambridge: Cambridge University Press, 1998), 194.

[10] Rawls, "The Idea of Public Reason Revisited," here cited from *University of Chicago Law Review* 64 (1999): 781. The reference to natural law here is specifically about John Finnis' natural law theory that might be seen to qualify as properly public, given its independence from theistic arguments and its attempts to make natural law universally accessible. But because, like Kant's and Mill's liberalism, it argues from a theory of the good life that is controversial and about which reasonable people may disagree, Rawls does not consider it properly public. This does not mean that these comprehensive doctrines are unreasonable, but just that their very comprehensiveness means that their adherents could not rely on them in political debates. For an alternative view, see George and Wolfe, eds., *Natural Law and Public Reason*.

[11] Rawls, *Political Liberalism*, 58.

that such disagreement stems simply from an exercise in "bad faith." Reasonable citizens affirm comprehensive doctrines that accept the burdens of judgment in that they recognize their inability to articulate a comprehensive conception of justice that would be compelling to others who embrace other reasonable comprehensive doctrines.[12] Thus, "the burdens of judgment set limits on what can be reasonably justified to others."[13]

Leif Wenar suggests that affirming Rawls' version of the burdens of judgment is not necessary for endorsing democratic essentials and thus ought not be a requirement of reasonableness.[14] He points out that the Catholic Church – clearly among the "reasonable romantics" Rawls thinks can be (and are) within the overlapping consensus[15] – can seemingly both support liberal toleration *and* assert the ultimate truth of its doctrines without affirming the burdens of judgment. The church (and it is not alone here) draws direct lines between its statements of faith and its embrace of liberal democratic politics, claiming that human rights, religious freedom, and the like are mandated by the nature of human freedom. Insisting on the burdens as a criterion of reasonableness may actually "exclude many with sincere religious beliefs," without any political benefit.[16]

Rawls might suggest that Wenar's claims are simply "political in the wrong way."[17] That is, rather than pointing out that there are groups of citizens who seem politically reasonable and then deriving from their comprehensive views a workable defense of a constitutional democracy,[18] Rawls' political liberalism is rooted in what he takes to be the essential ideas underlying a reasonably just and stable democratic society constituted by most any kind of (reasonable) value pluralism. The Catholic Church may indeed have its own reasons for supporting constitutional democracies, as do all reasonable comprehensive views, but Rawls'

---

[12] Rawls limits public reason's application to what he calls constitutional essentials and matters of basic justice. Freedom of speech and right to choose one's occupation would qualify as properly fundamental, while his difference principle would not (*Political Liberalism*, 215). For now, I ignore these distinctions.

[13] Rawls, *Political Liberalism*, 61.

[14] Leif Wenar, "Political Liberalism: An Internal Critique," *Ethics* 106, no. 1 (1995).

[15] Rawls, *Political Liberalism*, 170.

[16] Wenar, "Political Liberalism": 43. This is Nicholas Wolterstorff's point in his debates with Robert Audi over this very issue. See Audi and Wolterstorff, *Religion in the Public Square*. For claims that *only* theistic arguments provide solid grounds for defending human rights, see Michael J. Perry, *Toward a Theory of Human Rights: Religion, Law, Courts* (Cambridge and New York: Cambridge University Press, 2007).

[17] Rawls, *Political Liberalism*, 39–40.

[18] For this sort of overlapping consensus, see Klosko, *Democratic Procedures and Liberal Consensus*.

arguments suggest (to stick with Wenar's example) that any attempt by the church or its supporters to coerce non-Catholics solely on the basis of its own particular theological claims rests on the claim that their opponents' grounds are in some way essentially unreasonable and thus amenable to repression.[19]

So Wenar's critique does not obviously succeed. Yet, it highlights two important issues with respect to the burdens. First, the point of the burdens is that they provide a principled set of reasons why it is that the government's reach ought to be limited and in particular why it should not be in the business of enforcing wholesale one particular view of the world. But, second, nowhere does Rawls suggest that citizens will affirm the *same burdens of judgment*. Rawls provides a fairly perfunctory list of reasons why people could come to different conclusions about most anything.[20] But what he does not do is suggest that to affirm the burdens of judgment is to affirm a particular *reason* why contemporary democratic societies are constituted by a reasonable pluralism. Thus insofar as religious believers are willing to affirm democratic toleration in a principled manner (i.e. not just as the result of the current balance of political forces), and can readily be said to "endorse some form of liberty of conscience and freedom of thought,"[21] they seem to affirm, in some form, the burdens of judgment. To affirm some sort of political toleration is to affirm that there are good reasons to not coerce others even though you think they are, perhaps quite seriously, in the wrong.[22] Citizens who can do this are thus to that degree reasonable. If this claim is correct, then the burdens themselves do not require the prioritization of public reasons, or at least not obviously so. As long as a citizen thinks that she has good reasons (i.e. reasons that will not change when the political situation on the ground changes) to limit what it is that she could propose politically and those limits are in the range of accepted democratic practices, then her religious reasons – if she has any – are reasonable, at least with regard to the burdens of judgment. That suggests in turn that Rawls' argument for prioritization ought to hang on the other basic aspect of being reasonable – being willing to propose fair terms of cooperation.

To propose fair terms of cooperation means that as citizens deliberate politically, they should propose principles "that others may reasonably

---

[19] Rawls, *Political Liberalism*, 58–61. A corollary to this argument is that those who do profess unreasonable comprehensive views would seem in some measure to be amenable to repression. Or, as Rawls, puts it, "That there are doctrines that reject one or more democratic freedoms is itself a permanent fact of life, or seems so. This gives us the practical task of containing them – like war and disease – so that they do not overturn political justice" (ibid., 64 fn. 19).

[20] Ibid., 56–57.   [21] Ibid., 61.

[22] See chapter 6 for a much fuller discussion.

be expected to accept, so that all may benefit and improve on what every one can do on their own."[23] Reciprocity, or the willingness on the part of citizens to engage in a form of (self-interested) cooperation, turns out, then, to be the "essential social virtue" for Rawls, as it "underlies the capacity to propose, or to endorse, and then be moved to act from fair terms of cooperation for their own sake."[24] Proposing fair terms of cooperation and thus reasonableness just *is* practicing reciprocity. If we accept the idea of a democratic society as a system of social and political cooperation, and if we wish to practice reciprocity, then Rawls suggests that we need some way of persuading and justifying ourselves to one another that is in some sense independent of and politically superior to our own comprehensive views. Reciprocity – and thus reasonableness – requires a commitment to what he calls a freestanding political conception of justice.

For Rawls, a political conception of justice is a set of principles meant to govern a democratic society's basic institutions. It should be "freestanding" in the sense that "it is neither presented as, nor as derived from, such a [comprehensive] doctrine applied to the basic structure of society."[25] That is, it does not depend on any particular comprehensive doctrine for its justification, but rather it can be defended in terms that are "implicit in the public political culture of a democratic society," – the constitution, related founding documents, public political dialogues, and so on. Though it is does not depend on a society's comprehensive doctrines, the political conception is supported by them. Rawls calls it a kind of "module" that fits into the various reasonable comprehensive doctrines, but is not determined by any one of them.[26] So Catholics, Baptists, and Jews can all affirm the principle of religious liberty for their own reasons, but they are reasonable to the degree that they affirm that the principle of religious liberty can and ought to be defended and articulated in purely political terms, distinct from particular faith traditions, when citizens are engaging one another politically.

So what sorts of deliberative restraints does Rawls' idea of reciprocity impose? At first, he thought public reason required an exclusive view of deliberative norms, where "comprehensive doctrines are never to be introduced into public reason." But this exclusive view left him unable, he decided, to account for important democratizing movements that were inseparable from their comprehensive and religious foundations. (He had in mind the abolitionist and civil rights movements in the United States.) In its stead, he elaborated what he called an "inclusive"

---

[23] Rawls, *Political Liberalism*, 54.   [24] Ibid.
[25] Ibid., 12.   [26] Ibid.

view of public reason, where citizens may "present what they regard as the basis of political values rooted in comprehensive doctrine, provided they do this in ways that strengthen the ideal of public reason itself." This view suggests that "historical and social conditions" dictate when and how citizens might legitimately introduce non-public reasons into political debate. In "more or less well-ordered" societies, there is no reason for citizens to introduce non-public reasons, but in only "nearly well-ordered" or "not well-ordered" societies there may be. In the latter two societies, citizens may need to reassure one another about their commitment "to fundamental political values" or employ those comprehensive views in order to mobilize other citizens toward ending some great social evil (like slavery). These exceptions to the more general stipulations of public reason are justified, in the end, by the judgment that they "best [encourage] citizens to honor the ideal of public reason and [secure] its social conditions in the longer run in a well-ordered society."[27]

Eventually, Rawls settled on what he calls a "wide view of public culture."[28] This wide view states that "reasonable comprehensive doctrines, religious or nonreligious, may be introduced in public political discussion at any time, provided that in due course proper political reasons – and not reasons given solely by comprehensive doctrines – are presented that are sufficient to support whatever the comprehensive doctrines introduced are said to support."[29] This mixed approach suggests, first, that citizens are free to consult their religious or any other sorts of comprehensive views when thinking about or discussing even basic political issues. But they must check those reasons against whatever "public" ones they find convincing and be ready to introduce those when necessary. In this sense, then, Rawls' arguments for public reason end up in much the same place as Audi's, except that for Rawls public reasons are merely reasons that other citizens in their capacities as citizens could accept. No doubt these public reasons would all be secular (i.e. not depend on a particular conception of God or his commands), but not all secular reasons would qualify as "public." If the moral obligation is to be able to defend one's political proposals on grounds that other citizens (who do not share comprehensive views) could find persuasive, then those grounds – and not the religious ones – must have priority. Rawls' argument is not some prolegomena to a "naked public square," but it is for the most part quite firm in its insistence that political legitimacy requires public reasons.

---

[27] The quotations in this paragraph are from ibid., 247–51.
[28] Ibid., l–lvii.
[29] Rawls, "The Idea of Public Reason Revisited," 784–85. This last part he terms the "proviso."

Note the wiggle-room in that last sentence, though: "for the most part quite firm." As I noted above, Rawls allows that there may be historical circumstances which allow for a slight relaxation of the restraint obligation. The abolitionists did not violate their moral obligations vis-à-vis other citizens since the invocation of religious reasons was necessary to combat a great evil. Neither did the leaders of the American civil rights movement. Both were seeking to overcome some grave political injustice that required extraordinary popular mobilization, and both employed their religious rhetoric to make the political order more "well-ordered," closer to the day when such rhetoric would be unnecessary. But such admittedly (and thankfully) rare circumstances do not comprise the whole of Rawls' admitted exceptions. He also suggests that when citizens find themselves at odds with one another over basic political issues, invoking comprehensive doctrines and connecting those doctrines to democratic commitments might reassure other citizens and secure at least a provisional political agreement. In his last published writings on the matter of public reason, Rawls cited the controversies surrounding the question of public funding of religious schools as one salient example.[30] Here, he surmises, given the high potential for conflict and the likelihood that partisans on either side of the issue might come to doubt one another's basic democratic commitments, it is worth having citizens spell out more fully how their comprehensive views track their democratic political ones.

This last exception is, in one sense, a bit of an odd one. After all, if the worry is that citizens are likely to doubt their opponents' democratic credentials *without* having non-public views aired, it is hard to see what the airing of such views would really accomplish. If you think your opponent is a would-be theocrat or secularist bent on using the state to favor his particular view of the world, his reassurances that he is indeed in favor of constitutional democracy might seem like pretty weak tea. Indeed, you are likely to think his "public" claims all that much more fictitious. In any case, what is interesting here is how this fairly narrow second exception alerts us to Rawls' concerns regarding how citizens might respond if others refused to prioritize public reasons. Rawls is concerned about such refusal not just on account of how it runs counter to the moral claims citizens have on one another, but also because of how other citizens will *perceive* that refusal: they will take offense, and a democracy's civil comity will be likely compromised. Public reason is meant not just to make it possible in some abstract philosophical sense for laws to be justified to a morally pluralistic citizenry. It is meant to make it possible for citizens to actively *accept* laws as justified and to believe themselves

---

[30] Ibid., 785.

morally obligated to follow them, even if they do not find the particular laws in question the right ones. Public reasons thus serve a dual purpose: they make political coercion justifiable philosophically and they help reassure those who are being coerced (and by definition feel at least somewhat aggrieved) that the coercion is politically reasonable. Or, as I have characterized it, they help secure both moral and popular forms of legitimacy.

To consider Rawls' argument here more closely, consider the following example.[31] Jane holds a sincere belief that war is immoral. She holds this view *only* because, as a Mennonite Christian, she thinks that Jesus' teachings have permanently enjoined humans from using violence to achieve their ends. After careful reflection and wide reading, she concludes that the non-religious arguments for pacifism are unpersuasive, as they rely on absurd views about human nature or the expectation of justice. In deciding whether she should support an authorization of military force, is Jane committed, according even to the wide view of public reason, to not offering her pacifist views and either abstaining from or supporting the authorization of force? It is hard to see that she is not. Indeed, if whatever prudential calculations she makes come out in favor of military force, it is hard to see that she is not obligated to support the authorization. If citizens are morally obligated to offer reasons (and act on those reasons) only if they are compatible with public reasons that they themselves hold, Jane has little choice but to subordinate her religious views to her public ones if she wishes fulfill her obligations as a citizen.

Is this itself reasonable? Rawls supposes that when our political and comprehensive values clash, the political conception's "values [will] normally outweigh whatever other values oppose them, at least under reasonably favorable conditions that make a constitutional democracy possible."[32] But given the direct conflict between Jane's *religious* convictions that war is not ever justified and her *political* convictions that it is, it is far from a foregone conclusion that any generically reasonable person would choose in favor of her "public" reasons. Why does Rawls think that religious believers such as Jane should or will?

Believers like Jane *should* prioritize public reasons because refusing to do so evinces a lack of respect for their fellow citizens.[33] Rawls describes

---

[31] This example is similar to the one in Eberle, "Religion, Pacifism and the Doctrine of Restraint."

[32] Rawls, *Political Liberalism*, 155.

[33] This is the argument found in Joshua Cohen, "Moral Pluralism and Political Consensus," in *The Good Polity: A Normative Analysis of the State*, ed. Alex Hamlin and Philip Pettit (New York: Blackwell, 1993); Thomas Nagel, "Moral Conflict and Political Legitimacy," in *Morality, Harm, and the Law*, ed. Gerald Dworkin (Boulder, CO: Westview Press, 1994).

public reason as "the reason of equal citizens who, as a collective body, exercise final political and coercive power over one another in enacting laws and in amending their constitution."[34] Rather than offering reasons that reflect their status as co-equal holders of political authority, the believer who offers religious reasons treats her fellow citizen as someone with whom agreement cannot in principle be reached and must be coerced. The believer here has presumptively elevated fidelity to her own theo-political claims over and above fidelity to the premises and essentials of constitutional democratic government. The non-believer can, on this account, feel properly aggrieved and think the religious believer has violated her moral obligations because she has, even if she professes a commitment to "democracy," undermined the principal rationale for that democracy, namely that we are all equal holders of political authority and owe one another the respect that status demands. Religious reasons are morally improper in that their unreserved employment cuts against the very premise that makes us make ask about reasons for political coercion in the first place, the idea that political coercion must be *justified*. Jane should prioritize public reasons because to do otherwise runs counter to the respect she owes her fellow citizens on account of the democratic system she professes to support.[35]

In this sense, then, the Rawlsian case for deliberative restraint can be said to come down to the implications of the fact that we owe one another a certain sort of respect as fellow citizens in pluralist democracies. And so the question becomes: what is it about the respect we owe one another as citizens that carries with it an obligation to prioritize public reasons? As Christopher Eberle emphasizes (in the context of a fairly thoroughgoing critique of philosophical claims in favor of deliberative restraint), our status as rational creatures who care about what happens to us and who are averse to being coerced demands that we offer one another solid moral reasons for acts of political coercion.[36] But on his account this does not translate into an obligation that we prioritize public reasons, as he suggests that such a claim might well even conflict with Rawls' own justification of justice as fairness. In the Original Position we choose political principles behind a "veil of ignorance." Crucially, since we do not know what sort of person (race, gender, religion, and so on) we will be, Rawls thinks that we will be wary of choosing political principles that are

---

[34] Rawls, *Political Liberalism*, 214.
[35] If Jane were *not* in favor of democratic government, then Rawls' case against religious reasons largely goes away, since his argument is premised on what a constitutional democracy demands of us, not what some comprehensive moral claim does.
[36] See Christopher J. Eberle, "What Respect Requires and What It Does Not," *Wake Forest Law Review* 36 (2001).

unduly burdensome. We will avoid principles that infringe on our moral identities, on who we are and on the kinds of lives we might reasonably seek to lead. Of the many sorts of lives that ought to exist as reasonable possibilities for us, Eberle insists, is the life as a theist who has an "overriding and totalizing obligation to obey God" in all areas of life.[37] Prioritization would "require [these theists] to violate their deepest and most important commitments," meaning that it would be unreasonable for certain kinds of religious believers to endorse it.[38] No reasonable person who thought that she might be this kind of theist would sign onto a political conception that meant she could not live her life meaningfully, and unless Rawls wants to rule these integrationist lives out as obviously unreasonable, he cannot, perhaps, make Jane's claims (or, more broadly, the integrationists') out to be unreasonable without undermining his own argument for justice as fairness.[39] But to the degree that Rawls *affirms* the argument for public reason, he does mean to say, then, that Jane and integrationists more generally *are* unreasonable precisely in that the lives they seek to lead are incompatible with a legitimate, stable democratic polity since such lives do not include a commitment to public reason and deliberative restraint. To put things starkly, when Rawls asks if it is "possible for those holding religious doctrines, some based on religious authority, for example, the Church or the Bible, to hold at the same time a reasonable political conception that supports a reasonable constitutional democratic regime,"[40] his answer for Jane and other integrationists would have to be no.

But suppose that Jane, having been told that she is not just politically mistaken but unreasonable to boot, responds by suggesting that her fellow citizens are being unfair in their characterizations. She might acknowledge that they could find her invocation of her religious beliefs rather noxious, especially in a context where her preferred course of action could endanger the country's national security, but that she is willing to likewise accept that others might also have good reasons to employ their religious and other sorts of comprehensive views even when they run counter to what the best public reasons say. After all, she might point out, Rawls himself notes that "[Pacifists like Jane] do not think that the possibility of a people's voting to go to war is a sufficient reason for

---

[37] Eberle, *Religious Conviction in Liberal Politics*, 146.
[38] Ibid., 147. See also Weithman, *Religion and the Obligations of Citizenship*, 209.
[39] John Tomasi likewise suggests that Rawls' move to *Political Liberalism* means that liberals who affirm reasonable pluralism must be concerned with how citizens with only tenuously liberal private lives will be able to match those lives up with their liberal political commitments. See Tomasi, *Liberalism beyond Justice*.
[40] Rawls, "The Idea of Public Reason Revisited," 780.

opposing democratic government."[41] So in spite of the fact that the state may take actions she thinks entirely morally improper, she still conceives of it as legitimate and is willing to support it. Why could the same not be true of other citizens as well? Perhaps, she might suggest, if religious pacifists can sincerely support democratic government in spite of the fact that such government undertakes actions that the pacifist deems not just immoral in itself, but rooted in an unacceptable set of reasons, why could the same not be true of others? If it is the case that Jane and other pacifists can find democratic government legitimate *even if* it acts on the basis of principles they find immoral, it seems plausible enough to think that the same could be true of other citizens as well. Insofar as Jane is not trying to carve out for herself a special exemption, she might very well think that she is, in fact, fulfilling the demands of reciprocity, albeit in a way that Rawls thinks improper.

Rawls seems to think that this sort of claim is hardly a critique at all. In a discussion of similarly pacifist Quakers, Rawls claims that this sort of tension "illustrates how political values can be *overriding* in upholding the constitutional system itself."[42] He seems to think that insofar as Jane maintains her "allegiance to a just and enduring constitutional government,"[43] we can say that she has, in fact, prioritized public over religious reasons. If her claim is that war is fundamentally wrong (morally speaking) and yet she is willing to count as legitimate and participate in a government that wages war, then why not think that she has decided for political purposes that a "just" government may wage war though her religious convictions say otherwise? She has, on this account, prioritized public over religious reasons.

This is not be an implausible claim, but it would seem much more plausible to suggest that such an illustration shows precisely the opposite of what Rawls thinks it does, how even under conditions where religious values override public ones in citizens' own considerations, a "just and enduring constitutional government" can endure (and maybe even thrive). To think otherwise would seem to rely on making Jane out to be an unreliable interpreter of her own views, as if she cannot tell when she is giving priority to her religious views and when she is not. Why not suppose that in fact she could at the same time have the proper sort of respect for her fellow citizens, accept that they are free and equal like her, and believe that at certain points she has to give priority to her comprehensive religious beliefs? If being reasonable largely means practicing reciprocity, then perhaps Jane can plausibly escape the charge of being unreasonable, since she is not demanding anything of her fellow citizens

---

[41] Rawls, *Political Liberalism*, 393.   [42] Ibid., 394. Emphasis added.   [43] Ibid.

that she is not already willing to do herself. Jane's example thus raises the possibility – only the possibility at this point – that stable, legitimate democratic government is compatible with citizens employing at least some religious and other comprehensive claims in politics (provided, of course, that they are willing to extend the same right to others).

At least one difficulty here is that, however genuine Jane's democratic commitments, in order for the deliberative process to do its work vis-à-vis political legitimacy it is not enough that she is willing to live in a political system where others could employ their comprehensive views just as she insists on doing. Her fellow citizens must also agree to the more relaxed norms of restraint; otherwise, the civic relationship between Jane and her fellow citizens will in fact not be one of reciprocity, however much Jane insists that it can be. Instead, if her fellow citizens endorse the idea of public reason and Jane dissents, the other citizens will feel mistreated if they are coerced in accordance with Jane's political goals. This is not to say that Jane is *necessarily* being unfair in the employment of her religious views, but rather just that her fellow citizens may *think* her unfair if they endorse deliberative restraint. Jane – and integrationists more generally – must do more than just persuade others that their religious views are inextricably tied into their (democratic) politics. They must also persuade others that the political order as a whole will do better (or at least do fine) in the context of a more relaxed norm of deliberative restraint. Public reason, remember, means to make pluralist democracies legitimate morally and empirically: political outcomes will fall within a range that reasonable citizens *as citizens* can accept both in the sense that they are justified by certain sorts of reasons *and* in the sense that citizens understand that to be the case. Jane's gambit seems to work fairly well with respect to the former; it is with respect to the latter – how her fellow citizens will take her proposal in its practical expression – that things seem more delicate. And, indeed, Rawls includes in his argument for public reason a twofold set of claims pointing toward this very question, suggesting both that the willingness to embrace public reason plays a crucial role in constructing a well-ordered democratic society and that the refusal to embrace public reason would put the entire democratic project at serious risk.

The former comes out most clearly in Rawls' sociological "conjecture" regarding how his overlapping consensus and the accompanying widespread affirmation of the norm of public reason might come to govern a pluralist constitutional democracy. He describes a two-stage process. In the first stage, the polity moves from affirming certain liberal principles merely as a modus vivendi (e.g. as a result of the balance of powers or interests) to a "constitutional consensus." In this sort of consensus, liberal principles "are accepted simply as principles and not as grounded in certain ideas of society and person of a political conception, much less in a shared public conception."[44] Unlike in an overlapping consensus, political views are not justified by reference to a political conception of justice, but "depend solely on the comprehensive doctrine."[45] In other words, there are many citizens who – like Jane – refuse to prioritize public reasons but who maintain a sincere commitment to constitutional democracy.

Since a constitutional consensus lacks, Rawls thinks, the overlapping consensus's deep moral commitments, it will be unstable, thin, and things will almost inevitably move toward the overlapping consensus.[46] How? Since "most people's religious, philosophical, and moral doctrines are not seen by them as fully general and comprehensive,"[47] and they have a rational interest in framing their political appeals in terms of public reasons,[48] citizens will develop, perhaps without even quite realizing it, "an independent allegiance to the political conception that helps to bring about a[n overlapping] consensus."[49] In short, to the degree that citizens, including religious ones, are committed to something beyond a mere modus vivendi, they are quite likely to end up as an empirical matter affirming a freestanding political conception of justice and, hence, the particulars of public reason.

Rawls' empirically cast case for the progression to an overlapping consensus also has its dark converse: the implication that failing to move toward the overlapping consensus could (and most likely would) leave a society so disordered that it would be vulnerable to political failure. The introduction to *Political Liberalism*, for example, is chock-full of references to Europe's religious wars in the sixteenth and seventeenth centuries, mostly as the crucial motivation for the liberal tradition of political thought. Rawls makes the commonplace claim that the appearance of Christianity and especially the Reformation brought about the very problem that political liberalism is meant to solve. Unlike the ancient

---

[44] Ibid., 158. These liberal principles "guarantee certain basic political rights and liberties and establish democratic procedures for moderating the political rivalry, and for determining issues of social policy" (163).

[45] Ibid., 159.

[46] Ibid., 164–68. For a lengthy discussion of the relationship in Rawls between the overlapping consensus and political stability, see Barry, "John Rawls and the Search for Stability."

[47] Rawls, *Political Liberalism*, 165.

[48] They have a rational interest since, under conditions of pluralism, they "must enter the public forum of political discussion and appeal to other groups who do not share their comprehensive doctrine" (ibid.)

[49] Ibid., 168.

world, which "did not know ... the clash between Salvationist, creedal, and expansionist religions,"[50] medieval Christendom bequeathed to us the idea of a political order whose ends included the salvation of souls, an idea whose effects in a divided Europe was disastrous, to say the least. In the introduction to the paperback edition of *Political Liberalism*, Rawls even suggests that to put the work's central question "more sharply" means to ask, "How is it possible for those affirming a religious doctrine that is based on religious authority, for example, the Church or the Bible, also to hold a reasonable political conception that supports a just democratic regime?"[51] Clearly, political liberalism (and, by extension, public reason and deliberative restraint) is meant to stand in that tradition, a solution to the "problem" of religion's political mobilization.

But Rawls invokes the wars of religion not just to genuflect a bit toward liberalism's history, but more importantly to suggest that they (or something like them) remain a live possibility for us and that to eschew what he takes to be our democratic obligations is to put ourselves at real risk. He suggests that the legacy of Christianity and the Reformation was to introduce

into people's conception of their good a transcendent element not admitting of compromise. This element forces either mortal conflict moderated only by circumstance and exhaustion, or equal liberty of conscience and freedom of thought. Except on the basis of these last, firmly founded and publicly recognized, no reasonable political conception of justice is possible.[52]

The implication here should be fairly plain: *either* the political order will be governed by laws that are reasonable in that they do not depend for their justification on any particular religious claims *or* such an order will simply be forever in a state of civil war, though one moderated perhaps by "circumstance and exhaustion." If true, then other citizens would have good reason to dismiss Jane's suggestion that she and her fellow citizens could engage in a politics of respectful reciprocity in the context of a relaxed norm of public reason. Such efforts would merely serve to undermine the possibility of constructing a just political order and likely would do much worse.

If true. The case against what we might call a relaxed principle of reciprocity resolves to a two-headed empirical claim about the likely effects of either embracing or rejecting the norms of deliberative restraint. Jane does not treat her fellow citizens with disrespect simply in that she is unwilling to prioritize public reasons. By acknowledging that others may do so as well, she is plausibly placed in a situation of reciprocity

---

[50] Ibid., xxvii.   [51] Ibid., xxxix.   [52] Ibid., xxviii.

with them. The only way in which her refusal to abide by public reason evinces disrespect for others is if such a refusal puts the political system as a whole at risk. But those are empirical claims, claims that must be validated *as empirical claims* if we are to take them to be binding.

The religious conflict thesis and Europe's other religio-political conflict

Clearly, there is a great deal of disagreement in contemporary American society over what constitutes a just social and political order and, more specifically, over the norms of deliberative restraint. Citizens in modern democracies may not – and often do not – like the particular ends to which particular religious claims may be put, but they are far from united in thinking that such claims ought to be out of bounds morally. But that does not settle the matter for the restraint claim, since it seeks to describe the conditions within which reasonable citizens can endorse their political order in the proper sort of way. The task here, then, is to see if such norms actually are "realistic" in the way Rawls and others hope they are. That is, can the empirical claims implicit in the argument for deliberative restraint be validated, or is there evidence that should point us to something a bit different? In what follows, I make the case for the latter.

Plenty of scholarly and popular works have been written over the past several years about the connection between religion and violence. A key part of the liberal consensus on religion insists that religion's political presence makes for a dangerous civic life, or, as Robert Audi put it, bringing religion into politics leads to "a clash of Gods vying for social control. Such uncompromising absolutes easily lead to destruction and death."[53] To make a bumper sticker out of it, we might say that on this view religious politics seriously threatens religious war. But as Chris Eberle and Paul Weithman have both rightly noted, there has been precious little work substantiating this religious conflict thesis. The empirical claims are left largely unsubstantiated, I suspect, because they seem so plausible; indeed, they seem more like established facts than disputable claims. The specter of Europe's sixteenth and seventeenth century, not to mention our own day's violent conflicts, certainly make for a powerful presumption in its favor.

But inasmuch as Europe's sixteenth and seventeenth centuries do tell us something (and something dreadful) about religion's political effects, they do not tell us the whole story, even with respect to Europe.

---

[53] Audi, *Religious Commitment and Secular Reason*, 103. For a good collection of similar quotations, see Eberle, *Religious Conviction in Liberal Politics*, 154–55.

Rawls himself actually points his readers to a case, Weimar Germany, which he thinks reinforces his broader philosophical arguments. In *Political Liberalism*, Rawls cites Weimar's failure as a consequence not just of economic deprivation or political miscalculation but rather as following on from the widespread view that "a just and well-ordered democratic society is impossible" combined with the unwillingness of Germany's political elites to "[support] its constitution or ... cooperate to make it work."[54] In the introduction to his *Lectures on the History of Political Philosophy*, he expands a bit on that claim, suggesting that it was the distinctive pattern of Wilhelmine German political competition and especially the fact that its parties "held exclusive ideologies which made compromise with other groups difficult" that set the stage for the collapse of Weimar's constitutional democracy.[55] On this account, Germany's nascent democracy collapsed because its leaders were feckless and its political groupings had been long accustomed to a style of politics in which parties attempted to impose their particular moral vision on the rest of society instead of finding common ground with their opponents. Weimar Germany's failure, we might say, shows just how a refusal to move toward an overlapping consensus makes democratic failure a real, even likely, possibility.

Putting Weimar Germany's spectacular political failure into a historical and comparative context, however, suggests certain conclusions somewhat different from those Rawls offers, conclusions at odds with the restraint argument's empirical claims. In particular, this section examines the religious conflict thesis in light of the experiences of our cases of the European integrationists and focus on how these integrationists' political activities, especially their political parties, affected their respective countries' democratic consolidation. What emerges is that not only do the integrationists' parties not preclude democratic government or even often make it more difficult. They may sometimes actually be quite constructive politically. In fact, I suggest that it is the deeply *religious* nature of the parties in Belgium and the Netherlands that make them so politically helpful, as their powerful networks of affiliated associations helped tie members into their nascent democracies while giving their political leaders the flexibility to negotiate with their political opponents.

Among the few scholars who have tried to build empirical evidence into a theoretical argument, Paul Weithman has suggested that when the proponents of deliberative restraint argue that religion poses a threat to

---

[54] Rawls, *Political Liberalism*, lxi.
[55] Rawls, *Lectures on the History of Political Philosophy*, 8.

political stability, what they have in mind is that religion provokes "justified resentment" in others that issues in a breakdown of civility and trust.[56] But as he also notes, that sort of claim does not quite cut it, since any reasonably pluralist democratic system will invariably engender all sorts of "justified resentments" (over unfair tax policies, educational systems, and so forth) without fundamentally undermining the broader political system. He goes on to argue that taking the "long view" points to a pretty generous allowance toward politically mobilized religion, as the engagement of religious groups in the political process may "moderate their political positions to increase their chances of political success" and "reduce the polarization caused by the earlier adoption of positions that were regarded as extreme."[57] Weithman's argument strikes me as plausible and suggestive, but incomplete. It is one thing to argue that theorists have failed to make the argument as to how much resentment can be squared with a reasonably stable and just democratic government. It is quite another to argue that, therefore, religious citizens do not have much to concern themselves with the norms of deliberative restraint. What is missing here is any systematic analysis as to *how much* (or what kinds of) resentment are acceptable and how it is that formerly extreme positions can be modified and compromised. To fill this gap, I suggest focusing on how the integrationists' parties impacted their respective countries' democratic consolidations.

When political theorists talk about reasonable democratic regimes, they seem to mean something similar to what comparative social scientists mean when they consider a democracy *consolidated*, where democratic procedures and norms "become routinized and deeply internalized in social, institutional, and even psychological life, as well as in calculations for achieving [political] success."[58] Or, as one scholar has put it, where democracy becomes the "only game in town."[59] This is, I should note, conceptually distinct from a democratic *transition*, by which we typically mean the point at which an old authoritarian regime has fallen and a new, democratically elected one has been put in place. Though there is a good deal of disagreement over what constitutes the point at which a "transition" ends and the process of "consolidation" begins (or ends), it does seem important to keep the two distinct.[60] I focus here exclusively on

---

[56] Weithman, *Religion and the Obligations of Citizenship*, 160–61.
[57] Ibid., 162.
[58] Juan J. Linz and Alfred Stepan, *Problems of Democratic Transition and Consolidation: Southern Europe, South America, and Post-Communist Europe* (Baltimore, MD: Johns Hopkins University Press, 1996), 5.
[59] Di Palma, *To Craft Democracies*.
[60] For an overview (and criticism), see Gerardo L. Munck, "The Regime Question: Theory Building in Democracy Studies," *World Politics* 54, no. 1 (2001).

democratic consolidation because it seems to me obvious that religious political mobilization is compatible with the establishment of democratic procedures and because issues of consolidation most closely match the kinds of concerns political theorists voice when thinking about religion.

Conceptually, a consolidated democracy is one in which, Linz and Stepan suggest, three things hold:

[N]o significant national ... actors spend significant resources attempting to achieve their objectives by creating a nondemocratic regime ... a strong majority of public opinion holds the belief that democratic procedures and institutions are the most appropriate way to govern collective life [and] when governmental and nongovernmental forces alike ... become subjected to, and habituated to, the resolution of conflict within the specific laws, procedures, and institutions sanctioned by the ... democratic process.[61]

In short, a consolidated democracy is one in which political disputes are largely contained within constitutional norms and institutions that themselves have broad public support. Compare that to Rawls' definition of what counts as "stability for the right reasons":

(a) The basic structure of society is effectively regulated by the most reasonable political conception of justice.
(b) This political conception of justice is endorsed by an overlapping consensus comprised of all the reasonable comprehensive doctrines in society and these are in an enduring majority with respect to those rejecting that conception.
(c) Public political discussions, when constitutional essentials and matters of basic justice are at stake, are always (or nearly always) reasonably decidable on the basis of reasons specified by the most reasonable political conceptions of justice, or by a reasonable family of such conceptions.[62]

In both cases, a successful democracy means a democracy where political issues are decided within reasonably well-established political institutions, and outcomes enjoy a significant measure of popular legitimacy in large part because they were channeled through those institutions and represent the considered views of the citizens those institutions are meant to represent.[63]

---

[61] Linz and Stepan, *Problems of Democratic Transition and Consolidation*, 6.
[62] Rawls, *Political Liberalism*, 391.
[63] The match, of course, is not exact, as social science is not so directly concerned with the moral quality of the reasons brought out in political debates and so does not include Rawls' criterion (c), the overlapping consensus and its idea of public reason. But of course that is precisely what is at issue and so we can for now conceive of the two as being essentially equivalent.

The study of democratic consolidation has, of course, burgeoned into a major focus of comparative political science. Broadly speaking, three theories have dominated the discussion. *Precondition* theories argue that countries become and stay democratic as they modernize.[64] As economies and social systems become more complex and individuals achieve higher levels of wealth and education, authoritarian governments find it increasingly difficult to sustain themselves. *Cultural* theories, on the other hand, suggest that the chances for transitions and consolidation rest in the country's political culture, in the values, norms, and expectations that ordinary and elite citizens hold.[65] Finally, *institutional* theories propose that democracy succeeds largely because influential political actors first find it in their interest to agree to democratic procedures, which – if properly designed – then create a "virtuous circle" of reciprocating democratic politics.[66] Though certainly plausible, modernization theories simply have not been able to make the case that industrialization and economic development necessarily produce democracies.[67] Cultural theories also seem attractive, but it is extremely difficult to tease out exactly what one means by "culture" and exactly how that is supposed to

[64] Ruth Collier, *Paths toward Democracy: The Working Class and Elites in Western Europe and South America* (New York: Cambridge University Press, 1999); Seymour Martin Lipset, "Some Social Requisites of Democracy: Economic Development and Political Legitimacy," *American Political Science Review* 53, no. 1 (1959); Barrington Moore, *The Social Origins of Dictatorship and Democracy* (Boston: Beacon Press, 1966); Przeworski and Limongi, "Modernization: Theories and Facts"; Dietrich Rueschemeyer, Evelyn Huber, and John D. Stephens, *Capitalist Development and Democracy* (Chicago: Chicago University Press, 1992).

[65] Gabriel Almond and Sidney Verba, *The Civic Culture: Political Attitudes and Democracy in Five Nations* (Princeton, NJ: Princeton University Press, 1963); Samuel P. Huntington, *The Third Wave: Democratization in the Late Twentieth Century* (Norman, OK: University of Oklahoma Press, 1991); Robert D. Putnam, *Bowling Alone: The Collapse and Revival of American Community* (New York: Simon & Schuster, 2000); Robert D. Putnam, *Making Democracy Work: Civic Traditions in Modern Italy* (Princeton, NJ: Princeton University Press, 1993).

[66] Di Palma, *To Craft Democracies*; Guillermo O'Donnell and Phillippe C Schmitter, *Transitions from Authoritarian Rule: Tentative Conclusions about Uncertain Democracies* (Baltimore, MD: Johns Hopkins University Press, 1986); Przeworski, *Democracy and the Market*; Dankart A. Rustow, "Transitions to Democracy: Toward a Dynamic Model," *Comparative Politics* 2, no. 3 (1970).

[67] The most detailed and, in many ways, persuasive version of the modernization theory is Rueschemeyer, Huber, and Stephens, *Capitalist Development and Democracy*. In this work, they argue (using a large number of case studies from Europe and the Americas) that it is the mobilization of the working class that brings about the growth of democracy. Ruth Collier and James Mahoney showed pretty convincingly, however, that, even according to Rueschemeyer *et. al.*'s own data, their claims were not sustainable. See Ruth Berins Collier and James Mahoney, *Labor and Democratization: Comparing the First and Third Waves in Europe and Latin America* (Institute of Industrial Relations Working Paper no. 62) (Berkeley: Department of Political Science, University of California, Berkeley, 1995).

make a difference politically.[68] What's more, cultures change, sometimes radically, for a whole variety of reasons, and an explanation that focuses solely on cultural factors will likely be the subject of critiques looking for other, more fundamental causes.[69]

Though I cannot defend the claim fully here, it seems reasonable to say that while a certain degree of modern social and economic conditions certainly help with consolidating democracies, as do widely held values that favor the same, consolidations are better explained as the product of somewhat contingent circumstances in which political institutions, economic conditions, cultural values, and self-interest play off one another. Democracies become consolidated as new (or developing) political institutions acquire enough effectiveness to handle a society's political demands and that society's major social actors' values and interests do not push them toward rejecting the legitimacy of those same institutions. It sounds rather trite, but it is nonetheless all that much more true to say that democracies fail politically mostly on account of their politics, because their elites are incapable or unwilling to make things work, and because their citizens demand what cannot be delivered.

So the key question is how does integrationism's political mobilization of religion impact the prospects for democratic consolidation? In Belgium and the Netherlands, the two places where religious parties actually achieved majority status, not only were their democratic consolidations not precluded, but religious parties were key players in their construction and defense as well. Belgium's Catholic Party won a majority in the 1884 parliamentary elections, a majority that it would hold until World War I. The Netherlands' Catholic and Calvinist groups combined to gain a parliamentary majority in 1888 and again in 1901. They were strong enough to force their socialist and liberal opponents into the "Pacification" of 1917, setting the stage for the Netherlands'

[68] See, for instance, M. Steven Fish, "Reversal and Erosion of Democratization in the Postcommunist World," paper presented at American Political Science Association Meeting, Boston, MA, 1998. In this piece, Fish shows that the erosion of democratic gains in the former Soviet Union could be pretty well predicted by whether a particular country was historically Catholic/Protestant, Orthodox, or Muslim. But these cultural categories overlapped with other boundaries (economic, empires, etc.) that made it difficult to say for sure that culture was a "cause." Or, more precisely, it is difficult to say for sure what element of culture was the cause.

[69] Consider, for instance, the argument in ibid. and Samuel P. Huntington, "Religion and the Third Wave," in *Rendering unto Caesar: The Religious Sphere in World Politics*, ed. Sabrina Petra Ramet (Washington, D.C.: American University Press, 1995), where he suggests that one of the primary causes of the wave of democratization in Latin America and southern Europe in the 1970s and 1980s was the Catholic Church's formal embrace of democracy at Vatican II. Previously, Huntington notes, political scientists had long noted a "democracy gap" between Protestant and Catholic countries, with the latter clearly on the low side.

famed "pillarization."[70] The Catholic Party was in government perpetually from after 1917 until it combined with its Calvinist counterpart in the 1970s to form the Christian Democratic Appeal (the lead party in the Netherlands' current government). In both countries, then, the parties played significant political roles in both the transition to and consolidation of their respective democratic regimes.

In neither case did the parties seek to overturn their respective constitutional orders, even when they had the opportunity to do so. Once in power, Belgium's Catholic Party mitigated some of the worst (in the church's eyes) aspects of the liberal anti-clerical legislation, restoring educational privileges (and subsidies) to the church and re-establishing diplomatic relations with the Vatican. What it did not do, however, was to make Catholic schools the country's only school system; the new education laws provided for public support of the religious schools but maintained the need for public secular ones as well. Neither did the party make moves toward making Belgium a confessional state. The Catholic Party had a clear opportunity in 1884 to stifle Belgium's movement toward full democratization and, yet, against a significant number of reactionary Catholic notables and part of the episcopate, it refused to do so.[71] Rather, Belgium remained a liberal state with substantial guarantees for basic liberties and a robust set of subsidies for the majority Catholic Church. The Dutch parties likewise did not seek to overthrow the constitutional regime, and while none of these religious parties was especially enthusiastic about expanding the democratic suffrage, neither were they especially opposed.[72] Finally, each country's religious party helped defend its democracy against radical anti-democratic groups (like Belgium's Rex

[70] For more on this, see Rudy B. Andeweg, "Consociational Democracy," *Annual Review of Political Science* 3, no. 14 (2000); Bakvis, *Catholic Power in the Netherlands*; Herman Bakvis, "Toward a Political Economy of Consociationalism: A Commentary on Marxist Views of Pillarization in the Netherlands," *Comparative Politics* 16 (1984); J.C.H. Blom, "Pillarisation in Perspective," *West European Politics* 23, no. 3 (2000); Carlson-Thies, "Democracy in the Netherlands"; Hans Daalder, *Ancient and Modern Pluralism in the Netherlands* (Center for European Studies Working Paper no. 22) (Cambridge, MA: Center for European Studies, Harvard University, 1989); Daalder, "The Netherlands: Opposition in a Segmented Society"; Ertman, "Liberalization, Democratization, and the Origins of a 'Pillarized' Civil Society in Nineteenth-Century Belgium and the Netherlands"; Houska, *Influencing Mass Political Behavior*; Kalyvas, *The Rise of Christian Democracy in Europe*; Arend Lijphart, "Consociational Democracy," *World Politics* 21, no. 2 (1968); Lijphart, *Politics of Accommodation*; Val Lorwin, "Segmented Pluralism: Ideological Cleavages and Political Cohesion in the Smaller European Democracies," in *Consociational Democracy*, ed. McRae; McRae, ed., *Consociational Democracy*.

[71] Kalyvas, *The Rise of Christian Democracy in Europe*, 189–92. Kalyvas, "Democracy and Religious Politics" argues that because the church was influential it actually had a choice as to whether it would support Belgium's constitution or attempt to overthrow it.

[72] In fact, the ARP had split in the 1890s over the question of suffrage. The more conservative party members (mostly those who were still a part of the main DRC) opposed

movement) in the late 1920s and 1930s, deciding to cooperate politically with their political, especially socialist, opponents.[73] So it seems safe to say that the religious integrationists' political mobilization did not preclude democratic consolidation.

Even if, however, democracy is *possible* in the presence of religious parties, it might still be the case that they make it more difficult, perhaps so much so that prudence would counsel restraint. Though Austria's Christian Socials had helped establish the First Republic after the debacle of World War I, even cooperating with the Social Democrats in a coalition government, relations between the two parties deteriorated through the 1920s to the point that compromise looked impossible. Under pressure from right-wing paramilitaries and fascist parties in both Germany and Italy, the Christian Socials decided that ending Austria's democracy was preferable to cooperating with the socialists and overthrew the First Republic in 1933.[74] Germany's largely Catholic Center Party, organized to defend Catholics against Bismarck's *Kulturkampf*, became the largest party in the Reichstag and its leader, Ludwig von Windthorst, became a popular hero for Germany's Catholics. The Center participated in every Weimar government and provided four of its chancellors, but toward the end of the 1920s it lost its enthusiasm for constitutional government (to say nothing of democracy) and traded its existence for what can only be called a mess of pottage, fictitious Nazi promises to leave the church alone. The key distinction between the two sets of cases seems to be that in the former two, the religious parties and their opponents found ways to cooperate while in the latter two they did not.[75] What accounts for the fact that in Belgium and the Netherlands religious parties found ways to bridge the differences they had with their political opponents while the parties in Austria and Germany did not?

We can start by ruling out a few obvious explanations. We might think that the disparate outcomes merely reflect different political theologies.

the ARP's support of expanded suffrage and left to start the Christian Historical Union (CHU). The ARP and CHU continued to cooperate, however, in parliament and were eventually reunited when they and the remnants of the Dutch Catholic Party formed the Christian Democratic Appeal (CDA) in the 1970s.

[73] Giovanni Capoccia, "Defending Democracy: Reactions to Political Extremism in Inter-War Europe," *European Journal of Political Research* 39 (2001); Thomas Ertman, "Democracy and Dictatorship in Interwar Western Europe Revisited," *World Politics* 50, no. 3 (1998).

[74] Rath, "The Dollfuss Ministry: The Demise of the Nationalrat."

[75] I am here rather implicitly endorsing the idea that the interwar democracies survived or failed due to specifically political factors. There are, of course, plenty of theories as to why democracies failed in interwar Europe – economic conditions, cultural movements, political mistakes. What seems more or less persuasive to me are the newly emerging arguments that emphasize the importance of political leadership and the connection

Perhaps the Catholics in Germany and Austria were just less enamored with democracy. It is true that Austria's Christian Socials found the inspiration for their clerico-corporatist dictatorship in romantic Catholic thought, crystallized in an interpretation of Pius XI's *Quadragesimo Anno*.[76] But there is little evidence to suggest that Germany and Austria's religious political elites were *more* anti-democratic than Belgium's and Holland's. It is probably more accurate to say that none of the integrationists was particularly democratic in their orientation. In surveys of Christian Democratic parties, scholars have often refused to categorize *any* of the pre-World War II parties as properly democratic on the grounds that those parties all rejected some putatively fundamental democratic idea.[77] Kuyper's Anti-Revolutionary Party was anti-revolutionary in the sense of opposing the French Revolution and especially its promotion of popular sovereignty (as sovereignty, the Calvinists thought, belonged to God alone). Relying just on political theology as an explanation, moreover, cannot make sense of the Center's slide from a genuinely "liberal party"[78] in the nineteenth century to authoritarian enabler in the twentieth or the fact that Germany's Catholics were *more* resistant to radicalization at the end of Weimar than its Protestant majority.[79] While political theology surely makes a difference – the fact that the same intellectual currents pulsed through reactionary Catholic circles in both Spain and Austria in the 1930s is no coincidence – it cannot alone serve as an adequate explanation.

We also cannot sufficiently explain the different outcomes with reference to the structure of religious pluralism. We might very well think that a group's commitment to democratic constitutionalism will vary according to its majority/minority status. Rudy Andeweg suggests that the Netherlands' famous consociational democracy, and by extension the religious parties' willingness to accept democratic rule, emerged not out of any principled commitment to toleration or liberty, but out of

that leadership had to organizations within civil society. For general treatments along these lines, see Nancy Bermeo, *Ordinary People in Extraordinary Times: The Citizenry and the Breakdown of Democracy* (Princeton, NJ: Princeton University Press, 2003); Ertman, "Democracy and Dictatorship in Interwar Western Europe Revisited"; Zimmerman, "Political Breakdown and the Process of National Consensus Formation."

[76] Boyer, *Political Radicalism in Late Imperial Vienna*; Diamant, *Austrian Catholics and the First Republic*; Fogarty, *Christian Democracy in Western Europe, 1820–1953*; Hans Maier, *Revolution and Church: The Early History of Christian Democracy, 1789–1901* (Notre Dame, IN: University of Notre Dame Press, 1969).

[77] See, for instance, Irving, *The Christian Democratic Parties of Western Europe*. For worries about Christian Democratic Parties' democratic credentials even after World War II, see Gabriel Almond, "The Political Ideas of Christian Democracy," *Journal of Politics* 10, no. 4 (1948).

[78] Anderson, *Windthorst: A Political Biography*, 402.

[79] Richard F. Hamilton, *Who Voted for Hitler?* (Princeton, NJ: Princeton University Press, 1982).

the sociological fact that no single group could reasonably hope to gain a stable majority. Consociationalism on this account was the result of nothing more than rational political behavior under conditions of irremediable pluralism.[80] If a group finds itself in the minority, it will, as a matter of self-interest if nothing else, seek the protections of a constitutional democracy. If in the majority, the same group might be tempted to set democratic protections aside. Though this sort of explanation is quite plausible – the Center's historical emphasis on constitutionalism and religious and civil liberties can easily be attributed to its limited choices in the face of an aggressively hostile state – it does not do enough. It explains Austria's Christian Socials reasonably, but does not explain why Belgium's Catholic Party refused to overturn the country's liberal constitution. Nor does it help us understand why the Center refused to support anti-Semitic and anti-socialist legislation when doing so would have brought some relief from Bismarck's assault.[81]

Another version of the pluralist explanation focuses more on the reactions of political opponents. German historians have long claimed that the Center's success disrupted the "normal" pattern of class conflict and delayed German democracy. Its almost all-Catholic support was not limited to any one class, region, or even ethnicity, and given the antipathy with which many of Germany's Protestants and socialists viewed Catholics, alliances were difficult, if not impossible to sustain, meaning that no single party could effectively force democratic change. Likewise, Austria's Christian Socials and their socialist opponents were divided in every way: religious v. anti-clerical; urban v. rural; working class v. bourgeoisie and elite. The Christian Socials were the party of Catholics, rural Austrians, and Alpine aristocrats, while the socialists tended to be concentrated in big cities and among those who had become indifferent or opposed to religion. This left very little room for compromise, especially for the Christian Socials, who were being pressured by the *Heimwehr* and the German nationalists. Their conflict with the socialists became "total," and part of the reason that they could not mediate their conflict was that to compromise anything looked like compromising everything.[82]

But the parties' religious identity was as much a *product* as cause of conflict. At least in Belgium, Germany, and the Netherlands, the religious parties organized in the 1860s and 1870s because newly ascendant

---

[80] Andeweg, "Consociational Democracy."

[81] Anderson, *Windthorst: A Political Biography*, 251–60. This is not to say that nineteenth-century Center members did not have anti-Semitic feelings. What they did not do, at least under Windthorst's leadership, was to engage in the anti-Semitic demagoguery so common for that time.

[82] Frederick C. Engelmann, "Austria: The Pooling of Opposition," in *Political Oppositions in Western Democracies*, ed. Dahl.

political elites pursued policies meant to undermine or control their particular forms of religious faith. Liberal governments in all four countries sought, mostly through systems of public education, to reshape their citizens in order to make them properly "civic," meaning in practice weaning them away from their "obscurantist" and disreputable faith.[83] Nowhere was this more true than in Germany, where liberals and nationalists could agree on little except that German culture was irreducibly Protestant and that Catholics, on the basis of their Catholic-ness, could not participate in that culture.[84] So even if it is true that religious parties were politically inflammatory, they were so (at least in part) because their opponents had decided that they *would be* inflammatory. It hardly seems fair to single the integrationists out as politically disruptive.

Moreover, it seems as if the religious character of parties and the strength of organization that produced was, on balance, a real benefit to consolidation, not a problem. First, to the degree that the parties were more strongly constituted around religious identity and practice, they could construct broad cross-class coalitions, moderating their policy positions and helping to make them politically responsible. In Belgium, the Netherlands, and Germany, the parties were genuine coalitions originally organized around a common religious identity, meaning that they captured large portions of votes among a range of classes.[85] Austria's Christian Socials, on the other hand, found themselves deeply alienated from the country's urban working classes (and vice versa) in large part because the party originally organized more as a creature of nineteenth-century Viennese anti-liberal radicals rather than as a religious protest party.[86] Austria's peculiar combination of liberal anti-clericalism and close church–state cooperation meant that when the state began to pass legislation that threatened to strip the lower clergy of their social standing by secularizing schools, marriages, and other civil functions, these lower clergy became politically radicalized, but – crucially – not in defense of the faith.[87] Karl Lueger used Vienna's ubiquitous anti-Semitism to join

[83] Glenn, *The Myth of the Common School.*
[84] Smith, *German Nationalism and Religious Conflict.*
[85] To be sure, the parties were more successful among some strata than others. Holland's ARP was widely known as the party of the "little people," or the small shopkeepers or lower bourgeoisie. The Center, in turn, owed a good deal of its electoral strength to its ability to mobilize the peasant vote. But in all three cases, the parties could not do without some portion of their coalition. In the United States, as much as congregations and denominations tend to follow other cleavages, they are also pretty good at providing a place where cross-class contact happens much more frequently than in American society in general. See Robert Wuthnow, "The United States: Bridging the Privileged and the Marginalized," in *Democracies in Flux: The Evolution of Social Capital in Contemporary Society,* ed. Robert D. Putnam (Oxford: Oxford University Press, 2002).
[86] Boyer, *Political Radicalism in Late Imperial Vienna.*   [87] Ibid., 28–31.

together the lower clergy, artisans, and others threatened by the city's liberal politics to create the Christian Social Party and advance the interests of a particular social stratum, not religious community.[88] The Christian Socials were originally a party of social, not religious, protest. Later, when a religious identity was made more important politically, it simply completed the totalization of their conflict with the socialists. The irreligious roots of the Christian Socials made Austria's democratic failure *more* likely, not less, while in the other cases, the parties were actually less likely to wander into extremism, in large part *because* of their religious identity.

Second, the organization of the parties around religious identity and their tight links to other affiliated associations (newspapers, trade unions, and so on) gave those parties an institutional vigor and depth that reliably tied voters to the parties and, consequently, gave elites the freedom to negotiate with their opponents. When the religious hierarchy in Belgium decided in favor of the reasonably moderate conservatives prior to the 1884 elections (over the ultramontane radicals), the strong religious ties among Catholic voters made quashing the radicals relatively easy and reassured their liberal opponents that they had little intention of destroying Belgium's constitution.[89] In the Netherlands, the thoroughgoing "pillarization" effectively encapsulated individuals within their own particular subcultures, and since voters were so deeply embedded within their own pillar – with its churches, newspapers, radio stations, civic groups, and schools – voting largely became an expression of identity and not of reflective choice.[90] This produced a "deference" that made each pillar fairly stable and allowed elites a good deal of flexibility in political negotiations.[91] This was especially important in times of crisis, when obdurate political groups could very well have undermined Holland's ability to negotiate a solution to the "problem" of its

---

[88] Ibid., 206–37.

[89] For a fascinating comparison of Belgium in 1884 and Algeria in 1989, see Kalyvas, "Commitment Problems in Emerging Democracies." In the latter, he argues, the government canceled the final election because the main Islamic opposition party did not have the wherewithal to control its radicals, who threatened to make Algeria's nascent democracy a "one vote, one time" affair. In contrast, Belgium's episcopate could exert sufficient control over anti-liberal ultramontanes (closing down their newspapers, among other things) such that the Catholic Party's liberal opponents did not see the possibility of a Catholic win in apocalyptic terms. They could come back and contest the next election.

[90] Rutger S. Zwart, "Christian Democracy and Political Order in the Netherlands," in *Christian Democracy in the European Union*, ed. Emiel Lamberts (Leuven: Leuven University Press, 1997).

[91] See Lijphart, "Consociational Democracy"; Arend Lijphart, "From the Politics of Accommodation to Adversarial Politics in the Netherlands: A Reassessment," *West European Politics* 12, no. 1 (1989); Arend Lijphart, *Politics of Accommodation*, 2nd. edn. (Berkeley: University of California Press, 1975).

"segmented pluralism"[92] and, perhaps more importantly in this context, its ability to withstand the anti-democratic challenges of proto-fascist parties in the 1930s.[93]

Ironically enough, the parties' organizational strength, rooted in religious identity, gave them the capacity to at times even assert their political independence from their particular religious authorities as well. In 1887, the Center's vigorous opposition to the *Kulturkampf* had forced Bismarck to offer the Vatican an easing of the more onerous regulations (though not take them off the books) in return for the Center's cooperation on economic and military budgets. Both Bismarck and Rome excluded party leaders from these negotiations. Leo XIII agreed but when informed of the pope's wishes, the Center's charismatic leader, Windthorst, refused to go along. When the pope's explicit instructions to support Bismarck's budget leaked to newspapers, the party was caught in a bind.[94] If they acceded to Leo's order, they would be confirming what their enemies had always said, that they were nothing more than papal dupes. If they refused the pope, they risked undermining the very thing that sustained them politically – their Catholic identity. Windthorst did what seemed impossible: he retained the Center's loyalty to the church and confirmed its independence as a political party. In a speech to the Rhenish party conference in Cologne, he admitted that the pope had urged the Center to vote yes on the budget, but that such instructions were not binding since it concerned "secular" matters and "the Holy Father does not mix in these secular things. This principle we must maintain inviolable under all circumstances … for it is the basis of our political existence."[95]

[92] Daalder has long argued that pluralism was never the problem that Lijphart made it out to be, and that the Dutch pillarization was simply a continuation of Dutch political traditions. See Daalder, *Ancient and Modern Pluralism in the Netherlands*; Daalder, "The Netherlands: Opposition in a Segmented Society." That argument ignores, it seems to me, concerted efforts on the part of liberals and socialists alike to break up the pillarized system and to resist – almost at the cost of political breakdown in 1917 – the religious parties' attempts at securing public funding for their confessional schools. See Carlson-Thies, "Democracy in the Netherlands" for a detailed exploration of the roots of the 1917 "Pacification."

[93] As I noted earlier, Nancy Bermeo has argued recently that the interwar democracies survived and failed as a result of the political actions of their elites, not because of mass mobilization. In the Netherlands and Belgium in particular, the parties' strong hierarchical political controls and concomitant flexibility allowed them to join with the hated socialists in political cooperation and ensure that the nascent far-right movements were quashed. See Bermeo, *Ordinary People in Extraordinary Times*.

[94] Leo XIII had instructed the party leadership in two separate notes to vote for the *Septennat* (a seven-year military budget that Bismarck wanted in order to free him from accountability to parliament), copies of which were forwarded to Bismarck (either on Leo's instructions or by elements within the Vatican bureaucracy unsympathetic to the Center). When the Center appeared to stand firm against the *Septennat*, Bismarck leaked the notes, hoping to force their hand.

[95] Windthorst, quoted in Anderson, *Windthorst: A Political Biography*, 350–1.

The Center Party, he argued, was primarily a political party whose first duty was the defense of the church and its community's political interests, and thus it had a responsibility to listen to and follow the church's leadership as it could. But in "political" matters, whose definition Windthorst left artfully ambiguous, the party must proceed on its own expertise. The Center under Windthorst (and most of his successors) understood and defended the interests of its Catholic constituents better than the Vatican, if for no other reason than the party (under lay leadership) depended on those constituents in order to survive politically. Rather than thinking that political Catholicism meant simply what Rome said it meant, they began to develop for themselves *as Catholics* what a democratic political Catholicism might look like. Windthorst and the other party leaders could not support Bismarck's military budget because its burden would land disproportionately on the backs of German peasants, a significant Catholic constituency. They were sincerely interested in advancing German Catholics' political interests, and to do that they had to strike a balance between advancing the interests of Germans who happened to be Catholic and advancing the interests of the Catholic Church proper. As Margaret Anderson has noted, no one in the Center "wanted any bishop or priest to tell him how to vote in the Reichstag" (though, of course, they would always take care to listen to the bishops' opinions).[96] This is not to say that, as Kalyvas argues, they simply developed a necessarily "secular" political identity,[97] but rather that they developed their own political identity that was both democratic and religious, and achieved "the laicization of the Catholic milieu"[98] without disposing of its Catholicity.

As I noted in chapter 1, the Center's organizational apparatus began to disintegrate in the 1920s, as parish priests dropped their affiliation, trade unions exercised more independence, and the top leadership took on a deeper clerical hue. When Monsignor Kaas was elected to head the party in 1928, it signaled the end of an era, and especially the end of a politically independent German Catholic party. As even the party's regional elites

---

[96] Margaret Lavinia Anderson, "Interdenominationalism, Clericalism, and Pluralism: The Zentrumsstreit and the Dilemma of Catholicism in Wilhelmine Germany," *Central European History* 21, no. 4 (1988): 368. See also Margaret Lavinia Anderson, *Practicing Democracy*. There she describes how the Center's embrace of electoral politics "trained" German Catholics be good democratic citizens.

[97] See Kalyvas, *The Rise of Christian Democracy in Europe*, 222ff.

[98] Anderson, "The Kulturkampf and the Course of German History," 113. For a brief discussion of the role of religious parties and the development of a religious political identity, see Nancy L. Rosenblum, "Religious Parties, Religious Political Identity, and the Cold Shoulder of Liberal Democratic Thought," *Ethical Theory and Moral Practice: An International Forum* 6, no. 1 (2003).

became disconnected from the national leadership, the party became less interested in (and less capable of, for that matter) preserving Germany's fragile democracy and more interested in preserving the church's institutional integrity. In 1933, when Kaas negotiated the party's dissolution with the National Socialist government, he did so from the relative safety of Rome, where he had relocated without informing the rest of the party leadership. The formal announcement was largely a *coup de grâce* to a party that had already stopped functioning, though its remnants would re-emerge at the head of the Christian Democratic Union after the war. The Center folded because it failed to defend ordinary Catholics' interests, and not just the church's, sapping the source of its organizational strength, its identity as a religious party that pursued political interests. This, of course, is not to say that a more robust Center, or one not directed by the Vatican, could have saved Weimar, but it is to say that rather than being a hindrance to democratic consolidation, the party's religious identity and strong organizational ties look to be quite the opposite, a very real asset.

France, it seems to me, represents something of an instructive alternative. The 1789 Revolution did not produce, to put it mildly, a stable democratic politics, in part because the divisions between republican/ reactionary, democrat/authoritarian, and so on were inscribed with a profound religious/anti-clerical division. The *ancien régime* had been closely tied to the Catholic Church in France, and the revolutionaries were quick to make the church (and especially its property) a central target. They expropriated church property, forced clergy into humiliating acts of political submission (and murdered or forced into exile those who refused), and embarked on an ambitious, if not so well-executed, program of "dechristianization" of France.[99] Many Catholics, generally speaking, remained stubbornly opposed to the Republic and were only too glad to support its opponents throughout the nineteenth and twentieth centuries. These divisions were reinforced both by republicans and the church throughout the Second and Third Republics. For its part, the church consistently frustrated attempts on the part of Catholics to find ways to mediate the divisions between the two, condemning the proto-democratic theologians Lammenais and Montalembert in the 1832 encyclical *Mirari Vos*,[100] and ensuring that no mass Catholic

---

[99] For good summaries of the revolutionary period, see John McManners, *The French Revolution and the Church* (New York: Harper & Row, 1970); Harry W. Paul, *The Second Ralliement: The Rapprochement between Church in and State in France in the Twentieth Century* (Washington, D.C.: Catholic University of America Press, 1967), 1–7.

[100] Fogarty, *Christian Democracy in Western Europe, 1820–1953*, 156; Maier, *Revolution and Church*, 47.

political organization ever got off the ground.[101] Even when the church did decide to try and organize politically, as with Leo XIII's *Ralliement* in the late nineteenth century, it could not overcome its own internal divisions nor, it seems, give political organizations enough freedom to be successful.[102] Many activists who had been a part of the nascent French Christian Democratic parties drifted instead into the devoutly anti-republican *Action Française* (AF). Even after the Vatican condemned AF and embraced a kind of second *Ralliement* to the republic in the 1920s,[103] French Catholics were all too willing to support Vichy, some even seeing it as "the embodiment of their own aspirations for a Christian state."[104] French Catholicism was, as Margaret Anderson describes it, "the handmaiden of reaction,"[105] so furiously opposed to republicanism in all its (often anti-clerical) forms, it could not develop "coherent, internally consistent strategies for resistance."[106]

Absent a religious party or some sort of other mass political organization that could create some reasonable space within French republicanism for a Catholic subculture and invest Catholics into the wider political system, France's Catholics gravitated all too easily toward the anti-democratic extreme (and their anti-clerical republican opponents had little incentive to compromise). As Kalyvas notes, the failure to organize a religious party in France "greatly facilitated the rise of nationalism and antiliberalism among Catholics."[107] Religious citizens in Germany, Belgium, and the Netherlands thought their democratizing and democratic political orders legitimate in large part because those political orders had accommodated

---

[101] Ronald Eckford Mill Irving, *Christian Democracy in France* (London: Allen and Unwin, 1973); Kalyvas, *The Rise of Christian Democracy in Europe*, 118–25; James F. McMillan, "France," in *Political Catholicism in Europe, 1918–1965*, ed. Tom Buchanan and Martin Conway (Oxford: Clarendon Press, 1996), 38–41. The church prevented Albert de Mun from forming a French counterpart to Windthorst's Center Party in 1885, refused to give much support to various political efforts to create Christian Democratic political movements in the 1890s, and in 1910 condemned *Sillon*, founded by Marc Sangnier in 1899 as an attempt to defend Catholic interests against the anti-clericalism of the Third Republic.

[102] For an excellent discussion of the church's failures, see Kalyvas, *The Rise of Christian Democracy in Europe*, 150–60.

[103] See Paul, *The Second Ralliement*.

[104] McMillan, "France," 55. The French bishops were extremely loyal to the person of Pétain, even as they were not, for the most part, enamored of Vichy's disreputable cooperation with the Germans. See W.D. Halls, *Politics, Society and Christianity in Vichy France* (Oxford: Berg, 1995).

[105] Anderson, "The Divisions of the Pope," 42.

[106] John W. Boyer, "Catholics, Christians, and the Challenges of Democracy: The Heritage of the Nineteenth Century," in *Christian Democracy in 20th Century Europe*, ed. Gehler, Kaiser, and Wohnout, 34.

[107] Kalyvas, *The Rise of Christian Democracy in Europe*, 166. The general claim here is that the problem of consolidating French democracy was made more difficult because the republican government insisted on a rather rigid public secularism and pre-World War

them and given them space to develop their own views on democratic citizenship, views that their opponents could acknowledge as reasonable (if only barely so). French republicans could not do that, given that, generally speaking, Catholic political movements, at least until the 1920s, were as much anti-regime as anything else. Indeed, it seems not unreasonable to think that it was not until French Catholics formed the *Mouvement Républicain Populaire* (MRP) after World War II that French Catholicism and Republicanism came to be fully reconciled.[108]

The case of France helps us see clearly both sides of what explains the diversity of our outcomes. On the one hand, it was precisely the religious nature of the organizing in Germany, Belgium, and the Netherlands that made those parties so powerful and, for the most part, constructive democratically. In these countries, religious citizens tended to think their democratizing and democratic political orders legitimate in large part because those political orders had been forced (at least to some extent by the religious parties' electoral successes) to accommodate them and give them space to develop an affinity for democratic citizenship in ways that their opponents could acknowledge as reasonable (if only barely so). Moreover, their organized political participation tied them to the larger political order and helped make them, often quite surprisingly, democratic citizens within democratizing and democratic states. The failure to organize French Catholics politically *as Catholics*, conversely, left the Republican–Catholic divide yet to be overcome, and Catholics gravitated all too easily toward the anti-democratic extremes.

On the other hand, the democratically successful cases saw the religious political mobilization channeled through and controlled by networks of elites and organizations that, though united by a common religious identity, sought to advance distinctively *political* ends, not strictly otherworldly, spiritual ones.[109] In this way, then, the religious communities were able to bring faith to bear on political life in ways that respected the distinctiveness of politics without embracing it as wholly "secular." Religious parties in this sense were able to translate religious concerns

II political Catholicism insisted on the need for a confessional state, meaning that there was little middle ground between the two. For more, see William Bosworth, *Catholicism and Crisis in Modern France* (Princeton, NJ: Princeton University Press, 1962); Robert F. Byrnes, "The French Christian Democrats in the 1890s: Their Appearance and Their Failures," *Catholic Historical Review* 36, no. 3 (1950); Einaudi and Goguel, *Christian Democracy in Italy and France*; Halls, *Politics, Society and Christianity in Vichy France*; Irving, *Christian Democracy in France*; R.J. Wolff and J.K. Hoensch, eds., *Catholics, the State and the European Radical Right 1919–1945* (Boulder, CO: Westview Press, 1987).

[108] See Irving, *Christian Democracy in France*.

[109] James McMillan, "'Priest Hits Girl': On the Front Line in the 'War of the Two Frances'," in *Culture Wars: Secular–Catholic Conflict in Nineteenth-Century Europe*, ed. Christopher Clark and Wolfram Kaiser (New York: Cambridge University Press, 2003).

about education, church autonomy, or the like into goals and strategies that served those concerns but did so within the context of the developing democratic order. We can even understand the Center Party's complicity in Weimar's failure in these terms, for the party's late disaffection with the constitutional order and clear unwillingness to engage in the sort of compromise necessary to make that order succeed coincided with the elevation of Monsignor Kaas to party head in 1928. Kaas was the first priest ever selected to lead the Center and the party quickly turned to a policy of *Kulturpolitik*, refusing to trim its maximalist political demands, even when it became clear that such demands could be fulfilled only at the cost of Weimar's failure. Kaas negotiated the Center's political dissolution from the relative safety of Rome and in return for ultimately fraudulent Nazi promises to protect the institutional church.[110] The extent of the Center's culpability for Weimar's failure ought to be measured less in terms of its religiosity and more in terms of its clericalist shift.

The parties in Belgium, the Netherlands, and (for a time) Germany were successful in bridging their differences with their political opponents not *in spite* of their religious commitments and identity, but *because* the strength of those commitments gave them the tools and incentives to participate in and contribute to the development and maintenance of decent democratic order. While they were far from being democratic "heroes," these parties' histories show that the political mobilization of religion is not just compatible with a stable democratic order, it is sometimes even productive of it. The religious conflict thesis is just simply not true as a general proposition, and, indeed, it looks as if something quite different is the case. So what does this tell us in regard to deliberative restraint?

Considering political legitimacy again: a more restrained deliberative restraint

In his well-known 1997 law review article on the question of public reason, Rawls again focused his attention squarely on religious believers and asked how they might be able to fit within a reasonable liberal democratic political order:

How is it possible for those holding religious doctrines, some based on religious authority, for example, the Church or the Bible, to hold at the same time a reasonable political conception that supports a reasonable constitutional democratic regime? ... Referring to citizens holding religious doctrines as citizens of

---

[110] For a good discussion of this period in the Center's history, see Evans, *The German Center Party*.

faith we ask: How is it possible for citizens of faith to be wholehearted members of a democratic society who endorse society's intrinsic political ideals and values and do not simply acquiesce in the balance of political and social forces?[111]

His answer was that it is indeed possible for religious believers to both affirm the authority of either scripture or a church *and* to be "whole-hearted members of a democratic society" just so long as they can be "reasonable" and in particular affirm the norms of public reason. Absent that sort of affirmation, the best that they (and all of us, more generally) can expect is a political order to which we "acquiesce" but that does not really receive our "wholehearted" endorsement. In other words, absent a widespread and steady affirmation of the norms of public reason, i.e. deliberative restraint, Rawls and other deliberative theorists suggest that our moral and religious pluralism undermines even the possibility of legitimate democratic government. Instead, we are left with a continuing fight within a constitutional order where at best we cannot even agree on the terms of the fight and at worst inhabit a standoff where political peace is merely the product of a circumstantial "balance of political and social forces." To the degree we think it important, then, democratic political legitimacy under conditions of wide moral pluralism thus imposes on citizens a moral obligation to engage one another with reasons that all citizens as citizens can accept, an obligation to practice deliberative restraint. Or so the argument goes.

Stephen Carter has in contrast argued, "What is needed is not a require-ment that the religiously devout choose a form of dialogue that liberal-ism accepts, but that liberalism develop a politics that accepts whatever form of dialogue a member of the public offers."[112] While it is probably too much to ask liberalism to accommodate "whatever form of dialogue a member of the public offers," Carter's point emphasizes the questions I have been exploring in the last couple of chapters: why do Rawls and other proponents of deliberative restraint think that liberal democratic political legitimacy *depends* on that restraint? The answer seems to be that restraint allows citizens within liberal democratic societies to find in the rationale animating their own constitutional orders reasons that they themselves could accept, making their own political obligation plausible and securing political stability, in both the moral and ordinary senses of the word. This is a powerful and for many compelling line of argu-ment. But as I have argued in this and the preceding chapter, it contains a number of important, and I think insuperable, difficulties. There is,

---

[111] Rawls, "The Idea of Public Reason Revisited," 781–82. This is a question recycled from the introduction to the paperback edition of *Political Liberalism* (1996).

[112] Carter, *The Culture of Disbelief*, 230–31.

first, an epistemological problem in that the argument for deliberative restraint has difficulty in making persuasive distinctions between proper and improper political reasons. If the argument tries, as Robert Audi does, to make secularism the guiding criteria, such distinctions ultimately become self-defeating or depend (as with Habermas) on untenable sociological claims. The more plausible version of deliberative restraint, the one offered by Rawls and others, seems to avoid those difficulties by suggesting that there is something implicit in the nature of democratic polities themselves that both demands restraint and shows us what it means to execute such restraint, namely the respect we owe one another as citizens and equal holders of political authority. But even here, I have argued, the argument falters, as it relies on the idea that implicit in our democratic political practices is an expectation we have of one another regarding what that respect actually means. But those expectations turn out themselves to be reasonably controversial and are shaped by empirically cast claims about the likely outcomes should the restraint norms be widely embraced or dismissed. We think that respect requires deliberative restraint to the degree that "we" do in part because its embrace would push us toward Rawls' well-ordered democratic society and its dismissal would threaten us with religious conflict. But the easy acceptance of what I have called the "religious conflict thesis" is itself misguided, and so there seem to be good reasons to doubt that the expectations included in the restraint norm are themselves entirely reasonable. There may indeed be times in which recourse to religiously rooted claims is inadvisable and morally foolish, but as a broad claim about our moral obligations, deliberative restraint does not succeed.

Surely, though, proponents of public reason and deliberative restraint would lodge an objection here. Even inasmuch as I have shown that some sort of democratic polity can coexist with and even benefit from religion's political mobilization, such democracies fall quite short of Rawls' "well-ordered" society. Consider the fact that when the religious parties were successful participants in the construction of democratic polities in places like Belgium and the Netherlands (and, to a lesser extent, Germany), their success produced particular kinds of institutional outcomes, variations on what we might call structural pluralism.[113] In these sorts of democracies, the public sphere is largely divided according to particular identities, and to the degree that the state provides some public service, it does so in a fashion that respects, as much as it can, the autonomy of the communities that sustain those identities. The clearest example

[113] Veit Bader, "Religious Diversity and Democratic Institutional Pluralism," *Political Theory* 31, no. 2 (2003).

of this is in the Netherlands' "pillarized" consociational democracy that Arend Lijphart made so famous.[114] Though Dutch society had long been "segmented" by culture and religion,[115] the last half of the nineteenth and early part of the twentieth century saw that segmentation become institutionalized in both civil and political society. The country was portioned up into Catholic, Calvinist, and socialist pillars, each with its own newspapers, schools, trade unions, civic associations, and political parties, though all within the broader democratic polity.[116]

Pillarization was not a system endorsed enthusiastically by the country's socialist and liberal parties, but instead was the outcome the Catholic and Calvinist parties' political victories (or at least their ability to frustrate their opponents' political goals). Socialists and liberals in the early twentieth century could not get the kinds of constitutional changes they wanted (universal suffrage, mostly) without the cooperation of the religious parties and had to agree to fully fund religious schools as a means of breaking the deadlock, setting a precedent for pillarization's full development.[117] The socialists in particular were continually frustrated by their inability to "break out" of the system and gain a clear majority.[118] Pillarization was not, clearly, the product of an overlapping consensus. Neither, though, was the political order simply a modus vivendi.[119] Among the religious parties, at least, support for pillarization did not reflect merely considerations on the balance of power, but had real philosophical and moral depth. The pluralism of social and political life did not represent a disaster or a decline from some medieval ideal, but rather was the working out of Providence. Abraham Kuyper, in a series of lectures he delivered at Princeton in 1898, laid out a vision of society marked by what he called "sphere sovereignty," a set of claims not unlike

[114] Lijphart, "Consociational Democracy"; Lijphart, *Politics of Accommodation.*

[115] Daalder, *Ancient and Modern Pluralism in the Netherlands*; Hans Daalder, "The Consociational Democracy Theme," *World Politics* 26, no. 4 (1974); Daalder, "The Netherlands: Opposition in a Segmented Society."

[116] For example, 31 percent of Dutch children already went to denominational schools by 1900, a number that increased to 38 percent in 1910 and 62 percent by 1930. See Houska, *Influencing Mass Political Behavior*, 16.

[117] Carlson-Thies, "Democracy in the Netherlands"; Peter van Rooden, "Religious Developments in the Netherlands, *c.* 1750–2000," in *The Decline of Christendom in Western Europe, 1750–2000*, ed. McLeod and Ustorf.

[118] Kole Ruud, "The Societal Position of Christian Democracy in the Netherlands," in *Christian Democracy in the European Union*, ed. Lamberts. Religious parties were not excluded from government until after the 1994 parliamentary elections.

[119] The Belgian Catholics' acceptance of liberal constitutionalism was, at least at first, deemed by Rome to be a "hypothesis," as opposed to the preferred "thesis" of political confessionalism. In Belgian political Catholicism, however, this hypothesis seems to have been pretty persuasive, as its political leadership consistently refused to make the church's thesis a reality.

the ones advanced by Michael Walzer in *Spheres of Justice*.[120] Though the socialist and liberal parties (correctly) thought that pillarization injured their electoral prospects by keeping them from attaining a clear majority, that did not mean their commitment to constitutional democracy itself was dependent on the fact that they could not secure that majority. Like the religious partisans, they came to respect the democratic polity in its own right, though not for reasons that they shared, or could share, with the Catholics or Calvinists. Similarly for Belgium's Catholics, liberal constitutionalism, though doctrinally merely a "hypothesis" (versus the "thesis" of a confessional state preferred by the Vatican), seemed to have a pretty strong, one might say principled, hold on their political imaginations. Their consistent refusal to "confessionalize" the Belgian state reflected more than merely a pragmatic recognition of political pluralism; it reflected a real, if half-hearted, embrace of modernity.[121] Insofar as the structurally pluralist systems created in part by the integrationist parties represented a consensus at all, they are clearly of the constitutional kind, one in which liberal principles largely govern political life but do so more narrowly than the overlapping consensus's, and citizens affirm them on the basis of their own comprehensive views (or at least a good number of them do).[122]

Though they have their virtues, of course, democracies marked by a constitutional consensus only partially address the problems posed by moral and religious pluralism. In the constitutional consensus, liberal principles "are accepted simply as principles and not as grounded in certain ideas of society and person of a political conception, much less in a shared public conception."[123] Unlike in the overlapping consensus, political views are not justified by reference to a political conception of justice, but "depend solely on the comprehensive doctrine."[124] In other words, there are many citizens who seem to violate the norms of public reason while maintaining a real and principled commitment to a constitutional democracy. This sort of consensus suffers by comparison with

---

[120] For Kuyper's ideas, see Abraham Kuyper, "The Antirevolutionary Program," in *Political Order and the Plural Structure of Society*, ed. James W. Skillen and Rockne McCarthy (Atlanta, GA: Scholars Press, 1991); Kuyper, *Lectures on Calvinism*; Groen van Prinsterer, "Unbelief and Revolution," in *Groen Van Prinsterer's Lectures on Unbelief and Revolution*, ed. Harry Van Dyke (Ontario: Wedge Publishing Foundation, 1989 [1847]). I explore these ideas more fully in the next chapter.

[121] See Kalyvas, "Democracy and Religious Politics." He argues that Catholics did have the option of overturning Belgium's liberal constitutionalism and *chose* not to.

[122] Rawls, *Political Liberalism*, 158–68.

[123] Ibid., 158. These liberal principles "guarantee certain basic political rights and liberties and establish democratic procedures for moderating the political rivalry, and for determining issues of social policy" (163).

[124] Ibid., 159.

the overlapping one because the moral sources for those commitments remain at odds with one another and, Rawls surmises, is eminently liable to devolving into a mere modus vivendi, where the survival of liberal government hangs on the "happenstance" of how social groups are balanced against one another. Stopping short with a constitutional consensus leaves us without the moral and political resources necessary to deal justly with the sorts of problems occasioned by the of moral and religious pluralism we see in modern democratic societies.

It seems right, I think, to say that a constitutional consensus is less morally attractive in many respects than Rawls' overlapping one. But as he is so fond of reminding us (usually in the context of acknowledging that even in his more capacious political liberalism non-liberal ways of life will likely do more poorly than liberal ones) there is no social or political order "without loss."[125] And so even if foreclosing the possibility of an overlapping consensus is a genuine loss, it is a loss that ought to be weighed against whatever losses likewise might be incurred by moving (or attempting to move) to that overlapping consensus. Given that we *already* live under something that resembles a constitutional consensus[126] and that there continue to be those whose religious (and other non-public) views play an important, perhaps central, role in political deliberations, the choice to be made is not one simply between a constitutional and overlapping consensus. We must choose instead between accepting and working within a constitutional consensus and attempting *to move toward* an overlapping one.

Now, it might be the case that democracies marked by a constitutional consensus tend to move fairly naturally toward an overlapping one. I noted earlier how Rawls seems to have just this sort of expectation. But given that an important part of the overlapping consensus is the common affirmation of public reason, we would have good reason to expect that those who object to the norms of restraint will not think that there is anything at all natural or necessary about such a norm. The case of post-revolutionary France may once again be instructive here. Though the instability of the French republics no doubt has many causes, counted among them must be the mutual hostility between Catholicism and Republicanism that extended until well after World War II. Whatever the moral faults of French Catholicism (and there were many, to be sure), Republicanism's dogged insistence on *laïcité*, an especially rigid and uncompromising insistence on a public secularism perhaps most clearly embodied in the 1905 Act for the separation of church and state, clearly

---

[125] The idea is, of course, Isaiah Berlin's.
[126] Kurt Baier, "Justice and the Aims of Political Philosophy," *Ethics* 99, no. 4 (1989).

made it more difficult to reconcile the two camps.[127] We need not be alarmists to suppose that a similarly dogged insistence on public reason or deliberative restraint as a means of moving toward an overlapping consensus could have quite the opposite of its intended effect and make things worse rather than better. After all, if our scholars and public intellectuals tell the religious believer who eschews deliberative restraint that she is acting in ways fundamentally at odds with a constitutional democracy's moral premises, she may decide to embrace those norms. Or she may decide otherwise.

Consider our Mennonite Jane again. The restraint proponent (like Rawls) already hopes that her willingness to hold fast to her pacifist commitments – however unreasonable – is a one-off affair and that she could still be politically reasonable in the rest of her political views.[128] But suppose that Jane reflects on the matter and begins to wonder about the wisdom of public reason more generally. If it "misleads" her in matters of war and peace, who is to say that it is any more reliable on a range of other controversial questions? And if her fellow citizens continue to insist that fidelity to public reason is part and parcel of fidelity to democratic ideals, then why not think that she may come to think that much worse of those democratic ideals? Why not suppose that she will come to think it is hardly worth the effort to be reasonable at all? If religious commitments are at loggerheads with what the political order demands, it is possible that citizens will conclude that "Paris is worth a Mass,"[129] but it is also possible – probable, even – that they will not. And that, too, would be a real social and moral loss. Given the importance that religion has in so many people's lives and the reasonably just and stable democratic orders that were and are clearly closer to a constitutional consensus than an overlapping one, it is simply very hard to be persuaded that the calculus comes out in the overlapping consensus's favor.

But even to the degree that such a calculus comes out against the overlapping consensus, we are still left with a fairly perplexing conundrum: in

---

[127] A good biographical example of this might be the path taken by Jacques Maritain, who was associated with the quite anti-republican *Action Française* into the 1920s, in large part, it seems, on account of the perception that republicanism had little room for serious Catholic practice.

[128] He sketches out just such an argument with respect to those opposed to abortion rights. In *Political Liberalism*, he suggested in a footnote (243 fn. 32) that those who argued against a right to an abortion except in cases of rape or incest were therefore necessarily unreasonable on that point. But he hedges the claim by also suggesting that "a comprehensive doctrine is not as such unreasonable because it leads to an unreasonable conclusion in one or even in several cases. It may still be reasonable most of the time." So Jane's Mennonite faith may be reasonable most of the time.

[129] Supposedly said by France's Henry IV in 1593, as he renounced Protestantism in favor of Catholicism as part of a successful effort to win the throne.

what sense can we say that an order animated by a constitutional consensus is politically legitimate? Deliberative restraint is an attempt to circumscribe the range of arguments made in political life as a means to ensuring that political outcomes can be both morally and popularly legitimate. If we chuck aside the obligations to practice deliberative restraint, what is left of that effort? Well, recall again why it is that scholars turned to deliberation in the first place. Moral and religious pluralism made the more comprehensive sorts of justice-claims implausible. No longer could we hope to articulate a set of principles animating our political institutions and realistically hope that all rational adults ever *could* agree. Our pluralism cuts too deeply for that, even among those who seem to be quite reasonable fellow citizens. If that is the right way to think about the origins and contours of deliberative restraint, then what follows from my arguments in the past couple of chapters is that we must merely adjust a bit more extensively our thinking about political legitimacy to take account of the fact that religion's political mobilization does not represent the threat its liberal critics suppose.

First, consider the moral side of political legitimacy. Even though I remain unconvinced by the argument for deliberative restraint, one of its core intuitions remains largely untouched: the respect we owe to one another as persons simply by virtue of personhood does place limits on what we can justifiably propose and do politically. As Larmore argues,[130] it is the respect for persons that lies at the heart of liberal political thought, a respect that requires that we take seriously the claim that others make over their own lives. This means at a minimum that citizens must reflect carefully about the political proposals they make and support and reflect especially on the way in which their fellow citizens might respond to them. The moral critique of the modus vivendi model of democracy holds, then, at least this far: it is not enough that we give others a mere chance to participate in a political process, we must attend to their claims in a way that fulfills what Christopher Eberle (following Darwall) calls "recognition respect": "A citizen has recognition respect for her compatriots just in case she accords due moral weight in her deliberations to the fact that her compatriots are persons."[131] The fact that other citizens are persons means that they are the kinds of beings who care what happens to them and are capable of reflecting on and shaping their desires. In particular, because they have their own desires and can reflect on them, these other citizens are presumptively averse to being coerced, and this means that we have at least a prima facie obligation *not* to do

---

[130] Larmore, "The Moral Basis of Political Liberalism."
[131] Eberle, *Religious Conviction in Liberal Politics*, 85.

so. That obligation can only be overridden provided that we have a sufficiently weighty reason.

Chris Eberle's "ideal of conscientious engagement" suggests that citizens in a constitutional democracy are obligated to "pursue a high degree
of rational justification" for supporting a coercive policy and to "pursue
public justification" for those same policies.[132] In particular, he identifies
six formal constraints on a citizen in a liberal democracy:

(1) She will pursue a high degree of rational justification for the claim that a
favored coercive policy is morally appropriate. (2) She will withhold support
from a given coercive policy if she can't acquire a sufficiently high degree of
rational justification for the claim that the policy is morally appropriate. (3) She
will attempt to communicate to her compatriots her reasons for coercing them.
(4) She will pursue public justification for her favored coercive policies. (5) She
will listen to her compatriots' evaluation of her reasons for her favored coercive
policies with the intention of learning from them about the moral (im)propriety
of those policies. (6) She will not support any policy on the basis of a rationale
that denies the dignity of her compatriots.[133]

What distinguishes Eberle's proposal from the deliberative restraint
claims is that a citizen's decision about whether a particular law is morally appropriate (and thus deserving of his support) does not in the end
rest on the cognitive capabilities or comprehensive views of his fellow
citizens. Though Eberle does think that we owe it to our fellow citizens
not only to explain ourselves but also to try and find plausible arguments
that will persuade them of our position, we are in no way bound by their
views in the process of coming to our own. We should "attempt to provide [other citizens] with reasons they find convincing,"[134] but our pursuit of public justification, such as it is, is not a limiting factor on our own
reflections on whether the law is justified or not. Rather, we can come to
a conclusion about the morality of some coercive act only through doing
our best in employing our cognitive faculties and making our judgment
"from the perspective provided by [our] evidential set."[135] This ideal of
conscientious engagement, Eberle thinks, will not produce consensus,
but "provides citizens with the sort of guidance they need to do their
part in ameliorating the social disharmony generated by the application
of power in a pluralist society."[136]

So in this way of thinking about things, citizens have an obligation to
try and persuade each other of their respective positions and to propose
(or agree to) coercive political acts only provided that they are, as best
can be determined, morally appropriate. And as I have tried to show

---

[132] Ibid., 104–5.   [133] Ibid., 104–5.   [134] Ibid., 99.
[135] Ibid., 88.   [136] Ibid., 106.

over the past couple of chapters, determining what is morally appropriate might indeed include making recourse to religiously based claims. But Eberle's conscientious engagement does not mean to portend a kind of free-for-all, leaving citizens unencumbered morally and free to simply do as they wish politically. Citizens cannot just, willy-nilly, translate the claims of scripture or tradition, for example, into policy proposals. While there is no obligation per se to *prioritize* non-religious reasons, there is no sense that they are to be ignored; instead religious believers ought to consider non-religious evidence in addition to whatever religious views they find convincing.[137] Nor does conscientious engagement allow citizens to employ reasons or seek ends that deny the basic liberties or dignity of other citizens.[138] To do that would clearly run afoul of the "recognition respect" we owe one another.

Still, even if we allow that religious reasons can contribute constructively to reflections on what is morally appropriate for a liberal democratic government to do (no doubt still a controversial claim for many readers), we still must attend to the other element of political legitimacy and consider how religion's employment in political deliberations can help make a democratic order legitimate in the popular sense as well. For inasmuch as the evidence I have presented above regarding the European integrationist parties cuts against the widely held supposition that religion's political mobilization tends (almost inevitably) to civic strife, the very fact that such a supposition *is* so widely held means that believers who employ their religious views politically will quite plausibly do exactly what the restraint norm's proponents predict: incite serious political discord. That in itself is certainly not dispositive in thinking about our moral obligations, as simple discord is part and parcel of any recognizable democratic politics. But to the degree that the employment of religious claims makes some reasonable citizens doubt as a practical matter the particular government's legitimacy, things still do begin to tell against the use of those kinds of reasons.

Consider the worry – reflected in contemporary jeremiads warning of a looming theocracy in the US – that having citizens employing religious views politically is but a short step from having the state throw its weight behind those views themselves. Eberle suggests that citizens employing religious reasons should not be thought to pose much of a threat to pluralism or religious liberty more specifically because they, in fact, benefit from those conditions. Since religious vitality seems to depend in part on having "out-groups" against which a faith can be defined and since it

---

[137] Ibid., 327.
[138] Ibid., 105; Weithman, *Religion and the Obligations of Citizenship*, 137.

seems clear (in comparing the United States and Europe) that a robust religious liberty is empirically good for religion, he suggests that "politically active religious citizens … have a vested interest in refusing coercively to impose their favored religious orthodoxy on a diverse population."[139] But self-interest seems an awfully thin reed on which to hang something so important as religious liberty. Individuals often act against their interest, whether through ignorance, deception, or just plain stupidity. And those who may encourage religious political mobilization may not, after all, actually care that much about religious vitality per se, but instead care only about their own political success. Whatever the empirical truth about the positive effects of religious liberty, it is nonetheless the case that religious believers do often think that things would be better off if everyone were of their faith. (It would be a strange faith indeed that on the one hand claimed that God had commanded all human beings to worship in a certain way and to believe certain things and on the other hand sought to maintain a kind of social pluralism in order to remain "vital.") Non-believers might have little principled reason to believe the religious believers' claims about their support of religious liberty and would therefore quite plausibly view the believers' political proposals with some suspicion, especially if they are supported by religious reasons or affect issues dealing with religion.

The point here is simply this: even if citizens are doing their level best to develop and support morally appropriate political proposals, in a context where the merest hint of religion can make things highly "controversial," religious believers who consult and employ their religious beliefs when deliberating about such proposals risk significantly alienating their fellow citizens simply on account of that religious "taint." Because some citizens do endorse the norms of deliberative restraint and the issues to which religion seems to speak are our most highly contested, the employment of such claims seems likely to provoke a great deal of disagreement and even resentment. Reassuring other citizens that religiously rooted claims are not inklings of theocracy requires more than sociological assurances. It requires, I think, the institutionalization of precisely what the argument for deliberative restraint counsels against, religiously rooted political mobilization and engagement.

As I noted earlier, the thing that seems most clearly to divide my European cases into successful and unsuccessful ones (Germany being sort of in-between) is the degree to which the contending parties could find ways to bridge their differences, at least enough to sustain and protect a common constitutional framework. Part of the reason the successful

---

[139] Eberle, *Religious Conviction in Liberal Politics*, 27.

ones could do this was simply circumstantial: the extant political leadership made a decision to work within rather than against the existing political order.[140] But they were also successful, as Kalyvas points out, because the different sides *believed* that their opponents were committed to the preservation of that order.[141] Belgium is a good example of this phenomenon. Given the Catholic Church's rather unfavorable view of liberal constitutionalism (to say nothing of constitutional democracy), Belgium's liberals and socialists would have good reason to be suspicious of the Catholic Party's intent leading up to the 1884 election. Indeed, it would have been entirely reasonable for them to think the new party would seek to overturn the constitutional order and make Belgium a confessional state. And armed with such reasonable suspicions, it would have been not at all unwarranted to consider finding ways of excluding the Catholic Party from even participating in the electoral process. But they declined to do so, and they found the Catholic Party's assurances that they would not overturn the constitutional order credible precisely because the party and the Catholic hierarchy that stood with it demonstrated its control over a large swathe of the Catholic subculture by quashing the prospects of those who *did* want to overturn the political order. That is, Belgium's liberal constitutionalism survived the religious political mobilization of the 1870s and 1880s because that mobilization was institutionalized in and managed by political organizations committed to working within the constitutional order.

When thinking about how religious political mobilization might impact the popular side of political legitimacy – citizens' subjective sense of how much they think the existing political order is "theirs" – the great worry has to be that the religious groups' opponents will think their participation so much outside the boundaries of normal, legitimate democratic politics that they will come to see the mobilization not just as a threat to their preferred policy outcomes but as a threat to the democratic polity itself. While the evidence I have marshaled above certainly does not make such concerns entirely out of place, it just as certainly might make them a great deal less salient. Though of course groups can and do participate in deliberative and electoral institutions with an eye toward destroying them (Germany's National Socialists are the obvious example), a striking feature of my successful cases is how the religious groups' political opponents came to accept the legitimacy of those groups (and their political mobilization) in large part, it seems, because their political representatives proved reliable, if often despised, competitors and partners. Austria's socialists helped precipitate, in some sense, the country's political failures

---

[140] See Bermeo, *Ordinary People in Extraordinary Times.*
[141] Kalyvas, "Commitment Problems in Emerging Democracies."

when the persistently refused to cooperate with the quickly radicalizing Christian Socials. They (rightly) perceived that their opponents were not actually all that interested in forming a common front against German and Italian fascism, but instead were more interested in avoiding some responsibility for the country's deteriorating economic and political situation. The Christian Socials had proven themselves – in part because of their odd identity combining class, region, and religion – unreliable partners, and the socialists thought that colluding with them would turn out worse than the likely alternatives.

Religious political mobilization that institutionalizes itself in institutions like parties can go some distance toward mitigating those concerns, though it cannot entirely alleviate them. The religious parties created in Belgium, the Netherlands, and even Germany in the 1870s and 1880s did just that, showing themselves responsible and shoring up the existing political order when their absence (exemplified by the case of France) might have led at least portions of their communities into anti-systemic attitudes and groups. By bringing the religious impulse into a laicized (though not secularized, it is important to note) political organization, the parties and movements in parts of nineteenth- and twentieth-century Europe constructed political outcomes that defy the conventional wisdom about religion's political participation and demand a reconsideration of that conventional view's underlying rationale.[142]

Religion can be especially problematic politically. Robert Audi may exaggerate when he makes religion's political mobilization out to be little more than "a clash of Gods" that can easily "lead to destruction and death,"[143] but neither is he entirely wrong. The historical cases above, however, show that stable democratic regimes can be constructed and maintained even under very trying circumstances in the context of powerful religious political movements. So just as Rawls (and many other political theorists) revised what they took to be reasonable political views when faced with the "fact of reasonable pluralism," so too ought we to revise our conceptions regarding the norms of public deliberation and political legitimacy once we recognize that religion's participation in democratic politics does not inevitably issue in civil strife or political failure.[144] Once we recognize, that is, that if some of our fellow citizens hold religious views that have public import, rather than thinking those views

---

[142] In this sense, at least, Europe's religious parties are quite similar to their socialist competitors. See Przeworski and Sprague, *Paper Stones*.

[143] Audi, *Religious Commitment and Secular Reason*, 13.

[144] Rawls revised and relaxed his initial views on public reason as a result of realizing that they would, it seems, rule out of bounds abolitionist and civil rights activists, both of whom employed religious reasons centrally in their movements. See Rawls, *Political*

are a priori out of bounds simply because they are religious, we would do well to encourage their engagement within the extant institutions of deliberation and electoral contestation. Perhaps we should acknowledge the "fact of reasonable integrationism" and reconfigure our theorizing therein.

It would be foolish to deny that a democratic politics so conceived will be at times more contentious than the vision laid out for the overlapping consensus, or that allowing religion in will not thin out what we are able to hold in common politically. It is likely that the legitimacy that emerges from even just relaxing the norms of deliberative restraint along the lines of Eberle's conscientious engagement will look insufficient for its proponents. But to conclude this overly long chapter, it is probably worth asking why we should be so worried about falling short in this way. I have already acknowledged that accepting something like a constitutional consensus means accepting a political order that is, perhaps, morally less satisfying than one organized around an overlapping consensus. But given that the former looks quite capable of remaining stable (in the ordinary sense of the word) and protecting in the main the rights and liberties associated with constitutional democracies, I judged that the trade-off was worth making, especially since it seems to me that attempting to move toward the overlapping consensus itself has some significant moral costs and needlessly alienates citizens whose only fault is taking their faith more seriously than many liberal theorists think reasonable.

As I have sketched things out here, it might seem as though my disagreements with deliberative restraint remain a matter of degree, an artifact of differing judgments regarding what we might plausibly expect empirically when religion gets into politics. And in some sense, that is precisely true. The conventional view among liberal theorists is that religion's political mobilization portends political disaster: bad policy outcomes, heightened civic strife, even damage to political liberties. I am a good deal more sanguine (though without, hopefully, being naïve), but I think the differences I have explored over the past three chapters emerge from a deeper disagreement and that is over what we might reasonably expect regarding pluralist democracies' political legitimacy and, indeed, over the character of the democratic order itself.

Deliberative accounts of democracy appeal to many scholars, as I have noted before, not least because they make sense of what those scholars take to be an intuitively central feature of democratic politics, its moral connection to the idea of consensus. Rawls repeatedly makes his political liberalism out to be the best way to understand how the democratic functions as a "fair system of social cooperation," a term of art meant to illuminate how at its moral core democracy eschews coercion and points toward consensus as perhaps its most essential feature.[145] Deliberation will not actually produce consensus and even the most optimistic of its proponents do not expect it to, but its moral attractiveness hinges on the idea that its principles express the hope for a political world where "each, while uniting himself with all, may still obey himself alone and remain as free as before."[146] And truth be told, if such a thing *were* possible, it would be quite morally attractive. If it were possible.

But that really is quite the puzzle here. Since even deliberation's proponents recognize, even build upon, the idea that moral and religious pluralism are ineliminable in free societies and that real, substantive consensus is impossible, it remains quite unclear why we should ascribe to democratic societies a moral ideal that is then in the first instance eschewed. A fairer reading of modern democratic orders would seem to suggest that they are a messier and less philosophically coherent mix of cooperation and competition, as partisans both cooperate in the sense of operating within the context of a common political framework *and* compete in trying to impose not just particular policy prescriptions (by winning elections, mostly) but also a broader understanding of the framework itself. Rather than thinking that modern democracies are essentially cooperative, it seems more reasonable to recognize that they reflect how we are fundamentally and irredeemably divided on what the terms of that "consensus" should be. Democratic political life does mean cooperation in the sense of agreeing to common procedures for electing officials, evaluating the constitutional propriety of particular laws, and so on. But to the degree that citizens disagree over the particulars of those common procedures – what should be the scope for the Supreme Court's review of Congressional acts; how to draw the line between church and state; what is the proper extent of property rights? – then democratic politics reveals itself to be deeply, ineliminably, conflictual.

If democratic politics really is ineliminably conflictual, then it is near impossible, to my mind, to understand why norms of deliberative restraint, rooted as they are in a moral ideal of consensus, should govern that same political order. This does not mean that politics is simply about "interests and power" – Eberle's reflections on what we owe one another as persons would seem to cut against that claim – but it does mean our political theories cannot simply ignore their reality. And that suggests the best we

---

Liberalism, 249–52. He suggests that the abolitionists (and civil rights protesters) did not violate the essence of public reason though they did appeal to comprehensive, and religious, views in making their cases.

[145] See ibid., 15–22. For a rather tart critique of deliberation precisely along these lines, see Shapiro, "Enough of Deliberation."

[146] The quotation, of course, is from Rousseau's *The Social Contract*.

can hope for – perhaps the best we *should* hope for – is something a good deal less ambitious than what deliberation's proponents offer, something like a constitutional, rather than an overlapping, consensus. Perhaps the most we should be hoping for is a constitutional regime where citizens have good reasons (religious, philosophical, and otherwise) for endorsing the main outlines of the regime and agree at least that their disputes over its particulars ought to be decided within the contours of a constitutional order. In this sort of regime, legitimacy will come not so much out of a political order's reliance on a set of principles that all (or most) can affirm on the basis of a common set of reasons. Instead, citizens will come to see a democratic order as legitimate, and thus morally obliging, out of a mix of claims that include whether that order fits reasonably well with citizens' basic moral ideals, whether it protects their basic interests, and whether it gives fair play to their expressed policy outcomes.[147]

No doubt such a political order would be deeply unsatisfying to deliberation's proponents. It gives too much play to our pluralisms and largely eschews the "hope" that political life can be organized solely on a cooperative basis (even among people of good will). The argument for deliberative restraint seems premised on the view that if we wish to live together with one another in a pluralistic political community of free and equal citizens, we will be (or become) the sorts of people who reconfigure our views according to the politically reasonable needs of that political community. For many citizens – perhaps most – this is not an unreasonable argument. But for some, it is tantamount to treason, and religious treason at that, and unless the partisans of deliberative restraint can make more compelling the claim that an overlapping consensus is really as necessary for political legitimacy and stability as they make it out to be, it seems to me that we are better off dispensing with its inflated hopes and fears. Instead, we should accept that free societies are marked by such deep moral and religious distinctiveness whatever attraction the moral ideal of consensus might have for us, it is little more than a pipe dream and one whose claims can work to our political disadvantage. Religion need not be democracy's enemy, and by allowing religious citizens to participate more or less on their own terms in the political processes of electoral and deliberative contestation, we can help make sure it does not become such, making our democracies fair, stable, and, ultimately, legitimate.

[147] I have in mind something akin to the ideas advanced in George Klosko, *Political Obligations* (Oxford: Oxford University Press, 2005).

5   Religion and the problem of political autonomy

In the previous three chapters, I argued that the liberal concern regarding religion's political engagement and its effects on political legitimacy were overdrawn and that religious political mobilization could actually serve to buttress, not undermine, pluralist democracies. Democratic political legitimacy cannot depend on deliberative restraint, since restraint's moral claims are both unpersuasive on their own terms and dependent on unsustainable empirical claims. Key to my argument was my comparison of how some European religious political movements affected their respective countries' democratic prospects in the late nineteenth and early twentieth centuries. One way in which the more democratically beneficial movements in Germany, Belgium, and the Netherlands resembled one another was their penchant for constructing networks of affiliated churches, newspapers, trade unions, schools, and the like, creating "alternative civil societies"[1] that functioned as a strategy of "subcultural encapsulation."[2] This strategy was meant to protect against what they saw as the corrosive acids of modernity and to organize their social and cultural lives in ways reflective of what they thought their particular faith demanded. They sought to create, and largely succeeded, a subcultural order "integrated" around their faith.

What emerged in these cases were democratic societies marked by "segmented pluralism,"[3] where the various groups of citizens united around a powerful attachment to what Rawls might call "comprehensive doctrines" were allowed the opportunity to create their own, similarly

---

[1] The phrase is from Bermeo and Nord, eds., *Civil Society before Democracy.*

[2] See Smith and Emerson, *American Evangelicalism.* Here, the phrase is used to describe American evangelicals and their interestingly similar efforts to embed themselves in networks of churches, schools, media, and the like.

[3] For a political theorist's defense of this sort structural pluralism, see Bader, "Religious Diversity and Democratic Institutional Pluralism." We often take these sorts of structures to be at odds with the more freewheeling pluralism evident in contemporary American society, but that was not always the case. See Alan Ehrenhalt, *The Lost City: Discovering the Forgotten Virtues of Community in the Chicago of the 1950s* (New York: Basic Books, 1995).

organized, networks, the most developed of which was the Dutch pillarization. This had, I have suggested, some quite constructive political consequences, as it allowed elites in sharply divided societies to bargain effectively and marginalize those who might undermine the developing liberal and democratic political settlements. Hence, the argument that religion's political mobilization may benefit pluralist democracies' legitimacy depends in some measure on religious communities' capacity and willingness to pursue similar sorts of efforts. Otherwise, their fellow citizens might indeed harbor enough doubts regarding the believers' political aims to make religion's political employment destabilizing and thus delegitimizing.

Ironically enough, proponents of the liberal consensus on religion suggest that it is religion's tendency toward this sort of insularity that makes it politically problematic beyond the question of political legitimacy. Democracies require – as with any sort of regime – that its citizens possess a set of capacities, habits, and character traits in order for it to persist and thrive. The very thing that makes integrationist religious believers plausible as partners in the construction of stable, legitimate pluralist democracies also has the effect, the consensus contends, of undermining religious believers' capacity to acquire and exercise the civic virtues necessary for successful democratic politics. And so scholars within the consensus have argued much of late that liberal democratic states are justified, even obligated, to be engaged in systematic programs of what we can generically term "civic education" as a means of cultivating these virtues in their citizens, even if doing so means interposing in religious communities and attempting to shape their constitutive beliefs. This could include straightforward educational programs aimed at interrupting or reshaping the transmission of religious doctrines and practices or legal and fiscal restrictions or inducements that make the construction of certain kinds of religious institutions difficult or impossible. In short, what we can call the argument from civic virtue claims that because democratic polities depend in large measure on their citizens' beliefs, habits, and practices, those polities may properly use their limited coercive powers to shape those beliefs, habits, and practices, even if such shaping runs up against sincere religious liberty claims.

I examine this argument over the course of the next two chapters, critiquing it in regard to what liberal theorists deem the two most important political virtues, toleration and autonomy. I concede that there is good reason for liberal theorists to be concerned with integrationists (and, by extension, religious believers engaged in politics on the basis of their faith more generally), but it is too much to say that they simply make for bad citizens. Rather, the consensus claims in favor of civic virtue are themselves much too broadly argued and miss the ways in which religion can (though it certainly does not always) cultivate characteristics compatible with and even supportive of democratic politics. In this chapter, I defend integrationists against the charge that they lack the capacity to be properly autonomous and in the next I defend them against the idea that they are inevitably intolerant and contribute to a politics of oppression. In both cases, I show not only how the consensus's arguments are deficient but how the integrationists escape the indictments against them in large part *because* of their integrationism rather than in spite of it.

Liberalism and the virtues

Over the past decade, liberal theorists have evinced a strikingly renewed interest in the character and qualities of good citizens, or what they term civic virtue.[4] Though it is true that even classical liberal theorists like Locke, Kant, and Mill all emphasized the importance of virtue,[5] liberals have historically shied away from talking too much about the qualities and characteristics that individuals *ought* to possess. Virtue-talk was for liberalism's opponents, those who thought – with Aristotle – that political authority ought to have as a primary purpose the shaping and

---

[4] See, just for starters, Mehdi Aminrazavi and David Ambuel, *Philosophy, Religion, and the Question of Intolerance* (Albany: State University of New York Press, 1997); Ronald Beiner, ed., *Theorizing Citizenship* (Albany: State University of New York Press, 1995); Peter Berkowitz, *Virtue and the Making of Modern Liberalism* (Princeton, NJ: Princeton University Press, 1999); Walter Berns, *Making Patriots* (Chicago: University of Chicago Press, 2001); Harry Brighouse, "Civic Education and Liberal Legitimacy," *Ethics* 108, no. 4 (1998); Shelley Burtt, "The Politics of Virtue Today: A Critique and a Proposal," *American Political Science Review* 87, no. 2 (1993); Callan, *Creating Citizens*; Eamonn Callan, "Discrimination and Religious Schooling," in *Citizenship in Diverse Societies*, ed. Will Kymlicka and Wayne Norman (New York: Oxford University Press, 2000); John William Chapman and William A. Galston, eds., *Virtue* (New York: New York University Press, 1992); Richard Dagger, *Civic Virtues: Rights, Citizenship, and Republican Liberalism* (New York: Oxford University Press, 1997); Francis Fukuyama, *Trust: Social Virtues and the Creation of Prosperity* (New York: Free Press, 1995); William A. Galston, "Liberal Virtues," *American Political Science Review* 82, no. 4 (1988); Mary Ann Glendon and David Blankenhorn, *Seedbeds of Virtue: Sources of Competence, Character, and Citizenship* (Lanham, MD: Madison Books, 1995); David Heyd, ed., *Toleration: An Elusive Virtue* (Princeton, NJ: Princeton University Press, 1996); Loren Lomasky, "Toward a Liberal Theory of Vice (and Virtue)," in *Civil Society, Democracy and Civic Renewal*, ed. Robert K. Fullinwinder (Lanham, MD: Rowman & Littlefield, 1999); Stephen Macedo, "Charting Liberal Virtues," in *Virtue*, ed. Chapman and Galston; Stephen Macedo, *Liberal Virtues* (Oxford: Clarendon Press, 1990); Stephen Macedo and Yael Tamir, eds., *Moral and Political Education: Nomos XLIII* (New York: New York University Press, 2002); Susan Mendus, ed., *Justifying Toleration: Conceptual and Historical Perspectives* (New York: Cambridge University Press, 1988); Susan Mendus, *Toleration and the Limits of Liberalism* (Atlantic Highlands, NJ: Humanities Press International, 1989).
[5] See Berkowitz, *Virtue and the Making of Modern Liberalism*.

improving of citizens' moral lives. Liberalism was at least partly born of the conviction that, even if the standards of human excellence could be demonstrated, our perpetual (and sometimes reasonable) disagreement about those standards was too inflammatory and dangerous to resolve or enforce politically. One need not be a moral skeptic to think that societies characterized by wide moral and religious pluralism invite much danger in promoting a particular view of the good life to the exclusion of others.

In spite of this conviction, many have concluded that liberalism can be no more indifferent to citizens' character and capacities than its rivals. Under conditions of pluralism and social conflict, individuals' ability to cooperate with others (even just politically) with whom they deeply disagree demands more than just grudging forbearance or a barely repressed antipathy. It demands real virtue.[6] Indeed, to the degree that any liberal government is *limited* government, it will, perhaps, rely *even more* on citizens' character and habits than its competitors.[7] Finally, to the degree that the acquisition and exercise of any particular capacities are a necessary component of human flourishing, liberal democratic states will inevitably attend to them. They could no more ignore them than they could their citizens' physical security and still make a plausible claim to govern.

Besides the general virtues necessary for any political regime (loyalty, courage, law-abidingness) and those necessary for a liberal market society (entrepreneurship, adaptability, work ethic), a successful liberal politics, William Galston suggests, carries its own particular laundry list of political virtues: the ability to respect the rights of others, discernment

---

[6] Even grudging forbearance can be quite difficult and its achievement real virtue. See Judith Shklar, *Ordinary Vices* (Cambridge, MA: Harvard University Press, 1984).

[7] There is a bit of incongruity, perhaps, in contemporary liberals' appropriation of the idea of virtue. Classical discussions of virtue – and I have mainly Aristotle in mind here – situated the discussion of the virtues within the context of a larger teleological set of claims about the human good. The virtues were necessary in order to live the good life (though they were good in their own right as well). Among most contemporary theorists, the notion of a more or less unified and universal view of the human good has little appeal. Even those who follow Mill in extolling the importance of individuality or what I call below comprehensive autonomy are extolling a capacity that can – indeed, will – be put to various and competing ends. See Joseph Raz, *The Morality of Freedom* (New York: Oxford University Press, 1986). It may therefore be more accurate philosophically to talk in these contexts about *capacities* or *attributes* that make for good citizens (and good human beings) rather than talking about the virtues. Nonetheless, virtue-talk is thoroughly embedded in our theoretical discourse, and avoiding the term might muddy the discussion rather than clarify it. So I will use the term virtue here (and in the next chapter), though I will do it with a special eye toward individual capacities as they relate especially to a properly ordered democratic political life, though the question of the good life for humans more generally will not, as I note below, be irrelevant.

in political choice, moderation in political demands, and a commitment to public discourse.[8] Thomas Spragens similarly argues that what he calls "civic liberalism" requires that citizens be, among other things, independent, tolerant, deliberative, and self-restrained.[9] Stephen Macedo in turn emphasizes the need for tolerance, impartiality, "broad sympathies," and self-restraint.[10] Most of these are, at first glance, innocuous and uncontroversial. That is not true, ironically, for a virtue or capacity central to liberal political thought: autonomy. (It is even less true for toleration, which I take up in the following chapter.)

For civic republicans, autonomy stands coextensive with the idea of being actively engaged in collective self-government, or "sharing in self-rule."[11] Strong individualists like Mill argue that autonomy requires a studied dissociation from society's conventional opinions and a cultivated independence that promotes, even celebrates, distinctiveness and personal self-rule.[12] In a *Theory of Justice*, Rawls suggests that the principles of justice appropriate to a constitutional democracy carry with them a Kantian view of autonomy, namely "that a person is acting autonomously when the principles of his action are chosen by him as the most adequate possible expression of his nature as a free and equal rational being."[13] In particular, we should think of ourselves as deliberating and acting *autonomously* to the degree that we are doing so as if we ourselves were within the Original Position, fully ensconced behind a "veil of ignorance."[14]

Regardless of the differences among theorists concerning autonomy's precise definition, they are largely unified in the conviction that religion is mostly bad for its cultivation and exercise, a point often shared by liberalism's religious critics.[15] In modern pluralist societies, the maintenance and transmission of religious views may be difficult, given modernity's

---

[8] Galston, "Liberal Virtues," 224–27.

[9] Thomas A. Spragens, *Civic Liberalism: Reflections on Our Democratic Ideals* (Lanham, MD: Rowman & Littlefield, 1999), 214–30.

[10] Macedo, *Liberal Virtues*, 265–72.

[11] Sandel, *Democracy's Discontent: America in Search of a Public Philosophy*, 5. See also J.G.A. Pocock, *The Machiavellian Moment: Florentine Political Thought and the Atlantic Republican Tradition* (Princeton, NJ: Princeton University Press, 1975). For an attempt to marry liberalism and republicanism precisely on the point of autonomy, see Dagger, *Civic Virtues*.

[12] John Stuart Mill, *On Liberty, with the Subjection of Women and Chapters on Socialism*, ed. Stefan Collini (Cambridge and New York: Cambridge University Press, 1989); see especially chapter 3. For contemporary defenses of autonomy along the same lines, see Emily R. Gill, *Becoming Free: Autonomy and Diversity in the Liberal Polity* (Lawrence: University Press of Kansas, 2001); Raz, *The Morality of Freedom*.

[13] Rawls, *A Theory of Justice*, 222.

[14] For the relevant descriptions of the original position, see Sections 4 and 20–30 of Rawls' *A Theory of Justice*.

[15] See, for instance, Kraynak, *Christian Faith and Modern Democracy*.

seeming tendency toward forms of belief that, while not necessarily skeptical, are certainly more humble epistemologically. It looks quite unreasonable for any reflective believer (or non-believer, for that matter) to suggest that others' refusal to share his beliefs stems from mere cupidity or a willful refusal to acknowledge incontrovertible evidence.[16] Though, as I argue below, reasonable religious pluralism does not commit us to religious skepticism, it certainly does press in that direction. More to the point, modernity encourages – some might say demands – distinctly non-integrationist living and thinking. In chapter 1, I argued that Casanova's "public religion" was too constrained in its appreciation of religion's possibilities in the modern world. The power of his analysis, however, lies in its consonance with much of the structure of modern life. Very few integrationists press for a return to the pre-modern world of an organically conjoined life under religious tutelage. The (perhaps mythical) world of medieval Christendom is gone forever and any way of life that wants something more than to simply withdraw (Amish-like) must somehow make its peace with a world in which religious belief has become "optional," and its institutions and practices entreat us to "privatize" faith, sometimes in quite radical ways.[17] The upshot here is that being an integrationist, while still possible, is tough in the modern world; to borrow an image from Galston, trying to live an integrated life of any sort, never mind one oriented around a religious faith, is not unlike trying to swim upstream in a quick-flowing river.[18] It is possible, but difficult, and clearly requires all sorts of supportive institutions and strategies, ones that are specifically fitted to the modern world. The modern integrationist, as opposed to his medieval forebear, must figure out how to live as an integrationist and sustain that sort of community in an age where religion no longer plays an axiological political role.

This is, as I have described previously, precisely what Europe's religious integrationists attempted to do, building networks of schools, newspapers, trade unions, social clubs, and political parties organized around

---

[16] See the arguments in Habermas, "A Conversation about God and the World"; Habermas, "On the Relations between the Secular Liberal State and Religion"; Habermas, "Religion in the Public Sphere."

[17] Cf. the quite brilliant analysis in Taylor, *A Secular Age*, where he traces out how it came to be that the West shifted from a society in which religious unbelief was practically unknown to one in which belief was optional and even difficult. Taylor's story has any number of pathways, but among them is the often unintended psychological effects of institutional separation whereby different institutional elements asserted their independence and created expectations that their spheres of activity – intellectual life, the economy, politics, and so on – were themselves to be free of religious "taint" as well.

[18] He uses the image to good effect in William A. Galston, *Liberal Purposes: Goods, Virtues, and Diversity in the Liberal State* (Cambridge: Cambridge University Press, 1991).

and in defense of the faith.[19] These subcultural communities were not just a reflection of the integrationists' theological claims, though they were that.[20] More importantly for our purposes in this chapter, these strategies were also concerted attempts to forestall what these believers perceived to be the corrosive acids of modernity, in particular the modern tendency to valorize, maybe even idolize, the sort of Cartesian mode of moral and practical reflection that seeks to untether itself from any sort of historical, social, or religious contexts. In its stead, integrationists hoped that their encapsulation strategy would help nurture individuals for whom their religious commitments remain immune, in a sense, from the critical eye. That is, religious integrationists were (and are) deeply concerned that modern life had the effect of detaching individuals from the faith, if not in its entirety, at least in its comprehensiveness. Modernity encourages, as Taylor describes it, the development of a "buffered self," where we tend to try and stand apart from any of our particular commitments, even quite strongly held ones, and to be capable of choosing critically among the available options. The integrationists worked hard to make that mode of thinking unlikely, if not simply unavailable, to their communities, hoping instead that the faith, rather than the "buffered self," would remain undetached and at the center of everything else.

So it is easy to see why liberals concerned with autonomy might worry about integrationists, given that their social institutions are designed precisely to interfere with the cultivation of this sort of "choosing" self, at least with respect to the faith. Consider, for example, the quite strong views taken by a number of scholars about a couple of relevant court decisions. In *Wisconsin* v. *Yoder* and *Mozert* v. *Hawkins County Board of Education*,[21] religious parents (Old Order Amish in the former and fundamentalist Protestants in the latter) sought to have their children excused from general educational requirements on the basis of a conflicting

---

[19] Dobbelaere, "The Rationale of Pillarization." Steve Bruce, thoroughly convinced of the secularization thesis in all its aspects, suggests that religion could still survive, but only, he says, in a "ghetto." See Bruce, *Conservative Protestant Politics*.

[20] Cf. Pope Leo XIII's encyclical *Rerum Novarum* (1891), where he outlined the beginnings of modern Catholic social thought, a tradition perhaps marked above all by the persistent claim that Catholics had a responsibility grounded in the faith to build distinctively Catholic institutions – schools, trade unions, etc. – that would both reflect Church teachings and nurture the faith.

[21] 406 US 205 (1972) and 827 F.2d 1058 (6th Cir. 1987), respectively. The Amish parents wished to pull their children out of school after the eighth grade and integrate them into their farming communities. The Protestant parents were requesting that their children be excused from using an elementary school reader because they believed it to be detrimental to their efforts to pass along their faith to their children. The Supreme Court ruled for the Amish and the appeals court ruled against the Protestants.

religious obligation.[22] The concern in both cases was that unless their children were exempted from certain requirements (attending high school and using an elementary school reader, respectively), the parents believed that their children would be corrupted and lured away from the faith. The state ought not, their arguments went, engage in educational practices that tended to separate children from their parents' faith, even if those practices amounted to simply being exposed to other ways of life as a means of encouraging proper toleration.[23] The parents believed that there simply should not be some sphere of life autonomous from religious faith, and even the attempt to create such an autonomous space, or expose children to it, would be problematic, if not outright sinful. These sorts of integrationists, the consensus quite plausibly argues, are not conducive to the acquisition of autonomy, however you might define it.[24]

But if these integrationists are worrisome, much more so should be our European integrationists. Unlike the two American cases, the European integrationist challenge was both broader and deeper. The former more or less wanted to be left alone, especially with respect to the Amish. They were looking for exemptions from generally applicable laws, not organizing to change the laws themselves. Just as importantly, the Europeans' integrationism challenged the liberal consensus beyond just the question of formal education; they pursued strategies meant to affect all the spheres of social life. Schools are, of course, quite important when thinking about the question of autonomy (and toleration, for that matter), as they are above all else an effort on the part of the state to shape good citizens. But most of us are as deeply affected by the religious institutions we belong to (or do not), by the families into which we are born or adopted, by the neighborhoods where we live as we are by the schools we attend.[25] If we want to understand whether religious integrationism runs counter to the demands of civic virtue, we need to do much more than make an

---

[22] For the Amish, the parents wished to not send their children to public high schools, believing that exposure to that curriculum and environment would make it impossible for their children to embrace the Amish way of life. The *Mozert* parents wanted the school district to allow their elementary age children to opt out of a required reading program because, they believed, the nature of that reading program tended toward a kind of religious pluralism – or the view that no religion was necessarily any better than another.

[23] For a sympathetic reconstruction, see John Tomasi, "Civic Education and Ethical Subservience: From *Mozert* to *Santa Fe* and Beyond," in *Moral and Political Education*, ed. Macedo and Tamir.

[24] Cf. Gutmann, "Civic Education and Social Diversity"; Macedo, "Liberal Civic Education and Religious Fundamentalism."

[25] For evidence that it is *religious commitment* rather than level of education that is more likely to make Americans think it important to do something about poverty see Timothy T. Clydesdale, "Toward Understanding the Role of Bible Beliefs and Higher Education

argument about what sorts of exceptions might be appropriate vis-à-vis public education. We can also attend to the claims the religious integrationist makes across the institutions of civil and political society. We can, we might say, try and get an integrated view of the integrationist claim.

I consider here in this chapter whether religion and liberal autonomy are as much at odds as the theoretical tradition suggests by looking at the relationship between integrationism and the best understanding of autonomy. If it turns out that integrationism is compatible with (or even productive of) the acquisition of autonomy, liberal theorists might then have good reason to be less concerned about the specter of the religious conservative who "haunts liberalism today."[26] Alternatively, if religious integrationism produces lives overwhelmed with dependence, coercion, and domination, then liberals might have good reason to use the state to make those lives less available.[27] Below, I consider what relationship integrationism might have with autonomy, both as an aspect of human flourishing and, more narrowly, as an aspect of a reasonable democratic citizenship. I conclude that religious integrationism will not produce legions of Millian individualists, each celebrating their own eccentric, autonomous lives. But it will produce individuals with enough autonomy to make their lives go well (and, depending on one's perspective on these things, perhaps better than that). It will also go some ways toward helping make individuals politically autonomous, ironically enough, by embedding those individuals within institutions that, though thoroughly drenched in religious commitment, nonetheless engage politics something distinctive, a semi-separate "sphere," if you will. The upshot is that while liberals might have little reason to *celebrate* the emergence of a constitutionalist religious integrationism, neither should they have reason to despair, or have reason to support political efforts to interfere with its development.

Religious integrationism and personal autonomy

As I noted above, liberals have been generally reluctant to talk too much about virtue, in large part because they are convinced that government's legitimate roles do not include the cultivation and promotion of one

---

in American Attitudes toward Eradicating Poverty," *Journal for the Scientific Study of Religion* 38, no. 1 (1999).

[26] Spinner-Halev, *Surviving Diversity: Religion and Democratic Citizenship*, 24.

[27] As Stephen Macedo puts it in his distinctly clarifying style, "We [liberals] should not be concerned to make it equally easy for Fundamentalist Protestants and modernist Protestants to pass along their beliefs to their children" (Macedo, "Transformative Constitutionalism," 59.)

particular view of the good life. But liberalism cannot, it turns out, be wholly indifferent to the human good. In particular, it seems clear that any recognizably liberal government depends upon its citizens possessing at least autonomy's minimal requisites, what I call here "independence." Ignoring this basic element of human flourishing would put liberalism at risk of undermining a key component of its own rationale, its claim to connecting political legitimacy to consent. I argue below, though, that the same cannot be said of what we can call "comprehensive autonomy," an autonomy characterized by the maximization of personal choice, something akin to what Mill had in mind in *On Liberty*. Unlike independence, comprehensive autonomy is not necessary either for human flourishing or for the reasonable exercise of liberal democratic citizenship, and since its acquisition cannot then be thought a basic interest that all people possess and that the state is committed to protecting, it cannot serve as a basis for justifying the politically coercive reshaping of religious communities. Since integrationism can be productive of autonomy as independence, the fact that it is not likely to produce comprehensively autonomous people is not a reason to think integrationism incompatible with liberal autonomy, nor can it justify political intervention to secure the same.

As I discussed earlier at some length, liberalism is, among other things, a theory about legitimate government. In particular, it is a theory about the relationship between *consent* and legitimate government. Even if it is the case that consent as a strict criterion is an implausible standard, liberals still make political legitimacy dependent on whether it *could* be the object of consent. Liberal governments protect religious liberty not necessarily because every citizen affirms the principle of religious liberty but because no reasonable person would consent to a government that forced its citizens to worship against their conscience.[28] As Harry Brighouse points out, this principle of legitimacy means that citizens within liberal societies must be *able* to consent and, what's more, this consent must be "free and authentic."[29] In other words, "it must be true that citizens would give their consent if they were reasonable, informed, and not overly self-interested."[30] We might expand on that list a bit and say that free and authentic consent is not possible under conditions of

---

[28] See Madison's "Memorial and Remonstrance," where he argues for religious liberty on the grounds that our first duty is to worship God properly and since that duty precedes any duties we might have toward a political community, the political community cannot legitimately require that we worship improperly (or, presumably, worship at all). Locke's *Letter on Toleration*, of course, makes similar arguments.

[29] Brighouse, "Civic Education and Liberal Legitimacy," 721.

[30] Ibid., 720.

coercion or severe manipulation. Liberal states cannot send their citizens to re-education camps and claim that the resulting demonstrations of political loyalty mean anything. Though communist countries did (and still do in places like Cuba) have elections or other demonstrations of popular legitimacy, the very high turnout and vote totals do not signal any kind of consent (actual or tacit), because citizens under those sorts of conditions know quite well that to withhold a vote (or to vote incorrectly) is to invite state scrutiny, harassment, imprisonment, and even death.

It is not enough, however, that individuals be reasonably independent from state coercion; they must also be reasonably independent from sources of non-state coercion as well. If a man so dominates his wife that she simply parrots his political views and votes accordingly, then we cannot really say that it is even hypothetically possible that a government relying on her consent could be considered legitimate. Or, to be more precise about it, a liberal government could not reasonably claim itself legitimate so long as some portion of its citizens were so thoroughly dominated that they were not even minimally capable of rendering judgment on that government. For consent to be "free and authentic" it must in some way be the result of the individual herself reflecting on and deciding whether to give or withhold that consent. Of course, very few of us wake up every morning and think about whether we should extend or withhold our consent to government as we read the newspaper (though the thought might cross our minds, depending on the day's news). For the most part, we take our government's legitimacy for granted; we inhabit, perhaps unreflectively, a *presumption of legitimacy* and think that governments are, in general, legitimate until proven otherwise.[31] Nonetheless, on any liberal understanding, a government's legitimacy must have some relation to consent, and that must mean at the very least that it is possible that its citizens could decide *not* to support it.

Thus we can see how liberal legitimacy presupposes that its citizens have in some basic measure moral autonomy, what I have called "independence." My four-year-old son would not qualify even as

---

[31] Kukathas argues for a modulated view of consent, one that considers empirically how far it looks as if citizens in a particular society actually do consent to their government. To simplify a bit, if things are peaceful and lots of people participate in public life, we could reasonably think that there is a higher level of consent. See Chandran Kukathas, *The Liberal Archipelago: A Theory of Diversity and Freedom* (Oxford: Oxford University Press, 2003), 202–05. If there are riots and civil disobedience, we could reasonably think that the level of consent is lower. Of course, under certain kinds of extreme tyrannies – contemporary North Korea or Stalinist USSR – whatever public manifestations of consent might be observed would need to be rejected for the obscene spectacles they are (or, thankfully, were).

independent. He does not decide when he will go to bed, when and what he will eat for dinner, whether he can go outside to play in the rain, and so on, even though he has views on all these things and is quite willing to express them (sometimes with tears and sometimes without). We are happy to accommodate his wishes when we feel warranted, but feel no compulsion to respect them simply *because* they are his wishes; indeed, we coerce him in any number of ways every day. Young children just do not have the experience or wisdom to know when the choices they make will lead to disaster (or a ruined carpet, as the case might be). As he gets older, that will change as he becomes more capable of making (somewhat) responsible choices. If we treat him at twenty the same way we treated him at two, most everyone would (rightly) think us oppressive. We are often taken aback when we encounter someone who is so under the thumb of another that he does not make any of his own choices whether in trivial things like clothing or food or in more significant choices like the selection of a spouse or career. We might say that the person lacks an adequate capacity for autonomy, and believe that as such cannot be supposed to be capable of being even just a reasonable citizen. We might say further that his condition of subservience is so severe that his life as such is stunted. Not only is the lack of independence incompatible with any reasonable understanding of democratic citizenship, it is incompatible with most any understanding of human flourishing as well.

Even as stern a critic of autonomy liberalism as Chandran Kukathas argues that though, in his view, we do not have a basic interest in revising our ends (we might make bad choices, we might just live in circumstances that make it extremely unlikely, and so on), we still "have an interest in not being compelled to live the kind of life we cannot abide."[32] Even if it is the case "that the unexamined life may be well worth living,"[33] it still looks quite implausible to claim that autonomy, at least in the rather minimal sense of independence, really is not necessary for any sort of fulfilling human life.[34] Or, to redescribe this a bit differently, it is implausible to say that independence is not a basic interest that all human beings share, and as such the state has a responsibility for working to see that it is protected and, if necessary, promoted. Any putatively liberal theory of politics that denies this denies its own foundations, both political and moral, for how can a government of individual liberty, the rule of

---

[32] Ibid., 64.   [33] Ibid., 59.

[34] Even some of liberalism's most thoroughgoing critics affirm the importance of independence, albeit in particular forms. See Finnis, *Natural Law and Natural Rights*, 88; Alasdair C. MacIntyre, *Dependent Rational Animals: Why Human Beings Need the Virtues* (Chicago: Open Court, 1999), 71–76.

law, and *consent* be built on the back of dominance and dependence?[35] It cannot, for a government of the people must be a government of people who *can* consent. Autonomy as independence is for any liberal theory of politics a basic interest for all human beings and thus a proper object of political action (if necessary).[36]

Is integrationism compatible with this rather minimal understanding of autonomy, with independence? Consider some of the claims made by Groen van Prinsterer.[37] Prinsterer was in many ways the intellectual and spiritual godfather of what eventually became the Netherlands' ARP.[38] Prinsterer grew up in an aristocratic family, well educated and fairly comfortable with the latitudinarian Calvinism that dominated the upper strata of Dutch society. He underwent a conversion experience in the early 1830s and became quite evangelical, prompting him to write a series of treatises examining the flow of history from a distinctly (Calvinist) Christian perspective. In his most important work, "Unbelief and Revolution," he looked at the French Revolution and attempted to understand how its effects might be understood in the light of his Christian commitments to the idea of God's sovereignty and providential work in the world. His was a thoroughly integrationist view.

In Prinsterer's view, the French Revolution was, at bottom, an outworking of "practical atheism," or "unbelief applied to politics."[39] This he contrasted with what he thought of as the necessary Christian view, which begins with the question of *how* one ought "to submit unconditionally to the law of God."[40] What he calls the "Christian-historical position" originates, he thinks, with the Bible as "the infallible touchstone" that "indicates ... for nations and governments the foundations of justice and morality, of freedom and authority." To get at a *true* understanding of

[35] This sort of abject contradiction lay at the heart of our own Constitution and was only excised through a bloody civil war and decades of political struggle.

[36] There is, of course a very large literature concerning what I call here "basic interest." I cannot here even begin to elaborate a theory of basic interests, but for my purposes I do not think I need to. All I need to show is that independence is the kind capacity that all humans ought to possess and that it is necessary for a coherent theory of liberal politics (and that comprehensive autonomy is not).

[37] All of the citations from Prinsterer are from an excerpted version of his "Unbelief and Revolution," in Skillen and McCarthy, eds., *Political Order and the Plural Structure of Society*, 53–77. For the full version see *Groen Van Prinsterer's Lectures on Unbelief and Revolution*, ed. Van Dyke.

[38] For an account of Kuyper's role in organizing and leading the ARP through its early years, see Carlson-Thies, "Democracy in the Netherlands"; Fogarty, *Christian Democracy in Western Europe, 1820–1953*; D. Jellema, "Abraham Kuyper's Attack on Liberalism," *Review of Politics* 19, no. 4 (1957); Kalyvas, *The Rise of Christian Democracy in Europe*.

[39] van Prinsterer, "Unbelief and Revolution," in *Political Order and the Plural Structure of Society*, ed. Skillen and McCarthy, 59.

[40] Ibid., 61.

the world around us, we must "[surrender our] own wisdom" and submit unconditionally to Revelation.[41] This sort of submission would certainly seem at the very least to stand in tension with most any robust understanding of autonomy, as it seems to propose holding our critical faculties in abeyance (in some sense) when it comes to the claims of faith. Prinsterer's views helped shape the political movement whose initial aim was the establishment (and public funding) of schools that reflected these sentiments,[42] and so we might reasonably think that his sort of views help show integrationism to be incompatible with even autonomy as independence. That sort of concern would be reasonable, but mistaken.

Prinsterer claims that for the Christian, intellectual and moral inquiries must begin with the submission to the truths revealed in the Bible. But that is not the end of inquiry. As he says,

> The Christian would be wrong to imagine that, having the guidance of Scripture, he could do without learning. To be able to work at his appointed task diligently and conscientiously, the Christian too needs to have precise knowledge of the nature and function of his particular task. The fear of the Lord is the beginning of knowledge, but the beginning is not the whole of the matter; the whole of knowledge also embraces the other elements which embody the starting principle. The truth of the Gospel is the leaven, but to obtain nourishing and tasty bread there must be dough along with the leaven – if one appreciates solid substance.[43]

Prinsterer's religious integrationism was not a program for ignorance, indoctrination, or compulsion, but rather a view that Christians *as Christians* ought to think and learn as Christians, that their faith necessarily means accepting certain fundamental views as "basic" and then working from that view to understand its relationship with the world we can observe. Similarly, Abraham Kuyper, Prinsterer's successor, argued that the Christian acknowledgement of divine "ordinances" – laws governing both the physical and moral universe –

> brings with it a recognition that scientific discovery of the laws that rule the lives of nations would be completely adequate to establish an unsurpassable constitutional law if there were no sin. We regard as incontrovertible the assertion that the laws governing life reveal themselves spontaneously in life. In the very process of painting and sketching and performing and sculpting our artists discovered the laws for the artistic enterprise. And it enters no one's mind to consult the Bible or ecclesiastical authorities when it comes to learning what

---

[41] Ibid., 63.
[42] See Carlson-Thies, "Democracy in the Netherlands"; Glenn, *The Myth of the Common School*, 55–57.
[43] Prinsterer, "Unbelief and Revolution," in *Political Order and the Plural Structure of Society*, ed. Skillen and McCarthy, 60–61.

the purpose of art is ... The same is true of the laws which govern our thinking, the laws which govern commerce, and the laws which govern industry.[44]

This might not be model of academic inquiry or autonomy that many scholars think appropriate, but it is hard to say that these views do not also produce a workable sort of independence, at least enough to make consent (in the narrow form I described earlier) work and to be a part of a flourishing human life.

One way of seeing this is by examining the effects of contemporary Dutch religious schools, especially those run by Kuyper's spiritual and political successors. As a number of scholars have reported, it turns out that contemporary "evangelical" schools produce students who are as well equipped academically as their peers, closely tied to their religious communities, *and* good citizens.[45] Though this does not say anything directly about how these schools functioned in the late nineteenth and early twentieth century (since Dutch society has changed a great deal since then), such evidence is suggestive, and it certainly does not seem unreasonable to think that someone raised in these sorts of schools and formed by like institutions could make reasonable judgments about a government's political legitimacy. Those who do not share their perspectives may find their views off-putting, perhaps even one-sided and ill-informed, but they would plausibly qualify as independent.[46]

The same would not be true, I think, of integrationism considered in light of a more maximized version of autonomy, "comprehensive autonomy." As Will Kymlicka has pointed out, the bulk of the liberal tradition has historically affirmed the view that human freedom requires "[allowing] people to choose a conception of the good life, and then [allowing]

---

[44] Kuyper, "The Antirevolutionary Program," 245–46.
[45] See Geert Driessen and Frans Van der Silk, "Religion, Denomination and Education in the Netherlands: Cognitive and Noncognitive Outcomes after an Era of Secularization," *Journal for the Scientific Study of Religion* 40, no. 4 (2001); Roelande H. Hofman and Adriaan Hofman, "School Choice, Religious Traditions and School Effectiveness," *International Journal of Education and Religion* 2, no. 2 (2001); Geoffrey Walford, "Building Identity through Communities of Practice: Evangelical Christian Schools in the Netherlands," *International Journal of Education and Religion* 2, no. 2 (2001).
[46] The contrast with some contemporary Islamic *madrassas* that have been in the news is instructive, perhaps. In these schools, as I understand them, *only* the Koran is studied and the method of teaching is simply and only rote memorization. In the sort of Christian schools Prinsterer had in mind (and Kuyper and his followers helped create) the Bible was the center of a proper understanding of the world, but not the whole of that proper understanding. One obvious critique of this claim is that just because *these* religious integrationists are compatible with autonomy, that doesn't mean religious integrationism as a general phenomenon is. That may be true – and much of the rest of the chapter is dedicated in an indirect way to answering that critique – but at least for now, all I need to demonstrate is that it is possible to be a religious integrationist and have enough autonomy so as to qualify independent.

them to reconsider that decision, and adopt a new and hopefully better plan of life."[47] We all have a fundamental interest in living "good lives," and thus have a corresponding interest in being able to assess critically the life we *are* leading to see if it is actually good. Since we must presume that our judgments about the good life are fallible, we require "exposure to other ways of life" as a way of deciding "what is truly valuable," and this will necessarily both produce and require comprehensive autonomy.[48] This sort of autonomy is something to which each of us should have access and something that any recognizably liberal government will protect and even promote. Kymlicka suggests an analogue to religion: "A liberal society not only allows individuals the freedom to pursue their existing faith, but it also allows them to seek new adherents for their faith (proselytization is allowed), or to question the doctrine of their church (heresy is allowed), or to renounce their faith entirely and convert to another faith or to atheism (apostasy is allowed)." Similarly, "A liberal society ... not only allows people to pursue their current way of life, but also gives them access to information about other ways of life ... and makes it possible for people to engage in radical revision of their ends (including apostasy) without legal penalty."[49] Eamonn Callan puts it even more strongly, claiming (in the context of an argument about civic education) that children must, if their basic interest in comprehensive autonomy is to be protected, be engaged in schooling that

involves at some stage sympathetic and critical engagement with beliefs and ways of life at odds with the culture of the family or religious or ethnic group into which the child is born. Moreover, the relevant engagement must be such that the beliefs and values by which others live are entertained not merely as sources of meaning in *their* lives; they are instead addressed as potential elements within the conceptions of the good and the right one will create for oneself as an adult.[50]

The general idea here is that autonomy means being able to hold one's own conception of the good and being capable of standing apart, in some

---

[47] Kymlicka, *Multicultural Citizenship*, 80.
[48] Ibid., 92.   [49] Ibid., 82.
[50] Callan, *Creating Citizens*, 133. This is an instructive description, both because it shows how independence is an integral part of the liberal social and political order and how comprehensive autonomy often is not. Many liberal democratic states have had (and have) established religions (of the non-coercive type), and many educational programs attempt to teach their students something about a variety of religious beliefs. But I take it that it would be much more controversial to try and teach religion in public schools as a set of claims that students themselves ought to consider sympathetically as a real option for their own lives. I doubt seriously whether an autonomy liberal would be particularly happy if his son or daughter were required to read and consider as an opportunity for conversion C.S. Lewis' *Mere Christianity*. Neither, I suspect, would most religious parents be too thrilled about their children reading something like Bertrand Russell's *Why I Am Not a Christian*.

fashion, from that conception and revising it upon critical reflection. If children – or adults – lack the capacities which such engagement is supposed to develop, their lives will be stunted and perhaps even "ethically servile."[51] On this account, comprehensive autonomy is basic to human flourishing and any liberal polity worth the name will seek to promote it.

Clearly, liberals think that this sort of autonomy incompatible with integrationism (and integrationists presumably think likewise). But before we can write off religious integrationism as simply vicious, we need to ask whether comprehensive autonomy is indeed a basic interest that all persons must possess in order to flourish even minimally. Only *then* can we say something more definite about whether and how the state might protect that interest. So, can one live a good human life somewhere short of comprehensive autonomy?

Chandran Kukathas argues that you can. While there may be a good number of reasons why we would want to be able to assess and revise our ends, none of those reasons is universally compelling: "to think that we have a *basic* interest in being able to assess our ends is a mistake; some of us have *an* interest in being able to do so in some circumstances – but no stronger claim can be made."[52] We might come up with a better life by rationally reflecting on our views of the good life, or we might end up worse off than before.[53] Our basic interests lie not in the capacity to revise, but in the ability to live "according to conscience."[54] Human beings are peculiar creatures and what really seems to distinguish us from other animals is that we crave *meaning* from our lives, and Kukathas thinks that this suggests our basic interest is in living within the meaning we have for our lives, while being a rational reviser only suggests itself under certain circumstances and for certain sorts of people.

Suppose Kukathas' view a rough analogue of independence. Why do the proponents of comprehensive autonomy reject it as insufficient? Is

---

[51] Ibid., 152–57. Mill puts it a bit more strongly, arguing that "He who lets the world, or his own portion of it, choose his plan of life for him, has no need of any other faculty than the ape-like one of imitation. He who chooses his plan for himself, employs all his faculties. He must use observation to see, reasoning and judgment for foresee, activity to gather materials for decision, discrimination to decide, and when he has decided, firmness and self-control to hold his decision deliberate" (Mill, *On Liberty*, 59.) Who would volunteer for being "ape-like"?

[52] Kukathas, *The Liberal Archipelago*, 60. His is, of course, a minority view. Jeff Spinner-Halev argues for what he calls the "nonautonomous" life, but only in the context of a world in which those who live such a life could have a reasonable opportunity to leave it if they so chose. See Spinner-Halev, *Surviving Diversity*. Kukathas' freedom for exit is a good bit narrower.

[53] Kukathas, *The Liberal Archipelago*, 61–62.

[54] Ibid., 55. See also Swaine, *The Liberal Conscience*.

a life constituted merely by independence such a bad one that the liberal state should use its coercive powers to discourage it (or encourage something more robust, autonomy-wise)? Certainly it is the case that most people in most places in human history would not have counted as comprehensively autonomous. Is it plausible to think that something so "basic" to good lives has been opaque to so many? One answer is simply to suggest that however other people might have lived, for those of us who live now in modern pluralist societies, the notion that we could be non-culpably ignorant of other possibilities for us stretches the imagination to its breaking point. Very few of us (in developed democracies) inhabit the worlds of the isolated farmer or pious Muslim villager, and so it is no defense against autonomy, as Kukathas would have it, to say that comprehensive autonomy is good only under certain circumstances. If there are any circumstances under which it is a basic interest, even under Kukathas' view, it is ours.

The plausibility of a strong connection between comprehensive autonomy and the good life depends, I think, on the details of how we characterize comprehensive autonomy. As Callan points out, if comprehensive autonomy means what Michael Sandel thinks it means ("the unencumbered self"[55]), then we might indeed reasonably think that personal autonomy is not basic to a flourishing human life. Such a self depends, he rightly thinks, on a rather "bizarre metaphysics" and making autonomy out to be something it is not. Autonomy "does not demand that we can detach ourselves from all our ends. The requirement is only that we be capable of asking about the value of any particular end with which we currently identify and able to give a thoughtful answer to what we ask."[56] Instead of thinking of ourselves as "unencumbered," as Sandel's caricature suggests, we should think of ourselves as "revocably encumbered."

This might begin to look a bit more congenial to the religious integrationist than where we started, but it is clear that a gap remains – or, at least, Callan believes it does. His "sympathetic engagement" is meant precisely to stand against something like Prinsterer's unconditional submission to the "law of God." Indeed, Callan's argument might reasonably be read as a claim that the sort of views propounded by Prinsterer and his successors plausibly implicated them in a regime of "ethical servility" and, thus, political vice. For Callan, to be ethically servile is not only to maintain an "ignorant antipathy toward all alternatives to [our own]

[55] See Michael J. Sandel, *Liberalism and the Limits of Justice* (Cambridge and New York: Cambridge University Press, 1982).
[56] Callan, *Creating Citizens*, 54. See also Ian MacMullen, *Faith in Schools? Autonomy, Citizenship, and Religious Education in the Liberal State* (Princeton, NJ: Princeton University Press, 2007).

ethical ideal" but also to do so out of a settled disposition implanted by another.[57] That is, we are prevented from ever questioning our ends because we are so shaped by our parents, community, or schools that we lack even a basic capacity to do so. This is not a claim that we should be the kinds of people who can stand entirely outside of our moral, philosophical, or religious commitments, but rather a claim that we should be the kind of people who make those commitments in an awareness that they are *ours*. To be ethically servile is to be effectively under someone else's control, to inhabit a kind of intellectual and moral slavery. It is to live a bad life. The integrationist can avoid such servility, Callan suggests, only by taking steps that will themselves conflict with what is necessary to maintaining a cohesive religious view in a pluralist world, or what he calls "simple integrity."[58]

Simple integrity involves the "pursuit of the good inside a community of like-minded people … [in which] faith imposes the necessary harmony on the domain of responsibilities because its demands are accorded a paramount status in deliberation, and a coherent interpretation is provided of the significance of other attachments."[59] Under conditions of social and political pluralism, we are bound to take notice that others do not hold the same values and beliefs that we do, and to the extent that we think such differences obtain from something more than flawed reasoning or poor character we are unlikely to be able to conceive of ourselves as belonging integrally to a community simply organized around a single conception of the good. The result will be – and this is in part what Callan's educational proposals are meant to accomplish – that we will naturally "want to encompass many values" in our own lives, "and so instead of the tight cohesion of a life of simple integrity one ends up with a pattern rather more messy and unsteady, but perhaps richly fulfilling for all that."[60] Only by imposing a regime implicated in ethical servility can integrationists sustain the life of simple integrity under modern pluralism. Integrationists, like those represented in that ubiquitous *Mozert* v. *Hawkins* case, are thus caught in a powerful bind: they can pursue their integrationist goals, but only at serious cost to their own flourishing.

Let us grant that Callan and other advocates of comprehensive autonomy make a powerful, perhaps compelling, case against the sorts of claims that the *Mozert* parents made, especially their claims that their children should be shielded entirely from other religious points of view.

[57] Callan, *Creating Citizens*, 153.
[58] Callan's example is actually John Wesley, who proclaimed that we should think of the "Will of God [to] be our one rule of action … [and] our will is wholly to be given up to him, and all our affections to be regulated as he directs" (ibid., 150).
[59] Ibid., 60.   [60] Ibid., 67.

But let us not grant that this means, in turn, that they have shown that comprehensive autonomy is a necessary part of a flourishing human life and, thus, that religious integrationism stands convicted as vicious. There is, I think, still some conceptual distance between independence and ethical servility. Consider Callan's response to the argument that reasoning "from the basis of God's word as reflected in Scripture is [not] to abandon the exercise of critical rationality." After conceding that "a vigorous critical rationality is compatible with acceptance of Scriptural authority," he says that the *Mozert* parents were nonetheless unjustified in their complaints, for his concession "does not suffice to justify an education that would seek to expunge, so far as possible, all influences that conflict with what parents specify as the one correct interpretation of Scripture."[61] But here I do not think that the religious integrationists – at least as I have described them – so easily fall victim to that critique. As Kuyper notes,

the revelation of Holy Scripture is like a pair of glasses that enables him to read once again with his weakened eyes the partially obscured revelation of nature. It reveals to us the ground rules, the primary relationships, the principles that govern man's life together and his relationship to the most holy God, not information concerning the individual parts of the state as a whole. What life itself, distorted and derailed by sin, could no longer reveal, God in his love made known in his Word, also for our political life ... [But] we deny the church the right to establish political principles that would bind the state ... To establish these rules, what is necessary is not just knowledge of Revelation but also knowledge of the temperament of the people, of history, and of politics, and these the church does not possess.[62]

The parents in *Mozert* and *Yoder* could plausibly be viewed as imposing a regime of ethical servility on their children insofar as they sought, to the extent that it is possible, to insulate their children from any alternative views; indeed, it seems as though, especially with the parents in *Mozert*, that even exposure to alternative views was problematic. It is hard to see how that does children any good, given the presumptive inevitability that they will inhabit a community where, in fact, people do hold to any number of alternative views of life.[63] It is equally hard to see, though, that simply teaching children and living one's life (and constructing and inhabiting institutions that ran) *as though* your point of view were entirely true but with the acknowledgment that others think differently (and not

---

[61] Ibid., 237 fn. 8.

[62] Kuyper, "The Antirevolutionary Program," 250, 52.

[63] The critique does not seem to hold quite as well for the Amish, given that their future lives would not seem to offer as much in the way of pluralism, though what happens to those who decide not to stay in the community makes the question more difficult.

unreasonably so) is incompatible with a good human life.[64] In a way, the very thing that makes the European integrationists *more* threatening than the Amish or *Mozert* parents to the liberal consensus is also the thing that acquits them of the charge of ethical servility and political vice. Their vigorous *engagement* with the world around them, conjoined with the firmly held claim that such engagement begins (but does not end) with religious affirmation is a powerful contrast to the withdrawal strategies of the American integrationists in both the *Yoder* and *Mozert* cases. The point of pursuing a religiously integrated existence is not to *avoid* a world in which others disagree with you; its explicit articulation can be a *product* of engagement with that pluralistic world (though obviously it need not be).[65]

Religious integrationism simply need not be in thrall to the kind of servility that Callan (rightly) thinks inimical to our well-being and, as such, it escapes the claim that it is incompatible with a reasonable understanding of human flourishing. Religious integrationism (at least of a certain sort) should count as among the lives that individuals in liberal democratic societies might seek to live and thus a liberal state would not have reasons on grounds of comprehensive autonomy to interfere. Or, to put it a bit differently, comprehensive autonomy ought not count as a basic interest for liberal regimes, and since religious integrationism as I have described it here can be productive of at least independence, there is no reason for the state to intervene politically so as to make integrationism per se less available to its citizens.

Religious integrationism and political autonomy

Let me quickly review what I have argued so far. I suggested that a narrow form of autonomy – independence – sits reasonably well both with religious integrationism and the consent requirements associated with a liberal government's legitimacy. I then considered whether a more demanding kind of autonomy – comprehensive autonomy – might better capture what a liberal state should seek to protect as a basic human

---

[64] It might even be the case that religious integrationism would be, in some measures, *superior* to moral autonomy as a way of life. As William Galston has, rather famously, put it, "The greatest threat to children in modern liberal societies is not that they will believe in something too deeply, but that they will believe in nothing very deeply at all" (Galston, *Liberal Purposes*, 255.) In a world where trivial consumption threatens reflectiveness much more widely than integrationism, perhaps a closely held faith can be a salutary anchor.

[65] Prinsterer's essay "Unbelief and Revolution" was much more than some exegesis of scripture. It combined a commitment to scripture with an engagement with Europe's most important thinkers – Hobbes, Rousseau, Constant, and Guizot, to name a few.

interest and claimed that though people who are comprehensively autonomous can live good lives, human flourishing is not exclusively their province. Failing to be comprehensively autonomous does not commit the religious integrationist to ethical servility, and since comprehensive autonomy is not a basic interest, the liberal state need not promote it as such. In other words, integrationists' lives do not go badly absent comprehensive autonomy in such a way that a liberal state could be justified in coercing them into it.

The argument thus far seems to comport quite well with Rawls' considered views on autonomy as he began to reconceptualize them by the mid-1980s. In *A Theory of Justice*, Rawls originally argued that we should think of ourselves as autonomous in the sense that we should seek to act from principles that we come to hold "independent of natural contingencies and accidental social circumstances."[66] We should view ourselves, in other words, as always capable of stepping (metaphorically) into the Original Position and reasoning *as if* our gender, race, class, religion, and so on were hidden behind a veil of ignorance. Rawls came to think that this claim for a comprehensive moral autonomy left the broader claim for justice as fairness vulnerable and "unrealistic." In particular, as I explained previously, the claim for moral autonomy in *Theory* created a problem of stability within justice as fairness. Many citizens reasonably hold moral, religious, and comprehensive views that are "incompatible" with the sorts of comprehensive autonomy contained in, say, the liberalisms of Kant or Mill. "Many citizens of faith," he notes, "reject moral autonomy as a part of their way of life," and do so reasonably.[67] Tied to affirming a comprehensive autonomy "liberalism becomes but another sectarian doctrine" and thus unable to serve as means of adjudicating among a society's conflicting views.[68]

Rawls' response was to reconstruct justice as fairness as a purely political doctrine based on a conception of the "person as citizen" rather than the person as autonomous moral agent. As citizens, individuals "are regarded as capable of revising [their conception of the good] on reasonable and rational grounds ... [and] their public identity as free persons is not affected by changes over time in their conception of the good."[69] This sort of citizenship, he suggests, is compatible with being the sort of person who "regard[s] it as simply unthinkable to view [himself] apart

---

[66] Rawls, *A Theory of Justice*, 451.
[67] Larmore, "Political Liberalism"; Rawls, *Political Liberalism*, xlv.
[68] Rawls, "Justice as Fairness: Political Not Metaphysical," 409.
[69] Ibid., 405.

from certain religious, philosophical, and moral convictions, or from certain enduring attachments and loyalties."[70] It is plausibly compatible, we might say, with an integrationist religious view of life.

The *political* sort of autonomy is fully realized "by citizens when they act from principles of justice that specify the fair terms of cooperation they would give to themselves [as citizens] when fairly represented as free and equal persons [in the original position]."[71] This will in turn require that a reasonable education "include such things as knowledge of ... constitutional and civic rights so that ... [we are prepared] to be fully cooperating members of society and ... self-supporting; it should also encourage the political virtues so that [we] want to honor the fair terms of cooperation in their relations with the rest of society."[72] Though such an education may, he admits, have a deleterious effect on comprehensive views of the good that deny the goods of autonomy and individuality (or subordinate them to other goods), he thinks that as long as the state does not *intend* such an effect, then it is not unjust, though we might think it regrettable.[73] While a state that directly and consciously attempts to indoctrinate students into being Millian-style individuals might reasonably be rejected as unjustifiably disrespectful of citizens' non-individualist comprehensive views, one that merely attempts to ensure that citizens understand their rights within a liberal political system and are reasonably prepared to exercise them well would not. Citizens need to be prepared to think about and evaluate political proposals in some kind of critical manner, but they need not do so with respect to their own comprehensive beliefs. *Political* autonomy as a necessary virtue or capacity might then be more attractive to many religious believers than its comprehensive predecessor since it would not putatively require the capacity or inclination to look critically at that faith as the price of good citizenship.

Callan claims that this "contrast is bogus because the political virtues that implement the fair terms of cooperation impose educational requirements that bring autonomy through the back door of political liberalism."[74] In particular, Rawls' claim that citizens must affirm what he calls the burdens of judgment looks to be incompatible with the conviction that a particular comprehensive view is fully truth-disclosing. (Recall my earlier discussion of the burdens in chapter 2.) Citizens who affirm reasonable comprehensive views must as a part of that reasonableness also affirm that "[i]t is unrealistic – or worse, it arouses mutual suspicion and hostility – to suppose that all our differences are rooted

---

[70] Ibid.   [71] Rawls, *Political Liberalism*, 77.
[72] Ibid., 199.   [73] Ibid., 190–98.
[74] Callan, "Political Liberalism and Political Education," 21.

solely in ignorance and perversity, or else in the rivalries for power, status, or economic gain."[75] Even in optimal conditions of open and free inquiry, securing universal agreement about the good is not realistic, and we should think that such disagreement stems simply from reasoning in "bad faith." Affirming the burdens of judgment means affirming that there are limits to what can be justified to others politically, regardless of what we believe to be true. So even if we think a particular faith to be the true one, we do not, to the degree that we are reasonable, seek to use the state to impose it on others because we acknowledge that they may reasonably think another faith (or no faith) is true.

But in accepting these limits, Callan argues,

> citizens must become critically attuned to the wide range of reasonable political disagreement within the society they inhabit and to the troubling gap between reasonable agreement and the whole moral truth ... The upshot of all this is that Rawlsian political liberalism is really a kind of closet comprehensive liberalism ... To agree with Rawls is to accept a pervasive and powerful constraint (the burdens of judgment) on how we should think about the various convictions and practices that proliferate in the background culture of liberal politics and how we should form our own convictions and make our own choices in that setting.[76]

The result is that the only religious believers who could count as reasonable within political liberalism are "sophisticated fideists,"[77] who might precariously learn "to combine a vigorous faith with an intelligent humility about the possibility of its reasoned vindication."[78] Though religion might survive such an act, it is likely, he thinks, to become as thoroughly liberalized as if it had embraced comprehensive rather than political autonomy.[79] Thus, Rawls' attempt to accommodate the reasonable romantics comes to be nothing more than ethical liberalism in stealth mode, except this time it is made all the more effective because it does not rely on any controversial notion of the human good as comprehensively autonomous, but instead merely starts with the idea of free and equal citizens in a pluralist constitutional democracy. If Callan is right, then *political* autonomy actually poses a much stiffer challenge to religious integrationism than its comprehensive cousin, for religious integrationists could

---

[75] Rawls, *Political Liberalism*, 58.   [76] Callan, *Creating Citizens*, 41.

[77] Fideists can be defined as those who would accept, generally, the following proposition (within the Christian tradition): "An understanding of Christian theology which refuses to accept the need for (or sometimes the possibility of) criticism or evaluation from sources outside the Christian faith itself" (Alister McGrath, *Christian Theology: An Introduction* (Cambridge, MA: Blackwell, 1997), 570.)

[78] Callan, *Creating Citizens*, 38.

[79] Elsewhere, he avers that the fideists' lot is "to succumb over generations to [their] own internal tensions" (Callan, "Political Liberalism and Political Education," 20.)

only reject those autonomy claims if they were willing to reject liberal democratic government more generally. Religious integrationism – to the degree that it would remain integrationist – would on this account necessarily be incompatible with the acquisition of autonomy necessary for any reasonable citizen. If this argument is right, even if the integrationist can live a good human life generally, he cannot live as a good democratic citizen, and the liberal state may then have good grounds for intervening and making it difficult for integrationism to survive.

Is the religious integrationist really so condemned? In order for Callan to be right, he must be able to sustain two claims. First, it must be true that learning to reason autonomously with respect to politics (Rawls' political autonomy) is essentially the same thing as learning to reason autonomously with respect to the rest of one's life. And, second, Callan must then show that the autonomous reasoning he prefers is in fact corrosive to integrationism. Let me take the former claim first.

Callan claims that the skills and capacities we need to learn in order to be politically virtuous in the Rawlsian sense necessarily pull us toward a full comprehensive autonomy as well: "Learning to accept the burdens of judgment in the sense necessary to political liberalism is conceptually inseparable from what we ordinarily understand as the process of learning to be ethically (and not just politically) autonomous."[80] In one sense, this is undoubtedly true. Since being politically autonomous on Rawls' view means viewing ourselves, at least for political purposes, as the kinds of people who *could* change, leave, or enter a comprehensive view (or religious faith), it must be the case that we are able to view others (who are differently committed than we are) as living lives that are worthy of respect and maybe even admiration. It is no great insight on my part to suggest that such views tend to weaken, psychologically at least, our grip on what we take to be true.

But why does this drive us to some sort of comprehensive autonomy? The answer lies in how Callan characterizes the burdens of judgment. In his view, these burdens are a good deal more "subversive … than Rawls' anodyne discussion of them would suggest," in large part because Callan thinks that they require us to acknowledge (and act upon) the idea "that opposing views are equally reasonable, and that the political significance of the doctrine I cherish must be curtailed by deference to the reasonableness of beliefs I vehemently reject."[81] The idea here is that we claim to think that others' lives are worthy of political respect in part because

---

[80] Ibid., 22. Kymlicka, *Multicultural Citizenship*, makes a similar argument, noting that the problem for Rawls is that it is tough to "explain why anyone would accept the ideal of autonomy in political contexts unless they also accepted it more generally" (160).

[81] Callan, *Creating Citizens*, 34.

they are the kinds of people who can revise their ends and change their lives. If that is right, then we are seemingly destined to accept the notion that the reasonable differences among us stem not from any particular flaw in any one of us, but rather from the "contingencies of social position and experience."[82] Once we come to that view, then it is a short step to the view that we should regard our own view of the good as in large part a product of the "contingencies of social position and experience" and thus open to reasonably easy revision.

This is a powerfully argued position, and Callan is right to call attention to the way in which we may be (and often are) drawn into a position of ethical autonomy from an affirmation of political autonomy. But it is too much, I think, to say that such an outcome is inevitable. When Kymlicka similarly argues, "Accepting the value of autonomy for political purposes enables its exercise in private life" and that a system of political autonomy will favor "those who endorse autonomy as a general value,"[83] he may also be largely right, but that is not an argument that political autonomy necessarily entails comprehensive autonomy. The problem lies in Callan's view that we must consider other reasonable views as "*equally* reasonable." Since Rawls thinks that we should regard reasonable pluralism not as an "unfortunate condition of human life,"[84] Callan rules out as unreasonable many views that see at least some forms of moral pluralism as the result of sin or corruption. Unless we consider others as *equally* reasonable, and place great (even overriding) value on that reasonableness, then we will "open the door to contempt towards those who reasonably disagree with us,"[85] and he clearly thinks it hard – near impossible, really – to square such contempt with political respect.

Why should so much hang on the degree of one's cheerfulness toward moral pluralism? Callan suggests that we must prize the "respect for the limits of the reasonable ... [as] ... *the paramount virtue*"[86] if we are to be reasonable ourselves. The alternative, he seems to think, is that if we view our apostate neighbor as in some way less reasonable than ourselves, we will be tempted at some point to oppress him. No doubt that is sometimes true, and it is probably a necessary condition for undertaking such oppression that we view our neighbor with contempt. But is it really impossible (or implausible) for individuals of a variety of moral and religious (and non-religious) beliefs to cooperate politically, consider one another politically reasonable (and their lives worthy of a degree of respect), all the while thinking that others live lives that, while reasonable, are not *equally* reasonable as their own? This strikes me as not only

---

[82] Ibid., 35.   [83] Kymlicka, *Multicultural Citizenship*, 162.
[84] Rawls, *Political Liberalism*, 37.   [85] Callan, *Creating Citizens*, 37.
[86] Ibid., 37, emphasis added.

plausible, but perfectly in line with much of contemporary life. There is some real distance between thinking that others' lives are *equally* reasonable and that they are *unreasonable* and amenable to suppression, and Callan is simply wrong to try and conflate the two.

This leaves unanswered, though, Callan's second claim, that embracing political autonomy will necessarily be corrosive to one's non-autonomous comprehensive views, what Tomasi calls "spillover effects."[87] Callan presses on two points, one ethical and the other empirical. He claims, first, that "to retain a lively understanding of the burdens of judgment in political contexts while suppressing it everywhere else would require a spectacular feat of self-deception that cannot be squared with personal integrity."[88] Even if there is nothing illogical about distinguishing for oneself between being politically and morally autonomous, it might still be a bad way to live.[89] As I noted earlier, religious believers attempting to live with this conflict, Callan suggests, are forced to perform a kind of "high-wire act" where they risk falling either into denying the burdens of judgment (and becoming unreasonable) or giving up the view of their faith as truth-disclosing (and becoming ethically autonomous). They must instead learn to "combine a vigorous faith with an intelligent humility about the possibility of its reasoned vindication,"[90] and for Callan this precludes the kind of integrity important to any kind of ethical life.

It is probably true that anyone who wants to live productively in a modern pluralist society has to have an "intelligent humility" of some sort about her comprehensive view. There is little more grating than the well-schooled academic who glibly dismisses others' views as "archaic," "outmoded," or "obviously wrong," because, as such-and-such author has definitively shown, no literate person could believe that, and so forth. At least this much is true about the burdens of judgment: to presume that others disagree with you simply because they are reasoning in "bad faith," narrow self-interest, or ignorance is itself unreasonable. But that view does not commit you, as I argued earlier, to prizing the "limits of reasonableness" to such a degree that you abandon your own ethical commitments.[91] Even if that argument is unsound – and it has lots of

---

[87] Tomasi, *Liberalism beyond Justice*, 33–39.

[88] Callan, *Creating Citizens*, 31.

[89] Note here that this argument is distinct from the straightforward moral autonomy argument, because it does not say that one has to live a morally autonomous life to live a good life – Callan explicitly denies this – but rather that once you commit to being *politically* autonomous, holding that political autonomy in tension with a denial of moral autonomy leaves you with a fragmented life inconsistent with a life of integrity.

[90] Callan, *Creating Citizens*, 38.

[91] For similar arguments see Eberle, *Religious Conviction in Liberal Politics* and Nicholas Wolterstorff, "Why We Should Reject What Liberalism Tells Us," in *Religion and*

reasonable detractors – it is still hard to see why exactly we should agree with Callan that such "intelligent humility" is at odds with a plausible understanding of personal integrity. We all adjust how we present ourselves to others (in dress, language, and so on) depending at least in part on our surroundings. Sometimes we do it poorly – we simply bow to convention or peer pressure – but sometimes we do it out of conviction that such adjustment best reflects an appropriate balance between our ethical commitments and the other goods we seek with others. If, for instance, we have family members or co-workers whose political views we find noxious (or who might find ours so), we might simply avoid the topic altogether as a means to preserving that relationship. Sometimes the different parts of our lives do not fit together particularly well, but that does not amount to violating the (quite legitimate) good of integrity. It simply means we are making the best of the imperfect world in which we live. After all, if Callan wants to claim (as he does in critiquing Sandel and MacIntyre) that communitarians are too wedded to "simple integrity" and that something more complex, plural, and more tenuous is quite a reasonable (even attractive) way of life, then it seems a bit unfair of him to press the "personal integrity" ethical claim against the religious integrationist in turn.[92]

This leaves, however, the second "spillover" challenge to religious integrationism, a largely empirical claim that a society whose politics is organized around political autonomy creates sociological and psychological pressures that ineluctably move even the most obstinate among us toward ethical autonomy. Even if there is no logical connection between the two, and even if the integrationists' lives might still go well *as integrationists*, they will, on this account, nonetheless succumb. Liberalism making it possible for us to radically reconfigure our life – changing profession, family, or confession as we see fit and without political penalty – makes it that much more likely that we will in fact do so. Or, at least, that we will think of ourselves as the kind of people who *could* do so. As Stephen Macedo has provocatively suggested, "Liberalism holds out the promise, or threat, of making all the world like California."[93] (Presumably this means something other than enjoying sunny weather and being stuck in traffic.) If this is so and can reasonably be foreseen to be so (especially by the integrationists) then integrationism might indeed be thought problematic for liberal autonomy. For if a religious integrationist

---

Contemporary Liberalism, ed. Paul J. Weithman (Notre Dame, IN: University of Notre Dame Press, 1997).

[92] See Callan, *Creating Citizens*, 60–69.

[93] Macedo, *LiberalVirtues*, 278. He illustrates what he has in mind by sketching a picture of a man who abandons family and career to pursue a Buddhist religious vocation.

is committed to *being* an integrationist and is made to understand that his commitment to integrationism is empirically incompatible with a sincere commitment to liberal democratic politics, it is by no means obvious that the integrationist will choose his political over his religious commitments. Quite likely the opposite, actually, and he will take steps to protect his integrationist views, steps that, if the reactions to *Yoder* and *Mozert* are any guide, political liberals will likely find disturbing.

It should first be said that this claim has real intuitive appeal. It takes some effort to suppose that what you believe is ultimately true (to the exclusion of other views) and that others are nonetheless entitled to live by their different (and mutually exclusive) views just as you are. It is much easier to think that somehow we all have it a bit right and all have it a bit wrong, or, alternatively that you are right, the other fellow is wrong, and he should be coerced into thinking rightly. That is why, I suspect, so many young college students evince a kind of sophomoric relativism. Who wants to tell the guy down the hall that he's a sinner? Or a religious nut? It is much easier to acknowledge our differences, chalk them up to different life experiences, and have an "unintelligent humility" about one's own views. If even half of what Alan Wolfe argues about American religion is correct, moreover, scratch an evangelical (today's "sophisticated fideists") and what you will find, more often than not, are religious subcultures already deeply suffused with a comprehensive moral autonomy.[94] The structures of modern life and in particular the sense we have that moral and social pluralism is, to use Rawls' phrase, "reasonable" pull powerfully at our moral certitude.

Nonetheless, I think it is a mistake to say that liberal political autonomy will necessarily spill over into our non-public lives. Or, to be a little more precise about it, it is a mistake to think that there is nothing that can done within the bounds of political autonomy to curtail or dam up the spillover. In his reflections on *Mozert*, John Tomasi offers that the objecting parents were not perhaps as unreasonable as they might initially seem. As he notes, "The case record clearly states that the ... parents did *not* consistently object to the mere exposure of their children to the ideas in the reader, [but] ... objected consistently only to the *repetitiveness* and *depth* of the exposure."[95] This suggests to him that the parents were within

---

[94] See Wolfe, *The Transformation of American Religion*, where he details the ways in which he thinks American religion has been thoroughly overwhelmed by the liberal therapeutic culture. See also James Davison James Davison Hunter, *Evangelicalism: The Coming Generation* (Chicago: University of Chicago Press, 1987). Christian Smith thinks quite differently, arguing that evangelicals really do occupy a distinctive subcultural sociological space. See Christian Smith, *Christian America? What Evangelicals Really Want* (Berkeley: University of California Press, 2000); Smith and Emerson, *American Evangelicalism*.

[95] Tomasi, *Liberalism beyond Justice*, 92.

the realm of reasonableness in their objections, or at least some of them could have been, and that the informal compromises that many of the parents had worked out with their respective schools were sound within the context of the demands of political liberalism's view of citizenship.[96] The court's rejection of the parents' claims, and the broader implication that those claims were in principle unreasonable and illegitimate, represents an overreach on the part of the liberal state. What drives Tomasi's claims is not just a different evaluation of the facts (though that is certainly there) but rather a strikingly different view about what political liberalism's view of citizenship requires regarding autonomy.

Theorists like Callan and Gutmann conflate political and comprehensive liberalism only because they hold what Tomasi calls a "derivative" view of citizenship, where "Liberal citizenship, properly understood, involves only those attitudes, dispositions, and self-understandings that are directly derivable from the sets of rights and duties set out by one's political community."[97] Alternatively, Tomasi suggests that a "substantive" view of citizenship might implicate a good deal more than merely our rights or duties. It might also include "those socially constructive activities that implicate people's deepest ethical natures." In this view of liberal citizenship, "To be a good citizen is to be a good *person.*"[98] Rawlsian political liberalism does not merely reground the same claims about civic duties, rights, and obligations in more stable, purely political principles. More importantly, it suggests that in order for liberal politics to be successful in a world constituted by deep social diversity, it must attend to the skills, norms, and, yes, virtues necessary for politically reasonable citizens to "negotiate the *interfacing* of the public and the personal normative structures of their world."[99] Political liberalism's good citizens are not just good at exercising their rights and responsibilities politically, but they are also good at thinking through how those rights and responsibilities engage with their non-public lives and at making a success of those non-public lives in light of their public political commitments to a liberal polity. In particular, Tomasi suggests that good citizens must become skilled at learning to "reintegrate" those public and non-public lives so that they can both be good liberal citizens (properly autonomous, tolerant, and so forth) *and* good Catholics, Baptists, Marxists, feminists, or however they

---

[96] After some of the parents objected to the reader, some schools allowed students to opt out of the readers and spend the time in the library, where they would do similar kinds of work. In other cases, the readers were annotated with the disclaimer that students were not required to accept the normative claims implicit in the stories.

[97] Tomasi, *Liberalism beyond Justice*, 58.

[98] Ibid., 71.   [99] Ibid., 67.

identify in private life.[100] That is, when political liberals are thinking about the qualities of citizenship and educational or institutional strategies to produce them, they have to do much more than simply think about how these strategies will create good citizens, narrowly understood. Indeed, because political liberalism thinks it important that the political principles of justice cohere in some fashion with reasonable individuals' comprehensive views (via the overlapping consensus), political liberals must also think about how successful people will create their own (reasonable) views of citizenship.[101]

So the crux of what Tomasi calls the "formative project" is that political liberals have good reasons to help citizens find ways to make their private lives a success in light of the liberal political world they inhabit, especially those citizens whose private lives are decidedly non-liberal – like our integrationists. When the state engages in a direct strategy of civic education – say, through public schools – it should ensure that students are invited to consider how they think of their citizenship not just from a public point of view (though that is an important element) but also from their non-public view as well. Embracing political autonomy on the substantive view of citizenship, then, not only does not entail embracing comprehensive moral autonomy as well (for either ethical or psychological reasons), it also gives us good moral reasons to explore how citizens may make their non-public lives successful. Especially for those who do not embrace a comprehensive autonomy, like our integrationists, it gives us good moral reasons to see how they might successfully distinguish between the two and avoid the "spillover effect."

Political liberals might think this "impracticable,"[102] pointing out that in the kinds of widely diverse cultures we actually inhabit, attempts to attend to our particular claims leads to paralysis and inaction. This might be true – we can imagine some poor junior high school teacher attempting to teach a substantive-style civics class to a class of fourteen-year-olds – but such criticism focuses too quickly on what the state should do and ignores what it is that citizens can do on their own. More importantly, it focuses too much on the formal program of civic education to the neglect of the more pervasive and perhaps more important informal one, the direction and structure of civil society. In a critique of Michael McConnell's argument (on the basis of a more or less integrationist understanding) against the "democratic" control of schools, Nancy Rosenblum asks why it is that McConnell "stops short" with education? Why not extend the "structural pluralist" argument

[100] Ibid., 94.
[101] Cf. Weithman, *Religion and the Obligations of Citizenship*.
[102] Rawls, *Political Liberalism*, 194.

into the broader terrain of civil society?[103] Indeed, why not? Extending the argument thus, she thinks, reveals "the disjuncture between principled, comprehensive pluralism and strong, democratic public culture."[104] Perhaps that is so – depending on one's understanding of what is required for a strong democratic public culture – but it is not at all clear that the same is true if we focus more narrowly on political autonomy.

As I noted earlier, integrationism within the context of modern pluralist democracies seems to require (or at least occasions) the construction of a kind of "structural pluralist" institutionalism. We can see what this looks like in the networks of associations and institutions integrationists in Europe helped create and defend in the late nineteenth century: tightly linked parties, trade unions, newspapers, churches, social clubs, and employers' associations, all organized around a common religious identity and structured to reflect and nurture that identity. To the degree that they were successful – and they were for a good long time – our question on the autonomy claim, then, comes down to this: what sort of political identity do structural pluralist institutions produce and is such an identity one we might consider as being within the ambit of the politically autonomous? That is, can the sociological structures that might make integrationism a plausible and continuing option in pluralist democratic societies produce citizens whose civic attitudes and capacities suffice for them to be considered reasonable and politically autonomous participants in a common democratic political life?

Integrationism and the formation of a religious political identity

I argued in the previous sections that embracing political autonomy does not commit one to embracing comprehensive autonomy, but I

---

[103] Nancy L. Rosenblum, "Pluralism and Democratic Education: Stopping Short by Stopping with Schools," in *Moral and Political Education*, ed. Macedo and Tamir. McConnell's argument is in Michael W. McConnell, "Educational Disestablishment: Why Democratic Values Are Ill-Served by Democratic Control of Schooling," in *Moral and Political Education*, ed. Macedo and Tamir. Arguments similar to his can be found in the intellectual heirs of the Dutch Calvinist integrationists I discussed above. See Chaplin, "Can Liberal Democracy Accommodate Religious 'Integralism'"; Rockne McCarthy, James W. Skillen, and William A. Harper, *Disestablishment a Second Time: Genuine Pluralism for American Schools* (Grand Rapids, MI: Eerdmans Publishing, 1982). Rosenblum's argument is, I think, correct, but it too "stops short" in the sense that what is assumed is that the desire for a "strong democratic public culture" will necessarily trump the appreciation for pluralism, or, to use my formulation, the desire to live a more integrated life. My argument throughout this chapter has suggested (if only rather obliquely) that it is not unreasonable to be satisfied with a somewhat weaker democratic public culture if such a culture takes better account of our distinctly moral and religious selves.

[104] Rosenblum, "Pluralism and Democratic Education," 148.

have said too little so far about what constitutes a proper standard for strictly *political* autonomy. At the very least, it seems to require a knowledge and acceptance of our rights and liberties that we possess by virtue of our democratic citizenship and a willingness to view others has having the same rights and liberties we have.[105] Beyond that, however, things begin to get a bit murkier, especially if, as I argued in chapters 2 and 3, the standard of reasonableness need not imply an overriding commitment to public reason or deliberative restraint. We can clear the waters a bit, though, by reflecting on what is implied by our reasonable knowledge and capacity to exercise our rights and liberties. First, we must necessarily not be under the domination and social coercion of others. If, for instance, religious liberty is guaranteed under a liberal constitution, then we must necessarily know that we can leave or join a faith and not lose the goods tied to citizenship. We may, as Tomasi notes, refuse to *exercise* our rights, but we cannot alienate them, and this places limits on others' control over our lives (however much we might seek to give that control over).[106] Second, and I think this perhaps more important, we must come to respect the *distinctiveness* of politics as a practice meant to secure distinctively *political* goods. The first point about how rights create social limits implies as much. Once we recognize that we have certain rights and that this places limits on others (and ourselves), we must also come to accept the idea that the institution primarily charged with protecting these rights – the state – is not reducible to the society it governs and that our relationship to that state – our political identity – is not simply coextensive with our own more comprehensive identity. Though we need not understand our political identity as one that is freestanding with respect to our comprehensive one, neither can they be entirely conflated. A proper understanding of political autonomy must seemingly include, then, the development of a political identity that embraces democratic politics as a distinctive practice meant to secure the goods implied by our (and others') status as free and equal citizens.

Now note something important about the questions with which I ended the last section. My question primarily focuses on integrationism's civic effects, the formation of what Rosenblum has called a "religious political

---

[105] As I noted earlier, Rawls thinks that political autonomy will require that a reasonable education will "include such things as knowledge of ... constitutional and civic rights so that ... [we are prepared] to be fully cooperating members of society and ... self-supporting; it should also encourage the political virtues so that [we] want to honor the fair terms of cooperation in their relations with the rest of society" (*Political Liberalism*, 77).

[106] Tomasi, *Liberalism beyond Justice*, 48–55.

identity."[107] She suggests that one of the things that religious parties (and their accompanying subcultures) do – of which political theorists have been too little cognizant – is inculcate in their members a particular kind of political identity, a way of relating religious faith to political action that can be, though certainly need not be, good for democracy. So what sorts of political identities did these integrationist subcultures and their affiliated parties create and were they consonant with or productive of democratic political autonomy?

In his famous encomium to what he described as the Netherlands' consociational democracy, Lijphart argued that deference, which he defined as "an individual's acceptance of his position both in the social hierarchy and on the scale of political authority, accompanied by a low level of participation and interest in politics,"[108] was absolutely necessary for that pillarized society to work. In a society as deeply divided as was the early twentieth-century Netherlands, political elites needed a great deal of flexibility in negotiating political compromises. They could only exercise that flexibility, Lijphart suggests, because they could be reasonably sure that their voters would not desert them. Holland's citizens, especially its religious ones, he thought largely passive in their political life and all too willing to allow party and cultural elites to negotiate on their behalf without much input or, he says, accountability. Some commentators have even characterized Dutch elections before the mid-1960s as looking more like a "census" than a competitive election.[109] Now, it should be said that some of Lijphart's evidence for this is fairly thin[110] (at least by contemporary standards of social science), but suppose that for the most part he is right and that those citizens embedded within the religious subcultures tended to defer to that subculture's social and political elites in making their political choices. These voters had, we might say,

---

[107] The phrase is from Nancy L. Rosenblum, "Religious Parties, Religious Political Identity," pp. 36–38. See also Nancy L. Rosenblum, *On the Side of the Angels: An Appreciation of Parties and Partisanship* (Princeton, NJ: Princeton University Press, 2008), 319–67.

[108] Lijphart, *Politics of Accommodation*, 144–45.

[109] Houska, *Influencing Mass Political Behavior*, 58. Similarly, nineteenth- and early twentieth-century critics of Germany's Center Party often thought that many of the Center's voters, especially the poorly educated peasants, were simply doing the local priest's bidding. For accounts of such criticisms (and some illuminating anti-Catholic cartoons) see Margaret Lavinia Anderson, "Clerical Election Influence and Communal Solidarity: Catholic Political Culture in the German Empire, 1871–1914," in *Elections before Democracy: The History of Elections in Europe and Latin America*, ed. Eduardo Posada Carbó (New York: St. Martin's Press, 1996); Anderson, *Practicing Democracy*.

[110] On the basis of public opinion surveys, he said that the Dutch seemed more impressed with ambition and respect than other democratic citizens and less willing to start new political organizations to solve problems, but the differences among the countries are not large and it is rather unclear to me exactly how "ambition" and "respect" turn into deference. See Lijphart, *Politics of Accommodation*, 145–62.

a "deferential political identity." Trusting their political leaders primarily on the basis of a shared identity, the argument might go, these citizens deferred to those leaders' judgment.

Taken in one way, this looks to be quite problematic. If a religious subculture is so thoroughly subordinated to religious authority that citizens' religious political identities are not just political identities informed by religious views but are, instead, just simply religious views, then it is hard to see where those integrationist citizens might be exercising or capable of distinctive political responsibility. No plausible view of political autonomy fails to distinguish in some way between religious and political views, and if integrationism's civil society strategies require that believers hand over the capacity to make political judgments, then integrationism might rightly be judged wanting in political autonomy. To reconfigure Callan's phrase, the integrationists might not be ethically servile, but they might be so politically.

It seems to me, however, that this is very much *not* the case with the European integrationists. Ironically enough, it was their thoroughgoing integrationism, and in particular the extension of their religious views into political life, that made the crucial difference. As Lijphart (and others) have pointed out, one of the things that made these religious subcultures work was how their different organizations (trade unions, newspapers, broadcast associations, and so forth) were tightly interlinked through a network of reciprocal memberships, directors, and practical cooperation. These subcultures could only work as they did, however, because they were sustained by a common religious identity, and though this common identity and its propensity to "deference" sets off our alarms, it also produced powerful benefits for the development of a religious political identity compatible with a reasonable understanding of democratic citizenship.

Political deference did not mean that the parties were kings of the subcultures and that their leaders could just dictate whatever policies they happened to want.[111] Moreover, tight linkages among the different elements of these subcultures did *not* mean that they represented a uniform juggernaut. Indeed, what is so interesting about these subcultures is the degree to which their different elements, though united within a common identity, functioned relatively independently. Long before Michael Walzer made similar arguments, the Dutch Calvinist theologian and politician Abraham Kuyper argued, following Prinsterer, in favor of what he called "sphere sovereignty," the idea that "the family, the [sic] business, science, art and so forth are all social spheres, which do not owe their

---

[111] Ibid., 159, suggests that "the elite are mainly successful because they do in fact manage to satisfy their [followers'] expectations."

existence to the state, and which do not derive the law of their life from the superiority of the state, but obey a high authority within their own bosom; an authority which rules, by the grace of God, just as the sovereignty of the state does."[112] Though the state is still responsible to God, on Kuyper's view, to pursue its purpose (justice), it is nonetheless distinct from specifically religious authority. Instead, it is "only through the conscience of the persons invested with [political] authority" that states are to be governed.[113] The masthead to Kuyper's newspaper, *De Standaard*, declared his political goals: "A free church in a free state." Faith and politics, while never entirely separate, were also never conflated.

Consider also the Center Party's struggles in Germany throughout the first two decades of the twentieth century to maintain itself as an organizational and electoral force. Its success in beating back the *Kulturkampf* lessened the political salience of its Catholic identity and meant that its coalition was at risk of falling apart, especially in light of socialist inroads into its trade unions and the working-class vote, producing a number of intra-party conflicts. The most prominent of these conflicts, known as the *Zentrumsstreit*, was sparked by an article written by a Center leader, Julius Bachem, entitled "We Must Come Down from the Tower." The Center had used the image of a tower in its campaign literature as a way of projecting its image as a protector of the Catholic community. But inasmuch as the tower symbolized the Center's successes, especially during the *Kulturkampf*, it also symbolized its political isolation, as it continued to find it difficult, if not impossible, to build lasting coalitions with any of the other, mostly Protestant, parties. Bachem provocatively argued that if the Center was to survive as a political party, it needed to shed its Catholic confessional identity and pursue coalitions with (the largely Protestant) conservatives.[114] Among other things, this would mean nominating Protestant candidates even in heavily Catholic districts

---

[112] Kuyper, *Lectures on Calvinism*, 90. For further discussions on sphere sovereignty, see Jonathan Chaplin, "State and Civil Society in Christian Democracy: The Neo-Calvinist Perspective" (paper presented at the Meeting of the American Political Science Association, San Francisco, CA, 2001); Peter Heslam, *Creating a Christian Worldview: Abraham Kuyper's Lectures on Calvinism* (Grand Rapids, MI: Eerdmans Publishing, 1998); Luis E. Lugo, ed., *Religion, Pluralism and Public Life: Abraham Kuyper's Legacy for the Twenty-First Century* (Grand Rapids, MI: Eerdmans Publishing, 2000). This is, in some ways, quite similar to the British pluralist position in the early part of the twentieth century. See Paul Q. Hirst, "J.N. Figgis, Churches and the State," in *Religion and Democracy*, ed. David Marquand and R. Nettler (Oxford: Blackwell, 2000); Paul Q. Hirst, ed., *The Pluralist Theory of the State: Selected Writings of G.D.H. Cole, J.N. Figgis, and H.J. Laski* (New York: Routledge, 1989).

[113] Kuyper, *Lectures on Calvinism*, 104.

[114] Ronald J. Ross, *Beleaguered Tower: The Dilemma of Political Catholicism in Wilhelmine Germany* (Notre Dame, IN: University of Notre Dame Press, 1976), 35.

and demonstrating that "the Center was in fact a political, not a denominational, party."[115]

Bachem and his allies believed that a sincere attempt to deconfessionalize the Center would help them solve a longstanding issue for the Catholic community: the "Parity Question."[116] Subtle (and overt) discrimination, combined with Catholics' generally lower levels of education, had meant that Catholics were generally underrepresented in higher education, the civil service, and owners of industry. Bachem seemed to think that "If Roman Catholics were to attain parity in Wilhelmine society, the Centrum had to allay traditional Protestant fears concerning the party's connections to Rome."[117] That meant downplaying the kinds of *Kulturpolitik* that had occupied the Center for most of its existence and hoping that that such a move would allow it to form alliances with conservative Protestants whose *Mittelstand* constituencies would hopefully share their concerns.

Bachem's article unleashed a storm of controversy, as his critics accused him of abandoning the church and his allies responded by noting that the party had been consistently losing voters and that its only real option was to attempt to escape the confessional straitjacket and attract allies outside the Catholic milieu.[118] On the surface, as Anderson notes, it is difficult to see what all the fuss was about. The Center had always advertised itself as an inter-confessional party and had often included Protestants, even if only a few, in their caucus. Even an observer as sympathetic to Bachem's position as Ross admits that the "proposal was little more than a political stratagem"[119] whose most radical act would be to alter the Center's electoral rhetoric a bit. It is also unclear who Bachem and his allies thought were willing and ready to ally with even a formally deconfessionalized Center. Germany's popular Protestant League, formed in 1887 to combat Catholicism, fought long and hard to exclude Catholics – especially the ultramontane sort represented by the Center – from public life in Germany.[120] During the 1907 Reichstag election, anti-Catholic rhetoric soared to heights not seen since the *Kulturkampf*, Chancellor Bülow calling ultramontanism "the greatest enemy of our people and fatherland."[121] Anti-Catholicism meant that any party composed even mostly of Catholics would have a hard time in finding reliable political allies.

However Bachem and his allies might work to reshape the Center's electoral message, the simple fact remained that the Center depended

---

[115] Anderson, "Interdenominationalism, Clericalism, and Pluralism," 353.
[116] Ross, *Beleaguered Tower*, 38.   [117] Ibid., 33.
[118] Ibid., 38.   [119] Ibid.
[120] Smith, *German Nationalism and Religious Conflict*, 126–38.
[121] Quoted ibid., 141.

fundamentally on its religious identity and, more practically, on its clerical allies and their organizational infrastructure for its political life. Priests acted as information conduits, ran many of the party's affiliated organizations, acted as editors of Catholic publications, and could dispense (or withhold) the kinds of social and political patronage at the local level absolutely necessary for the very decentralized and fissiparous Center to hold together.[122] It seems implausible to think either that the conservative Protestants Bachem hoped to attract could generate the kind of electoral support that Catholic candidates could or that the priests and other Catholic organizations would work very hard to elect them. In the early 1900s, for example, the Center saw its vote totals decline, in part because its voters were repeatedly asked to switch their votes among conservatives, socialists, and liberals, depending on local circumstances.[123] Simply put, given the nature of Germany's confessional divide, especially Catholicism's minority status and Protestants' hostility, the Center could survive only as a confessional party.

Surely Bachem and his allies understood this? They were not mere political neophytes, after all, and even their opponents, though more attentive to the church's requests, understood the Center's identity as a political party. To take one example, on Easter Tuesday in 1907, a group of "integrationists" (as Evans calls them) met in Cologne to draft a set of principles in opposition to Bachem's. They emphasized closer ties to the episcopacy and urged the Center to pursue its interests "in harmony with the basic principles of the Catholic world-outlook."[124] Nonetheless, even theirs was a *political* Catholicism – Anderson notes that no one in the Center "wanted any bishop or priest to tell him how to vote in the Reichstag."[125] She argues, in fact, that Bachem's opponents were just more critical "towards the social and political status quo" and thought that the calls for inter-denominationalism "could only signify an undignified willingness to mute unpopular *Catholic* demands, such as the repeal of the Jesuit law, in exchange for social acceptance within the national consensus."[126] They thought, in essence, that only the "vigorous assertion of [Catholic] particularity" could acceptably safeguard

---

[122] Anderson, *Practicing Democracy*, 108–10.

[123] Stanley Suval, *Electoral Politics in Wilhelmine Germany* (Chapel Hill: University of North Carolina Press, 1985), 67. In the German voting system, a candidate had to win a majority of the votes cast, meaning that run-offs were quite common. In areas where Catholics were a minority, the Center could not hope to win a seat and so often made electoral alliances with their opponents to provide votes in the second round.

[124] Evans, *The German Center Party*, 200.

[125] Anderson, "Interdenominationalism, Clericalism, and Pluralism," 368.

[126] Ibid., 363.

the Catholic community and that "the Center was there in order that Catholics themselves not 'disappear'."[127]

The *Zentrumsstreit* overlapped with and to some degree reinforced a contemporaneous dispute over workers' associations. Catholic workers' associations had been formed as early as the 1850s as means of providing religious education and social melioration to workers thrown into the often brutal world of early industrial Germany. These associations were controlled by clerics, eschewed strikes as instruments of class warfare, and emphasized strongly their Catholic identity – to the exclusion of cooperation with similarly situated Protestants. In the face of socialist successes in organizing both Protestant and Catholic workers, organizers put together inter-confessional "Christian" trade unions that were a good bit more militant and willing to strike. Worried that such unions fostered "religious indifference," the German bishops published a pastoral letter in September 1900 extolling the virtues of the workers' associations and criticizing the unions.[128] The majority of the Center came down firmly on the side of the unions, worried that the only way they could hope to stall the socialists' successes in organizing Catholic workers was through inter-denominational unions. Pope Pius X issued the encyclical *Singulari Quadam* in 1912, which expressed a preference for the workers' associations – unsurprising, given Pius' strong promotion of "integrationist" theology – but nonetheless declined to condemn inter-denominational trade unions and by 1913 they simply overwhelmed the workers' associations and the conflict largely subsided.[129]

The *Zentrumsstreit* and related conflicts turned out, then, not to be so much about inter-denominationalism versus integrationism per se, but rather about the sorts of *political* goals and issues the Center and its allies ought to emphasize. Party leaders, though they had a good bit of flexibility in their day-to-day political negotiations, were not free to disregard the interests of their constituents, voters who were constituents, we should note, largely by virtue of their confessional attachment. When party leaders did disregard those interests or attempted to run roughshod over them, the "religious vote" simply went elsewhere. Recall Windthorst's agile speech in which he affirmed the Center's political identity but retained its religious character.

The point here is that the very things that make the European integrationists so interesting and seemingly dangerous from the liberal

---

[127] Ibid., 374–75.
[128] Thomas M. Bredohl, *Class and Religious Identity: The Rhenish Center Party in Wilhelmine Germany* (Milwaukee, WI: Marquette University Press, 2000), 152–54.
[129] Evans, *The German Center Party*, 200.

consensus's perspective are also the very things that make it productive of this sort of political capacity. European integrationists, especially in the Netherlands and Germany, built robust religiously oriented subcultures meant to encompass believers within structures consonant with the faith. Thinking these structures inconsistent with the development of political autonomy, while a reasonable inference, misses the ways in which the subcultural institutions were (a) closely tied to the faith and yet also independent of its ecclesiastical control and (b) closely tied to one another and yet often in competition for the chance to shape the institutions' political goals and strategies. These subtle sociological tensions went some way, I think, toward teaching believers how to judge their political options *as* political options – that is, how to grasp some political autonomy.

Rosenblum has recently emphasized the ways in which the development of a *partisan* political identity pays real democratic dividends.[130] This seems true to an even greater degree with respect to *religious* political parties. Key to her analysis, it seems to me, is how parties as parties draw their followers into the broader political system and by virtue of their *partisan* nature implicitly commit those followers to respecting the basis of democratic politics. Once the religious subcultures committed themselves via their political parties to pursuing their public goals through politics and especially through competing in elections, managing coalitions, and deliberating in parliamentary bodies, they implicitly, if all that much more powerfully, reshaped their own political identities. It is no surprise that the Catholic Church largely opposed the formation of the Center and its sister parties, since their success would challenge the church's claim to be the faithful's sole representatives.[131] Anderson especially emphasizes how the Center's political activity engendered a kind of "habituation" in the exercise of democratic politics; Center followers learned to be, as she notes, democrats before there was democracy.[132] And even if Kalyvas may not quite be right to say that a secular political identity was the inevitable outcome of party formation, he is right to say that the parties induced a rather robust political independence. Again, the alternative here would seem to be France, where the church's tight control of social and political movements not only prevented the movement's success, but also meant that ordinary Catholics did not have the opportunity to develop a political identity that was both Catholic and distinctively political. Rather, they had to choose between the two, with deeply troubling effects.[133]

[130] Rosenblum, *On the Side of the Angels*, chapter 7.
[131] Kalyvas, *The Rise of Christian Democracy in Europe*, 18ff.
[132] Anderson, *Practicing Democracy*, 150.
[133] See Kalyvas, *The Rise of Christian Democracy in Europe*, 115–66.

Conclusion

When liberals consider what set of attitudes, habits, and virtues they think citizens in liberal democracies require, some sort of autonomy is almost always at the top of that list. And almost just as often, religion is thought damaging to the same. This is certainly not an unreasonable claim, and I think it even true with respect to what I have called comprehensive autonomy. This sort of celebration of individual choice – Mill is still its most eloquent advocate – runs up against many religious views that make obedience and submission to God a central element of the good life. This conflict is probably especially true for integrationists, who tend to construct elaborate institutional barriers in order to thwart autonomy's seductive attractiveness. If comprehensive autonomy is a basic interest that all humans share, then the integrationists can quite plausibly be thought to run afoul of that and thus can be the object of political intervention. But as I have argued, comprehensive autonomy is not properly a basic human interest, though a narrower form of autonomy – independence – is. Though it is likely that there *are* integrationists who run afoul of even independence, these European integrationists did not, and in the powerfully pluralistic cultures in which most of us now live (and which make integrationist institutions necessary) it is hard to imagine many doing so.

More interestingly, perhaps, the experience of the European integrationists should suggest to us that integrationism and its mobilization on the basis of religious belief and identity in political life is not destructive of political autonomy, but quite consonant with and perhaps constructive of it as well. The parties exercised and their followers developed a sort of political autonomy that, though not separating politics from everything else, distinguished it sufficiently to qualify the integrationists as citizens in good standing. Politics has its proper "sphere." Parties (and their supporters) must learn how to reason *politically* about politics, and even if that reasoning politically necessarily includes considerations of how religious views matter, politics on this account does not simply reduce to religious dogma. In a world constituted by reasonable pluralism, not only must citizens learn to reason politically about politics; they must also learn to integrate that reasoning into their personal, sometimes quite non-liberal lives. Otherwise, they will always be tempted into dispensing with their political liberalism or their non-political views, a temptation whose outcome could end quite badly for political liberalism. This, it seems to me, is what the European parties and their associated subcultures did well. Rather than making religious individuals choose between their faith and their politics, they rather artfully found ways to connect the two without obviously sacrificing either. The sorts of institutions and social norms necessary for making integrationism a plausible option in a pluralistic world *are* compatible with a reasonable understanding of political autonomy, and maybe even at times productive of it, precisely because in the process of mobilizing, organizing, and participating in democratic or proto-democratic politics, they learned to give politics its distinctive place in the light of their religious commitments.

6 Making the most of conflict: religion and political toleration

Suppose that it is true, as I have argued in the previous chapters, that religious believers in pluralist liberal democratic societies may not only consult their religious views when deliberating about or taking political action, but that they may do so independently of other, putatively public views, all without endangering the possibility of political legitimacy. Suppose further, if just to humor my argument, that this political mobilization of religion, ensconced within institutions designed to buttress them against modernity's pressures, is quite compatible with and sometimes even productive of political autonomy. Even if there are good reasons for thinking that religious beliefs do not threaten legitimacy or the capacity for autonomy, many liberal theorists rightly worry that those beliefs could and will have oppressive political consequences, in particular undermining liberalism's traditional protections for pluralism and diversity. In short, the worry goes, religion can still pose a significant problem for a regime of political toleration.

You can hardly peruse a book on religion and politics – never mind *liberal* politics – without running into plenty of ominous rehearsals of how religion embodies, breeds, and institutionalizes intolerance. Distinctly *intolerant* religious views (to understate it pretty strongly) combined with political ambition to drive the destructive religious wars in Europe in the sixteenth and seventeenth centuries. When Islamic terrorists behead "infidels" in a bid to secure a theocratic *umma*, it is no slur to think them intolerant (and their intolerance deeply abhorrent). Only in the 1960s did the world's largest religious body, the Roman Catholic Church, officially endorse religious liberty, though many Catholics had endorsed it in practice long before that. Survey upon survey shows a negative relationship between religious belief or practice and tolerance, especially among those purported paragons of American intolerance, evangelical Protestants.[1]

---

[1] See Klosko, *Democratic Procedures and Liberal Consensus*. Christian Smith tempers that view a bit, though it is still clear that, in general, conservative Protestants at least are less tolerant than others. See Smith, *Christian America?*.

We should not be surprised that holding strong religious beliefs seems to conduce toward intolerance. Most religious traditions involve a divine being who legislates out of perfect knowledge, wisdom, and goodness not just about matters "spiritual," but about matters temporal as well. Believers' religious views make serious claims about things central to who we are as human beings, and if they honestly believe that others are mistaken – to the point of risking condemnation in both this life and the life to come – it is certainly not unreasonable to think that they should be "encouraged" to repudiate those mistakes. It is much easier, psychologically speaking, to let others live as they so choose, to be "tolerant," if you are skeptical about whether any way of life is right or true.[2] So it is not surprising that, historically speaking, tolerance has been the exception rather than the rule.[3]

Even if Galston is not quite right to say that liberalism is all about the protection of pluralism, it does seem right to say that such protection constitutes one of liberalism's core purposes.[4] The circumstances of pluralism occasion tolerance in two senses. First, citizens need to be "personally" tolerant, capable of putting up with or enduring the everyday frictions that come with living in a society where others live lives substantially different from your own, what Nancy Rosenblum calls the "democracy of everyday life."[5] Second, those attitudes must connect to political norms and institutions, providing for what we can call "political" tolerance. Both sorts are crucial, and neither is straightforwardly reducible to the other. No set of democratic institutions could long survive a political culture in which rival groups were bent on killing one another at the least provocation. And if personal tolerance is not matched by its political correspondent, we could end up in a society marked by the conjoining of a sometimes easy comity with significant public injustice and oppression.[6]

---

[2] Though, as a number of people have pointed out, a thoroughgoing skepticism does not necessarily translate into tolerance since we might be skeptical of the value of tolerance as well. Hobbes' *Leviathan* is certainly one example of how skepticism regarding the good life for humans can result in something less than toleration. Cf. Richard Tuck, "Scepticism and Toleration in the Seventeenth Century," in *Justifying Toleration*, ed. Mendus.

[3] This last point is especially true if we restrict tolerance to its relatively narrow liberal meaning. See Michael Walzer, *On Toleration* (New Haven: Yale University Press, 1997).

[4] See Galston, "Two Concepts of Liberalism."

[5] Nancy L. Rosenblum, "The Democracy of Everyday Life," in *Liberalism without Illusions: Essays on Liberal Theory and the Political Vision of Judith N. Shklar*, ed. Judith N. Shklar and Bernard Yack (Chicago: University of Chicago Press, 1996).

[6] One need only reflect on the many stories that emerged from the segregated American South of whites who had close, genuine friendships with blacks and seemingly thought nothing incongruous about supporting those blacks' disenfranchisement and political oppression.

In thinking about the question of religion and political tolerance more closely, we will see that the connection between religion and political intolerance is neither direct nor easy. Again focusing on the cases of Europe's religious integrationists, I argue that even if integrationists (and religious believers in general) tend to be less tolerant than other kinds of citizens, such intolerance does not straightforwardly translate into a system of *political* intolerance. In keeping with the argument I have made in the earlier chapters (especially chapter 5), I suggest that when liberal democratic societies have integrationist citizens, their political organization, rather than being a threat to political toleration, may indeed be crucially productive of it. Though it sounds quite counterintuitive, such organization and mobilization can actually (and sometimes ironically) have the effect of making political tolerance a plausible, though by no means inevitable, political outcome.

I proceed below in three steps. First, I develop an argument as to what it is that we should mean philosophically by tolerance, settling on the view that sees tolerance as a practice of judgment in which we adjudicate among competing and irreconcilable goods and come to understand which goods ought to be forgone in favor of others. I then ask what that understanding might mean for a system of political tolerance, arguing in favor of "substantive neutrality," a view that the commonplace liberal claim that the state should not favor one way of life over another provides good reason for it to take affirmative steps to ameliorate the negative effects of its aspirationally "neutral" institutions. Finally, employing the case studies of the European integrationists, I suggest how religious integrationism in particular might indeed be productive of this sort of political tolerance. These integrationists' histories illustrate how it is that the moral and religious conflict that makes political toleration so important can also make it plausible, provided that a democratic society's partisans are given the opportunity to engage those differences politically. As with the chapters that precede it, this chapter does not mean to suggest that religion per se, or even politically organized religion per se, necessarily produces political toleration. Rather, it merely suggest ways in which it can produce – and has helped produce – such an outcome, thus showing how the confidence of the liberal consensus is misplaced and in need of some significant revision.

What do we mean by tolerance?

Before we can say much about the relationship between religion and political toleration (for good or ill), we need first to get a clear fix on what it is we mean by "toleration," for it is one of those terms whose meaning appears intuitively obvious and yet deeply disputed. Long a central issue in liberal political thought, it has become a rhetorical weapon in the so-called "culture wars" – being thought intolerant is a major blow to one's credibility for some, while for others tolerance is a sure sign of mushy-minded libertinism – and as such it has been the subject of much renewed discussion and debate.[7] Generally speaking, when we think of tolerance or the practice of toleration, we tend to have in mind the idea of putting up with some practice or belief that we find morally objectionable or inappropriate.[8] It is a mistake to say – though as we will see some persist in this mistake – that we tolerate someone's race or sex, as there simply are no plausible moral grounds for objecting to those

[7] See, for instance, Aminrazavi and Ambuel, *Philosophy, Religion, and the Question of Intolerance*; J. Budziszewski, *True Tolerance: Liberalism and the Necessity of Judgment* (New Brunswick, NJ: Transaction Publishers, 1992); A.J. Conyers, *The Long Truce: How Toleration Made the World Safe for Power and Profit* (Dallas, TX: Spence Publishing, 2001); Ingrid Creppell, *Toleration and Identity: Foundations in Early Modern Thought* (New York: Routledge, 2002); Richard Dees, "Establishing Toleration," *Political Theory* 27, no. 5 (1999); Noah Feldman, "Morality, Self-Interest, and the Politics of Toleration," in *Toleration and Its Limits*, ed. Melissa Williams (New York: New York University Press, 2008); George P. Fletcher, "The Instability of Tolerance," in *Toleration: An Elusive Virtue*, ed. David Heyd (Princeton, NJ: Princeton University Press, 1996); N. Fotion and Gerard Elfstrom, *Toleration* (Tuscaloosa: University of Alabama Press, 1992); Anna E. Galeotti, *Toleration as Recognition* (New York: Cambridge University Press, 2002); David Heyd, "Is Toleration a Political Virtue?," in *Toleration and Its Limits*, ed. Williams; David Heyd, ed., *Toleration: An Elusive Virtue* (Princeton, NJ: Princeton University Press, 1996); J. Horton, "Toleration as a Virtue," in *Toleration: An Elusive Virtue*, ed. Heyd; Michael Ignatieff, "Nationalism and Toleration," in *The Politics of Toleration: Tolerance and Intolerance in Modern Life*, ed. Susan Mendus (Edinburgh: Edinburgh University Press, 1999); Preston T. King, *Toleration* (London: Frank Cass, 1998); Mendus, ed., *Justifying Toleration*; Susan Mendus, "My Brother's Keeper: The Politics of Intolerance," in *The Politics of Toleration*, ed. Mendus; Susan Mendus, *The Politics of Toleration in Modern Life* (Durham, NC: Duke University Press, 2000); Mendus, *Toleration and the Limits of Liberalism*; Susan Mendus and David Edwards, eds., *On Toleration* (New York: Oxford University Press, 1987); Glen Newey, *Virtue, Reason and Toleration: The Place of Toleration in Ethical and Political Philosophy* (Edinburgh: Edinburgh University Press, 1999); Hans Oberdiek, *Tolerance: Between Forbearance and Acceptance* (Lanham, MD: Rowman & Littlefield, 2001); T.M. Scanlon, "The Difficulty of Tolerance," in *Toleration: An Elusive Virtue*, ed. Heyd; Jeff Spinner-Halev, "Hinduism, Christianity, and Liberal Religious Toleration," *Political Theory* 33, no. 1 (2005); Walzer, *On Toleration*; Mary Warnock, "The Limits of Toleration," in *On Toleration*, ed. Mendus and Edwards; Bernard Williams, "Toleration: An Impossible Virtue?," in *Toleration: An Elusive Virtue*, ed. Heyd; Melissa Williams, "Tolerable Liberalism," in *Minorities within Minorities: Equality, Rights, and Diversity*, ed. Avigail I. Eisenberg and Jeff Spinner-Halev (Cambridge and New York: Cambridge University Press, 2005).

[8] David Heyd, "Introduction," in *Toleration: An Elusive Virtue*, ed. Heyd. Of course, we also say that we tolerate things that don't quite rise to the level of being morally objectionable. I can be said to "tolerate" a friend's perpetual lateness, and the objection can be more one of annoyance than the idea that habitual lateness represents some kind of moral failure. We can, I think, ignore for now this sort of tolerance, since its political impact is rather negligible and its relation to religious beliefs quite tenuous.

sorts of characteristics.[9] You might as well object to someone's height or the length of her nose. It might be proper, on the other hand, to say that we tolerate someone whose views or acts we find objectionable, if, to stick with the example, her views or acts were related to a particular racial or sexual identity. It is not the race or sex per se, but the activities or ideas emerging (perhaps accidentally) from those physical facts that can be the proper object of moral evaluation. It nearly goes without saying that a good many people have difficulty in making this admittedly fine distinction, and that they all too often claim that they are making moral judgments about activity or views when in fact those judgments are simply cover for an unjustified antipathy toward persons' (largely) unchangeable characteristics. Many are, perhaps rightly, suspicious of toleration precisely because it seems to track with claims to "hate the sin and love the sinner," and they suspect that the hate for "sin" all too easily overwhelms love for the "sinner."[10] Nonetheless, unless we are to embrace antinomianism and give up on the practice of moral judgment altogether – something that would make tolerance entirely irrelevant – we will inevitably make these sorts of often difficult distinctions.

Notice something important that follows from this. To the degree that toleration is inextricably linked to what we find morally objectionable, we are bound to take into account others' capacity to act on their own accord. In a word, we are bound to take into account others' individual agency and autonomy; how else would it make sense to suggest that we might rightly make the actions or beliefs of another person the object of moral judgment while making her largely immutable characteristics strictly out of bounds? For some, the claim for autonomy almost entirely drives and conditions the argument for toleration. Hans Oberdiek argues that toleration is necessary so that men and women might best develop their "individuality" and pursue their "self-directed life."[11] Oberdiek's claim is but an updated version of John Stuart Mill's justly famous argument in *On Liberty*, where Mill looks to maximize political *and* social toleration as a means to protecting and encouraging human individuality. In the previous chapter, I argued that autonomy properly understood (as independence) was indeed an indispensable feature of the human good, but I also argued that its maximization, Millian-style, counted as merely one of the good lives humans might live. It was not the sole one (or even, necessarily, the best one). As Susan Mendus has pointed out, there are any number of problems with the maximal autonomy claim, not least

---

[9] Horton, "Toleration as a Virtue."

[10] This is obviously the case with contemporary debates over homosexuality.

[11] Oberdiek, *Tolerance*, vi, 120. See also Gill, *Becoming Free*; Kymlicka, *Multicultural Citizenship*.

that it might require some rather unsavory and illiberal practices to make those who are incapable of exercising their individuality or for some reason refuse to do so become capable or willing.[12]

Indeed, we might just say that the signal problem with making toleration simply a handmaid to the maximal autonomy claim is that it narrows toleration's scope too much and that decoupling toleration from an exclusive reliance on autonomy can make toleration more capacious and more defensible rather than less. Moshe Halbertal argues, in the course of criticizing Will Kymlicka's autonomy-based claim for group rights, that by focusing on what is "important and central in … life" rather than what is putatively "chosen" rationally we can better describe the kind of harm that can come to people who are the objects of intolerance. On this account intolerance harms us by "robbing [us] of the possibility of continuing a way of life that harbors great meaning for [us] as individuals"[13] rather than just undermining our ability to *choose* some way of life. What is crucial to recognize here, though, is that this does *not* mean that autonomy is somehow unimportant. Halbertal suggests that toleration concerned exclusively with protecting autonomy misses the ways in which thing that are "unchosen" also hold great meaning for us and cites as an example the story of Paul's conversion to Christianity on the road to Damascus (as related in Acts 9). Halbertal points out that Paul's conversion was not simply the product of rational reflection and that to "tolerate" such a conversion simply in terms of autonomy misdescribes what it is that is being tolerated. That does not mean that Paul had no choice in the matter, though, a point that Halbertal seems to miss. After his vision on the Damascus road, Paul traveled on to Damascus, joined the Christians there, and began preaching, putting his own life in danger. At each point along the way, he had and made a choice (and if tradition is to be believed, paid for those choices with a martyr's death). Conversion can be said to be tolerated, if it is, because it corresponds to something in us that is amenable, in some sense, to change, even if "choice" does not exhaust the description of conversion. The very idea of conversion relies upon this point. Toleration is inextricably tied to moral evaluation and individual autonomy, though the latter is, as we will see, but one of many competing goods that factor in.

The idea of tolerance also indicates that the practice in question is itself within our moral and practical reach. As Preston King puts it, tolerance

---

[12] Mendus, *Toleration and the Limits of Liberalism*, 65–66. See also Joseph Hamburger, *John Stuart Mill on Liberty and Control* (Princeton, NJ: Princeton University Press, 1999).

[13] Moshe Halbertal, "Autonomy, Toleration, and Group Rights," in *Toleration: An Elusive Virtue*, ed. Heyd, 109–10. This argument is similar to Kukathas, *The Liberal Archipelago*.

"presupposes a *power* to act out the objection" to a particular practice and the decision to not act on that power.[14] Tolerance is, he notes, quite distinct from "acquiescence," where we accept something because it is futile to do otherwise. If my neighbor decides to paint her house bright pink, I cannot be said to tolerate her choice of color; I have no plausible means of forcing her to do otherwise, besides perhaps remarking that it made her house look like it was something you could buy at a toy store. If, on the other hand, she parked her cars on her front yard, in contravention of a city ordinance banning the practice, I could decide whether to call the proper authorities and have her ticketed or not. (Whether these examples rise to the level of moral objections is perhaps another discussion.) Similarly, I cannot be said to tolerate the way that Saudi Arabia systematically mistreats women, since there is nothing I can do directly about it. That does not mean I cannot find the practice objectionable (I do); it just means that it is not a question of tolerance, at least not on an interpersonal scale.[15] So toleration has the character of declining to take action against what we view as morally objectionable when, if we chose, we could act and have some expectation of preventing it or at least limiting its scope or effects.

Tolerance is *unnecessary* in two sorts of situations: (a) where everyone agrees on what is moral, and (b) if everyone agrees that *nothing* is moral or immoral. If (b) is true, as I noted, there is no need to even talk about tolerance, for there is nothing that can be the object of reasonable moral opprobrium.[16] But that is also the case if (a) is true, for if everyone actually agrees on what is moral, then no one can rightly object to being coerced on those moral grounds. Some seem to look forward to just that kind of situation, suggesting that toleration an inherently paradoxical and incoherent concept, less a virtue and more a relic of outmoded moral judgmentalism.[17] Bernard Williams, for one, has famously noted:

The difficulty with toleration is that it seems to be at once necessary and impossible. It is necessary where different groups have conflicting beliefs – moral, political or religious – and realise that there is no alternative to their living together. [It is impossible] because people find others' beliefs or ways of life deeply unacceptable. In matters of religion, for instance ... the need for toleration arises because one of the groups, at least, thinks that the other is blasphemously, disastrously, obscenely wrong ... It is because the disagreement

---

[14] King, *Toleration*, 24.
[15] Whether it is a case of tolerance on an inter-governmental scale is a completely different question and would involve discussions of the capacity (and willingness) of the United States to force large-scale social change.
[16] Bernard Williams, "Tolerating the Intolerable," in *The Politics of Toleration*, ed. Mendus.
[17] Heyd, "Is Toleration a Political Virtue?"

goes this deep that the parties to it think that they cannot accept the existence of the other. We need to tolerate other people and their ways of life only in situations that make it very difficult to do so. Toleration, we may say, is required only for the intolerable. That is its basic problem.[18]

Toleration seems thus, even at its best, a puzzling conjunction of claims. We are asked to tolerate what is "intolerable," to allow that which we find immoral and wrong to persist or even thrive. If something is truly wrong, then how can we be asked to tolerate it? As Williams has suggested, when we think of toleration as a philosophical or moral idea – he says "value" – this puzzle becomes less opaque when we realize what toleration means is just a balancing of competing goods.[19]

The claim that toleration is paradoxical rests on the odd conjunction that we are to tolerate the "intolerable," and put that way, it does seem like a paradox. But the conjunction looks that way only because it elides the distinction between what is "wrong" and what is "intolerable."[20] The two are not the same thing. Or, at least, they need not be the same thing. We can make sense of the practice of toleration by realizing that it is precisely about understanding when, if ever, the two ought to be separated. A decision to tolerate (or not) does not hang immediately on a conviction about whether some practice is right or wrong. It would be morally wrong, for example, for me to shove my daughter because she did not want to eat her broccoli, though I am clearly in the right about the fact that eating broccoli would do her good. It would be right, however, for me to shove her as a means of getting her out of the way of an onrushing truck. In the former case, I am right, but what I am right about does not entitle me to use coercive force. In the latter, I am right *and* justified in using such force. If toleration is indeed conceptually incoherent or paradoxical, then it has to be shown – not assumed – that our everyday sort of distinctions between "intolerable" and "wrong" do not make sense on their own terms.

The idea of toleration as paradox does help remind us of something important. I noted in the introduction to this chapter that tolerance is occasioned by pluralism. But that is not quite right. Rather, toleration is occasioned by the sort of pluralism that includes genuine and persistent moral disagreement. We can imagine a sort of pluralism in which toleration was unnecessary because the pluralism is too superficial to matter morally, what some have called a kind of "funny hat" pluralism, where the distinctions among us are merely superficial and unconnected to any

---

[18] Williams, "Tolerating the Intolerable," 65.   [19] Ibid.
[20] I should note here that this elision is not a part of Williams' argument. My thanks to Dennis Thompson for his correction on my earlier misreading.

real moral differences or disagreements. Tolerance, *pace* Rousseau, is the way we find to live with one another precisely when we think each other condemned (or profoundly morally wrong).

King seems right, then, when he suggests that the apparent paradox dissolves once we realize that in practicing toleration what we are doing is, in fact, balancing a set of "competing objections."[21] We may, for example, object to someone's religious beliefs, either because we think them wrong or we think them morally noxious, but we tolerate them – when we do – because we think that our objection to denying someone her religious liberty is stronger. If those beliefs include something that we find absolutely unacceptable – say, sacrificing infants – then the religious liberty claim loses out and we are justified in our intolerance. As William Galston has remarked in a different context, there is no religious liberty for the (human-sacrificing) Aztec.[22] Similarly, J. Budziszewski argues that "true tolerance" means "an evil must be tolerated in just those cases where its suppression would involve equal or greater hindrance to goods of the same order, or any hindrance at all to goods of higher order."[23]

All activity is oriented toward some good, but in the world in which we live goods are often in conflict; in choosing to pursue one good, we lose the opportunity to pursue another.[24] Going to graduate school instead of, say, law school means forgoing a reasonable chance at employment and good pay. Toleration is, we might say, just a species of the more general practice of adjudicating among competing and irreconcilable goods, and we distinguish it as a separate practice because inherent in whatever sort of moral calculus we make we must necessarily include the respect we owe other persons simply as persons. When reflecting on whether to tolerate some practice or not, central among the competing claims we must balance is this sense that each person possesses as a person a degree of agency, and autonomy demands a great deal of circumspection on our part. When deciding whether to indulge in some chocolate ice cream or engage in physical exercise, we may attempt to balance out all sorts of goods: the pleasure of good ice cream, the good of physical well-being, the time involved, and so on. But, generally speaking, we are the only ones concerned. In deciding whether to tolerate some practice, on the other hand, the decision inherently involves others, and especially

---

[21] King, *Toleration*.   [22] Galston, *Liberal Pluralism*.

[23] Budziszewski, *True Tolerance*, 13.

[24] Isaiah Berlin has, of course, written extensively on this. Ironically enough, so have a number of decidedly non-liberal natural law theorists. See Finnis, *Natural Law and Natural Rights*; Robert P. George, *Making Men Moral: Civil Liberties and Public Morality* (New York: Oxford University Press, 1993); Robert P. George, ed., *Natural Law Theory: Contemporary Essays* (New York: Oxford University Press, 1992); George, ed., *Natural Law, Liberalism, and Morality*.

involves taking consideration of other individuals' capacity to make their own decisions and be responsible for them.[25] Liberal democratic societies have rightly come to value very strongly the idea that our lives are pretty much our own, that we should be free to live them as we see fit, and that we should do so without undue interference from others. Of course, all of the interesting questions hang on what constitutes "undue," and it is these that the practice of judgment associated with toleration tries to get right.

Suppose I have a neighbor who enjoys viewing pornography in the privacy of his home, and that I think that viewing pornography is both intrinsically and instrumentally harmful.[26] It predisposes him or reinforces tendencies toward committing immoral sexual acts and makes the neighborhood less inviting for families, since there will always be the possibility that children will see it. Suppose further that I decide that the threats posed (intrinsic and instrumental) are grave enough that I should at least consider doing something to dissuade him from continuing. A moment's reflection reveals three options:

(1) I could approach him privately and urge him to quit watching the pornography, appealing to his reason and sense of decency, perhaps even offering to help him avoid the opportunities for viewing it, if he feels like he is "addicted" to it.
(2) I could threaten to expose him to public shaming if he did not quit, telling his friends and neighbors, maybe even writing letters to the newspaper or taking out advertisements.
(3) I could take physical action to prevent him from gaining access to the pornography. I could cut his cable television line, intercept his mail, and sneak into his house and disable his video players.

Option (3) is obviously impermissible. Even if it were the case that we as a society were to decide that viewing pornography should be illegal, I would not be justified in taking it upon myself to enforce such a decision. To do so would be to trespass on the sorts of activities that we generally

---

[25] Chris Eberle calls this "recognition respect" in Christopher J. Eberle, "Religion and Liberal Democracy," in *The Blackwell Guide to Social and Political Philosophy*, ed. R.L. Simon (New York: Blackwell, 2002).

[26] As one of my anonymous reviewers noted, this is in itself a controversial claim, since to someone who does not think there is a plausible moral objection to pornography, the rest of the argument may not make much sense. To the degree that someone thinks that there are *no* immoral self-regarding acts (a view that I think even Mill would reject) then it is perhaps hard to see how to get a toleration argument going. But I doubt very many people hold such a view or that the line between self- and other-regarding acts is possible to police effectively. And so given the range of moral disagreement extant in modern democracies, if readers do not find pornography morally objectionable, they are welcome to substitute something else, perhaps religious integrationism.

and rightly regard as the province of the state. A claim to the contrary collapses the distinctiveness of politics I defended in the last chapter. Option (2) does seem permissible, assuming no problems with libel or defamation laws, though such private exposés are rare, especially when they concern people who are not celebrities or public figures. Why are they so rare? They might be rare because we are simply unsure about how we feel about things like pornography; that would be the answer we might expect if Williams' "paradox" is correct, and no doubt that is sometimes the case. Given the pervasiveness of pornography in modern culture, to stick with my example, we would be hard pressed to say that most people really consider it immoral (a bit distasteful, perhaps, but not immoral). Or, it might be that we do not want others to return the favor. If I expose my neighbor's pornography habit, he might in turn expose some practice of mine I wish to keep private. I suspect both sorts of considerations play into our calculations, but there is another, perhaps more interesting, way of describing our decisions.

Consider a more obvious moral wrong. Suppose that I have a brother who is an out-and-out racist. He deems black people to be fundamentally inferior sorts of beings. Now, I might warn new acquaintances of his execrable views, but I also might decide not to denounce him in public as a means to changing these views. (If he ran for public office that would likely be a different story.) Why not? After all, it might change his mind and that would be an undeniably good thing. But it also might irreparably disrupt our relationship, and we alienate our families – generally speaking – only with great reluctance. We usually value the good, we might say, of family relationships more than the good of convincing a family member to change a wrong opinion. (That this is not always true merely reinforces the difficulty of toleration and, as I argue below, its status as a practice of judgment.) Similarly, then, we might decline to publicly shame our neighbor because we value him as a neighbor. If I denounced him, he might be shamed into giving up his pornography and perhaps he even might thank me (at some point), but it is quite likely that he would also feel quite intruded upon and angry. Indeed, it is hard to see how, as these things usually go, any kind of friendship could continue. In like manner, though option (1) is certainly less "dangerous" to our relationship, if I persisted with trying to persuade him to give up the pornography by mentioning it every time I saw him, sending him books on pornography's dangers, and so on, it is quite likely that he would find himself again quite annoyed and our relationship would be put at risk.

The point here is that to the degree that I decide to "tolerate" my neighbor's taste for pornography, I do so with an eye to the kinds of goods I am securing through that practice of toleration. (The same would be formally true if I decided not to tolerate my neighbor's attraction to pornography.) It is quite reasonable to think that the goods of friendship and community are worth more than hoping my neighbor develops what I consider proper views on sexuality. But the goods are competing and seemingly irreconcilable. I cannot likely try to get him out of his pornography habit while expecting him to remain a good friend. Toleration is best understood, then, as the practice of adjudicating among competing and incompatible goods in the context of behaviors or views that we find morally objectionable.[27]

Note something interesting about the way I have described toleration. It is not toleration itself that we are, strictly speaking, actually interested in. After all, we are at least as interested in when we should be intolerant as when we should be tolerant. We are interested in, rather, the practice of moral judgment, in the adjudication of "competing objections" or competing goods, as I have put it. Heyd is right in some sense, then, to say that toleration is not really a virtue.[28] Unlike courage, deciding to tolerate someone or something is not always appropriate. Similarly, when Oberdiek complains that toleration is inherently unstable, the instability does not come from toleration per se but from the difficulty in getting the moral judgments right.[29] Getting toleration right, what Budziszewski calls "true tolerance,"[30] requires getting our moral judgments right.

That is, I hardly need say, a condition that makes toleration very difficult indeed. The practice of judgment, as Charles Larmore has pointed out,[31] involves (though is not entirely defined by) the invocation of stories and examples as means to help inform our decidedly tenuous decisions about difficult and much controverted moral matters. We invoke those stories and examples out of recognition that moral judgments all too often tread very fine lines about which there is abundant reasonable disagreement. Strict analytic reasoning may very well provide strongly persuasive arguments, but when even the most abstract of thinkers – Larmore cites Kant in this regard – feel compelled to include examples and stories, we can be sure that we are, for better or worse, just simply the sorts of creatures whose moral judgments are tied in some important way to our own stories and examples.[32] Moral reasoning on this account is not *reduced to* stories and examples, but we cannot do it without them.

---

[27] At least in this way, this view lines up with the objections Waldron levies against typical liberal toleration claims in Jeremy Waldron, "Toleration and Reasonableness," in *The Culture of Toleration in Diverse Societies: Reasonable Toleration*, ed. Catriona McKinnon and Dario Castiglione (New York: Manchester University Press, 2003).

[28] Heyd, "Is Toleration a Political Virtue?"   [29] Oberdiek, *Tolerance.*

[30] Budziszewski, *True Tolerance.*   [31] Larmore, *Patterns of Moral Complexity.*

[32] This is, I take it, part of what we are to learn from those who emphasize "narrative" and "tradition." See Stanley Hauerwas, *A Community of Character: Toward a Constructive*

Consider for the moment why we might be so inclined toward such practices. Part of the answer is clearly that we are interested to think about how abstract principles might work in practice. Rawls' shifts in his view of public reason (detailed in chapter 4) emerged out of his reflections on what his exclusive view might mean practically, reflections driven primarily by a consideration of antebellum abolitionist and the civil rights movements. What makes sense in the abstract can suddenly seem rather absurd or unpalatable in the particular. But part of the answer, and this is the part that Alasdair MacIntyre and Charles Taylor have been so influential in developing, is also that the moral claims we invoke and the ways in which we adjudicate among those moral claims (or even decide what counts as a moral claim) is itself a process embedded in particular communities with particular histories. We need not advert to a crude historicism to recognize that our moral judgments rely in important ways on histories within which we find ourselves. Nor need we advert to a crude Whig view of those histories to recognize how those histories can serve to improve our moral judgments. Mark Twain is said to have remarked on how much smarter his father became between the time Twain was a teenager and when he was in his twenties. Even if the quotation is apocryphal, it illustrates something quite true: namely, that we expect, as a general rule, that those with more experience, more history under their belt, will have better judgment. In dealing with someone who cannot seem to learn from his mistakes, we shake our heads and, eventually, throw up our hands in frustration – experience *should* lead to better judgment. We tell stories and use examples in our practice of moral judgment not just as a way of seeing how our principles might apply practically but just as importantly as a way of embedding ourselves in the lessons those borrowed histories might offer. We might think of this account of examples and stories as a kind of history shortcut, allowing us to benefit from their lessons and thus (hopefully) improving our judgments.

So judgment depends in part upon history and the lessons therein. If toleration does, as I have argued, involve the practice of judgment about competing and incompatible moral goods, then it too is thus tied inevitably to stories and examples – to history. Notice what emerges here: we have a picture of toleration that can no longer be reduced to some easy or even straightforward formula. We see why it is so difficult, impossible really, to draw a bright line between, say, "self-regarding" and "other-

Christian Social Ethic (Notre Dame, IN: University of Notre Dame Press, 1981); Alasdair C. MacIntyre, *After Virtue: A Study in Moral Theory*, 3rd edn. (Notre Dame, IN: University of Notre Dame Press, 2007); MacIntyre, *Dependent Rational Animals*; MacIntyre, *Whose Justice? Which Rationality?*

regarding" actions or between acts that cause "harm" and those that do not. We see why simply invoking "autonomy" or "liberty" or some such value cannot solve the problem of toleration, for the choice to tolerate (or not) depends profoundly on contextual details that make us value one good over another. Finally, we see why it is that we so often get that judgment wrong, deciding to tolerate things that we should not and not tolerating things that we should. Toleration's critics are right to be suspicious of the practice, but we should be suspicious for the very reasons we should tolerate: we are fallible, limited creatures who inevitably engage in moral judgments about competing and irreconcilable goods, judgments that are embedded in historical moments and thoroughly suffused with examples and stories meant to enrich those judgments without any sure expectation that we will always get them right.

Political toleration and the argument for substantive neutrality

Tolerance is unavoidable in an interpersonal context, and even if we do not always figure out how to make those judgments properly, we all do make allowances for one another in our daily lives. Or, if we do not, we very quickly become social pariahs. The preachy scold who is quick to point out every transgression and attempts to browbeat others into compliance is more likely to be the subject of mocking satire than sincere emulation. We avoid them when we can and merely endure them when we cannot; we do not seek them out.[33] Political toleration is a rather different matter. Most of us do not "choose" our political communities any more than we choose our families. We are for the most part born into a particular community and must, especially in modern democracies, decide whether and how to tolerate one another politically within those (mostly given) contexts. There is no avoiding one another here, and the stakes are even higher than in our personal lives.

In interpersonal matters, getting toleration wrong might lead to tragic, but limited consequences. Broken friendships, disrupted families, and the like are nothing to cheer about, but neither are they socially catastrophic in the way that a mistaken political decision can be. When a state decides that some activity should not be tolerated, it uses its coercive authority to inflict punishment, impose financial burdens, and so on. These are weighty acts and for the individuals concerned, possibly disastrous. Additionally, political toleration is much more difficult to get

---

[33] This may not be precisely true, at least in cases where the "preachy scold" is scolding only others and not us. We are probably all too likely to seek those out.

right, as it involves a third actor, the state. In thinking about whether to tolerate something personally, the considerations typically only involve a couple of people and the consequences rarely move beyond circles of friends and acquaintances. *Political* toleration means thinking about how an organization that typically holds a monopoly of coercive force in a given area should treat morally controversial questions, something made even more difficult in contemporary liberal societies. For one thing, we disagree quite deeply on what constitutes moral and immoral behavior. This is especially obvious (in contemporary American culture, at least) when it comes to sex, but it hardly stops there, and where the state is supposed to be responsive to the citizenry at large, such disagreement makes it extremely tough to distinguish what the state should and should not be tolerating. What's more, once the liberal state decides to tolerate some practice (or refuses to), it creates what we might call the problem of precedent.[34] Since political decisions in liberal states are generally embodied in law, the political decision on whether to tolerate some practice often ends up extending far beyond the particular question at hand.[35] Take, for instance, the US Supreme Court's decision in *Griswold* v. *Connecticut*. Though directly about the propriety of a state regulating the sale of contraceptives, the decision introduced the right of privacy into the Court's jurisprudence. This led – with a few twists and turns along the way – to what amounted to a finding of sexual liberty as a constitutionally protected right in *Lawrence* v. *Texas*.[36] When courts or legislatures make a decision about a particular issue, they necessarily invoke principles whose evolution and application are not always easy to discern (for good and for ill).

This is especially problematic if toleration is indebted to a practice of moral judgment for which the correct answer is not only disputed but also often indeterminate.[37] When political systems make "mistakes,"

---

[34] Judicial adherence to precedent is obviously not problematic in itself and is a great boon to the rule of law. I just mean to suggest that sometimes precedent can lead us in unexpected directions, directions that are difficult to change precisely *because* they are rooted in precedent and the rule of law.

[35] Eugene Volokh, "The Mechanisms of the Slippery Slope," *Harvard Law Review* 116 (2003).

[36] *Griswold* v. *Connecticut*, 381 US 479 (1965) and *Lawrence* v. *Texas*, 539 US 558 (2003). This is, of course, a rather too hasty gloss on how the court has treated privacy, especially as regards sex, but I think the broader point largely right.

[37] Just to be clear, when I suggest that the "correct answer" is disputed and essentially indeterminate, I do not mean to embrace the rather silly idea that because many of our moral choices involve the adjudication of conflicting and irreconcilable goods, we can say little or nothing about the quality of those moral choices. Even where reason underdetermines our choices – and that is not always the case – we can still say a great deal about whether choices are better or worse than others we might have made.

especially in the context of toleration, they make them in a way that can lock in injustices for generations to come. They make them as institutions, incorporating those mistakes into their constitutive rules. Justice Henry Brown's decision in *Plessy* v. *Ferguson*, for example, locked in segregation for decades, only being overturned in law (though not in practice) by *Brown* v. *Board of Education*. Institutions are "sticky" in the sense that the outcomes they produce are in part dictated by the shape of the institutions themselves, and to the degree that the institutions are a product of significant mistakes, the error can be multiplied over time. When the state makes mistakes about what it tolerates and does not – and it will inevitably make mistakes – it will then be engaging in a practice of political oppression or even endangering its own foundations (to the degree that such mistakes produce Locke's "seditious commotions"). Neither is a particularly attractive prospect, and given how difficult it is to change political institutions, especially when those institutions are intertwined with widespread cultural practices (think here again of racial segregation), mistakes in political toleration can be costly indeed.

Perhaps, then, the state should not be in the toleration business at all. Libertarians have long urged the state to remove itself as far as possible from the sorts of decisions that would require "toleration." So, to take a contemporary issue of some controversy, instead of having the state "tolerate" homosexual relationships and perhaps grant them marital status (or something akin to it), the state would simply get out of the marriage business altogether.[38] Whatever its abstract merit – and I think there is a good deal to be said for it – it is not clear that such recommendations can actually do much to help us think about how to structure *our* social and political life. If it were plausible to think that the state could withdraw from its involvement in social and economic life, then perhaps the libertarian claims could be made good. But there is little evidence to suggest that the state – anywhere – is about to get out of the business of regulating marriage, health care, child care, economic transactions, education, and a whole host of other areas intimately connected to discrete – and morally controversial – ways of life. Quite the opposite, and as long as the state is involved in regulating those things, it will inevitably make decisions about the range of lives that are available, and which are more available than others. And it will make those decisions – also inevitably – in part on the basis of citizens' collective (or majoritarian) sense of things. That is, the liberal democratic state will inevitably be in the business of political toleration.

---

[38] Cf. Michael Kinsley, "Abolish Marriage: Let's Really Get the Government out of Our Bedrooms," *Washington Post*, July 3, 2003.

The most common way liberal theorists have attempted to make toleration an effective political principle is with the idea of neutrality.[39] Ronald Dworkin argues that "political decisions must be, so far as possible, independent of any particular conception of the good life, or of what gives value to life."[40] Similarly, Bruce Ackerman suggests, "A power structure is illegitimate if it can be justified only through a conversation in which some person (or group) must assert that he is (or they are) the privileged moral authority."[41] Generally speaking, the idea of neutrality suggests that the liberal state, insofar as it can, should not favor one way of life over another, thus making the state as tolerant as possible toward the diverse and incompatibly plural ways of life that populate any modern society. Rawls implies that his political liberalism is, in one sense, but an extension of Locke's *Letter Concerning Toleration*.[42]

Broadly speaking, there are two kinds of liberal neutrality, the "neutrality of effect" and "neutrality of intent." The former argues that state action can be considered properly neutral provided that it has an equal impact on those affected; "disparate impact" arguments in legal scholarship more or less embody this sort of neutrality. Rawls argues that a neutrality of effect is "impracticable" as a matter of "commonsense political sociology," noting that it is very difficult – he says it is "futile" – to figure out exactly how basic political institutions affect the long-term fortunes of distinct ways of life and that in any case every sort of society involves "social loss."[43] Instead, he offers that neutrality is violated only when "the well-ordered society of political liberalism fails to establish, in ways that existing circumstances allow – circumstances that include the fact of reasonable pluralism – a just basic structure within which permissible forms of life have a fair opportunity to maintain themselves and to gain adherents over generations."[44] The state that is properly neutral, and thus gives effect to political toleration, does not as a matter of course *intend* to disadvantage any particular way of life, at least among those deemed permissible within liberal democratic societies. As he says elsewhere in his revised discussion of public reason, "Central to the idea of public reason is that it neither criticizes nor attacks

---

[39] For a rather exhaustive critique of the very idea of neutrality, see George Sher, *Beyond Neutrality: Perfectionism and Politics* (Cambridge and New York: Cambridge University Press, 1997). For a response that acknowledges the force of Sher's critiques but nonetheless shows why neutrality continues to have so much currency, see Andrew Koppelman, "The Fluidity of Neutrality," *Review of Politics* 66, no. 4 (2004).

[40] Ronald Dworkin, "Liberalism," in *A Matter of Principle*, ed. R.M. Dworkin (Cambridge, MA: Harvard University Press, 1985), 191.

[41] Ackerman, *Social Justice in the Liberal State*, 10–11.

[42] Cf. Rawls, *Political Liberalism*, 10.   [43] Ibid., 193–200.

[44] Ibid., 198. I should note that Rawls expresses some discontent with the term "neutrality" because it inevitably seems to call to mind the idea of neutrality of effect. See Rawls, *Collected Papers*, ed. Freeman, 460. Nonetheless, he continued to use it.

any comprehensive doctrine, religious or nonreligious, except insofar as that doctrine is incompatible with the essentials of public reason and a democratic polity."[45] Liberal political toleration in this sense requires the neutrality of intent, which means that the liberal state goes as far as it can – while remaining liberal – to avoid importuning those ways of life compatible with a just and stable liberal political regime.

Of course, the very fact that Rawls distinguishes his version of neutrality from a neutrality of effect tells us that some ways of life will inevitably do better than others. He suggests that ways of life permissible under a liberal polity may still "fail to gain adherents" and perhaps even disappear, but that such an outcome, while it might be lamentable, does not necessarily rise to the level of injustice. As long as a liberal society's basic institutions are not "arbitrarily biased" against those ways of life and that the conditions leading to those ways' decline or demise are not themselves unjust, there is little more to be said.[46] Others have not been quite as sanguine as Rawls, suggesting that this sort of benign neglect amounts, in fact, to some very serious injustice. Instead, they argue that a liberal state has the responsibility to ensure that groups of citizens, especially those who have historically been the object of discrimination, feel properly included in the wider political community. Rather than neutrality, the state should pursue what they call recognition.

Recall that one of the things essential for the practice of toleration was some negative moral evaluation. In order to say that you tolerate something, you need to think it morally objectionable. So to the degree that liberal neutrality is meant to instantiate a regime of political toleration, it suggests to those whom it tolerates that their acts or views are thought by the state (or perhaps just the citizens at large) to be disreputable or unsavory. Since those being "tolerated" in a liberal democratic society are likely also to be largely excluded from significant social or political influence – otherwise, they would likely not need political toleration – they are likely to find themselves doubly marginalized. This, as Anna Galeotti points out, has the practical effect of undermining their civic standing by making it impossible for those who are the object of toleration to develop the kind of self-respect deemed necessary by the proponents of recognition for the effective exercise of civic duties.[47] Rather than simply encouraging mutual toleration, the state should, she says, "make all citizens feel positively at ease with their full-blown identities in public as well as private."[48] It should extend, through subsidies, legal protection, or

---

[45] Rawls, "The Idea of Public Reason Revisited," 767.
[46] See Rawls, *Political Liberalism*, 196–99.
[47] Galeotti, *Toleration as Recognition*, 12.   [48] Ibid., 105.

some sort of affirmative cultural policy, political recognition: state action designed to provide material and psychological support for disparate and competing religious, ethnic, or cultural identities.

The demand for recognition emerges from what Charles Taylor has called the quest for "authenticity." The idea here is that the claims for equality, which have long underwritten liberal politics, have evolved in recent times. Rather than claiming that human beings deserve equal respect because they possess some characteristic – rational capacity, *imago Dei*, and so on – we each deserve respect as a creature who has "the potential for forming and defining one's own identity, as an individual, and also as a culture."[49] Since individuals and cultures develop dialogically, the argument goes, and are thus dependent on others' perceptions of them for their flourishing, the demand is that "we all *recognize* the equal value of different cultures; that we not only let them survive, but acknowledge their *worth*."[50] Politically speaking, this means that the state should take positive action to affirm and support distinctive identities, adapt educational curricula, subsidize cultural institutions, and protect cultural traditions with legal exemptions, guaranteed representation, or group vetoes over policy, to give just a few examples.

Recognition has the real virtue of taking account of the ways in which an ostensibly neutral set of political institutions can serve to reinforce or even create social inequalities that can then have pernicious political consequences. But it has real problems as well. It oversimplifies the connection between civic capacities and cultural esteem[51] and neglects the ways in which mediating institutions like families, churches, and parties create cultural identity, making state action less necessary and more problematic.[52] It can very quickly, as both Taylor and Galeotti recognize, run afoul of even the most basic liberal commitments.[53] Arguments in favor of recognition also seem to ignore or (at best elide) the zero-sum

---

[49] Taylor and Gutmann, *Multiculturalism*, 42.
[50] Ibid., 64.
[51] For an argument that American evangelicals thrive in part on the perception that they are an "out-group" under siege from the broader culture see Smith and Emerson, *American Evangelicalism*. Such perceptions reinforce subcultural boundaries and can serve to police inter-cultural disputes.
[52] Rosenblum, *Membership and Morals*, 329–31. I say "more problematic" because political attempts to subsidize cultural identity necessarily have the effect of selecting one version of that identity and probably have the effect of subtly changing that cultural identity in ways that help it secure those subsidies.
[53] Taylor declines to endorse the most robust version of recognition, but rather suggests that we should approach diverse cultures with the "presumption" that they are equally worthy of respect and make judgments to the contrary only after we've delved more deeply therein. For her part, Galeotti suggests that recognition could be "symbolic" and thus avoid running afoul of basic liberal commitments.

quality of some political conflicts: extending recognition to one group means derecognizing another.[54]

Perhaps most importantly, the argument for recognition founders on a tension that stands at the heart of its claims. It claims that in modern democratic societies there exist diverse and contesting ways of life on whose fortunes purportedly neutral laws will have disparate – and unjust – effects. But it then argues that to compensate for (or to avoid) such injustices, laws should be altered and public resources committed to ameliorating those effects. What is lacking is any reasonable argument as to *why* or *how* those laws will be altered or resources committed. Why will the members of these diverse and contesting cultures agree to extend to one another these sorts of resources if, in fact, they are as diverse and contesting as the recognition argument suggests? Indeed, if the marginalized cultures are really as marginalized and despised as advertised, it is hard to see how a practical program of recognition gets off the ground at all, except to the degree that these diverse and contesting ways of life are actually not all that diverse or contested. If, as Galeotti put it, the goal of recognition is to "make all citizens feel positively at ease with their full-blown identities in public as well as private,"[55] that can only happen so long as those identities are relatively easily compatible with one another. Recognition tends to involve the extension of public benefits (money, employment set-asides, legal exemptions, and so on) to minority groups that have historically been the object of social marginalization and ostracism. These benefits must garner, I take it, some reasonably significant levels of political support. It must be the case that some large portion of the population clearly accepts the necessity of extending recognition, and most citizens must already view minority groups at least somewhat positively, meaning in effect that problem for which recognition is meant to be a solution is pretty marginal itself. It seems to me that the argument for recognition, ostensibly an attempt to provide a more capacious response to cultural pluralism, in fact relies on reconstructing the scope of that pluralism so narrowly as to make it largely irrelevant to the kinds of moral conflict that toleration is meant to address.

Recognition fails, then, as an alternative to neutrality, since the preconditions for its political success make it largely unnecessary. Thinking through the recognition claim does, however, point up an important

---

[54] Consider something as relatively innocuous as public holidays. In deciding who or what gets honored with holidays, the state goes some way toward "recognizing" one element of a pluralistic culture over another. To the degree that the state decides to adjust those holidays to shift its recognition, it is likely that some groups will feel slighted as they "lose" their holiday.

[55] Galeotti, *Toleration as Recognition*, 105.

element of the neutrality of intent. The arguments for recognition are rooted in the commonplace observation that institutions can systematically and predictably disadvantage groups of people even if they are not meant to do so. The claim for recognition takes that to mean that the whole edifice of neutrality ought to be overthrown or significantly reconstructed. Rawls (among others) argues, alternatively, that the neutrality of intent is the right way to make toleration politically effective because it fulfills what justice requires and is, unlike the neutrality of effect (and recognition), practical. The neutrality of intent fulfills the requirements of justice because it treats various ways of life fairly. That is, it is not "arbitrarily biased" against some ways of life, biased in ways unnecessary to political liberalism.[56] If, for example, only "individualistic" views of life could survive under a regime of political liberalism, and such disparate effects were not the result of what was required to make such a liberalism work, then, Rawls admits, the neutrality of intent would be violated. It would be unfair to those for whom individualism conflicted with other basic moral views. The mere fact, on the other hand, that some ways of life prosper and others fall into desuetude is not, he thinks, in itself a problem with a neutrality of intent. As long as the institutions do not aim at promoting one way of life over another, no one is done an injustice, even if her way of life does not prosper.

Suppose, though, that some people find it systematically more difficult than others to pursue their way of life because liberalism's political institutions exact what John Tomasi has called an "unequal psychological tax."[57] That is, even though their political views qualify them as citizens in good standing, these citizens find themselves systematically frustrated in pursuing their non-political ends. Alan Wolfe, for example, has argued in a series of books that the United States' economic, educational, political, and cultural institutions have made it quite difficult for the people I have called religious integrationists to sustain themselves, meaning that American religion has become, he thinks, thoroughly suffused with liberal individualism, moral relativism, and a therapeutic culture.[58] If the integrationists are, as I have argued, largely morally and sociologically compatible with liberal politics, and Wolfe is right that they suffer unequally in their attempts to live out their integrationism, should we think that a problem for a neutrality of intent?

As Rawls points out, ways of life might do poorly under political liberalism for one of two reasons. First, they might be "in direct conflict

---

[56] Rawls, *Political Liberalism*, 197.   [57] Tomasi, *Liberalism beyond Justice*, 35.
[58] Wolfe, *Moral Freedom*; Wolfe, *One Nation, after All*; Wolfe, *The Transformation of American Religion*. I should note that he emphatically thinks this a good thing.

with the principles of justice."[59] Slaveholders will find their lives frustrated in liberal societies, but, of course, that is nothing to be concerned about; the fact that ways of life dependent on injustices incompatible with any reasonable sort of liberal politics will not do well under liberal institutions is part of the reason for upholding those institutions in the first place. Second, some ways of life "may be admissible but fail to gain adherents under the political and social conditions of a just constitutional regime."[60] Examples of this type include "certain types of religion" that "can survive only if [they control] the machinery of state and [are] able to practice effective intolerance."[61] Since this sort of religion could only survive provided that the state violates a central liberal claim – religious liberty – its passing (or radical change) might be lamented, but cannot be considered unjust.

Rawls' second example here is a strange one, for it does not seem to differ in principle from the first. In both cases, a way of life or comprehensive view can only be sustained through a political injustice that any liberal democratic regime is fundamentally committed to preventing.[62] More to the point, what does Rawls mean by saying that the coercive religion is "admissible" under a liberal regime? Perhaps he means that a liberal state need not outlaw such a religion, as opposed to its duty to outlaw slaveholding, but in the context of trying to understand whether political liberalism is fair to different ways of life, it is an unhelpful example, to say the least. The question that needs solving is when political institutions systematically disadvantage some people over others, whether they do so for justifiable reasons. So if the establishmentarian religion does poorly, then *by definition* there is not a problem, but that does not mean much more than saying that political institutions animated by liberal principles are unfavorable to those who oppose them. It says nothing about the integrationists, especially to the degree that they are compatible with liberal politics.

Stephen Macedo has taken up this question at some length, but interestingly enough seems to fall victim to this same tendency. Whether he is discussing liberalism's effects on fundamentalists in Tennessee or Roman Catholics in the United States,[63] his answer is largely the same: the religious believers' views are largely incompatible with liberalism properly

---

[59] Rawls, *Political Liberalism*, 196.
[60] Ibid.   [61] Ibid.
[62] As Alfred Stepan has pointed out, of course, an established church is not in itself incompatible with liberal democratic government. See Stepan, "Religion, Democracy, and the 'Twin Tolerations'." A *coercive* establishment, where membership is compulsory, is another matter altogether.
[63] See, respectively, Macedo, "Transformative Constitutionalism," and Macedo, *Diversity and Distrust*.

understood and the fact that these views will do poorly in a liberal society is no problem for liberalism. Whether his moral and sociological claims are true is largely irrelevant here, as they do not take up what seems to me the truly interesting and important question: should there be anything to be done if liberalism systematically disadvantages ways of life that *are compatible* with liberalism properly understood? Is the neutrality of intent truly fair if it has disparate and predictably disparate effects? Liberalism seems committed to being fair to the different ways of life within its borders and if it looks like some of those ways of life do poorly *because* of liberalism's institutions, then it seems quite plausible to say that we should at least explore ways to make liberalism's requirements less burdensome or more equitable.[64]

Rawls declaims any such attempt. He rightly argues that any set of social institutions will necessarily favor some ways of life and disfavor others. No one could reasonably expect to achieve a full "neutrality of effect," even if that were desirable. But Rawls goes further, and suggests that it "is futile to try to counteract these effects and influences, or even to ascertain for political purposes how deep and pervasive they are. We must accept the facts of commonsense political sociology."[65] Macedo likewise throws up his hands at the possibility of saying anything useful empirically about how social life and political institutions interact.[66] This is a strange conjunction of claims. We must, Rawls tells us, "accept the facts of commonsense political sociology" and believe (a) that the effects of political institutions are deep and pervasive and (b) that it is futile to try and counteract such effects. If we take Rawls at his word here, then we are left with the rather puzzling idea that we know that political institutions have lots of non-political effects, but we cannot really know what those effects are – or, at least, how "deep and pervasive" they are – and we certainly cannot do much of anything about them, except, it seems, rely on them to underpin our liberal political institutions.[67]

---

[64] I have been influenced greatly in this argument by Tomasi, *Liberalism beyond Justice.*

[65] Rawls, *Political Liberalism*, 193.

[66] In the course of arguing that parents should not have a right to opt their children out of a reading program meant to inculcate important civic virtues, he suggests (not implausibly) that judgments in how well educational programs actually teach these virtues "seem intrinsically hard to settle" as empirical matters. Oddly enough, however, he is – in the same paragraph – quite sure (as an empirical matter, I suppose) that a "Liberal civic education is bound to have the effect of favoring some ways of life or religious convictions over others" (Stephen Macedo, "Community, Diversity, and Civic Education: Toward a Liberal Political Science of Group Life," *Social Philosophy and Policy* 13, no. 1 [1996]: 485.)

[67] Rawls notes, in a discussion of public reason, that his argument for political liberalism relies at least in part on the "hope … that the political conception and its ideal of public reason are mutually sustaining, and in this sense stable." They can be so as long as "A

It is almost certainly true that we cannot discern *precisely* how political institutions affect social and private life, and it is probably true that our ability to design political institutions to effect particular goals is inevitably partial, but we can still say a great deal about how institutions do in fact have their effects. If all shops are closed on Sundays, Christians probably have a comparative advantage over religions that have their worship services on other days. If all children are forced to go to secular schools, probably fewer of them will be religious than if some had gone to the religious schools of their choice. Public education in the United States and elsewhere is constructed precisely out of the conviction that we can rely on certain kinds of institutions to effect personal and social change.[68] Further, even if no one intended for a particular set of institutions to be unequal in their effects, once such effects are evident, refusing to adjust those institutions to account for those effects clearly then becomes part of "intent." "Commonsense political sociology" can tell us a great deal about how institutions shape social life, and even if it is far from perfect, a set of institutions whose design turns out to favor one way of life over another cannot, it seems to me, plausibly be called neutral, even if they are not intended, strictly speaking, to act in that manner. And to the degree that the possible adjustments are themselves compatible with liberal principles and not productive of greater problems, political institutions absent those adjustments cannot be considered properly neutral or fair.

So it seems to me that Tomasi is right to suggest that once liberals have committed themselves to a neutrality of intent, they are then also committed to ensuring that such neutrality is truly as neutral as it can be; they must be concerned with political institutions' non-political effects.[69] But surely, Rawls and others might complain, this simply leads us back to some kind of neutrality of effect, a standard that I agreed above was "impracticable." It is impossible to delineate with sufficient clarity whether some people's lives go well and others go poorly as a result of political institutions, technological shifts, cultural trends, or any of the other bewilderingly myriad ways that societies change. Moreover, it is not even often clear whether people's lives are going well, going poorly, or simply changing. Multiplying these uncertainties across groups of people

well-ordered society publicly and effectively regulated by a recognized political conception fashions a climate within which its citizens acquire a sense of justice inclining them to meet their duty of civility and without generating strong interests to the contrary" (*Political Liberalism*, 252). In other words, political liberalism works as long as political institutions are as effective as he deems them to be in producing "just" citizens. His argument is thus triply puzzling.

[68] Cf. Glenn, *The Myth of the Common School.*
[69] Tomasi, *Liberalism beyond Justice.* See especially 40–56.

produces some real sympathy for Rawls' (and others') unwillingness to tread in such territory. Fools and angels indeed: it may not be exactly "futile" to try and discern how things are going for particular groups of people (and say something about why that is), but it is quite difficult, and any attempt will likely become a part of political disputes rather than simply a set of observations about them.[70]

Nonetheless, it is not so obvious what sort of force the "practicability" objection should have, especially when we are considering disparate effects on ways of life politically compatible with liberalism. *If*, for instance, political institutions *could* be arranged so as to have perfectly equal effects on the various ways of life compatible with political liberalism, what reason could there be for not doing so? What is striking about Rawls' discussion of the neutrality of effect is the absence of a moral argument: the critique is entirely practical. There is nothing in Rawls' argument to suggest he thinks there is anything *morally* wrong with thinking about neutrality this way, it is just too hard to make it work. If that is right, then practicability ought to be understood as a prudential warning against expecting too much out of a system of political neutrality; it is not a knock-down argument against mitigating political institutions' disparate effects on people's ways of life. It is perhaps unavoidable that political institutions will unfairly advantage some ways of life over others, while it is just as unavoidable that a liberalism properly understood will seek to mitigate that unfairness as a means of making toleration politically effective.

Again, as Tomasi has argued, citizens of diverse and incompatible ways of life must be afforded the opportunity to make a success of their lives as they see them; liberal states must find ways to "flatten" the disparate psychological taxes they impose on their diverse citizens. Without compromising their commitment to basic liberal claims about justice, political liberals should do what they can to mitigate or ameliorate the unequal consequences of laws or political practices. This might include, he suggests, approving vouchers as a means of distributing educational monies, revamping pedagogical practices, altering marriage laws, and even signing up for something like President Bush's "Faith-Based Initiative."[71] Even integrationists, to the degree that they are compatible with a political

---

[70] This is especially true of the various "culture wars" claims. Both sides have an interest in arguing their existence or non-existence, since the question is itself a part of the cultural debate.

[71] Tomasi, *Liberalism beyond Justice*. Tomasi doesn't endorse the administration's initiative, but does argue that political liberals have good reasons to endorse the philosophical impulse behind it. See John Tomasi, "Why Political Liberals Should Be Compassionate Conservatives" (paper presented to the American Political Science Association, Washington, D.C., September 2003).

liberalism, must have a fair chance to live out their integrationism. Rather than a neutrality of intent, liberal states seeking to make toleration politically effective should be committed to what Stephen Monsma and Douglas Laycock, among others, have called "substantive neutrality."[72] In this view of neutrality, the liberal state should take care that its actions do not advantage or disadvantage any particular way of life, insofar as that way of life looks to be compatible with the continuation of the liberal polity. In doing so, it makes toleration politically effective by securing the goods necessary for politics and then doing its best to honor citizens' desires to live their lives as they see fit.

But again the prudential concerns loom large. Indeed, it looks like the critiques I made of recognition would apply equally well to this idea of substantive neutrality. Who will judge whether some "way of life" is compatible with liberalism? How will you identify "ways of life"? How can you tell whether some state action is responsible for decline versus some other cause? How will you line up political support for this? Consider for a moment the political fate of President Bush's faith-based initiative. Though the administration has been able to effect some administrative changes that make it easier for religious groups to compete for federal monies, it could not get any significant changes through Congress.[73] Some of the administration's most important supporters – conservative Protestants – were either hesitant about the proposal or outright opposed it both because they feared the strings that would inevitably follow the money and because they opposed public monies going to religious groups they found objectionable. More broadly, other opponents worried that the use of federal money in religious contexts would undermine liberty protections and provide public support for groups whose ends were at odds with a liberal democratic political order.[74] These sorts of difficulties are not just the product of partisan wrangling, though they obviously are that. They are also emblematic of the political difficulties any program of substantive neutrality will have under robustly

---

[72] Douglas Laycock, "Formal, Substantive, and Disaggregated Neutrality toward Religion," *Depaul Law Review* 39 (1990); Michael W. McConnell, "Believers as Equal Citizens," in *Obligations of Citizenship and Demands of Faith*, ed. Nancy L. Rosenblum (Princeton, NJ: Princeton University Press, 2000); Steven Monsma, "Substantive Neutrality as a Basis for Free Exercise–No Establishment Common Ground," *Journal of Church and State* 42, no. 1 (2000). The context for these arguments is the interpretation of the First Amendment to the US Constitution.

[73] Amy E. Black, Douglas L. Koopman, and David K. Ryden, *Of Little Faith: The Politics of George W. Bush's Faith-Based Initiatives* (Washington, D.C.: Georgetown University Press, 2004).

[74] Among many others, see Emily R. Gill, "Religious Organizations, Charitable Choice, and the Limits of the Freedom of Conscience," *Perspectives on Politics* 2, no. 4 (2004);

pluralist conditions. To the degree that individuals' and groups' moral commitments include a negative appraisal of others' commitments (even if they deem the commitments "reasonable" they still might think them wrongheaded), we should not be surprised that support for this sort of public funding would be difficult to come by. Social and political conflicts make substantive neutrality quite hard to achieve. But conflict, it turns out, may also be its best ally.

Conflict, substantive neutrality, and religious integrationism

Stanley Fish and J. Budziszewski (an odd couple if ever there was one) have each in his own way quite severely criticized the idea of liberal neutrality.[75] They both argue that since no political order can truly be neutral toward the various ways of life within it, to hang anything of significance on such a standard is foolhardy or worse. Fish goes so far as to say that to the degree that liberalism is organized around the chimera of neutrality, it "does not exist." Budziszewski decries the attempt to organize liberal politics so as to get as close as we can to achieving neutrality when we know as a matter of course that such neutrality is in principle impossible: "In neutrality, we are not speaking of what we can think, but never bring about, like a perfect circle; we are speaking of what we *cannot consistently think*, like a square circle. There is no 'partial' neutrality for the same reason that there is no 'partially' square circle."[76] Susan Mendus suggests further that toleration becomes an issue for us only when reason runs out and shows itself incapable of producing definitive resolutions: "Where reason cannot operate, we must, it seems, turn to politics."[77] Though I think these critiques of neutrality overplayed and especially do not share the view that tolerance and intolerance lie outside of reason (though reason underdetermines their resolution), their claims point us to something important. Namely, they alert us to the important role that politics, and especially political conflict, can and must play in developing and sustaining systems of political neutrality and, by extension, political toleration.

I argued above that toleration is best understood philosophically as emerging out of a practice of moral judgment about competing and

Kathleen Sullivan, "Religion and Liberal Democracy," *University of Chicago Law Review* 59, no. 1 (1992).

[75] Budziszewski, *True Tolerance*; Stanley Fish, "Liberalism Doesn't Exist," *Duke Law Journal* 6 (1987).

[76] Budziszewski, *True Tolerance*, 116.

[77] Mendus, ed., *The Politics of Toleration*, 5.

irreconcilable goods, always with an eye toward others' independence and autonomy. The puzzle of *political* toleration is to find a way to make the state act like a reasonable moral actor who can do a good job in making such judgments. We are quite wary of assigning even the democratic state this sort of role, both because its popular responsiveness makes it vulnerable to capture by popular (and sometimes quite noxious) political passions and because the institutionalization of its decisions in law and practice makes its mistakes that much more pernicious. There are, then, at least two distinct prudential problems in making substantive neutrality work: first, you must be able to reliably and justly identify the ways in which political institutions treat different ways of life unfairly; and, second, you must be able to ameliorate that unfairness – if you can – without damaging core liberal protections for all.

In this section, I outline the ways in which these prudential problems can be overcome and describe how religious integrationism can and – in the case of the European integrationist parties – *did* help make that a success (though certainly not always). The very thing that makes political toleration necessary – social and political conflict – is also the thing that makes substantive neutrality plausible; its prudential problems, moreover, are closely connected to their solutions. Conflicts over injustices, real and perceived, can produce political mobilization and organization as a means to redressing those injustices, especially when those injustices *can* be redressed politically. Additionally, social and political conflict within the context of systems of electoral contestation and deliberation, can "teach" citizens the distinctions between the sorts of goods that the state ought properly to secure (i.e. public goods) and those it ought not (i.e. private goods). In short, political conflict, properly arranged, may do reasonably well in putting issues of justice on the table, so to speak, while at the same time tempering political demands to keep things within the bounds of liberal democratic politics. Let me explore each aspect in turn.

We might think of the first prudential problem as a problem of political inputs. If you think that political toleration requires taking account of how institutions favor some ways of life over others (and then adjusting them accordingly), one difficult problem is gaining a clear understanding of whether and how those institutions actually are impacting discrete ways of life. Not only will it be difficult to disentangle political causes from the myriad other causes (technological, cultural, and so on) that impact us, but it will also be the case that cultural "leaders" will have an incentive to overstate (or fabricate entirely) the measure of the impact as a means to securing to themselves whatever kinds of resources might then flow from the state. Nonetheless, the most clear and clearly understood source of information about the nature of injustices (and their possible amelioration) comes from within the aggrieved communities themselves. Consider, for example, the Netherlands' 1917 "Pacification." As I sketched out earlier, Holland's Catholic and orthodox Calvinist communities began organizing politically as early as the 1870s, when liberal governments attempted to secularize the public school systems. Kuyper's "Anti-School League," was founded in 1873 and eventually grew into the Anti-Revolutionary Party (ARP), Europe's first mass political party. By the turn of the century, the coalition of Catholic and Calvinist parties[78] had a clear goal: the equalization of public funding among private and public schools. Though religious parties' political victories had forced their opponents to allow some state funding for private religious schools, public schools were still at a fiscal advantage.

As World War I ground to a halt, Dutch politics seemed immobilized. Liberals and socialists controlled the government, but they could not make the constitutional changes they wanted, especially those expanding suffrage, without the cooperation of the religious parties. But these parties would not endorse the expansion of suffrage without it being tied to a solution for the "school question." Eventually, the parties reached a compromise where the constitution was amended to make suffrage universal and to equalize funding for schools, whether they were public or private (though private schools did have to meet certain requirements in order to receive state funding). Over the next few decades, this sort of proportionality rule was extended to include radio and television broadcasts, medical care, and anything else that was the object of government spending. The moral idea behind this system was that, within limits, individuals and groups had the right to organize their lives around their core, sometimes religious, beliefs and to the degree that government programs touched on those lives, the state should structure those programs in ways amenable to such organization. In practice, this meant establishing some minimal standards for the receipt of public funds and then allowing communities to use those funds to achieve the particular end as they saw fit.[79]

Similarly in Germany, though the Center could not stop Bismarck's *Kulturkampf* legislation, it could organize enough social and political opposition through parliamentary action, newspapers, and local obstructionism that Bismarck was forced to reach out to the Vatican to try and

---

[78] The Catholics were a collection of electoral leagues, as they would not officially have a party until 1926 and the Christian Historical Union had split off from the ARP over the issue of suffrage.

[79] For example, schools that wished to receive public funds had to teach certain curricular subjects – Dutch language, history, etc. – but beyond that were free to structure their schools in keeping with their particular views (Calvinist, Catholic, socialist, and so on).

negotiate a truce.[80] The interesting thing here is that had the fate of Germany's Catholics been left to negotiations between Bismarck and ecclesial authorities (including the Vatican), it is likely that things would have been much worse for Germany's Catholics. Some of Germany's leading bishops seemed quite willing to accept what amounted to Erastian control in return for political peace and German support for the Vatican's tenuous political position in Italy. Though religion is often cast (rightly at times) as toleration's opponent, it is worth remembering that it has just as often been intolerance's object and that religion's political organization, while certainly no panacea, can serve to blunt such oppression.

This will hardly reassure those who worry about religion's tendency toward intolerance. No one reasonably denies that religion can be a force for relieving injustice – note the role of black churches in the United States' civil rights movement[81] or the Catholic Church's role in Poland's Solidarity trade union. As I noted in the Introduction, however, surveys repeatedly show that there is a correlation between traditional religious views and an unwillingness to tolerate disliked groups. People of whatever persuasion who believe that certain kinds of moral norms are not only superior but universally applicable as well can quite plausibly be expected to think that, as the old Catholic saying goes, "error has no rights." And to the degree that such views generate and sustain political mobilization, it is quite reasonable to think that these movements may be expected to go beyond such legitimate defense and edge into politically oppressive ends. It is also reasonable to think this true of integrationist political movements in particular, even if they sometimes do defend religious communities against unjust political actions. Austria's Christian Socials overthrew the democratic First Republic and established a corporatist dictatorship at least in part on the basis of such reasoning. Though this is a reasonable concern, I think I can make a plausible case that religious integrationism can actually *strengthen* rather than weaken the odds of avoiding such oppression. Integrationism's organization of subcultural communities around religious belief and identity not only effectively organizes those communities in defense of their political interests but also tempers the reach of those interests in ways constructive of political toleration more generally.

---

[80] I discussed this and Windthorst's agile response to it in chapter 3.
[81] David L. Chappell, *A Stone of Hope: Prophetic Religion and the Death of Jim Crow* (Chapel Hill: University of North Carolina Press, 2004); Frederick C. Harris, "Something Within: Religion as a Mobilizer of African-American Political Activism," *Journal of Politics* 56, no. 1 (1994). More broadly, see Stark, *For the Glory of God*, where he argues that though religious belief (monotheism in particular) is to blame for serious outrages, it is also responsible for very real progress.

In the example I used earlier to help flesh out what we mean by toleration philosophically, I described how I might tolerate my (quite fictional) neighbor's consumption of pornography on the grounds that to do otherwise might damage other goods I regard more highly than his proper conduct – namely, our friendship or his capacity to choose for himself how he should spend his time (i.e. his autonomy). Integrationists plausibly pose a problem for making toleration politically effective here in that they are already, by virtue of being integrationists, committed to seeing *all* goods as intimately connected to their faith. And since those beliefs will often include negative appraisals of others' lives, integration-ists can be reasonably thought likely to commit what we can call the "theocratic mistake." By drawing too tight a connection between, say, the divine moral law and its enforcement via political authority, the theocrat assigns to politics a set of responsibilities it does not have and that liber-alism (rightly) finds odious. If part of the divine moral law, for example, truly includes the proper worship of God, it is still a mistake to give the state the authority to regulate or control worship. Such an act improperly supposes worship a public good that should (or even can be) secured via physical coercion.

Some have suggested that since many religious believers are amenable to this kind of "theocratic mistake," any sustainable regime of political toleration will require not only that believers abjure the theocratic claim, but that they set aside their negative views about others altogether. In the course of an argument suggesting that the difference between Rawls' political liberalism and others' comprehensive liberalisms is practically nonexistent, Amy Gutmann argues that a properly constructed civic education will "educate all children to appreciate the public value of toleration."[82] This requires, she thinks, more than simply a "live-and-let-live" attitude. It requires "mutual respect," or "a reciprocal positive regard among citizens who pursue ways of life that are consistent with honoring the basic liberties and opportunities of others."[83] Fair equality of opportunity in, say, employment cannot plausibly be achieved so long as those who are in socially dominant positions harbor distaste for those who are different from them.

In one respect, Gutmann's argument rings true. Widespread racism will inevitably confound any attempt at ensuring the objects of that racism receive a fair shake at landing good jobs. Even if some employer is formally and conscientiously committed to treating all applicants fairly, if some group is the object of even just negative stereotyping, it is quite

---

[82] Gutmann, "Civic Education and Social Diversity," 559.
[83] Ibid., 561.

plausible to think that members of that group will not be treated fairly. But it seems to me that Gutmann here conflates some rather important distinctions. As I noted early on, it is incorrect to say that we tolerate someone's race; race is a largely immutable category about which moral judgment is irrelevant.[84] Extending the argument, moreover, to religion or other sorts of similar kinds of belief systems makes her claims quite untenable. Religion is not like race or sex. There is, of course, an unchosen element to religious belief (or non-belief): most grow up in households where children do not choose whether or where to attend worship, and we come to many of our basic beliefs through a complex combination of socialization, reflection, and experience. Unlike race or sex, however, we can (and do) change our religious beliefs.[85] More importantly, integral to most religious belief is the idea that our belief is superior to another's, or, to put it a bit more starkly, that our religious beliefs are true and others' are false.

If Gutmann's arguments were correct, then the scope of social diversity permissible in a liberal democratic society would be pretty thin: no one could, at least to the degree that they would be considered a citizen in good standing, hold that their religious views were superior to others'. Democracy would then seem to depend, then, on its citizens being "religious pluralists," accepting the view that all (or most) religious traditions are equally valid means of worshiping God or exploring the meaning of human life. Perhaps Gutmann thinks that is true, but as I pointed out in chapter 5, the politically proper demand that we extend one another respect as free and equal citizens does not translate into the improper demand that we then consider others' basic moral views as reasonable as our own. (Though it probably does require that we think their views have a certain level of reasonability.) It seems patently *unreasonable* to say that liberal democracies work well only when their citizens accept Rousseau's dictum that those who believe each other damned cannot live with one another. To the contrary, people *do* live in democratic societies where they think each other damned, and it is silly to pretend otherwise.

There is, then, no special political virtue in being a religious pluralist, but – sticking with Gutmann's framework – we would be rightly disturbed if a local grocery store refused to hire Muslims or, more broadly, if anti-Muslim sentiment were so widespread and so deeply entrenched that immigrants from predominantly Islamic countries had difficulty in

---

[84] This doesn't mean, of course, that questions emerging from racial issues aren't subject to moral judgment, but, rather, that it is incoherent – to say the least – that you might think someone morally objectionable on account of his race.

[85] People can, of course, change their sex and even racial appearance through medical interventions.

finding anything but the most menial work. Gutmann's arguments have, in this respect, a certain intuitive appeal. It is likely to be true that an employer will be less likely to discriminate against particular religious believers if he himself does not take any particular religious view to be true or others false. He simply will not have much motivation to think anything of those views at all, and multiplied across a society, such sentiments are probably more likely to "support social justice" in the way that Gutmann thinks of it.[86] More broadly, things probably *would* go better politically if individuals had a 'positive mutual regard' for one another. But that does not settle the matter here at all.

Consider why we think religious discrimination is wrong – and where we think it is not. In the case of, say, the grocery store, a refusal to hire Muslims wrongs them in making religious identification a prerequisite for a job where no such prerequisite is rationally plausible. We protect individuals' access to employment out of the conviction that it is a good that everyone requires for taking care of their basic needs and thus a proper object of public action. Access to employment is thus, in this sense, a public good that should not, generally speaking, be affected by religious affiliation (or disaffiliation, as the case may be). But note the "generally speaking," for the exceptions here are revealing. The Catholic Church would certainly not act immorally if it refused to hire a Muslim or a Protestant as a theologian. Religious institutions have bona fide reasons for limiting certain positions to religiously qualified individuals, and though the definition of what counts as a bona fide religious position may not always be clear,[87] very few dispute the idea that such positions are reasonable exceptions to the general rule of non-discrimination. What's more, there may be *non-religious* jobs whose functions require activities that individuals' religious identifications disqualify them from. Suppose that a liquor company is looking for a marketing executive; a devout Muslim or Mormon who thinks alcohol immoral would rightly be thought a bad fit for such a position. (Why they would apply for such a job is another question.) An Orthodox Jew would be a bad choice for refereeing a college football game (since these are mostly played on Saturday afternoons). Similarly, if a bank was interested in expanding its retail operations in a largely black neighborhood, it would make good sense to hire someone who was black to work in that position, even if

---

[86] Gutmann, "Civic Education and Social Diversity," 562.

[87] Cf. *Presiding Bishop v. Amos*, 483 US 327 (1987), where a janitor at a Mormon-run gymnasium was dismissed because he was no longer in good standing with the church. The janitor challenged the ruling and the Supreme Court upheld the firing. For an argument suggesting both that the gym should not have been allowed to discriminate and that churches need a good bit of space to practice discrimination, see Nancy Rosenblum, *Membership and Morals*, 73–116.

that means, technically speaking, it would be discriminating against non-blacks in its employment search.

So when the grocery store owner who believes an applicant's religious views to be false and perhaps even immoral discriminates against that person on account of those religious views, we ought to say that he acts improperly not in that he thinks her religious views to be false but in that he misidentifies the goods being secured through employment. In particular, he makes the mistake of thinking that the properly public good of access to employment is, in fact, a non-public good whose allocation can be determined at least in part by reference to religious identity. Now, of course, the store owner who viscerally hates Islam (or religion in general) is unlikely in any case to give its adherents fair treatment, and if such hatred is widespread then Muslims will have a difficult time in gaining fair access to employment. Nonetheless, if a liberal democratic regime can be secured in a way that is minimally damaging to ways of life compatible with liberal democratic politics, then it should be.[88] If Muslims' access to employment opportunities can be protected without impugning others' religious views, then they should be. If this is right, then the question to which we have come is whether integrationists can (and did) avoid the theocratic mistake. Can they be induced to distinguish between the goods that are properly public and those that are not and therein develop a set of political views and practices that extends to other citizens a reasonable toleration and prevents the state from unduly impinging on those other citizens' efforts to secure their own, non-public goods? In short, can integrationists come to understand, in the context of their religious views, that the state has only a limited responsibility and should not be used to secure properly non-public goods?

Consider again the Dutch case. As I noted in the last chapter, Lijphart argues that what made the pillarized system work was the way in which the political leaders of the different pillars could negotiate with one another over highly contentious issues (e.g. public funding for religious schools) with the confidence that they had a good deal of latitude in what their constituents would find acceptable. This meant, in fact, that political life came to possess a degree of practical independence from other parts of life, an independence that perhaps not coincidentally reflected important theological claims. As I noted earlier, the Calvinist (and ARP

---

[88] Tomasi, *Liberalism beyond Justice*. He suggests that the way to think about this is like the just war theory's "doctrine of double effect." There, it is morally licit to kill non-combatants but only in the context of going after a legitimate military target. You may not *intend* to kill non-combatants, and, what's more, you must do what you can to minimize those casualties.

leader) Abraham Kuyper was perhaps the most explicit here, arguing that because the state derived its authority from God, it had a responsibility to govern "in a Christian way" but that could only happen "through the conscience of the person invested with authority."[89] That is, though the state has a divine mandate, its purposes are not, in the way we usually think of these things, religious. More to the point, the state should not, he thinks, infringe on the sovereignty of the churches and regulate matters of religion, since "*the government lacks the data of judgment*" and was not created in order to pursue religious goals; neither are the churches to infringe on the state's prerogatives. Politics is to be, he suggests, its own particular practice, with – to use my language here – its own goods and purposes.[90]

Of course, politics is not an entirely autonomous practice, either theologically or sociologically. Political life, as with all of the different "spheres" of life, has a purpose ordained by God and is morally responsible therein.[91] Moreover, those political elites could not be entirely pragmatic, for the tight linkages between the parties and the other parts of the pillars (churches, newspapers, trade unions, and so on) necessarily meant that their flexibility had to be employed in the service of the pillars and their members. So this particular configuration of integrationism embodied the idea that politics had a set of divine purposes, but that those purposes were distinct from, say, the purposes of the church. Integrationists could thus commit themselves to the idea that the state secured goods that were not strictly religious without having to accept the idea, contrary to their integrationism, that politics was something quite unconnected to God's divine mandate.

The subcultural encapsulation of these religious communities further reduced the temptation to make the theocratic mistake. Recall that part of the argument for recognition was the claim that since individuals and cultures develop dialogically, political toleration was insufficient because it carried some negative evaluations of those being tolerated. But even to the degree that toleration inflicts (or allows) a real harm, the argument for recognition is persuasive only if such harms are best mitigated politically. In integrationist communities, by virtue of the fact that they are so well encapsulated, the close ties within the communities may go

---

[89] Kuyper, *Lectures on Calvinism*, 104.
[90] Ibid., 105. The state, Kuyper argues has three broad duties: "1. Whenever different spheres clash, to compel mutual regard for the boundary lines of each; 2. To defend individuals and weak ones, in those spheres, against the abuse of power over the rest; and 3. To coerce all together to bear the *personal* and *financial* burdens for the maintenance of the natural unity of the state" (97).
[91] See my discussion below on the ways in which religious believers tend to see the "moral order" as one of the goods that ought to be secured by the state.

some distance toward mitigating these harms, especially if their political arms are successful in securing some sort of accommodation. The insularity of integrationism, quite reasonably thought by many to be a real threat to regimes of political toleration, actually reduces the likelihood, it seems to me, that those same integrationists will think that the state is the proper vehicle for instantiating wholesale their religious views.

So it seems as though it is possible to meet the two main prudential objections to substantive neutrality. Politics can help identify and ameliorate injustices and, properly arranged, can also temper tendencies to use the state to secure goods it ought not, preventing damage to liberalism's core protections. And what's more, integrationist communities have demonstrated – at least in the European cases – that they can serve to strengthen the prospects for political toleration rather than weaken it. Integrationism stands at least plausibly acquitted of the charge of intolerance. Nonetheless, there are some important caveats to this acquittal we need to keep in mind.

First, politics can serve as a reasonably effective means to political toleration provided that the groups in question already accept the political system as basically legitimate and other groups as more or less reasonable fellow citizens (though they may think that the political system in need of significant revision). Michael Walzer calls acceptance of "peaceful coexistence" the "moral minimum" for toleration, and though I have argued that democracies do not require the robust reasonableness of Rawls and others, they cannot do without *some* sort of reasonableness.[92] In Belgium for example, the Catholic Party's 1884 election victory could only have taken place because the Catholic Church and the party had made it quite clear that they would abide by the limits of Belgium's liberal constitution. Kalyvas argues that the contrast with the aborted 1989 Algerian elections could not have been more stark, as the ruling secularists cancelled elections that Islamists were poised to win.[93] The Islamists' opponents did not trust that they would stay within the extant political order or even allow further elections. As I noted in chapter 4, deeply opposed groups can still live within the same political order as long as they all accept that order's basic outlines and feel confident that their opponents do as well.

It helps, of course, if the structure of social cleavages is such that no one group can reasonably hope to dominate political life. Holland's 1917 constitutional agreements came about as they did in part because neither the religious parties nor their liberal and socialist opponents could muster the kind of majority necessary to amend the constitution to their

---

[92] Walzer, *On Toleration*.
[93] Kalyvas, "Commitment Problems in Emerging Democracies."

liking. Similarly, the Center's leadership, and Windthorst in particular, could temper some of German Catholics' popular antipathy toward Jews and socialists and refuse to support nineteenth-century legislation targeting either by citing Catholics' comparable minority status. Being the object of *Kulturkampf*-like legislation can focus the mind rather powerfully on the benefits of political toleration.

Still, even if the integrationist – by dint of theological reflection and practical experience – can buy the idea that some goods are properly public and others not (and thus not a proper object of politics), liberals quite reasonably worry that religious believers have the propensity to view the actual scope of public goods more expansively than liberals typically do. Paul Weithman has suggested that this primarily involves the believers' propensity to include the "moral order" as among the goods that political authorities might rightly be made to secure.[94] None of us, or very few of us anyway, live our moral lives in isolation from one another, and even if the recognition claim that we develop dialogically is overblown (as I suspect it is) we are nonetheless all quite profoundly affected by those around us. In particular, we are profoundly affected by their moral views and practices, and to the degree that they differ from our own, we may often find ourselves relaxing our own moral conceptions to accommodate them. When the political system, moreover, decides to tolerate some practice, say, by lifting legal restrictions, it has the tendency to induce in people the sense that the practice is morally acceptable, or at least that the practice is not *as* worthy of moral opprobrium as once was thought. Pluralist societies governed by a rather latitudinarian toleration have the tendency, we might say, of making latitudinarians of all of us. This is, after all, why the integrationists sought (and seek) to construct encapsulating social institutions, and why liberals find them so concerning. To the degree that integrationism gets mobilized politically and is interested in securing a social and political order that makes integrationism plausible, we might reasonably think that among the goods the integrationists will seek to secure will be those conducive to the construction of a "moral order" in line with their religious views.

---

[94] Paul J. Weithman, "Review of George Klosko, *Democratic Procedures and Liberal Consensus*," *Ethics* 112, no. 3(2002). See also Klosko, *Democratic Procedures and Liberal Consensus*; Smith, *Christian America?* I should note that it is not just believers who are amenable to this tendency. In a very interesting article, T.M. Scanlon expresses his sincere difficulty with religious toleration, given that he would be "very unhappy if [toleration] leads in time to my society becoming one in which almost everyone is, in one way or another, deeply religious, and in which religion plays a central part in all public discourse … What I fear is not merely the legal enforcement of religion but its social predominance" ("The Difficulty of Tolerance," 230).

So even if the integrationists are not so interested in using the state to enforce their faith per se (as Rawls seems to be primarily concerned about), they might very well be interested in using the state to help construct or maintain a certain set of moral expectations, perhaps at the cost of others' ways of life. Take, for instance, contemporary debates over the legal status of homosexual relationships. Most liberals, I take it, are in favor of extending those relationships the same recognition afforded to heterosexual ones. Opposition to such actions comes mostly (though not exclusively) from conservative religious believers (who, as I noted, often seem to have integrationist tendencies). The arguments against same-sex marriage are certainly not always strictly religious (i.e. "God made marriage to be between a man and a woman") but they are largely consonant with religious claims, and among these non-religious arguments is the idea that broadening the legal definition of marriage will have the effect of diminishing marriage's importance across the whole of the society. Though it is not always clear how this is supposed to happen, the premise behind it is, I take it, a concern for the broader moral order. Similar stories could be told as well about believers' propensity to be less tolerant with respect to issues of speech, assembly, and the like; they are, it seems, simply more concerned to live out their lives in accordance with a particular moral order and that is made easier or more plausible in a society that supports that order or simply takes it for granted.

I think there are a few things to be said about this concern. First, and perhaps most importantly, it should be said that there are good reasons to worry. Religious believers do, it seems, tend to have a more "moralistic" view of politics and thus expect more from the political order than, generally speaking, do non-believers, and some of the goods that believers will seek to have the state secure will dismay liberals. For those whose views incline toward the libertarian end of things, this will seem like especially bad news indeed. At least since John Stuart Mill, liberals have been concerned with the power of social consensus to impede the pursuit of individual lives. The idea of having the state reinforce that consensus makes things even worse.

There are a few reasons, however, why this tendency might not be so worrisome. First, if toleration in general really is a practice of adjudicating among competing and irreconcilable goods and political toleration is the attempt on the part of the state to treat its citizens fairly through substantive neutrality, then we should not be surprised at disagreement, even among those broadly committed to liberal democratic politics, over the relative priority of different goods and the scope we accord to individual autonomy. The decision to have the political system protect certain kinds of behavior (if by no other means than simply refusing to persecute or outlaw it) has *always* been controversial, and perhaps rightly so. Toleration is always something of a risk, for as it increases the breadth and depth of permitted human activity, it makes the bet that such an increase will not carry with it unreasonably pernicious social and political consequences.

Consider, very briefly, the history of religious toleration in the West. Though the medieval world may not have been quite the "persecuting society,"[95] it was far from a religiously tolerant one. The Reformation and the dawn of the modern world both made religious toleration possible and more urgent, but nowhere did religious toleration spring immediately into existence. Far from it. Rather, it developed incrementally, first as attempts to find grounds for coexistence among some Protestant and then Protestant and Catholic churches and only later as principled deference to the right of each individual to worship (or not) as she pleases.[96] Locke's rather famous (or infamous) argument denying toleration to Catholics and atheists was rooted not in religious antipathy (though that may have been there with respect to Catholics), but in political calculation: neither could be trusted, he thought, to keep their commitments to the commonwealth. Religious toleration came to triumph, as it were, because of principled arguments about the nature of religious faith, its relation to political life, and the *practical experience* of religious liberty's consequences. Arguing against toleration was not necessarily the product of religious conviction; the seemingly skeptical Hobbes, after all, thought – as did many of his contemporaries – that a common religious confession was essential for social stability. Only when that was shown not to be true *empirically* could religious toleration make real political headway.[97]

Second, to the degree that my arguments for substantive neutrality as the best instantiation of political toleration available are persuasive, it is no criticism per se to say that religious believers will include a concern for the moral order in their political goals. The very idea of substantive neutrality already assumes that the social and political orders are

---

[95] See John Christian Laursen and Cary J. Nederman, eds., *Beyond the Persecuting Society: Religious Toleration before the Enlightenment* (Philadelphia: University of Pennsylvania Press, 1998).

[96] See Perez Zagorin, *How the Idea of Religious Toleration Came to the West* (Princeton, NJ: Princeton University Press, 2003).

[97] The sources of religious toleration, of course, are complex and varied. They include pragmatic bargaining among religious groups, theological developments, and religious skepticism. But if it were the case that religious toleration was incompatible with a reasonably stable social order, it seems unlikely that we would value it as much as we do today. The Catholic experience seems especially important here. Catholicism's experience with religious liberty in the US and its notable absence in communist Eastern Europe was a powerful source for the church's embrace of religious liberty at Vatican II.

closely related and that the political order ought to be judged at least in part on how it affects our ability to live our moral lives as we see fit. That politically mobilized religious believers might make this difficult or impossible for others *is* a reason for concern – and a reason for thinking them intolerant – but the idea that they focus on the moral order as such is not.

Third, to the degree that the democratic societies actually *are* pluralist ones, there might be even less to worry about than we suppose. To take a page from Madison's argument in *Federalist* no. 10, what we are worried about here is the evil of "faction," or the propensity of some part of society to try and dominate the rest. But how likely is it that any particular "faction," especially a religiously informed one, could put together a large enough electoral coalition to inflict real damage on the sorts of liberties that liberalism rightly prizes? Consider, again, the homosexual marriage debate. The debate in the United States is over whether and how to grant legal recognition to same-sex relationships, *not* over whether and how to enforce a certain sort of sexual morality. Even absent the Supreme Court's decision in *Lawrence* v. *Texas*, it seems highly unlikely, near impossible actually, that anyone could cobble together a political movement strong enough to reassert, say, a ban on certain sexual practices and actually enforce it. As Steve Bruce has pointed out, modernity has (seemingly permanently) fractured our religious communities, meaning that it is very unlikely sociologically that religious believers could sufficiently overcome their denominationalism and tendency to split to sustain a serious and seriously worrying political movement.[98] Our response to the problem of faction ought not be to attempt to rid ourselves of factions but rather to set factions against one another and have their competition help to secure the public good.

Ironically, perhaps, politically mobilized integrationism seems to me well placed in just this manner. Because, as I argued in chapter 5, its social and political institutions are tightly woven together and because its political elites have some reasonable amount of freedom, they can adjust their positions pragmatically and seek accommodation with their political opponents. When communities, even rather intolerant ones like integrationists, make a commitment to participate in and abide by an electoral political process, they are drawn into a kind of institutionalized negotiation over what kinds of things the state ought to be doing and ought not. That is, they are drawn into a political process of adjudicating

---

[98] Bruce, *Conservative Protestant Politics.* He notes, as an aside, that Pat Robertson did especially poorly in the 1988 Republican primaries, even in his home state of South Carolina, partially perhaps because he is a Pentecostal.

among competing goods, and out of that can come a system of political toleration (though, of course, it may not).[99]

Finally, consider the following. The Netherlands has a well-deserved reputation for being a very tolerant country and has been so for a very long time.[100] In part, no doubt, this was the product of changes in religious belief (toward latitudinarianism and beyond), but as should be clear by now, Holland also contained a rather large number of religious believers who felt quite strongly about their faith and were mobilized politically very early on. These things went together, to the degree that they did, in large part because the country's system of pillarization relocated the context of the "moral order" away from the national political system toward what we now think of as civil society. That is, because the Dutch opted for their system of structural pluralism, their integrationists posed little threat to the rest as far as their attempts to secure their moral order were concerned. Just as social and political conflict makes toleration a practical and moral necessity, so such conflict can make it a possibility – and religious integrationism can even make it likely.

Conclusion

The question of toleration remains a central one for liberal democracies, all the more so as the scope of moral and religious pluralism has widened and deepened. Popular accounts often tend to equate toleration with a kind of moral latitudinarianism, an easy live-and-let-live attitude. Properly speaking, however, toleration is much more demanding, for it requires a studied willingness to hold to one's own moral claims while declining press those claims against others (provided toleration is actually called for). Like toleration more generally, political toleration understood as substantive neutrality takes its cues not from the infallible, universal dictates of Reason or natural law or whatever, but instead from the moral and political concerns of actually existing citizens who not only must make judgments about how their political institutions will proceed but must bear the consequences as well. Of course, it nearly goes without saying that such commitments are not automatic or completely

---

[99] We can draw a parallel here with Europe's socialist parties, which largely began as revolutionary parties but were "tamed" by the emerging democratic electoral systems. See Przeworski and Sprague, *Paper Stones*. For the argument that such tendencies work for parties more generally, see Rosenblum, *On the Side of the Angels*.

[100] Kees Aarts, Stuart MacDonald, and Elaine Rabinowitz, "Issue and Party Competition in the Netherlands," *Comparative Political Studies* 32, no. 1 (1999); J.C.H Blom and Emiel Lamberts, *History of the Low Countries* (New York: Berghan Books, 1999); Daalder, *Ancient and Modern Pluralism in the Netherlands*; Rooden, "Religious Developments in the Netherlands, *c.* 1750–2000."

secure. If, for instance, the Catholic Church in Belgium had decided against accommodation, the outcome might have been quite tragic – and certainly not amenable to political toleration. Political toleration developed mostly out of democratic political conflict is a risky venture. It will likely get many things wrong. It would be tempting to think that we could do without such risk and place the adjudication of competing goods in the hands of experts or judges or guardians. But if we take moral pluralism seriously – a precondition of being concerned about toleration in any case – then we have to take seriously the idea that there exist a range of goods whose public status will be genuinely disputed and not simply disputed out of bigotry or vice. The best way to give voice to that disagreement and come to a reasonable political accommodation that can be revised if things turn out badly is through politics, not through its avoidance.

Such a system is likely to make few people happy, but since political toleration in liberal democratic government means, if it means anything, that we should not expect the whole truth as we see it reflected in politics, I count that as a good thing, not a defect. Religious integrationism *is* compatible with the development of political toleration, and perhaps even productive of it as well.

Conclusion: toward a better sort of liberal democracy

Few issues seem to vex liberal political theorists as much as those concerning religion's place in contemporary democratic political life. In one sense, the continuing controversies are surprising. It is as settled as anything can be, after all, that political authorities may not coerce citizens into professions of faith and that church and state, even if they need not be separated as strongly as they are in the United States, must be distinct enough to give one another "freedom of movement."[1] Religious liberty is a "first liberty" without which no state can reasonably be called liberal or democratic.[2] Its benefits, both political and religious, are so obvious and attractive that religious traditions long thought inimical to its charms have become significant, perhaps leading, proponents of its protection and expansion.[3]

In another sense, however, the controversies should not surprise us. Though Locke was right to suggest that declining to make the state responsible for securing our religious salvation would lower the temperature of political conflicts, he was wrong to think that the conflicts would be rare.[4] Religions have always had something to say about the way we ought to dress, what foods we should (or should not) eat, how we should raise our children and care for our elderly, how we should make and spend our money, and how we should identify and treat our neighbor. In short, religion has always had something to say not just about the life hereafter, but also about our lives in the here and now, both individually and collectively. And that makes religion inevitably and inextricably political.

---

[1] Stepan, "Religion, Democracy, and the 'Twin Tolerations'.".
[2] William Lee Miller, *The First Liberty: America's Foundation in Religious Freedom*, expanded and updated edn. (Washington, D.C.: Georgetown University Press, 2003). Though the claim to religious liberty is not seriously contested, there are those who argue for non-coercive establishments out of the conviction that some sort of establishment – be it religious or secularist – is inevitable and it is better to be up-front about that fact. For arguments along these lines, see Graham Walker, "Illusory Pluralism, Inexorable Establishment," in *Obligations of Citizenship and the Demands of Faith*, ed. Nancy L. Rosenblum (Princeton, NJ: Princeton University Press, 2000).
[3] Hertzke, *Freeing God's Children*.   [4] Locke, *A Letter Concerning Toleration*.

This remains the case even in many democratic societies where the state and market have assumed (or, as the case may be, taken away) some of religion's historical socio-political functions and challenged its right even to make normative judgments on putatively public matters. Indeed, to the degree that the modern regulatory state continues to extend its reach far beyond what Locke could have imagined, the conflicts are unlikely to cease anytime soon.

This is especially true if I am right to say that what I have called religious integrationism continues to be a significant and growing presence in the democratic world. Most any religious tradition will make claims about human sexuality, children, economics, and so on, but a good number of traditions in the democratic West have largely acceded to the idea that any number of spheres of human activity are beyond their normative and institutional reach. (Or, at least, they have decided that their traditional sources of authority are outdated and require modification according to what is "rational" and "scientific" and the like). Religion for them has become an almost entirely private affair, concerned solely with the interior spiritual life of the individual, and sometimes they are even unwilling to make and enforce normative claims *within* religious communities, never mind outside of them.[5] As Alan Wolfe has provocatively suggested, some portion of American religion, far from being opposed to liberalism, has in fact thoroughly embraced it.[6] As I have described them, integrationists largely reject this embrace, claiming instead that all the spheres of one's life ought to be governed in accordance with the faith, not the other way around.

At first (and maybe second and third) blush, these believers will seem especially dangerous, politically speaking. The theocrat is a kind of integrationist, and if there is one thing that any sort of liberal can agree on, it is that theocracy is fundamentally incompatible with liberalism or democracy. That is surely right (and the incompatibility also surely works to theocrat's disfavor) but that does not conclude the matter. Most religious believers within contemporary liberal democratic societies – even those who might fall into the category of integrationists or who have integrationist tendencies – do not see themselves nor can they obviously be categorized as liberal democracy's opponents. Quite the opposite, and to the degree that they form political movements or seek political changes,

---

[5] See Wade Clark Roof and William McKinney, *American Mainline Religion* (New Brunswick, NJ: Rutgers University Press, 1994); Robert Wuthnow, *The Restructuring of American Religion: Society and Faith since World War II* (Princeton, NJ: Princeton University Press, 1988).

[6] Wolfe, *The Transformation of American Religion*. Of course, the question for Wolfe is *how much* of American religion does he actually capture.

they do so *within* their society's democratic political institutions. Their presence (and political success) challenges some key elements of what many, perhaps most, political theorists working in the liberal democratic tradition have concluded regarding the proper relationship between religion and liberal democratic politics. That is, they challenge what I have called the liberal consensus on religion.

Liberals are famous, of course, for not having a consensus about much of anything. Among other things, they disagree on the grounds and extent of individual rights (though not their existence or importance), on the relative importance of and relationship between liberty and equality, and even whether liberalism is best understood as a theory of government or something more comprehensive. What liberals generally do not disagree about is the sorts of threats they think religion poses to the construction of legitimate, stable, and free constitutional democracies. Both because religion has a particularly potent capacity to inspire political action and because its fundamental claims cannot be rationally adjudicated, strictly speaking, liberal political thought suggests that it makes a poor basis for justifying and shaping our political life. Under conditions of religious and moral pluralism, that poverty can become disastrous. Religiously inspired political movements competing in the public square can all too easily, the argument goes, turn political conflict into religious war.

Moreover, the consensus points out that many religious traditions are, even within liberal democratic societies, quite illiberal themselves. They seem to disdain the sort of critical rationality liberals tend to prize, take views on gender relations and sexuality that many liberals find distasteful or outright immoral, and often make submission to authorities (textual and ecclesiastical) a key element of their moral and religious thinking. However much liberals might be committed to sustaining a public–private distinction and keeping the state out of the latter, these sorts of characteristics they find especially worrisome, especially in light of their ability to shape not just individuals' private identities, but their public ones as well. How we think and act as citizens, after all, cannot be entirely dissociated from how we think and act privately. Illiberal religions make for illiberal citizens, or so the consensus argues.

These diagnoses have given rise to corresponding strategies, theoretical articulations of what ought to be done to protect liberalism from its religious threats. First, liberal political thought has attempted to construct a public political sphere largely independent of religious influence or presence. On this account, even if liberal democracies need not evince a complete separation of church and state, they must in principle be justifiable to all citizens as citizens. Under conditions of moral and religious pluralism, this means justifying our political authorities without reference to the dictates of religious faith and instead through reasons that are broadly shared or "public." Second, liberal theorists have argued that the religious traditions themselves, to the degree that they are privately illiberal, need reshaping to make them productive of good citizenship. Good citizens are not just born, they are formed. They are formed by institutions – educational, civic, and others – that inculcate attitudes and habits of mind supportive (or not) of the establishment and maintenance of free societies. Though liberals disagree on the amount and sort of reshaping necessary, with some suggesting that believers need only reconceptualize how they relate their religious and political views and others suggesting something much more intrusive and thoroughgoing, they do agree that some reshaping is in order.

This book has challenged this consensus in the context of the integrationist challenge generally and in the context of four historical European cases of integrationism more specifically. Religious integrationists in the Netherlands, Belgium, Germany, and Austria all created powerful networks of schools, trade unions, newspapers, and political parties (among many other things), largely in response to nineteenth-century liberal political efforts to secularize public life and, in the process, reshape their extant religious traditions. No other integrationist movements in modern times have built such powerful subcultural communities, nor have any others acquired as much political power as these, winning parliamentary majorities in Belgium and the Netherlands and pluralities in Germany and Austria. How these integrationist movements impacted their respective countries' democratic prospects and the role they played in shaping their followers' political attitudes and habits of mind can tell us a great deal about the consensus's strengths and weaknesses.

These empirical observations serve to provoke and augment my broader philosophical critiques of the consensus, critiques that suggest the consensus fails in overestimating both religion's political threat and the plausibility of its corresponding prescriptions for ameliorating those threats. I have shown that the powerful claims made in favor of deliberative restraint overestimate both the possibilities for achieving a certain conception of legitimacy in the presence of significant moral and religious pluralism and the dangers in allowing religion to participate in public political life. Moreover, I have argued that while religious integrationists are not, perhaps, ideal liberal citizens, neither are they so deficient in their civic capacities to warrant state intervention. Most interesting is how it is *precisely* religion's political organization and mobilization, coupled with integrationism's robust institutionalism, that seems to make its democratic beneficence possible.

It is not this book's argument that religion, to say nothing of religious integrationism, is always and everywhere a friend to democracy; that would be obviously false. But it is its argument that religion *can* be a boon to democratic government and that liberal theorists interested in making their democratic orders more durable should be more welcoming of religion's political mobilization, with at least one significant caveat. These cases do nothing to injure the supposition that absent some appreciation for the broad legitimacy of the extant political system and a general willingness to work within it, religious political movements – like any other sort of political movement – are incompatible with democratic politics. Revolutionary theocrats need not apply; even if we might be able to justify the liberal order to them,[7] we do them no injustice by saying that they are a threat to the democratic order. These cases do, however, help distinguish the integrationist from the theocrat and injure the supposition that political mobilization on the basis of religion damages democratic prospects. Indeed, it seems as though it is precisely that organization that goes some way toward helping make integrationism more democratically constructive, not less. In other words, it is the thing the consensus finds most threatening that makes religion least worrisome democratically.

One useful way to think about this rather ironic dynamic is in terms of politically mobilized religion's *internal* and *external* effects.[8] Externally, to the degree that the integrationists were successful at organizing themselves and achieving some electoral success, they went some distance toward reshaping the broader political and social order, often helping create what I have termed a structurally pluralist democratic society. In these sorts of societies, the state allowed subcultural communities a great deal more space within which they could organize themselves according to their own particular moral and religious principles. The most developed of these was obviously the Netherlands, where twentieth-century Dutch society organized around discrete "pillars" that encompassed broad swathes of the social order. These structures reflected both theological and philosophical claims (crystallized in Kuyper's neo-Calvinist "sphere sovereignty" but with similarities to Catholic views on "subsidiarity" as well[9]) and the political realities of deeply divided pluralist societies. Internally, the integrationists' peculiar combination of subcultural

---

[7] See Swaine, *The Liberal Conscience.*

[8] I am borrowing here generally from Warren, *Democracy and Association.*

[9] For newer neo-Calvinist and Catholic views along these lines, see Chaplin, "State and Civil Society in Christian Democracy"; Jeanne Heffernan Schindler, *Christianity and Civil Society: Catholic and Neo-Calvinist Perspectives* (Lanham, MD: Lexington Books, 2008); James W. Skillen, *In Pursuit of Justice: Christian-Democratic Explorations* (Lanham, MD: Rowman & Littlefield, 2004).

encapsulation and internal social pluralism worked to produce citizens who recognized that politics had a particular role to play, one that was both connected to and yet distinct from their most basic religious (and moral) convictions. Citizens were "schooled," as it were, to regard politics as organized around securing a set of distinctive goods, perhaps most importantly goods that were not simply reducible to correlative (basic) religious ones.

Absent any significant political organization, believers in places like the Netherlands and Germany could not have achieved the success they did, and absent that success, as the case of France suggests, they might very well have been forced to choose between anti-system activities and the deep reshaping of the faith. Moreover, the cases where *religion* was emphasized more, not less, were the cases where the integrationists were most successful (democratically speaking), as the emphasis on a common religious identity made the construction of political coalitions across class and ethnicity more plausible. This emphasis on religious identity both made the parties more responsive to their communities' interests (religious and temporal) and made them more independent of ecclesial hierarchies, as the political effectiveness of religiously informed organizing gave party leaders political credibility. In short, they could get things done and keep their followers with them. The liberal consensus is wrong, then, to suppose that religion's political mobilization endangers liberalism's moral and philosophical foundations or liberal democracy's practical prospects. Quite the opposite, actually.

Whither liberalism?

If my claims are correct, then it seems as if the consensus is in need of some fairly serious revision. Religion's political participation should be welcomed, maybe even encouraged, along the same lines as other groups. But if that is correct, the implications extend beyond the contours of how liberalism treats religion. As should be clear by now, my strategy in this book has not been to accept what liberals say should be liberalism's proper standards and ask if religion in some form measures up. To do that would concede too much to the tradition, especially since significant strands of that tradition emerged out of engagement with and critique of religion. My strategy was to put the liberal tradition into conversation with religion – and a particularly challenging form of religion at that – and show where some of liberalism's basic claims look to have overreached themselves. Thus while the argument here centers primarily on religion, it necessarily ends up saying something (and, hopefully, something important) about liberal political thought more broadly. And, indeed, in picking up the various strands of argument scattered throughout the previous six chapters it becomes clear that looking closely at liberalism's consensus on religion ends up pressing us toward a reconceptualization of how we think about liberalism itself. Though I can hardly draw in this space anything like a detailed picture of what the revised conception of liberalism might look like, there are important themes that stand out, especially with regard to political legitimacy and civic virtue.

Take first the question of political legitimacy. We should not, it seems to me, give up on the claims of political obligation altogether and reduce our normative theorizing to articulating merely the implications of self-interest (rightly understood or not). We should not, in other words, become satisfied with a mere modus vivendi.[10] We should, however, take more seriously the question of how political institutions might accommodate the diverse and often conflicting ways of life that populate any modern free society. As I suggest at the end of chapter 4, taking pluralism more seriously implies at the least that we set aside as "unrealistic" the expectation that citizens committed to democratic government will find each other's political proposals reasonable only if they are backed by mutually shared reasons. It is simply implausible, given the shape and extent of modern pluralism, to expect anything more than what Rawls has described as a constitutional consensus.[11]

This thinner consensus does not, again, simply obviate our obligations, and though it is wrong to say that we should exercise restraint as the deliberative argument would have it, it does not follow that we should view ourselves as free to deliberate and act politically in any way we happen to see fit. (Or, at least, we are not free to the extent that we are committed to making liberal democratic politics work.) Even as persistent and rigorous a critic of the claim for deliberative restraint as Chris Eberle has argued that since other citizens are beings who deserve what he calls (following Darwall) "recognition respect" they can be coerced only on the basis of (and thus we can pursue only political objectives justified with reference to) morally credible reasons.[12] We cannot go around seeking willy-nilly whatever ends we happen to desire. Our fellow citizens

---

[10] This is what I take to be one of the more important claims in Raymond Geuss, *Philosophy and Real Politics* (Princeton, NJ: Princeton University Press, 2008). He is right, though, to score Rawls and others as insufficiently attentive to the unfortunate (and often bloody) reality of political life. Whether Geuss' repeated invocation of Lenin, the architect of the twentieth century's bloodiest regime, offers much of an improvement is quite another question.

[11] It is possible, of course, that even the United States may see a large-scale secularization. If so, then perhaps we could expect an overlapping consensus, though that would only come about, in that case, because of a narrowed pluralism.

[12] Eberle, *Religious Conviction in Liberal Politics*, 87–105.

deserve more than that (and we deserve more than that from them). These moral reasons are reasons that, according to Eberle, meet a "high degree of rational justification" as judged from within our own "evidential set" and are in accord with the "canons of rationality." Paul Weithman has similarly argued that citizens may draw on their non-public views in debating political issues and voting, provided that "they *sincerely believe* that their government would be justified in adopting the measures they vote for ... and are prepared to indicate what they think would justify the adoption of the measures."[13] These formulations have, I think, a great deal to say for them, but the trick is to say something clear and convincing about those canons and their relation to religious views both so that religious believers can grasp and apply their obligations with some consistency and so that those who do not share their religious beliefs will still see them (and their proposals) as fellow citizens who are acting in good faith politically.

Recall that public reason and other versions of deliberative restraint mean to make political coercion justified both morally and practically: laws must meet a certain moral standard and we must in practice understand them as such. Even if Eberle and Weithman can satisfy the first part, the second remains very much in doubt. We all have too much experience with others offering arguments they take to be nothing but what is "rational" but which we recognize as rooted in particularistic or sectarian bases. Given the mistrust of religion (especially within elite circles, where deliberative restraint has a great deal of valence) it seems important that we can describe a means for religious citizens to articulate views that meet reasonable moral criteria and that their fellow citizens can see as such. How can religious citizens who think themselves compelled to think and act politically on the basis of those religious beliefs demonstrate to their fellow citizens who do not share those beliefs that they offer their proposals in good faith?

Consider two examples that Rawls cites in the last iteration of his public reason argument: debates over the public funding of religious schools and competing grounds for justifying public relief of poverty.[14] In the former, Rawls suggests that in debates over whether the state ought to provide funding for religious schools, there is a danger that the debates could become so vexatious that "those on different sides are likely to come to doubt one another's allegiance to basic constitutional and political values" (154). Those opposed to public funding will, I suppose, worry that those in favor are interested mostly in using the state's resources to

---

[13] Weithman, *Religion and the Obligations of Citizenship*, 121, emphasis added.
[14] All page citations in this section are from Rawls, ed., *The Law of Peoples*.

propagate their faith, something the state has no business doing.[15] In the latter, Christians taking the parable of the Good Samaritan to mean that the state should provide poverty relief can be moved to support such relief by those religious convictions "but go on to give a public justification for this parable's conclusions in terms of political values," something like Rawls' own difference principle, for example (155). In cases like these, believers can reassure their opponents (and vice versa, though it is less clear what this might look like) that their religious values which encourage religious schooling and poverty do in fact support a "reasonable [conception] of political justice" and contribute to an overlapping consensus," thus "[strengthening] the ties of civic friendship" (155).

But these examples show themselves to be either entirely trivial or unhelpful to the question at hand. If it is relatively easy for the religious advocate of poverty relief to translate his argument "in terms of political values," then the matter hardly seems worth arguing about.[16] If, on the other hand, the religious believer can persuade his fellow citizens that his policy proposals, while fundamentally dependent on religious claims, nonetheless are consonant with a reasonable understanding of democratic politics, it is hard to see what the point of the public reason argument is in the first place. The key problem that employing religious reasons poses is that it makes the political outcome dependent on reasons that others cannot – absent a religious conversion – accept, undermining rather than strengthening "the ties of civic friendship." The problem with Rawls' example is that it flies in the face of what public reason is supposed to do, namely, reassure citizens that political outcomes are based on values and ideas that they themselves hold, even if they do not support the particular principle in question. On the public reason argument, it is not enough for religious believers to simply make the argument that their religious views comport with democratic essentials. They must be able to support their political views with public reasons; otherwise, their fellow citizens will have reason to doubt their democratic bona fides and, if coerced according to the believers' political views, reason to think the political order to that degree illegitimate. Rawls' examples simply do not touch the truly central question at hand here: how can religious believers employ their religious beliefs politically without alienating their fellow citizens and undermining even the possibility of democratic legitimacy? It looks hopeless.

---

[15] This seems to be the way that Rawls characterizes the debate in Rawls, *Political Liberalism*, 248–49.

[16] Though there might be some interesting questions regarding the ethics of such translation. See Greenawalt, *Private Consciences and Public Reasons*.

It would be hopeless if we took the liberal consensus to be true, but Europe's religious integrationists suggest something quite different, even perhaps the converse. Rather than thinking that democratic legitimacy and stability are to be found in some elusive dream of consensus, the integrationists illustrate how legitimacy and stability are more the product, not precondition, of democratic politics.

In my discussion of the religious parties' effects on democratic consolidation, I argued that they should not be blamed for their divisiveness, as they were no more to blame than any other party. But they were divisive. Germany's Center Party was quite controversial precisely because it was so Catholic and its Catholicism made it a difficult political ally (from the other parties' perspectives, as they generally seemed to think Catholicism deeply retrograde). In response, the parties could have done something along the lines that Rawls' public reason argument suggests: they could have thinned out their religious affiliation and made themselves something more class- or region-based. That is, as I recounted, what the *Zentrumsstreit* was all about, as some of the Center leadership proposed making the party less Catholic in hopes of attaining real majority status. But that strategy was doomed to failure, mostly because, in the Center's case, the party's opponents were too invested in their anti-Catholicism to allow such a broadening. It was not until the disasters of the Nazi era thoroughly discredited the largely Protestant conservative parties that the Christian Democratic Union could serve as a largely ecumenical party. The Center and the other religious parties served the cause of democratic consolidation (to the degree that they did) by proving themselves to be responsible contestants within the constitutional order and by carving out space for their communities within which those communities could survive and even flourish. That is, rather than restraining themselves as deliberation's proponents suggest, these parties helped consolidate their respective democracies via democratic politics itself.

Here is the broader (philosophical) point: public reason and deliberative restraint are meant to buttress the moral and practical elements of political legitimacy. But they neglect to their discredit the practical side of things, meaning that they overestimate religion's propensity to disrupt democratic stability and underestimate its potential for the converse. Attending more closely to the practical aspects of political legitimacy shows that we should trust – have faith, we might say – that the institutions and practices of constitutional democracies can handle the tempestuous conflicts of something akin to a constitutional consensus. Democracies do not self-destruct because citizens disagree over the proper boundaries of church and state or even – as Rawls himself reminds us – over questions of war and peace.[17] But we can press the point further. It is not just that constitutional orders can handle more conflict than deliberative restraint supposes. Those political conflicts and the partisan electoral efforts associated with them are, in fact, key to securing political legitimacy in the first place. By investing themselves in the political order and seeking to effect a particular interpretation of its norms and principles, partisans make that order theirs and in so doing often solidify its legitimacy, the exceptions notwithstanding.[18] Deliberative restraint's strategies do not just fail to make democracies secure; they can actually work against them by drawing overly bright lines to participation and insisting on implausible moral requirements. Rawls suggests at one point that constitutional democracies ought to work at containing unreasonable views "like war and disease,"[19] and no doubt that is sometimes correct. Our firm anti-democratic partisans should not be given the chance to win power, but these are fairly rare in most contemporary democracies and taking the same stance toward plausibly reasonable citizens is simple foolishness. Instead, we should be encouraging religious believers whose faiths have some sort of public import to organize and participate politically, not to withdraw.

Note here how this meets up rather nicely with the other half of the liberal consensus, the question of civic virtue. The consensus suggests that religion – and especially seemingly the politically mobilized sorts of religion we have been considering – threatens democracies in the sense of making bad citizens. Politically mobilized believers can help establish and sustain legitimate democracies, though, precisely by virtue of their political mobilization and organization. But they can only do so (as with all of us) provided that they learn to think about politics as something distinct, if not separate, from their more basic beliefs. Political legitimacy in a society where some significant portion of the population has integrationist views can only happen, seemingly, if those integrationists can fruitfully distinguish between politics and the other parts of their lives. That requires, I hope to have shown, a decent amount of social

---

[17] Habermas' rather bizarre suggestion that there should be parliamentary procedures for excising religious speech within legislative bodies so as to preserve the idea (or fiction) that a law actually met his deliberative standards suggests that he too is overly worried about democratic failure. See Habermas, "Religion in the Public Sphere." At least Habermas has the excuse of living in the shadow of Weimar's failure; it is really quite difficult to see why Rawls and other American thinkers are similarly worried.

[18] The affinity here with Rosenblum's arguments ought to be clear. See Russell Muirhead and Nancy L. Rosenblum, "Political Liberalism vs. 'The Great Game of Politics': The Politics of Political Liberalism," *Perspectives on Politics* 4, no. 1 (2006); Rosenblum, *On the Side of the Angels*; Rosenblum, "Religious Parties, Religious Political Identity."

[19] Rawls, *Political Liberalism*, 64 fn. 19.

"space" within which the integrationists can organize those other parts of their lives as they see fit.[20] Religious believers, like many other citizens, are much less likely to impose their particular ways of life on others if afforded the opportunity to freely organize their own lives (and, often, their children's lives as well).

Ironically enough, the consensus view – that the liberal state has an obligation to try and interfere in those lives[21] – works in just the opposite manner. By attempting to force a kind of "congruence"[22] on these non-liberal subcultural communities, the consensus actually teaches something quite, well, illiberal: namely, that there is very little, if any, distinction to be made between politics and the rest of our lives. If Macedo is right and liberalism must work to shape "the soul as well as the body,"[23] integrationists might be excused for thinking that they would be justified in doing what their opponents accuse them of desiring: imposing their particular way of life on others. The consensus, ostensibly an effort to secure pluralist democracies, again can work against its own purposes, as its own efforts cut against the very ideas that should sustain it.

The lessons for liberal democratic thought here are twofold. First, liberalism needs to be more attentive to the range and depth of moral and religious pluralism extant in contemporary democratic societies. Liberalism has almost always been more sensitive and accommodating of pluralism than its competitors, especially the twentieth-century varieties. But in its anxiousness to grapple with an invigorated set of pluralisms that refused to keep their distinctive views safely in private life, liberalism trimmed its accommodations for religious believers (while seemingly expanding it for ethnic, racial, and other minorities).[24] That is a mistake, and liberal political theorists should reconsider how to accommodate believers, even those whose views do not win them many fans in the halls of academia and whose political efforts liberals may find noxious or worse. This will require that liberalism attend especially to the sorts of

---

[20] There are, of course, limits to this. Attempting to detail them would take us too far afield into debates surrounding liberal multiculturalism.

[21] See, for example, Macedo, "Transformative Constitutionalism"; Susan Moller Okin, "Comment on Nancy Rosenblum's 'Feminist Perspectives on Civil Society and Government'," in *Civil Society and Government*, ed. Nancy L. Rosenblum and Harry Post (Princeton, NJ: Princeton University Press, 2002).

[22] I borrow this term from Rosenblum, *Membership and Morals*.

[23] Macedo, "Transformative Constitutionalism," 64.

[24] See Kymlicka, *Multicultural Citizenship*; Will Kymlicka, *Politics in the Vernacular: Nationalism, Multiculturalism, and Citizenship* (Oxford and New York: Oxford University Press, 2001); Will Kymlicka and Wayne Norman, eds., *Citizenship in Diverse Societies* (New York: Oxford University Press, 2000).

institutions and structures that make distinctive lives possible and both abstain from interfering in those institutions and structures and provide support (under some conditions). It will not do, for example, to blithely say that you may live as you wish and organize your life around diverse sets of values, but that the state may legitimately attempt to impose its quite substantive moral values on your children or that the state may interfere in how religious organizations may organize themselves internally, and so on. But neither will it do for the state to simply leave us alone and then use its enormous resources to favor one way of life over another; clearly, something like Tomasi's psychological "tax-flattening" plan is necessary.[25]

This attentiveness does not issue simply from the moral demands of fairness, however. If it is right to say – as I do in the Introduction – that religious integrationism remains a serious and even growing force in democratic life world-wide, then there is a practical aspect to this accommodationism as well. The point of liberal political strategies is to ensure that constitutional democratic orders persist and flourish over the long term, and key to that flourishing is how citizens in those democracies come to understand their own political orders and their place in it. Democracies will do well (in this respect, at least) to the degree that citizens are able and willing to make distinctions between politics and the rest of their lives. This is especially true in democracies beset by wider and deeper sorts of pluralisms than ever before; if some portion of the electorate comes to believe, and tries to act on this belief, that the state is the proper vehicle for enforcing the "one true faith" (to pick an example out of the air), that democracy will be in danger. It might be possible – indeed, it has been possible – to persuade some, maybe most, to privatize their distinctive views and avoid the problem altogether. But it would be unwise to count on that strategy, as the experience of the past few decades reminds us. Religion – and other sorts of pluralisms – is not so easily tamed, and a better practical strategy would tend toward accommodation, not confrontation. The hope would be that, given space to order themselves more or less freely, religious believers

---

[25] Tomasi, *Liberalism beyond Justice*. See chapter 5 for more discussion. Veit Bader has also worked in recent years to develop arguments in this direction. See Veit Bader, "Associative Democracy and Minorities within Minorities," in *Minorities within Minorities: Equality, Rights, and Diversity*, ed. Eisenberg and Spinner-Halev; Veit Bader, "Democratic Institutional Pluralism and Cultural Diversity," in *The Social Construction of Diversity*, ed. Danielle Juteau and Christine Harzig (Oxford: Berghan Books, 2003); Veit Bader, "Religion and States: A New Typology and a Plea for Non-Constitutional Pluralism," *Ethical Theory and Moral Practice: An International Forum* 6 (2003); Bader, "Religious Diversity and Democratic Institutional Pluralism"; Veit Bader, "Religious Pluralism: Secularism or Priority for Democracy," *Political Theory* 27, no. 5 (1999).

would feel less compulsion to order others' lives and learn to understand politics as a distinctive practice designed to secure limited temporal goods.

The second lesson for liberal political thought is that it needs to be more trusting in the institutions and procedures of constitutional democracies. In a word, liberalism needs to appreciate more fully how *politics* and political contestation fit into its aspirations. As Gaus and Vallier have recently suggested, proponents of deliberation (and liberals more generally, it seems) have been too focused on the quality of what motivates our political activities and too little focused on how institutions help shape outcomes.[26] They have been too focused, we might say, on inputs as opposed to outputs. But this is a problem created by more than just inattention. The source of liberalism's deliberative turn and its focus on the sorts of reasons we might offer one another politically is its rather broad merger with the democratic tradition, made most explicit in Rawls' political liberalism.[27] Democracy as an ideal, at least as understood by its deliberative proponents, carries with it an aspiration to consensus, the hope that we can obey all and just ourselves at the same time. It is the aspiration to consensus and the view that coercion, conflict and the like are signs of moral and political failure. We are stuck with such failures, it seems, but they are, in this new kind of liberal dispensation, to be hemmed in and avoided if at all possible.

Conflict and coercion are not to be lauded in and of themselves, of course. It would be better, all things considered, for us all to respond to reason and persuasion as opposed to force. But the plain fact of the matter is that in modern democracies we disagree and disagree deeply over a number of quite contentious issues. It does democracy no credit to suggest that it cannot handle the political debates that roil our public deliberations – democracies are not all Weimars-in-the-making and we should stop treating them as if they are delicate flowers, always ready to fail. Rather, we should recognize that political debate, electoral contestation, and the like are a good way to flesh out our disagreements and find ways to live with one another as free and equal citizens. Liberalism should, then, at the least temper its fear of political conflict and think about ways to employ it to the ends of free, stable, and legitimate constitutional democracies.[28]

---

[26] Gaus and Vallier, "The Roles of Religious Conviction in a Publicly Justified Polity."
[27] See Cohen, "A More Democratic Liberalism."
[28] The Madisonian element here should be obvious. See *Federalist* no. 10 and his discussions of factions.

Two tentative applications

The reasonable reader who has read this far might wonder how it is I can make such an effort to rehabilitate religious political mobilization and say so little about the world's two most visible – and controversial – contemporary examples of religion's politicization, religious conservatives in the United States and Islamic activists around the globe. At least since the late 1970s – with the 1979 revolution in Iran and the emergence of conservative protestant political organizations in the US – few, if any, intersections of religion and politics have occasioned nearly as much commentary and analysis as these two. If the arguments of the preceding six chapters work, as I hope they do, to redirect some of liberalism's views regarding religion's political activities then surely they should be able to say something about the issue's two most prominent and controversial examples.

It is a fair concern, and by way of concluding I offer here some tentative thoughts regarding how my rough alternative to the liberal consensus sketched out above might inform our reflections on both. What I suggest, perhaps unsurprisingly, is that we have good reasons to be hopeful regarding at least some elements of both cases. Neither political Islam nor American religious conservatives offer insurmountable obstacles to the construction and sustenance of constitutional democracies; to the contrary, both may actually turn out to be quite beneficial, though each in their own way. Two caveats, though, before I begin. First, both phenomena have elicited a tremendous amount of commentary and analysis, and what I offer below is but the thinnest of glosses on that vast literature. I do not mean this to be definitive or complete; indeed, given the fact that both are ongoing phenomena, it would be unwise in the extreme to pretend otherwise. What follows is merely meant to be suggestive and hopefully helpful in assisting our considerations on both. Second, in considering these two phenomena together, I do not mean to suggest that the two are linked in any essential way, except perhaps that both mean to employ religious views politically. There has been over the last decade or so a recurrent tendency to lump the two together, typically as a way of discrediting the American Christian Right politically.[29] Whatever one thinks substantively of the Christian Right, tarring them as the "American Taliban" or worse is frankly stupid and hardly worth a rebuttal.[30] Nothing in what follows is meant to suggest otherwise.

---

[29] This is obviously true in Phillips, *American Theocracy*; Sullivan, *The Conservative Soul*.

[30] For that matter, as I suggest below, neither is it the case that all sorts of political Islam are mere stalking horses for "Talibanic" politics.

So how does my thinly sketched alternative to the liberal consensus help us to think about the relationship between political Islam and constitutional democracies? It is a difficult question, not least because of the wide variety of cases it includes. Should Muslim cab drivers in Minneapolis be excused from carrying passengers with liquor in their luggage? Should the liberal state recognize (and thus endorse) Islamic marriages and divorces? Should Muslim demands for protections against "hateful" criticisms of Islam be accepted? Are Islamist political parties good or bad for democracies? Can *sharia* law coexist with democratic liberties? And so on and so on. The first problem with thinking about political Islam is that the issues included in the phrase "political Islam" are themselves so vast and varied as to be practically impossible to grasp effectively. To make things more manageable, suppose we can think about political Islam in three different sorts of cases: (1) political Islam as a revolutionary movement, dedicated to a more or less strict theocratic state (as in Iran or Saudi Arabia); (2) political Islam as a political movement within tenuously democratic or pseudo-democratic states (as in Turkey and Indonesia); and (3) political Islam within established democracies (as in Western Europe or the United States).

As to the first case, political Islam as a revolutionary movement, nothing in what I have offered above should suggest anything other than what is commonly believed, namely, that such movements as al Qaeda and the like are simply and fundamentally incompatible with democratic government. Europe's religious integrationists might not, as I have noted, have been democratic "heroes" in the sense of working consciously to effect democratic progress, but their willingness to work politically within the extant constitutional order contributed powerfully (if perhaps ironically) to democratization. There is no such modesty to the Islamic radicals who are willing to blow up buildings, murder innocent civilians, behead captives, and the like in service to some vision of a pan-Islamic theocracy. And there should be very little modesty in the liberal response to such movements: Rawls' admonition to contain unreasonable doctrines like "disease and war" seems much too mild in these sorts of cases.[31]

But the radical, revolutionary case hardly covers the full spectrum of political Islam. Consider the Islamic political parties that now populate most majority-Muslim countries in the Middle East and elsewhere. These parties, in ways not entirely unlike Europe's integrationists, seek to apply their specifically religious claims politically within constitutional,

---

[31] To my mind, a much better liberal response is Paul Berman, *Terror and Liberalism*, 1st. edn. (New York: Norton, 2003).

and sometimes democratic, orders.[32] But these parties are not, or are not all, straightforward analogues to the integrationists or their Christian Democratic successors.[33] Most of the political parties in majority-Muslim countries that claim – or are reliably identified by their opponents as deserving – the Islamic label emerged from (or are still a part of) the Muslim Brotherhood (MB), a radical Islamic movement that began in Egypt in the 1920s and sought (or seeks, depending on how one views its goals) to impose strict *sharia* law. There is good reason to worry, as Algeria's military thought in canceling elections that the country's Islamic party was likely to win, that such parties contest elections on the principle of "one man, one vote, one time."[34] A party whose purpose is to impose a political settlement that effectively precludes future electoral contestation is not, I hardly need say, a boon to democratic government. Bassam Tibi, for example, makes the quite plausible claim that "Islamist" parties cannot be properly democratic since, theologically, accepting pluralism and the possibility of political shifts away from Islam looks to be profoundly incompatible with a distinctively Islamic view of politics.[35] On this account, one can be democratic or one can be Islamist. One cannot be both.

This is, as I said, not implausible, but it depends on a fairly narrow view of what counts as Islamist, almost to the extent that it amounts to a false dichotomy. If indeed an Islamic party is Islamic to the extent that it seeks to put in place a "totalitarian order" in which "difference appears as heresy and placed within the ambit of that which is sacred and hence nonnegotiable"[36] then we would be well advised to look askance at such movements, whatever they might *say* about their political goals. But there are two ways in which such a strong dichotomy between Islamic (or Islamist) parties and democratic rule looks less obvious than Tibi makes it out to be. First, consider that for the most

---

[32] Robert Hefner, *Civil Islam: Muslims and Democratization in Indonesia* (Princeton, NJ: Princeton University Press, 2000); Marina Ottaway and Amr Hamzawy, *Getting to Pluralism: Political Actors in the Arab World* (Washington, D.C.: Carnegie Endowment for International Peace, 2009); David L. Phillips, *From Bullets to Ballots: Violent Muslim Movements in Transition* (New Brunswick, NJ: Transaction Publishers, 2009); Jillian Schwedler, *Faith in Moderation: Islamist Parties in Jordan and Yemen* (New York: Cambridge University Press, 2006); Sultan Tepe, *Beyond Sacred and Secular: Politics of Religion in Israel and Turkey* (Stanford, CA: Stanford University Press, 2008).

[33] Turkey's Justice and Development Party (AKP) explicitly claims that it is little more than a parallel to Germany's Christian Democratic Union. I suggest below that Germany's Center Party would be a better analogy.

[34] That quip is from Edward Djerejian, "The US and the Middle East in a Changing World," address at Meridian House International, *US Department of State Dispatch*, June 8, 1992. Quoted, among many other places, in Berman, "Taming Extremist Parties."

[35] Bassam Tibi, "Why They Can't Be Democratic," *Journal of Democracy* 19, no. 3 (2008).

[36] Ibid., 45.

part, Islamic parties have had no chance to actually exercise political authority. To the extent that they participate in elections and parliaments, they remain walled off from real political authority and the accountability that goes with it. Perhaps the Islamists would do precisely what Tibi thinks they would do, perhaps following the lead of Iran, where the regime combines narrowly competitive elections with a theocratic dictatorship, but we really do not know, since almost none of them has been afforded the opportunity.[37]

Second, in the only instance where a putatively Islamic party has actually been afforded the opportunity to rule, Turkey's AKP, it has done so in a way that might assuage some of Tibi's concerns.[38] Though it is certainly far from making for a knock-down argument in favor of *more* Islamic political mobilization, the AKP's record for now suggests that hope rather than fear ought to guide our reflections on Islamic parties. The AKP is the latest in a series of Islamic (or Islamist) political parties that have percolated through Turkish politics at least since the late 1960s.[39] Winning 363 out of 550 seats in parliamentary elections in 2002 and then 46 percent of the vote in 2007, the AKP has now established itself as the majority party in Turkey's contentious, sometimes quite tenuous, democracy. It has accomplished this in spite of the ways in which its undeniably Islamist orientation stands in tension with the officially proclaimed secularism of the Turkish republic.

Modern Turkey emerged from the tottering ruins of the Ottoman Empire, and clearly high among Mustafa Kemal Atatürk's priorities was an emphasis on dissociating the new republican political order from Islam. To that end Atatürk abolished the caliphate, closed religious schools, and replaced the traditional *sharia* law with European civil codes. To question or challenge Turkey's public secularism was, in effect, to challenge Turkey's republican government, a point made by the Constitutional Court in 2008 when it overturned a constitutional amendment allowing the wearing of the Islamic head-scarf by women in universities. Indeed, the AKP narrowly avoided the fate of its predecessors the same year when the Court narrowly (by one vote) decided not to ban the party for its challenge to public secularism.[40]

---

[37] A point made by Amr Hamzawy and Nathan J. Brown, "A Boon or a Bane for Democracy," *Journal of Democracy* 19, no. 3 (2008).

[38] Some might conceivably suggest that Hamas also fits the bill with its election victory in Gaza. If so, that would be a mark in Tibi's favor. I would place them in the revolutionary radical category above.

[39] For the complicated history, see Tepe, *Beyond Sacred and Secular*, 159–226.

[40] The court found that the party did violate the constitution's guarantees of secularism, but declined to disband it and force its leaders out of politics for five years. Instead, the

To our ears, the idea of *banning* a political party because it is too religious may sound odd, even rather oppressive.[41] But if it is the case that Turkish democracy depends in some fundamental way on the maintenance of public secularism, then the AKP may indeed be problematic, since it is clearly an organization that means to advance a religiously rooted view of the public order, even if it describes itself as just another center-right political party in the mold of Germany's Christian Democratic Union. The evidence offered by the past several years of AKP rule suggests something quite different, though. At the very least, the AKP has adapted itself (and its Islamist impulses) to the constraints of a democratic order and, what's more, done a great deal to advance and enlarge the scope of basic liberties (speech, religion, association, and so on) that were much less well protected under the previous, fully secular, governments.[42] It is true that it pursued these policies in light of both the lure of possible EU membership and the credible threat of a military coup if it strayed too far from the Kemalist path.[43] So we should not infer from the case of the AKP that Islamic parties are inevitably or even likely to be beneficial democratically.

But given these reasonably strong institutional constraints, it seems (at least at this point) that the party has begun to tread along the same pathways as Europe's integrationists. In seeking to make its Islamist program attractive to an electoral majority (and acceptable to the ever-brooding military), the AKP offered a broadly conservative program that advanced policies along the whole range of political issues.[44] In so doing, it began to reshape its followers' political identities and, indeed, their religious identities as well.[45] It may very well be the case, as a number of worried observers suggest, that the AKP's leaders are playing a kind of double game, professing their democratic bona fides while waiting for the moment to impose an undemocratic Islamist polity. But even if that *is* the case, we should not be surprised if such intentions, should they exist, never come

court halved the amount of money the party received from the state. Combined with warnings from the military establishment, it was clearly a shot over the bow.
[41] That is the position of Amitai Etzioni, "Turkey's Dilemma: How Secularism Is Threatening Democracy," *Commonweal* (August 2008). For some very interesting reflections on the grounds on which democracies might quite legitimately ban political parties, see Rosenblum, *On the Side of the Angels*, 412–59.
[42] See Ihsan Dagi, "Turkey's AKP in Power," *Journal of Democracy* 19, no. 3 (2008).
[43] See Zeyno Baran, "Turkey Divided," *Journal of Democracy* 19, no. 1 (2008); Dagi, "Turkey's AKP in Power"; M. Hakan Yavuz, *Secularism and Muslim Democracy in Europe* (Cambridge: Cambridge University Press, 2009).
[44] Gamze Cavdar, "Islamist New Thinking in Turkey: A Model for Political Learning," *Political Science Quarterly* 121, no. 3 (2006).
[45] See Ihsan Dagi, "Transformation of Islamic Political Identity in Turkey: Rethinking the West and Westernization," *Turkish Studies* 6, no. 1 (2005); Husain Haqqani and Hillel Fradkin, "Going Back to the Origins," *Journal of Democracy* 19, no. 3 (2008).

to fruition. Europe's integrationists had no intention of helping secure their respective countries' democratizations; often, they intended something quite the opposite. But the logic of electoral competition and the requirements of parliamentary and democratic government can exert a powerful pull and reshape intentions, sometimes in ways that surprise even the most reflective of political agents. Turkey's AKP, easily the most successful and powerful of the world's numerous Islamic political parties, has not put Turkey's democracy in peril and in many ways looks to have made it more secure. Though we should be clear about the potential for reversal (especially under, say, difficult economic conditions), we should also be clear that the arguments offered in the previous six chapters give us reasons to be rather hopeful.

That leaves one last type of political Islam to be considered, politically mobilized Muslims within established democracies, especially those in North America and Europe. Again, nothing in what I have argued previously should be taken to suggest that those actors who use terrorism and other forms of political violence to advance a vision of some sort of Islamic theocracy are to be tolerated in the least. There is no accommodation to be had with such groups, and democratic governments are foolish if they think that integrating them into political structures would be a wise strategy.[46] Prudence may counsel restraint in dealing with such radicals, but we should recognize it as the prudence of choosing the least bad option.[47] More interesting with regard to the sorts of challenges the liberal consensus is meant to address are those Muslims who might plausibly fit into a democratic order but whose substantive views on social, economic, and political issues make them quite distinctive – and threatening to many.[48] The key question

---

[46] Sheri Berman has suggested that we might fruitfully learn from the ways in which some of Europe's communist parties were "tamed" over the course of the twentieth century. See Berman, "Taming Extremist Parties." The key here, though, was that Italy and France's communist parties, which had significant electoral support in the post-World War II era, were shut out of any real political power until they temporized their revolutionary ideology and distanced themselves from the Soviet Union. See also Rosenblum, *On the Side of the Angels*. For my part, I think banning political parties is generally a mistake, at least insofar as it just drives conspirators underground or provides incentives to infiltrate "mainstream" parties (e.g. Henry Wallace's Progressive Party). But mainstream parties should be unwilling to cooperate or have anything to do with parties whose orienting doctrines put them fundamentally at odds with a constitutional democracy's basic values. Recall that the religious parties in Belgium and the Netherlands were crucial in defending democracy in the 1930s precisely because they, along with their liberal and socialist opponents, drove the extremists (on both left and right) out of political society.

[47] See Philip Jenkins, *God's Continent: Christianity, Islam, and Europe's Religious Crisis* (New York: Oxford University Press, 2007), 205–32.

[48] See, for example, the highly charged arguments in Bruce Bawer, *Surrender: Appeasing Islam, Sacrificing Freedom* (New York: Doubleday, 2009); Bruce Bawer, *While Europe*

that seems to divide analyses regarding these populations is whether these democracies' Muslim populations are merely distinctive or whether they fall into what I have termed the revolutionary category, a question whose importance obviously has greater salience in relation to the terrorist attacks in New York, Washington, London, and Madrid (and attempts in many other places). Those who are pessimistic with respect to Muslims in Western democracies generally think that they are broadly sympathetic to the radicals' aims (if not always with their ends) while the optimists see a much greater (and growing) divide between the two.

I have neither the expertise nor the space here to adjudicate this very complex matter, but there are a couple of ways in which my extended critique of the liberal consensus (and alternative rendering) might offer some interesting insights, especially on the question of Muslims in Europe, where the issue seems much more politically explosive.[49] First, note that the European integrationists' political mobilization was beneficial democratically when religious believers who decided to engage politically did so within religiously oriented organizations, most notably religious political parties. This sort of representation seems less available to contemporary Muslims in Europe, as they constitute a much smaller percentage of the population and there is a much stronger norm against religious politics than in the United States.[50] More problematic still, Europe's Muslims are not organized in a way that conduces

---

Slept: How Radical Islam Is Destroying the West from Within, 1st. pbk. edn. (New York: Broadway Books, 2006); Claire Berlinski, *Menace in Europe: Why the Continent's Crisis Is America's, Too* (New York: Crown Forum, 2006); Melanie Phillips, *Londonistan* (New York: Encounter Books, 2006); Mark Steyn, *America Alone: The End of the World as We Know It* (Lanham, MD: Regnery, 2006). For more hopeful views see Fetzer and Soper, *Muslims and the State in Britain, France, and Germany*; Jenkins, *God's Continent*.

[49] In what follows, I focus mostly on political Islam within Europe, as Muslim political activity has been much less of an issue in the USA, even if the "War on Terror" has been a much bigger one. Part of the reason for the disparity is population, as the American Muslim population is much smaller proportionately (well below 1 percent), or perhaps America's longer experience with immigration and pluralism.

[50] According to Philip Jenkins, France has the highest percentage of Muslims in Western Europe at around 8 percent. Some of the smaller states in the East have more. See Jenkins, *God's Continent*, 16. Numbers for the USA vary widely but a recent Pew Forum poll put the number at 0.6 percent. See http://religions.pewforum.org/pdf/affiliations-all-traditions.pdf. On the different expectations governing public discourse in Europe, it is enough to quote former British Prime Minister Tony Blair in a recent speech at the US National Prayer Breakfast: "I recall giving an address to the country at a time of crisis. I wanted to end my words with 'God bless the British people'. This caused complete consternation. Emergency meetings were convened. The system was aghast. Finally, as I sat trying to defend my words, a senior civil servant said, with utter distain: 'Really, Prime Minister, this is not America you know.'" The full text of the speech is available at http://tonyblairoffice.org/2009/02/full-text-of-tony-blairs-speec.html.

toward cohesive political mobilization. Unlike Catholics and even most Protestants, they do not fit easily into more or less hierarchically ordered political networks, meaning that it is much more difficult for them to mobilize politically as a group.[51] At first blush, this might seem like an advantage; popular fears of Muslim political goals would no doubt not be assuaged by the image of a strongly unified Islamic political movement running candidates, making demands, conducting demonstrations, and so forth.

But first blushes can be deceiving, and European Muslims' general inability to cohere around a common political organization means that Muslims themselves have a limited capacity to exert control over members' political activities. Those inclined to more radical sorts of politics are therefore much less constrained than they might be otherwise, and, indeed, to the degree that Muslims in Europe feel aggrieved, the lack of broad political organizations would actually seem to create incentives to radicalism.[52] Europe's nineteenth-century Christian parties successfully participated in their respective democratic consolidations in part, as I have noted, because they could exert more or less effective control over their communities' political efforts. At the very least, they could establish boundaries and reassure nervous opponents that they would be reliable political partners in their nascent parliamentary and democratic regimes.[53] Absent those sorts of political organizations, Muslims will continue to find it difficult to press their interests effectively within normal democratic politics and will be bedeviled by political entrepreneurs eager to exploit frustrations via ever more radical political goals. Given the general suspicion with which many Muslims are viewed and the very real conflicts with Islamic terrorist groups, the difficulties in political organizing will likely make the position of political Islam a thorny well into the future.[54]

But even if European (or American) Muslims were able to overcome these structural–institutional barriers, they might still prove problematic politically insofar as their political mobilization would tend to make for a heightened sense of overlapping, as opposed to cross-cutting, cleavages.

---

[51] See Carolyn M. Warner, "Religion and the Political Organization of Muslims in Europe," *Perspectives on Politics* 4, no. 3 (2006). Warner points out that Islam is, for the most part, a quite decentralized religion. There is no Vatican or Synod with which the state or other political groups can negotiate.

[52] For an argument showing how it is that organization helps keep radicals in check see Rosenblum, *Membership and Morals*.

[53] Again, Kalyvas' contrast between 1884 Belgium and 1989 Algeria is most instructive. See Kalyvas, "Democracy and Religious Politics."

[54] This is, I should note, true entirely independently of the degree to which Muslims support revolutionary efforts. Even if Muslims are within the political mainstream (if still quite distinctive) they will likely find it difficult to advance their political interests and police those tempted toward radicalism.

Especially in Europe, Muslims are almost entirely relatively new immigrants (at least in the last two or three generations) and are almost all from North Africa, Asia, and the Middle East.[55] This means that when Europe's Muslims do press political demands, they stand as both a religious and ethnic group, perhaps strengthening rather than mitigating political conflict. As I noted in the case of Austria, part of the reason for the First Republic's failure was the way in which the divisions between the Christian Socials and socialists became "total." On one side were the Christian Socials (rural, Catholic, Alpine) and the other were the socialists (urban, working class, secular). Unlike in Germany, where the Center's cross-class and multiethnic constituencies pushed it toward political compromise, Austria's Christian Socials were vulnerable to radicalization and confrontation. This religious–racial combination has confounded many a discussion of Europe's Muslims and makes their political position that much more difficult. Neither of these factors – Muslims' lack of natural political organization and their racial–religious overlap – means that political Islam is somehow an inevitable or even likely threat to European democracy, but they do mean that Europe's Muslims may have a more difficult time in finding their political voice within their respective democratic orders for reasons rather independent of their particular political theologies or social norms.[56]

If political Islam has raised all sorts of difficult political questions in Europe, in the United States it has been the rise of religious conservatives, often grouped under the label Christian Right (CR), that has roiled our political waters. Made up mostly of theologically conservative Protestants – but with a strong number of Catholics and even some Jewish believers – the CR emerged out of the tumult of the late 1960s and 1970s as a political movement with both defensive and constructive goals.[57] These conservatives sought to protect their private

---

[55] This is less true in the United States, where some portion of American Muslims are native-born African Americans.

[56] In this, then, I tend more toward Philip Jenkins than, say, Mark Steyn. This is not to say, of course, that the degree to which Europe's Muslims favor radical political options (i.e. terrorism and/or some sort of theocratic regime) does not matter or does not make things much more difficult. If even just a small percentage of Muslims are sympathetic toward al Qaeda or toward political norms clearly incompatible with a constitutional democracy, then things will be even more difficult. My point is merely that even if such numbers are vanishingly small, political Islam in Europe will find things difficult to navigate.

[57] The literature is vast and unwieldy. For a sample, see Steve Brint and Jean Schroedel, eds., *The Christian Conservative Movement and American Democracy: Evangelicals, the Religious Right, and American Politics* (New York: Russell Sage Foundation, 2009); Michael Cromartie, *Disciples and Democracy: Religious Conservatives and the Future of American Politics* (Grand Rapids, MI: Eerdmans Publishing, 1994); Sara Diamond, *Not by Politics Alone: The Enduring Influence of the Christian Right* (New York: Guilford Press,

schools and broadcast rights against what they deemed improper state interference as well as to roll back (or redirect, as the case may be) changes in the American social and political order, especially regarding the role of women, abortion, sexual liberty, and other issues that might be included in the "moral culture" (or "social issues.") The CR has gone through a number of permutations as its leading organizations – the Moral Majority, Christian Coalition, and so on – have risen, splintered, and fallen back into obscurity, provoking repeated claims that its influence was ebbing or dead.[58] Many of these claims were motivated, perhaps, less by sober consideration of evidence and more by hope, given that most scholars (it seems safe to say) have viewed the CR with a mixture of frustration, horror, and contempt. It is difficult to say whether the latest rounds of obituaries will prove any more accurate than the previous ones, but the arguments I have developed above offer us some reasons to appreciate the CR (and its difficulties) and grasp a bit more clearly the role it plays in American politics quite independently of our normative and moral evaluations of its objectives.

The first thing to note is that the CR, viewed rather broadly, emerges out of social conditions not unlike those of Europe's integrationists. Like parts of late nineteenth-century Europe, the United States of the 1960s and 1970s was in the grip of tremendous social, economic, and political changes, and the CR organized in large part as a means of pushing back against newly empowered elites who were, on one telling, attempting to secularize the public order and make religion something private and "trivial."[59] It is not often appreciated, but as Jon Shields has recently emphasized, one thing the CR did was to bring a whole category of religious voters into the electoral system.[60] The core of the CR, conservative Protestants, had largely abandoned the world of politics following

1998); Green *et al.*, eds., *Religion and the Culture Wars*; Green, Rozell, and Wilcox, *The Christian Right in American Politics*; Rozell and Wilcox, *God at the Grass Roots*; Wilcox, *Onward Christian Soldiers?*

[58] See, for example, Steve Bruce, *The Rise and Fall of the New Christian Right* (Oxford: Clarendon Press, 1988).

[59] Carter, *The Culture of Disbelief*. The highly regarded sociologist Peter Berger has suggested that if India is the world's most religious society and Sweden the least, then the United States is a country of Indians ruled by Swedes. For some evidence at least on the liberal side of the political spectrum, see Bolce and De Maio, "Our Secularist Democratic Party."

[60] Jon A. Shields, *The Democratic Virtues of the Christian Right* (Princeton, NJ: Princeton University Press, 2009), 115–45. See also Jeffrey C. Isaac, Matthew F. Filner, and Jason C. Bivins, "American Democracy and the New Christian Right: A Critique of Apolitical Liberalism," in *Democracy's Edges*, ed. Ian Shapiro and Casiano Hacker-Cordon (Cambridge: Cambridge University Press, 1999).

their cultural and political defeats in the 1920s and 1930s.[61] That did not mean that their faith was "private" or "non-political," but rather that they were content to remain ensconced within their own communities and institutions, regardless of the injustice swirling around them.[62] The CR represented the means through which many (though certainly not all) religious conservatives began to participate politically and exercise their office of citizenship.

Of course some (maybe many) might think that whatever the goods of electoral participation, it is sometimes a double-edged sword. While we may appreciate how the CR may have been the means through which conservative Protestants (and their allies) came to participate in American democracy, it is the ends they seek, not their participation as such, that worries so many. As one scholar argued to me in discussing this project, the problem is not so much that individuals and groups employ their religious views politically (that seems well-nigh inevitable), but rather that they employ them toward goals that seem to run counter to views that many liberals take to be axiomatic. The CR opposes abortion rights, fought to defeat the Equal Rights Amendment, is lukewarm (at best) regarding women's full participation in the workforce, opposes homosexual marriage, and so on and so on. What's more, its adherents tend to grasp at just one issue (abortion) or a couple (abortion and homosexuality) and act as if that is the end-all, be-all of politics.[63] Even if they do not threaten in any sense of the word to impose a "theocracy,"[64] they are often at odds with liberalism's defenders, both academic and public. In this case, I suspect that the CR's critics would be happy to trade off some participation for their own substantive political goals.

That would be a mistake, I submit, for it would attempt to do politically what the liberal consensus has attempted to do philosophically: construct a public political order independent of citizens' basic moral, religious,

---

[61] See George M. Marsden, *Fundamentalism and American Culture*, 2nd. edn. (New York: Oxford University Press, 2006); Mark A. Noll, *Religion and American Politics: From the Colonial Period to the 1980s* (New York: Oxford University Press, 1990).

[62] This is the "uneasy conscience" of Carl F.H. Henry's 1947 call for fundamentalists and "neo-evangelicals" to engage the surrounding culture, a call that most historians cite as a seminal moment in the development of the CR. See Carl F.H. Henry, *The Uneasy Conscience of Modern Fundamentalism* (Grand Rapids, MI: Eerdmans Publishing, 1947). The prevailing view among Henry's fundamentalists was that politics (and the broader culture) was a corrupt and dirty business and that Christians were better served by remaining within their own communities and institutions, free from the taint of "the world."

[63] For a critique along these lines from within the evangelical camp, see Ronald J. Sider, *The Scandal of Evangelical Politics* (Grand Rapids, MI: Baker, 2008).

[64] For a clear and witty take-down of the theocratic canard, see Ross Douthat, "Theocracy, Theocracy, Theocracy," *First Things* 165 (2006).

and philosophical views. Perhaps that is plausible if the religious views (as in mainline Protestantism) more or less match up with the prevailing liberal sentiment or if the religious views (as in pre-CR conservative Protestantism) are already oriented toward privatism and political quiescence. But if those conditions do not hold, then such efforts are the product of political fantasy and, indeed, are likely to do more harm than good. Again, organization retards radicalism and keeps those who might otherwise slide into revolutionary activity within normal political ambits.[65] Moreover, if we reject or weaken the moral claims attendant to the liberal consensus that try to construct a high wall of separation between religious (and other basic) claims and the political order, we are left with the question of how, then, religious believers (and citizens more broadly) ought to relate the two. Instead of a high wall or bright line, we have a rather muddy field.

This is, to many, a frustrating and unfortunate situation, but the response is not, as I have argued, to hope that a wall or line will suddenly appear to deliver us from our troubles. Nor is it to hope that religion will just go quietly into the night (or at least the closet). Rather, the proper response is to think about ways in which citizens themselves might pick their way across that muddy field, developing for themselves a rough and ready sense of how to both distinguish and relate the spheres of faith and politics. This is, of course, a site for moral reflection, for thinking about how individuals can best fulfill their political obligations while not abandoning or betraying their faith (or similar sorts of basic views). But as should be obvious by now, this sort of moral reflection does not occur in a vacuum. Rather, we develop and refine our reflections in conversation with our attempts, individual and collective, at putting our presumptive conceptions to work politically. That is, in our fallible, often tenuous attempts at developing our own conceptions regarding how (and if) to apply our basic views politically, we start off with a sort of presumptive conception and wrestle with it philosophically and in light of how it seems to work as a guide to real politics.

Recall my earlier discussion of political toleration in chapter 6. I argued that we should not be surprised that political toleration has a kind of progressive cast, in that we come to a decision about what to tolerate (and what not) based not just on abstract moral arguments but also (and maybe more importantly) on our judgments about how such toleration will

---

[65] Of course, by saying it "retards," I implicitly acknowledge that this is only a probabilistic effect and says nothing about "radical" organizations that have revolutionary purposes. Even those kinds of organizations might be better than nothing, though, as in joining an organization you commit yourself to its maintenance, often tempering your plans therein.

work out practically. Religious toleration and the protection of religious liberty has advanced as far as it has not, I suspect, because Locke's *Letter on Toleration* is so widely available, but because toleration works out very well practically. European democracies afford expression less protection than the US does at least in part because of their experience with fascism and World War II. But as Tocqueville averred, we solitary individuals are, for the most part, poorly equipped to execute these sorts of reflective exercises well.[66] We often lack the time, knowledge, philosophical inclination, or even the desire to think carefully enough on our own to do the job adequately well, never mind excellently.[67] We cannot pick our way across the muddy field on our own, and at least part of what we need to do it well are civic and political associations. This is part of how political organizations – and especially political parties – serve democratic purposes, shaping our political identities such that we learn how to advance our interests and visions while at the same time accepting the inevitable uncertainties of democratic politics.[68] Though clearly not the whole story, political organizations play a key role in helping make (or remake) us into democratic citizens, as they provide the avenues for our political participation and the arenas in which we can try out successive conceptions of how that citizenship ought to be conceptualized.

As Shields points out, that is exactly what CR organizations have done over the past few decades. Whatever the CR's faults – and they have been documented in plenitude by its critics (and supporters, for that matter) – it has at least this much to be said for it: it helped mobilize a sizeable swathe of voters and turn them into persistent contributors to the democratic order, and it contributed, albeit through its failures as much as its successes, to the development of a ever more thoughtful and sophisticated religiously rooted conception of politics. Shields documents quite nicely how the CR worked to pull conservative Protestants especially out of their tendencies toward political indifference and separationism. In 1972, only 59 percent of conservative evangelicals bothered to vote, as opposed to 73 percent of all eligible voters. By 2004, 77 percent of conservative evangelicals turned out, as opposed to 79 percent of all voters.[69] Though no doubt the CR organizations cannot take all the credit for this

[66] He is most worried about how democratic individualism turns into mass conformity: "after having broken all the shackles once imposed upon it by classes or by individual men, the human mind would shackle itself tightly to the general will of the majority" (Tocqueville, *Democracy in America*, vol. II, part I, ch. 2).

[67] For a rather depressing account of how poorly informed most voters are see Bryan Douglas Caplan, *The Myth of the Rational Voter: Why Democracies Choose Bad Policies* (Princeton, NJ: Princeton University Press, 2007).

[68] Rosenblum, *On the Side of the Angels*, 356–68.

[69] Shields, *The Democratic Virtues of the Christian Right*, 123–4.

quite remarkable shift, neither can we plausibly think them irrelevant. To the degree that it is better to have more participation (especially electoral participation) than less, it seems clear that the CR has had some positive democratic effects.

Of course, the CR's critics can admit that and still suggest (again) that simply participating is not enough. It is just as important *how* individuals and groups participate, what sorts of ends they pursue politically, and here, many will quite plausibly suggest, the CR comes up woefully short. But Shields documents how it is that even the most vocal and provocative CR organizations, those dealing with the fraught question of abortion, work quite hard to train their activists to think politically and indeed deliberate with their opponents as fellow democratic citizens.[70] They do not become perfect deliberators – no surprise there – but they do evince some of the political virtues liberals are so insistent play a key role in democratic life. And, indeed, broadening our view somewhat suggests that the story Shields tells about anti-abortion protest groups has a wider corollary in the development of conservative Protestants' political thinking, both popular and intellectual.

On a popular level, it takes very little time to recognize the quite sizeable difference between, say, Jerry Falwell's fulminations against "secularism" or the "obliterat[ion of] the Judeo-Christian influence on American society" and the National Association of Evangelicals' recent publication, "For the Health of the Nation: An Evangelical Call to Civic Responsibility."[71] Instead of overly sure pronouncements about getting America "back" to its Christian roots, to "the simple faith on which [it] was built,"[72] the NAE talks about Christians' responsibility to engage politically as a means of advancing "justice" and the "common good." No longer are the issues at hand only abortion or homosexuality or a strong national defense, though these are still central concerns. Rather, the new "Evangelical Call" emphasizes "commitments to the protection and well-being of families and children, of the poor, the sick, the disabled, and the unborn, of the persecuted and oppressed, and of the rest of the created order." This shift in, or broadening of, popular evangelical

---

[70] Ibid., 104–14.

[71] Jerry Falwell, "An Agenda for the 1980s," in *Piety and Politics: Evangelicals and Fundamentalists Confront the World*, ed. Richard John Neuhaus and Michael Cromartie (Washington, D.C.: Ethics and Public Policy Center, 1987); Jerry Falwell, *Listen, America!* (New York: Doubleday, 1980). The NAE document is available online at www.nae.net. Of course, the NAE is not at all the divisive partisan political actor that Falwell was, but that is part of the point. If one wanted to get a start on thinking about what it is that politically mobilized evangelicals think *today* about political matters, you would be well served to start with the NAE.

[72] Falwell, "An Agenda for the 1980s," 111.

political emphasis is matched by a similar deepening of academic evangelical political thought. Mark Noll's 1994 lament that the "dismal" state of evangelical political reflection was, perhaps, beginning to turn around looks plausible fifteen years hence.[73] Though it is a commonplace (and true) that evangelicals lack a cohesive "tradition" of political thought (unlike Roman Catholics) the development of political thought among religious believers over the last decade or so has been remarkable. Kuyperian neo-Calvinists,[74] Anabaptists,[75] and evangelical natural law thinkers[76] have all begun (if still in fits and starts) to deepen and enrich theologically conservative believers' thinking on politics.[77]

Of course, some of these thinkers would not, sometimes quite emphatically, identify themselves with anything resembling the politics of the CR. So it would be a mistake to suggest that the CR's political trajectory over the past three decades has straightforwardly produced better popular and intellectual religious political reflection. But it *has* perhaps done so inadvertently, at least in the sense that its failures have been as "productive" as its successes. Suppose we could imagine, for instance, an American political history for the past three decades in which conservative Protestants remained on the sidelines politically and culturally. Gone, no doubt, would be a great many irritants for the liberal consensus, but also gone would be the impetus for much recent reconsideration of how religious conservatives ought to relate to the democratic political order. It is as much (if not more) the occasion of their political failures as their successes that has prompted whatever reconsiderations there are among this group.[78] The point here is this. Serious moral reflection about

---

[73] Mark A. Noll, *The Scandal of the Evangelical Mind* (Grand Rapids, MI: Eerdmans Publishing, 1994).

[74] See Jonathan Chaplin, "Can Liberal Democracy Accommodate Religious 'Integralism'"; Chaplin, "State and Civil Society in Christian Democracy"; Schindler, *Christianity and Civil Society*; Skillen, *In Pursuit of Justice*.

[75] Sider, *The Scandal of Evangelical Politics*.

[76] J. Budziszewski, *Written on the Heart: The Case for Natural Law* (Downers Grove, IL: InterVarsity Press, 1997); J. Daryl Charles, "Protestants and Natural Law," *First Things* (December 2006); J. Daryl Charles, *The Unformed Conscience of Evangelicalism: Recovering the Church's Moral Vision* (Downer's Grove, IL: InterVarsity Press, 2002); Michael Cromartie, ed., *A Preserving Grace: Protestants, Catholics, and Natural Law* (Grand Rapids, MI: Eerdmans Publishing, 1997); David L. Weeks, "The Uneasy Politics of Modern Evangelicalism," *Christian Scholar's Review* 30, no. 4 (2001).

[77] For a survey of how American Christians, only some of whom could be reasonably connected to the CR, see politics, see Sandra Joireman, ed., *For the Sake of Conscience: Some Evangelical Views of the State, Christian Views of the State* (New York: Oxford University Press, 2009).

[78] For an example of this phenomenon, see Cal Thomas and Ed Dobson, *Blinded by Might: Why the Religious Right Can't Save America* (Grand Rapids, MI: Zondervan, 2000). This re-examination of the CR's tactics and priorities came after the Clinton impeachment imbroglio, widely seen as a defeat for the CR.

one's political conceptions always takes place in the context of a "conversation" between basic philosophical, moral, and religious commitments and the ways those commitments seem to work themselves out practically in everyday politics. If the CR had never emerged in the late 1970s, we would have, I think, a much poorer set of political conceptions among these religious conservatives than we do now. Opponents of the CR can hold fast to most all of their critiques and *still* acknowledge that there have been some plausible *democratic* benefits to its emergence and political trajectory.[79]

But while thinking about the CR in light of my philosophical arguments and the cases of the European integrationists suggests some reasons to appreciate the CR, it also suggests some ways in which the CR suffers by comparison. The two chief complaints against the CR seem to be that it lacks the capacity (or willingness) to compromise and that it unreasonably (and illegitimately) seeks to impose a particular set of values on others. The CR, on these critiques, is so strongly committed to its particular goals – especially on issues relating to abortion and sexuality, but not exclusively those – that it cannot find a way to cooperate effectively with those on the other side of the issues; instead, it simply attempts to impose them through legislative or administrative fiat. We might say that the CR's critics charge that it lacks a proper appreciation for political autonomy and toleration and thus threatens political legitimacy. Hence the oft-heard "theocracy" charge.

While particular charges are often overstated and the CR interpreted as uncharitably as possible, the CR's tendencies on both counts ring true. But this does not really count against my broader argument. Rather, it merely highlights the ways in which the argument shows how important political organization is to making religiously motivated politics work. The most significant institutional difference between the CR and Europe's integrationists is that the CR is *not* a political party but instead a social movement closely allied to the GOP.[80] This has at least two problematic consequences: it means the CR is less capable

---

[79] For a complementary take, see Isaac, Filner, and Bivins, "American Democracy and the New Christian Right." Whether the CR's critics judge the benefits to be, in the end, outweighed by the drawbacks is, of course, quite another matter.

[80] Clyde Wilcox has captured the relationship between the CR and the GOP quite nicely with the metaphor of co-evolution. Neither simply "uses" the other but they are dependent (in some sense) on the other. See Clyde Wilcox, "Of Movements and Metaphors: The Co-Evolution of the Christian Right and the GOP," in *The Christian Conservative Movement and American Democracy*, ed. Brint and Schroedel. For other discussions, see Bruce, *The Rise and Fall of the New Christian Right*; Geoffrey Layman, *The Great Divide: Religious and Cultural Conflict in American Party Politics* (New York: Columbia University Press, 2001).

290 Faith in Politics

institutionally of reshaping the political order and thus less secure in its own subcultural sphere, both consequences making it more likely that the CR will vitiate its critics' concerns. It may seem odd in the extreme to argue that the CR's critics are right to say that it has these politically bad tendencies in relation to political autonomy and toleration and then turn around and suggest the source is the fact that the CR is not successful enough politically. It is odd, but let me briefly sketch the case for oddness.

I suggested in chapters 5 and 6 that the European integrationists successfully helped consolidate democratic government in part because they were successful in reshaping its democratizing orders in a structurally pluralist direction. This meant that these countries' religious communities enjoyed politically protected social space within which they could more or less live their integrationist lives while at the same time allowing others to live differently. Because the American electoral system so strongly favors broad coalition parties, there was and is very little opportunity for the CR to exert much real political influence. Add to that the ways in which many of the CR's signature issues, especially abortion, have been remanded to the judicial branch, and the result has been that the CR both lacks the effective means to impact seriously political outcomes and pursues its objectives as an all-or-nothing manner.

The easiest issue with which to illustrate what I mean is education. The European integrationists all started off as efforts to defend some form of religiously inflected education against secularizing elites. They subsequently developed into political parties and by different means forced their opponents to compromise on educational matters, most obviously in the Netherlands, where Kuyper's ARP was able to equalize state funding for both private and public schools without giving up religious schools' distinctiveness. Compare that to the United States, where nineteenth-century Catholics were forced to create their own network of religious schools and twentieth-century efforts to allow for wider pluralism within publicly funded schools has been, for the most part, stymied.[81] Given, say, the sorts of judicial results in *Mozert v. Hawkins*, religious conservatives in the US have either simply opted out of the public educational system altogether (via private religious schools or homeschooling) or have mounted political campaigns to reshape public schools to their liking, even if the success of such campaigns would quite plausibly mean treading on other citizens' consciences. Part of

[81] See Glenn, *The Myth of the Common School*; McGreevy, *Catholicism and American Freedom*.

the reason for this all-or-nothing strategy is surely the way in which American political institutions (and, indeed, American culture) lean quite strongly against the kinds of structurally pluralist outcomes reached in Europe.

The American order has any number of advantages, but it seems reasonable on this account to say that one of its disadvantages lies precisely here, and it goes beyond any particular battle. When the liberal consensus's partisans insist that a constitutional democracy's public order must be tilted against a set of citizens and they consistently resist efforts to carve out social spaces for those who live lives not in line with robust definitions of personal autonomy and the like, we should not be surprised when those citizens then turn around and attempt to do the same (if in quite different directions). More to the point, the lack of structurally pluralist options – or, more precisely, their political difficulties – leaves the CR's partisans without an institutional framework within which they can learn effectively how to distinguish well the sorts of goods and ends proper to democratic politics. In short, the CR's political weaknesses, rooted in the American order and its status as a social movement, has made its members less likely to develop the proper set of democratic civic virtues, especially as regards political autonomy and toleration.[82]

The CR in the United States and political Islam in Europe (and elsewhere) are but two manifestations of religion's widespread political re-emergence. For those of us who value the achievements of constitutional democratic governments – the protection of individual liberties, political and social equality, the rule of law, democratic accountability, and so on – few issues are as important to those governments' future and democracy's global fate than the place of religion. We are very far indeed from the days when political and social theorists could merely assume that religion was destined to either disappear or retreat into the inner sanctums of private conscience. We are right in the middle, instead, of the days when religiously inspired political movements pose a, perhaps *the*, significant challenge to the spread and consolidation of democratic government. The burden of this book has been to show that there is a great deal more space within the contours of liberal democracies for many (though certainly not all) religiously inspired politics and that those liberal democracies that find ways to accommodate and

---

[82] For an argument attempting to show that when CR members move into "normal" party and political institutions, they do in fact show some development along those lines, see Kimberly H. Conger and Bryan T. McGraw, "Religious Conservatives and the Requirements of Citizenship: Political Autonomy," *Perspectives on Politics* 6, no. 2 (2008).

engage such efforts will do better than those that do not. Religion is not democracy's enemy, and if democracy's liberal defenders might reconsider some of their very serious concerns regarding religion's political mobilization, we might very well take a few steps toward polities that are indeed stable, legitimate, and free. That seems like something worth working toward.

Bibliography

Aarts, Kees, Stuart MacDonald, and Elaine Rabinowitz. "Issue and Party Competition in the Netherlands." *Comparative Political Studies* **32**, no. 1 (1999): 63–99.

Ackerman, Bruce A. *Social Justice in the Liberal State*. New Haven: Yale University Press, 1980.

Almond, Gabriel. "The Political Ideas of Christian Democracy." *Journal of Politics* **10**, no. 4 (1948): 734–63.

Almond, Gabriel, and Sidney Verba. *The Civic Culture: Political Attitudes and Democracy in Five Nations*. Princeton, NJ: Princeton University Press, 1963.

Aminrazavi, Mehdi, and David Ambuel. *Philosophy, Religion, and the Question of Intolerance*. Albany: State University of New York Press, 1997.

Anderson, Margaret Lavinia. "Clerical Election Influence and Communal Solidarity: Catholic Political Culture in the German Empire, 1871–1914." In *Elections before Democracy: The History of Elections in Europe and Latin America*, ed. Eduardo Posada Carbó. New York: St. Martin's Press, 1996.

———. "The Divisions of the Pope: The Catholic Revival and Europe's Transition to Democracy." In *The Politics of Religion in an Age of Revival: Studies in Nineteenth-Century Europe and Latin America*, ed. Austen Ivereigh. London: Institute of Latin American Studies, 2000.

———. "Interdenominationalism, Clericalism, and Pluralism: The Zentrumsstreit and the Dilemma of Catholicism in Wilhelmine Germany." *Central European History* **21**, no. 4 (1988): 350–78.

———. "The Kulturkampf and the Course of German History." *Central European History* **19**, no. 1 (1986): 82–115.

———. "The Limits of Secularization: On the Problem of the Catholic Revival in Nineteenth-Century Germany." *Historical Journal* **38**, no. 3 (1995): 647–70.

———. *Practicing Democracy: Elections and Political Culture in Imperial Germany*. Princeton, NJ: Princeton University Press, 2000.

———. *Windthorst: A Political Biography*. New York: Oxford University Press, 1981.

Andeweg, Rudy B. "Consociational Democracy." *Annual Review of Political Science* **3**, no. 14 (2000): 1–20.

Atkin, Nicholas, and Frank Tallett. *Priests, Prelates and People: A History of European Catholicism since 1750*. New York: Oxford University Press, 2003.

Audi, Robert. "The Place of Religious Argument in a Free and Democratic Society." *San Diego Law Review* **30** (1993): 677–702.

    Religious Commitment and Secular Reason. Cambridge and New York: Cambridge University Press, 2000.

    "The State, the Church, and the Citizen." In *Religion and Contemporary Liberalism*, ed. Paul J. Weithman. Notre Dame, IN: University of Notre Dame Press, 1997.

Audi, Robert, and Nicholas Wolterstorff. *Religion in the Public Square: The Place of Religious Convictions in Political Debate.* Lanham, MD: Rowman & Littlefield, 1997.

Bader, Veit. "Associative Democracy and Minorities within Minorities." In *Minorities within Minorities: Equality, Rights, and Diversity*, ed. Avigail I. Eisenberg and Jeff Spinner-Halev. New York: Cambridge University Press, 2005.

    "Democratic Institutional Pluralism and Cultural Diversity." In *The Social Construction of Diversity*, ed. Danielle Juteau and Christine Harzig. Oxford: Berghan Books, 2003.

    "Religion and States: A New Typology and a Plea for Non-Constitutional Pluralism." *Ethical Theory and Moral Practice: An International Forum* **6** (2003): 55–91.

    "Religious Diversity and Democratic Institutional Pluralism." *Political Theory* **31**, no. 2 (2003): 265–94.

    "Religious Pluralism: Secularism or Priority for Democracy." *Political Theory* **27**, no. 5 (1999): 597–633.

Baier, Kurt. "Justice and the Aims of Political Philosophy." *Ethics* **99**, no. 4 (1989): 771–90.

Bakvis, Herman. *Catholic Power in the Netherlands.* Kingston: McGill-Queen's University Press, 1981.

    "Toward a Political Economy of Consociationalism: A Commentary on Marxist Views of Pillarization in the Netherlands." *Comparative Politics* **16** (1984): 315–34.

Baran, Zeyno. "Turkey Divided." *Journal of Democracy* **19**, no. 1 (2008): 55–69.

Barber, Benjamin R. *Strong Democracy: Participatory Politics for a New Age.* Berkeley: University of California Press, 1984.

Barry, Brian M. *Culture and Equality: An Egalitarian Critique of Multiculturalism.* Cambridge, MA: Harvard University Press, 2001.

    "John Rawls and the Search for Stability." *Ethics* **105** (1995): 874–915.

Bawer, Bruce. *Surrender: Appeasing Islam, Sacrificing Freedom.* New York: Doubleday, 2009.

    While Europe Slept: How Radical Islam Is Destroying the West from Within, 1st. pbk. edn. New York: Broadway Books, 2006.

Beiner, Ronald, ed. *Theorizing Citizenship.* Albany: State University of New York Press, 1995.

Benhabib, Seyla, ed. *Democracy and Difference: Contesting the Boundaries of the Political.* Princeton, NJ: Princeton University Press, 1996.

Berger, Peter L. *The Desecularization of the World: Resurgent Religion and World Politics.* Washington, D.C.: Ethics and Public Policy Center, 1999.

The Sacred Canopy: Elements of a Sociological Theory of Religion. New York: Anchor Books, 1969.

Berkowitz, Peter. "John Rawls and the Liberal Faith." *Wilson Quarterly* **26**, no. 2 (2002): 60–70.

Virtue and the Making of Modern Liberalism. Princeton, NJ: Princeton University Press, 1999.

Berlinski, Claire. *Menace in Europe: Why the Continent's Crisis Is America's, Too.* New York: Crown Forum, 2006.

Berman, Paul. *Terror and Liberalism*, 1st. edn. New York: Norton, 2003.

Berman, Sheri. "Taming Extremist Parties: Lessons from Europe." *Journal of Democracy* **19**, no. 1 (2008): 5–18.

Bermeo, Nancy. *Ordinary People in Extraordinary Times: The Citizenry and the Breakdown of Democracy.* Princeton, NJ: Princeton University Press, 2003.

Bermeo, Nancy Gina, and Philip G. Nord, eds. *Civil Society before Democracy: Lessons from Nineteenth-Century Europe.* Lanham, MD: Rowman & Littlefield, 2000.

Berns, Walter. *Making Patriots.* Chicago: University of Chicago Press, 2001.

Beyme, Claus von. *Political Parties in Western Democracies.* Aldershot: Gower, 1985.

Black, Amy E., Douglas L. Koopman, and David K. Ryden. *Of Little Faith: The Politics of George W. Bush's Faith-Based Initiatives.* Washington, D.C.: Georgetown University Press, 2004.

Blom, J.C.H. "Pillarisation in Perspective." *West European Politics* **23**, no. 3 (2000): 153–64.

Blom, J.C.H, and Emiel Lamberts. *History of the Low Countries.* New York: Berghan Books, 1999.

Bohman, James. "Public Reason and Cultural Pluralism: Political Liberalism and the Problem of Moral Conflict." *Political Theory* **23**, no. 2 (1995): 253–79.

Bohman, James, and William Rehg, eds. *Deliberative Democracy: Essays on Reason and Politics.* Cambridge, MA: MIT Press, 1997.

Bolce, Louis, and Gerald De Maio. "Our Secularist Democratic Party." *Public Interest*, no. 149 (2002): 3–21.

Bosworth, Willi am. *Catholicism and Crisis in Modern France.* Princeton, NJ: Princeton University Press, 1962.

Bowman, William D. "Religious Associations and the Formation of Political Catholicism in Vienna, 1848 to the 1870s." *Austrian History Yearbook* **27** (1996): 65–76.

Boyer, John W. "Catholics, Christians, and the Challenges of Democracy: The Heritage of the Nineteenth Century." In *Christian Democracy in 20th Century Europe*, ed. Michael Gehler, Wolfram Kaiser, and Helmut Wohnout. Cologne: Routledge, 2002.

Culture and Political Crisis in Vienna: Christian Socialism in Power. Chicago: University of Chicago Press, 1995.

Political Radicalism in Late Imperial Vienna: Origins of the Christian Social Movement 1848–1897. Chicago: University of Chicago Press, 1981.

"Religion and Political Development in Central Europe around 1900: A View from Vienna." *Austrian History Yearbook* **25** (1994): 13–57.

Bredohl, Thomas M. *Class and Religious Identity: The Rhenish Center Party in Wilhelmine Germany.* Milwaukee, WI: Marquette University Press, 2000.

Brighouse, Harry. "Civic Education and Liberal Legitimacy." *Ethics* **108**, no. 4 (1998): 719–45.

Brint, Steve, and Jean Schroedel, eds. *The Christian Conservative Movement and American Democracy: Evangelicals, the Religious Right, and American Politics.* New York: Russell Sage Foundation, 2009.

Bruce, Steve. "Christianity in Britain, R.I.P." *Sociology of Religion* **62**, no. 2 (2001): 191–204.

  Conservative Protestant Politics. New York: Oxford University Press, 1998.

  God Is Dead: Secularization in the West, Religion and Modern World. Malden, MA: Blackwell Publishers, 2002.

  The Rise and Fall of the New Christian Right. Oxford: Clarendon Press, 1988.

Bruce, Steve, ed. *Religion and Modernization: Sociologists and Historians Debate the Secularization Thesis.* Oxford: Oxford University Press, 1992.

Budziszewski, J. *True Tolerance: Liberalism and the Necessity of Judgment.* New Brunswick, NJ: Transaction Publishers, 1992.

  Written on the Heart: The Case for Natural Law. Downers Grove, IL: InterVarsity Press, 1997.

Burleigh, Michael. *Earthly Powers: The Clash of Religion and Politics in Europe from the French Revolution to the Great War,* 1st. edn. New York: HarperCollins Publishers, 2005.

  Sacred Causes: The Clash of Religion and Politics, from the Great War to the War on Terror, 1st. edn. New York: HarperCollins, 2007.

Burtt, Shelley. "In Defense of *Yoder*: Parental Authority and the Public Schools." In *Political Order: Nomos XXXVIII,* ed. Ian Shapiro and Russell Hardin. New York: New York University Press, 1996.

  "The Politics of Virtue Today: A Critique and a Proposal." *American Political Science Review* **87**, no. 2 (1993): 360–68.

Byrnes, Robert F. "The French Christian Democrats in the 1890s: Their Appearance and Their Failures." *Catholic Historical Review* **36**, no. 3 (1950): 286–306.

Byrnes, Timothy A. *Catholic Bishops in American Politics.* Princeton, NJ: Princeton University Press, 1991.

  Transnational Catholicism in Postcommunist Europe. Lanham, MD: Rowman & Littlefield, 2001.

Caciagli, Mario. *DC, Christian Democracy in Europe: Barcelona 1992.* Barcelona: ICPS, 1992.

Callan, Eamonn. *Creating Citizens: Political Education and Liberal Democracy.* New York: Clarendon Press, 1997.

  "Discrimination and Religious Schooling." In *Citizenship in Diverse Societies,* ed. Will Kymlicka and Wayne Norman. New York: Oxford University Press, 2000.

  "Political Liberalism and Political Education." *Review of Politics* **58**, no. 1 (1998): 5–34.

Caplan, Bryan Douglas. *The Myth of the Rational Voter: Why Democracies Choose Bad Policies*. Princeton, NJ: Princeton University Press, 2007.

Capoccia, Giovanni. "Defending Democracy: Reactions to Political Extremism in Inter-War Europe." *European Journal of Political Research* **39** (2001): 431–60.

Carlson-Thies, Stanley. "Democracy in the Netherlands: Consociational or Pluriform?" unpublished dissertation, University of Toronto, 1993.

Carter, Stephen L. *The Culture of Disbelief: How American Law and Politics Trivialize Religious Devotion*. New York: Basic Books, 1993.

God's Name in Vain: The Wrongs and Rights of Religion in Politics, 1st. edn. New York: Basic Books, 2000.

Cary, Noel D. *The Path to Christian Democracy: German Catholics and the Party System from Windthorst to Adenauer*. Cambridge, MA: Harvard University Press, 1996.

Casanova, José. "Church, State, Nation and Civil Society in Spain and Poland." In *The Political Dimensions of Religion*, ed. Saïd Amir Arjomand. New York: State University of New York Press, 1993.

Public Religions in the Modern World. Chicago: University of Chicago Press, 1994.

Cavdar, Gamze. "Islamist New Thinking in Turkey: A Model for Political Learning." *Political Science Quarterly* **121**, no. 3 (2006): 477–97.

Chambers, Simone. "How Religion Speaks to the Agnostic: Habermas on the Persistent Value of Religion." *Constellations* **14**, no. 2 (2007): 210–23.

Chaplin, Jonathan. "Beyond Liberal Restraint: Defending Religiously Based Arguments in Law and Public Policy." *University of British Columbia Law Review* **33**, no. 3 (2000): 617–46.

"Can Liberal Democracy Accommodate Religious 'Integralism': A Dialogue with Nancy Rosenblum." Paper presented at American Political Science Association Meeting, Philadelphia, PA, 2006.

"State and Civil Society in Christian Democracy: The Neo-Calvinist Perspective." Paper presented at the Meeting of the American Political Science Association, San Francisco, CA, 2001.

Chapman, John William, and William A. Galston. *Virtue: Nomos XXIV*. New York: New York University Press, 1992.

Chappell, David L. *A Stone of Hope: Prophetic Religion and the Death of Jim Crow*. Chapel Hill: University of North Carolina Press, 2004.

Charles, J. Daryl. "Protestants and Natural Law." *First Things* (December 2006), available online at www.firstthings.com/article/2007/01/protestants-and-natural-law-39.

The Unformed Conscience of Evangelicalism: Recovering the Church's Moral Vision. Downer's Grove, IL: InterVarsity Press, 2002.

Chaves, Mark. "Intraorganizational Power and Internal Secularization in Protestant Denominations." *American Journal of Sociology* **99**, no. 1 (1993): 1–48.

"Religious Pluralism and Religious Participation." *Annual Review of Sociology* **27**, no. 1 (2001): 261–82.

"Secularization as Declining Religious Authority." *Social Forces* **72**, no. 3 (1994): 749–74.

Clydesdale, Timothy T. "Toward Understanding the Role of Bible Beliefs and Higher Education in American Attitudes toward Eradicating Poverty." *Journal for the Scientific Study of Religion* **38**, no. 1 (1999): 103–18.

Cohen, Joshua. "Deliberation and Democratic Legitimacy." In *Deliberative Democracy: Essays on Reason and Politics*, ed. James Bohman and William Rehg. Cambridge, MA: MIT Press, 1999.

"Democracy and Liberty." In *Deliberative Democracy*, ed. Jon Elster. Cambridge: Cambridge University Press, 1998.

"Moral Pluralism and Political Consensus." In *The Good Polity: A Normative Analysis of the State*, ed. Alex Hamlin and Philip Pettit. New York: Blackwell, 1993.

"A More Democratic Liberalism: Political Liberalism." *Michigan Law Review* **92**, no. 6 (1994): 1503–46.

"Procedure and Substance in Deliberative Democracy." In *Democracy and Difference: Contesting the Boundaries of the Political*, ed. Seyla Benhabib. Princeton, NJ: Princeton University Press, 1996.

Collier, Ruth. *Paths toward Democracy: The Working Class and Elites in Western Europe and South America*. New York: Cambridge University Press, 1999.

Collier, Ruth Berins, and James Mahoney. *Labor and Democratization: Comparing the First and Third Waves in Europe and Latin America* (Institute of Industrial Relations Working Paper no. 32). Berkeley: Department of Political Science, University of California, Berkeley, 1995.

Conger, Kimberly H., and Bryan T. McGraw. "Religious Conservatives and the Requirements of Citizenship: Political Autonomy." *Perspectives on Politics* **6**, no. 2 (2008): 253–66.

Conway, Martin. "Belgium." In *Political Catholicism in Europe, 1918–1965*, ed. Tom Buchanan and Martin Conway. Oxford: Clarendon Press, 1996.

"Introduction." In *Political Catholicism in Europe, 1918–1965*, ed. Tom Buchanan and Martin Conway. Oxford: Clarendon Press, 1996.

Conyers, A. J. *The Long Truce: How Toleration Made the World Safe for Power and Profit*. Dallas, TX: Spence Publishing, 2001.

Cooke, Maeve. "A Secular State for a Postsecular Society? Postmetaphysical Political Theory and the Place of Religion." *Constellations* **14**, no. 2 (2007): 224–38.

Creppell, Ingrid. *Toleration and Identity: Foundations in Early Modern Thought*. New York: Routledge, 2002.

Cromartie, Michael. *Disciples and Democracy: Religious Conservatives and the Future of American Politics*. Grand Rapids, MI: Eerdmans Publishing, 1994.

Cromartie, Michael, ed. *A Preserving Grace: Protestants, Catholics, and Natural Law*. Grand Rapids, MI: Eerdmans Publishing, 1997.

Daalder, Hans. *Ancient and Modern Pluralism in the Netherlands* (Center for European Studies Working Paper no. 22). Cambridge, MA: Center for European Studies, Harvard University, 1989.

"The Consociational Democracy Theme." *World Politics* **26**, no. 4 (1974): 604–21.

"The Netherlands: Opposition in a Segmented Society." In *Political Oppositions in Western Democracies*, ed. Robert A. Dahl. New Haven: Yale University Press, 1966.

Dagger, Richard. *Civic Virtues: Rights, Citizenship, and Republican Liberalism.* New York: Oxford University Press, 1997.

Dagi, Ihsan. "Transformation of Islamic Political Identity in Turkey: Rethinking the West and Westernization." *Turkish Studies* 6, no. 1 (2005): 21–37.

"Turkey's AKP in Power." *Journal of Democracy* 19, no. 3 (2008): 25–30.

Dalton, R.J., and M.P. Wattenberg, eds. *Parties without Partisans: Political Change in Advanced Industrial Democracies.* Oxford: Oxford University Press, 2000.

Dauenhauer, Bernard P. "A Good Word for a Modus Vivendi." In *The Idea of a Political Liberalism: Essays on Rawls*, ed. Victoria Davion and Clark Wolf. Lanham, MD: Rowman & Littlefield, 2000.

Dees, Richard. "Establishing Toleration." *Political Theory* 27, no. 5 (1999): 667–93.

Deveaux, Monique. *Cultural Pluralism and Dilemmas of Justice.* Ithaca, NY: Cornell University Press, 2000.

Dewey, John. *A Common Faith.* New Haven: Yale University Press, 1991 [1934].

Di Palma, Giuseppe. *To Craft Democracies: An Essay on Democratic Transitions.* Berkeley: University of California Press, 1990.

Diamant, Alfred. "Austria: The Three *Lager* and the First Republic." In *Consociational Democracy: Political Accommodation in Segmented Societies*, ed. Kenneth D. McRae. Toronto: McClellan and Stewart, 1974.

Austrian Catholics and the First Republic: Democracy, Capitalism, and the Social Order, 1918–1934. Princeton, NJ: Princeton University Press, 1960.

Diamond, Larry, and Richard Gunther, eds. *Political Parties and Democracy.* Baltimore, MD: Johns Hopkins University Press, 2001.

Diamond, Sara. *Not by Politics Alone: The Enduring Influence of the Christian Right.* New York: Guilford Press, 1998.

Dobbelaere, Karel. "The Rationale of Pillarization: The Case of Minority Movements." *Journal of Contemporary Religion* 15, no. 2 (2000): 181–200.

Dombrowski, Daniel A. *Rawls and Religion: The Case for Political Liberalism.* Albany: State University of New York Press, 2001.

Douthat, Ross. "Theocracy, Theocracy, Theocracy." *First Things* **165** (2006): 23–30.

Driessen, Geert, and Frans Van der Silk. "Religion, Denomination and Education in the Netherlands: Cognitive and Noncognitive Outcomes after an Era of Secularization." *Journal for the Scientific Study of Religion* **40**, no. 4 (2001): 561–73.

Dryzek, John S. *Deliberative Democracy and Beyond: Liberals, Critics, Contestations.* New York: Oxford University Press, 2000.

Dworkin, Ronald. "Liberalism." In *A Matter of Principle*, ed. R.M. Dworkin. Cambridge, MA: Harvard University Press, 1985.

Life's Dominion: An Argument about Abortion, Euthanasia, and Individual Freedom, 1st. edn. New York: Knopf, 1993.

Eberle, Christopher J. "Basic Human Worth and Religious Restraint." *Philosophy and Social Criticism* 35, no. 1–2 (2009): 151–81.

"Religion and Liberal Democracy." In *The Blackwell Guide to Social and Political Philosophy*, ed. R.L. Simon. New York: Blackwell, 2002.

"Religion, Pacifism and the Doctrine of Restraint." *Journal of Religious Ethics* **34**, no. 2 (2006): 203–24.

Religious Conviction in Liberal Politics. New York: Cambridge University Press, 2002.

"What Respect Requires and What It Does Not." *Wake Forest Law Review* **36** (2001): 305–51.

Ehrenhalt, Alan. *The Lost City: Discovering the Forgotten Virtues of Community in the Chicago of the 1950s*. New York: Basic Books, 1995.

Einaudi, Mario, and François Goguel. *Christian Democracy in Italy and France*. Hamden, CT: Archon Books, 1969.

Elshtain, Jean Bethke. "The Bright Line: Liberalism and Religion." *New Criterion* **17**, no. 7 (1999): 4–14.

"State-Imposed Secularism as a Potential Pitfall of Liberal Democracy." Paper presented at the Religious Liberty Conference, Prague, Czech Republic, 2000.

Elster, Jon. *Sour Grapes: Studies in the Subversion of Rationality*. New York: Cambridge University Press, 1983.

Engelmann, Frederick C. "Austria: The Pooling of Opposition." In *Political Oppositions in Western Democracies*, ed. Robert A. Dahl. New Haven: Yale University Press, 1967.

Ertman, Thomas. "Democracy and Dictatorship in Interwar Western Europe Revisited." *World Politics* **50**, no. 3 (1998): 475–505.

"Liberalization, Democratization, and the Origins of a 'Pillarized' Civil Society in Nineteenth-Century Belgium and the Netherlands." In *Civil Society before Democracy: Lessons from Nineteenth-Century Europe*, ed. Nancy Bermeo and Philip Nord. Lanham, MD: Rowman & Littlefield, 2000.

Etzioni, Amitai. "Turkey's Dilemma: How Secularism Is Threatening Democracy." *Commonweal* (August 2008): 11–12.

Evans, Ellen Lovell. *The Cross and the Ballot: Catholic Political Parties in Germany, Switzerland, Austria, Belgium and the Netherlands, 1785–1985* (Studies in Central European Histories). Boston: Humanities Press, 1999.

The German Center Party, 1870–1933: A Study in Political Catholicism. Carbondale, IL: Southern Illinois University Press, 1981.

Falwell, Jerry. "An Agenda for the 1980s." In *Piety and Politics: Evangelicals and Fundamentalists Confront the World*, ed. Richard John Neuhaus and Michael Cromartie. Washington, D.C.: Ethics and Public Policy Center, 1987.

Listen, America! New York: Doubleday, 1980.

Feldman, Noah. "Morality, Self-Interest, and the Politics of Toleration." In *Toleration and Its Limits*, ed. Melissa Williams. New York: New York University Press, 2008.

Fetzer, Joel S., and J. Christopher Soper. *Muslims and the State in Britain, France, and Germany* (Cambridge Studies in Social Theory, Religion, and Politics). New York: Cambridge University Press, 2005.

Finke, Roger, and Rodney Stark. *The Churching of America: 1776–1990*. New Brunswick, NJ: Rutgers University Press, 1992.

Finnis, John. *Natural Law and Natural Rights*. New York: Oxford University Press, 1980.

Fiorina, Morris P., Samuel J. Abrams, and Jeremy Pope. *Culture War? The Myth of a Polarized America*, 2nd. edn. New York: Pearson Education, 2006.

Fish, M. Steven. "Reversal and Erosion of Democratization in the Postcommunist World." Paper presented at American Political Science Association Meeting, Boston, MA, 1998.

Fish, Stanley. "Liberalism Doesn't Exist." *Duke Law Journal* 6 (1987): 997–1001.

Fletcher, George P. "The Instability of Tolerance." In *Toleration: An Elusive Virtue*, ed. David Heyd. Princeton, NJ: Princeton University Press, 1996.

Fogarty, Michael Patrick. *Christian Democracy in Western Europe, 1820–1953* (International Studies of the Committee on International Relations, University of Notre Dame). Notre Dame, IN: University of Notre Dame Press, 1957.

Fotion, N., and Gerard Elfstrom. *Toleration*. Tuscaloosa: University of Alabama Press, 1992.

Freeman, Samuel Richard. *Justice and the Social Contract: Essays on Rawlsian Political Philosophy*. New York: Oxford University Press, 2007.

Freston, Paul. *Evangelicals and Politics in Asia, Africa and Latin America*. New York: Cambridge University Press, 2001.

Fukuyama, Francis. *Trust: Social Virtues and the Creation of Prosperity*. New York: Free Press, 1995.

Fung, Archon. "Democratic Theory and Political Science: A Pragmatic Method of Constructive Engagement." *American Political Science Review* 101, no. 3 (2007): 443–58.

Galeotti, Anna E. *Toleration as Recognition*. New York: Cambridge University Press, 2002.

Galston, William A. *Liberal Pluralism*. Cambridge: Cambridge University Press, 2002.

Liberal Purposes: Goods, Virtues, and Diversity in the Liberal State. Cambridge: Cambridge University Press, 1991.

"Liberal Virtues." *American Political Science Review* 82, no. 4 (1988): 1277–90.

"Two Concepts of Liberalism." *Ethics* 105, no. 3 (1995): 516–34.

"Value Pluralism and Liberal Political Theory." *American Political Science Review* 93, no. 4 (1999): 769–78.

Garnett, Richard W. *Religion, Division, and the First Amendment* (Notre Dame Law School Legal Studies Research Paper 05–23). Notre Dame, IN: Notre Dame Law School, 2004.

Gaus, Gerald F., and Kevin Vallier. "The Roles of Religious Conviction in a Publicly Justified Polity: The Implications of Convergence, Asymmetry and Political Institutions." *Philosophy and Social Criticism* 35, no. 1–2 (2009): 51–76.

Gehler, Michael, Wolfram Kaiser, and Helmut Wohnout, eds. *Christian Democracy in 20th Century Europe*. Cologne: Routledge, 2002.

Genovese, Eugene. *A Consuming Fire*. Athens: University of Georgia Press, 1999.

George, Robert P. *The Clash of Orthodoxies: Law, Religion, and Morality in Crisis*. Wilmington, DE: ISI Books, 2001.

"The Concept of Public Morality." *The American Journal of Jurisprudence* **45**, no. 17 (2000).

Making Men Moral: Civil Liberties and Public Morality. New York: Oxford University Press, 1993.

George, Robert P., ed. *Natural Law, Liberalism, and Morality: Contemporary Essays*. New York: Oxford University Press, 1996.

George, Robert P., ed. *Natural Law Theory: Contemporary Essays*. New York: Oxford University Press, 1992.

George, Robert P, and Christopher Wolfe, eds. *Natural Law and Public Reason*. Washington, D.C.: Georgetown University, 2000.

Gerlich, Peter, and David F.J. Campbell. "Austria: From Compromise to Authoritarianism." In *Conditions of Democracy in Europe, 1919–39: Systematic Case Studies*, ed. Dirk Berg-Schlosser and Jeremy Mitchell. New York: St. Martin's Press, 2000.

Geuss, Raymond. *Philosophy and Real Politics*. Princeton, NJ: Princeton University Press, 2008.

Gill, Anthony. "Religion and Comparative Politics." *Annual Review of Political Science* **4**, no. 1 (2001): 117–38.

Gill, Emily R. *Becoming Free: Autonomy and Diversity in the Liberal Polity*. Lawrence: University Press of Kansas, 2001.

"Religious Organizations, Charitable Choice, and the Limits of the Freedom of Conscience." *Perspectives on Politics* **2**, no. 4 (2004): 741–55.

Glendon, Mary Ann. *Abortion and Divorce in Western Law. The Julius Rosenthal Foundation Lectures, 1986*. Cambridge, MA: Harvard University Press, 1987.

Glendon, Mary Ann, and David Blankenhorn. *Seedbeds of Virtue: Sources of Competence, Character, and Citizenship*. Lanham, MD: Madison Books, 1995.

Glenn, Charles. *The Myth of the Common School*. Amherst: University of Massachusetts Press, 1988.

Goldberg, Michelle. *Kingdom Coming: The Rise of Christian Nationalism*, 1st. edn. New York: W.W. Norton & Co., 2006.

Grant, Ruth W. "Political Theory, Political Science, and Politics." *Political Theory* **30**, no. 4 (2002): 577–95.

Green, John C., James L. Guth, Corwin E. Smidt, and Lyman A. Kellstedt, eds. *Religion and the Culture Wars: Dispatches from the Front*. Lanham, MD: Rowman & Littlefield, 1996.

Green, John C., Mark J. Rozell, and Clyde Wilcox. *The Christian Right in American Politics: Marching toward the Millennium*. Washington, D.C.: Georgetown University, 2003.

Prayers in the Precincts: The Christian Right in the 1998 Elections. Washington, D.C.: Georgetown University, 2000.

Greenawalt, Kent. *Private Consciences and Public Reasons*. New York: Oxford University Press, 1995.

Guth, James L., Lyman A. Kellstedt, John C. Green, and Corwin E. Smidt. "American Fifty/Fifty." *First Things* **116** (2001).

Gutmann, Amy. "Civic Education and Social Diversity." *Ethics* **105** (1995): 557–79.

Gutmann, Amy, and Dennis F. Thompson. *Democracy and Disagreement.* Cambridge, MA: Belknap Press, 1996.

Habermas, Jürgen. "A Conversation about God and the World." In *Time of Transitions,* ed. Ciaran Cronin and Max Pensky, 149–69. Malden, MA: Polity, 2006.

"Equal Treatment of Cultures and the Limits of Postmodern Liberalism." *Journal of Political Philosophy* 13, no. 1 (2005): 1–28.

"A Geneaological Analysis of the Cognitive Content of Morality." In *The Inclusion of the Other: Studies in Political Theory,* ed. Ciaran Cronin and Pablo de Greiff, 75–103. Cambridge, MA: MIT Press, 1999.

The Inclusion of the Other: Studies in Political Theory, ed. Ciaran Cronin and Pablo de Greiff. Cambridge, MA: MIT Press, 1999.

"On the Relations between the Secular Liberal State and Religion." In *Political Theologies: Public Religions in a Post-Secular World,* ed. Hent De Vries and Lawrence Sullivan. New York: Fordham University Press, 2006.

"'Reasonable' Versus 'True,' or the Morality of Worldviews." In *The Inclusion of the Other: Studies in Political Theory,* ed. Ciaran Cronin and Pablo de Greiff, 75–103. Cambridge, MA: MIT Press, 1999.

"Reconciliation through the Public Use of Reason: Remarks on John Rawls's Political Liberalism." *Journal of Political Philosophy* 92, no. 3 (1995): 109–31.

"Reconciliation through the Use of Public Reason." In *The Inclusion of the Other: Studies in Political Theory,* ed. Ciaran Cronin and Pablo de Greiff. Cambridge, MA: MIT Press, 1999.

"Religion in the Public Sphere." *European Journal of Philosophy* 14, no. 1 (2006): 1–25.

The Theory of Communicative Action, vols. I–II, trans. Thomas McCarthy. Boston: Beacon Press, 1984–7.

Halbertal, Moshe. "Autonomy, Toleration, and Group Rights." In *Toleration: An Elusive Virtue,* ed. David Heyd. Princeton, NJ: Princeton University Press, 1996.

Haldane, John. "The Individual, the State and the Common Good." *Social Philosophy and Policy* 13 (1996): 59–79.

Halls, W.D. *Politics, Society and Christianity in Vichy France.* Oxford: Berg, 1995.

Hamburger, Joseph. *John Stuart Mill on Liberty and Control.* Princeton, NJ: Princeton University Press, 1999.

Hamburger, Philip. *Separation of Church and State.* Cambridge, MA: Harvard University Press, 2002.

Hamilton, Richard F. *Who Voted for Hitler?* Princeton, NJ: Princeton University Press, 1982.

Hamzawy, Amr, and Nathan J. Brown. "A Boon or a Bane for Democracy." *Journal of Democracy* 19, no. 3 (2008): 49–54.

Haqqani, Husain, and Hillel Fradkin. "Going Back to the Origins." *Journal of Democracy* 19, no. 3 (2008): 13–18.

Harris, Frederick C. "Something Within: Religion as a Mobilizer of African-American Political Activism." *Journal of Politics* 56, no. 1 (1994): 42–68.

Harris, Sam. *The End of Faith: Religion, Terror, and the Future of Reason.* New York: W.W. Norton & Co., 2004.

Letter to a Christian Nation. New York: Knopf, 2006.

Hatch, Nathan O. *The Democratization of American Christianity.* New Haven: Yale University Press, 1989.

Hauerwas, Stanley. *A Community of Character: Toward a Constructive Christian Social Ethic.* Notre Dame, IN: University of Notre Dame Press, 1981.

Haynes, Jeffrey. *Religion in Global Politics.* New York: Longman, 1998.

Religion in Third World Politics. Boulder, CO: Lynne Rienner Publishers, 1994.

Hefner, Robert. *Civil Islam: Muslims and Democratization in Indonesia.* Princeton, NJ: Princeton University Press, 2000.

Henry, Carl F.H. *The Uneasy Conscience of Modern Fundamentalism.* Grand Rapids, MI: Eerdmans Publishing, 1947.

Hertzke, Allen D. *Freeing God's Children: The Unlikely Alliance for Global Human Rights.* Lanham, MD: Rowman & Littlefield, 2004.

Heslam, Peter. *Creating a Christian Worldview: Abraham Kuyper's Lectures on Calvinism.* Grand Rapids, MI: Eerdmans Publishing, 1998.

Heyd, David. "Introduction." In *Toleration: An Elusive Virtue,* ed. David Heyd. Princeton, NJ: Princeton University Press, 1996.

"Is Toleration a Political Virtue?" In *Toleration and Its Limits,* ed. Melissa Williams. New York: New York University Press, 2008.

Heyd, David, ed. *Toleration: An Elusive Virtue.* Princeton, NJ: Princeton University Press, 1996.

Hirst, Paul Q. "J.N. Figgis, Churches and the State." In *Religion and Democracy,* ed. David Marquand and R. Nettler. Oxford: Blackwell, 2000.

Hirst, Paul Q., ed. *The Pluralist Theory of the State: Selected Writings of G.D.H. Cole, J.N. Figgis, and H.J. Laski.* New York: Routledge, 1989.

Hofman, Roelande H., and Adriaan Hofman. "School Choice, Religious Traditions and School Effectiveness." *International Journal of Education and Religion* 2, no. 2 (2001): 144–65.

Horton, J. "Toleration as a Virtue." In *Toleration: An Elusive Virtue,* ed. David Heyd. Princeton, NJ: Princeton University Press, 1996.

Houska, Joseph J. *Influencing Mass Political Behavior: Elites and Political Subcultures in the Netherlands and Austria.* Berkeley: Institute of International Studies, University of California, 1985.

Hunter, James Davison. *Culture Wars: The Struggle to Define America.* New York: Basic Books, 1991.

Evangelicalism: The Coming Generation. Chicago: University of Chicago Press, 1987.

Hunter, James Davison, and Alan Wolfe. *Is There a Culture War? A Dialogue on Values and American Public Life* (Pew Forum Dialogues on Religion and Public Life). Washington, D.C.: Pew Research Center and Brookings Institution Press, 2006.

Huntington, Samuel P. *The Clash of Civilizations and the Remaking of World Order.* New York: Simon & Schuster, 1996.

"Religion and the Third Wave." In *Rendering unto Caesar: The Religious Sphere in World Politics,* ed. Sabrina Petra Ramet. Washington, D.C.: American University Press, 1995.

The Third Wave: Democratization in the Late Twentieth Century. Norman, OK: University of Oklahoma Press, 1991.

Ignatieff, Michael. "Nationalism and Toleration." In *The Politics of Toleration: Tolerance and Intolerance in Modern Life,* ed. Susan Mendus. Edinburgh: Edinburgh University Press, 1999.

Irving, Ronald Eckford Mill. *Christian Democracy in France.* London: Allen and Unwin, 1973.

The Christian Democratic Parties of Western Europe. London: Allen and Unwin, 1979.

Isaac, Jeffrey C., Matthew F. Filner, and Jason C. Bivins. "American Democracy and the New Christian Right: A Critique of Apolitical Liberalism." In *Democracy's Edges,* ed. Ian Shapiro and Casiano Hacker-Cordon. Cambridge: Cambridge University Press, 1999.

Jellema, D. "Abraham Kuyper's Attack on Liberalism." *Review of Politics* **19**, no. 4 (1957): 472–85.

Jenkins, Philip. *God's Continent: Christianity, Islam, and Europe's Religious Crisis.* New York: Oxford University Press, 2007.

The Next Christendom: The Coming of Global Christianity. New York: Oxford University Press, 2002.

Joireman, Sandra, ed. *For the Sake of Conscience: Some Evangelical Views of the State, Christian Views of the State.* New York: Oxford University Press, 2009.

Jordan, Jeff. "Religious Reasons and Public Reasons." *Public Affairs Quarterly* **11**, no. 3 (1997): 245–54.

Juergensmeyer, Mark. "Holy Orders." *Harvard International Review* **25**, no. 4 (2004): 34–39.

The New Cold War? Religious Nationalism Confronts the Secular State. Berkeley: University of California Press, 1993.

"The New Religious State." *Comparative Politics* **27**, no. 4 (1995): 379–91.

Terror in the Mind of God: The Global Rise of Religious Violence. Berkeley: University of California Press, 2000.

Kalyvas, Stathis N. "Commitment Problems in Emerging Democracies: The Case of Religious Parties." *Comparative Politics* **32**, no. 4 (2000): 379–99.

"Democracy and Religious Politics: Evidence from Belgium." *Comparative Political Studies* **31**, no. 3 (1998): 292–311.

The Rise of Christian Democracy in Europe. Ithaca, NY: Cornell University Press, 1996.

Kekes, John. *Against Liberalism.* Ithaca, NY: Cornell University Press, 1997.

A Case for Conservatism. Ithaca, NY: Cornell University press, 1998.

Kelley, Erin, and Lionel McPherson. "On Tolerating the Unreasonable." *Journal of Political Philosophy* **9**, no. 1 (2001): 38–55.

King, Gary, Robert O. Keohane, and Sidney Verba. *Designing Social Inquiry: Scientific Inference in Qualitative Research.* Princeton, NJ: Princeton University Press, 1994.

King, Preston T. *Toleration.* London: Frank Cass, 1998.

Kinsley, Michael. "Abolish Marriage: Let's Really Get the Government out of Our Bedrooms." *Washington Post,* July 3, 2003, 23.

Klemperer, Klemens von. *Ignaz Seipel: Christian Statesman in a Time of Crisis.* Princeton, NJ: Princeton University Press, 1972.

Klosko, George. *Democratic Procedures and Liberal Consensus*. New York: Oxford University Press, 2000.

Political Obligations. Oxford: Oxford University Press, 2005.

"Rawls's Argument from Political Stability." *Columbia Law Review* **94**, no. 6 (1994): 1883–98.

Koppelman, Andrew. "The Fluidity of Neutrality." *Review of Politics* **66**, no. 4 (2004): 633–48.

Krause, Sharon R. *Civil Passions: Moral Sentiment and Democratic Deliberation*. Princeton, NJ: Princeton University Press, 2008.

Kraynak, Robert P. *Christian Faith and Modern Democracy: God and Politics in the Fallen World*. Notre Dame, IN: University of Notre Dame Press, 2001.

Kukathas, Chandran. *The Liberal Archipelago: A Theory of Diversity and Freedom*. Oxford: Oxford University Press, 2003.

Kuyper, Abraham. "The Antirevolutionary Program." In *Political Order and the Plural Structure of Society*, ed. James W. Skillen and Rockne McCarthy. Atlanta, GA: Scholars Press, 1991.

Lectures on Calvinism. Grand Rapids, MI: Eerdmans Publishing, 2000 [1906].

Kymlicka, Will. *Multicultural Citizenship: A Liberal Theory of Minority Rights*. New York: Clarendon Press, 1995.

Politics in the Vernacular: Nationalism, Multiculturalism, and Citizenship. Oxford and New York: Oxford University Press, 2001.

Kymlicka, Will, and Wayne Norman, eds. *Citizenship in Diverse Societies*. New York: Oxford University Press, 2000.

Lafont, Christina. "Religion in the Public Sphere: Remarks on Habermas's Conception of Public Deliberation in Postsecular Societies." *Constellations* **14**, no. 2 (2007): 239–59.

Larmore, Charles. "The Moral Basis of Political Liberalism." *Journal of Philosophy* **96**, no. 12 (1999): 559–626.

"Political Liberalism." *Political Theory* **18**, no. 3 (1990): 361–91.

Larmore, Charles E. *Patterns of Moral Complexity*. New York: Cambridge University Press, 1987.

Lauersen, John Christian, and Cary J. Nederman, eds. *Beyond the Persecuting Society: Religious Toleration before the Enlightenment*. Philadelphia: University of Pennsylvania Press, 1998.

Laycock, Douglas. "Formal, Substantive, and Disaggregated Neutrality toward Religion." *Depaul Law Review* **39** (1990): 993–1018.

Layman, Geoffrey. *The Great Divide: Religious and Cultural Conflict in American Party Politics*. New York: Columbia University Press, 2001.

Levy, Jacob T. "Liberal Jacobinism." *Ethics* **114** (2004): 318–36.

The Multiculturalism of Fear. New York: Oxford University Press, 2000.

Lijphart, Arend. "Consociational Democracy." *World Politics* **21**, no. 2 (1968): 207–55.

"From the Politics of Accommodation to Adversarial Politics in the Netherlands: A Reassessment." *West European Politics* **12**, no. 1 (1989): 139–53.

Politics of Accommodation. New Haven: Yale University Press, 1967.

Politics of Accommodation, 2nd. edn. Berkeley: University of California Press, 1975.

Linker, Damon. *The Theocons: Secular America under Siege*, 1st. edn. New York: Doubleday, 2006.

Linz, Juan J., and Alfred Stepan. *Problems of Democratic Transition and Consolidation: Southern Europe, South America, and Post-Communist Europe*. Baltimore, MD: Johns Hopkins University Press, 1996.

Lipset, Seymour Martin. "The Indispensability of Political Parties." *Journal of Democracy* 11, no. 1 (2000): 48–55.

"Some Social Requisites of Democracy: Economic Development and Political Legitimacy." *American Political Science Review* 53, no. 1 (1959): 69–105.

Locke, John. *A Letter Concerning Toleration*. Amherst, NY: Prometheus Books, 1990 [1689].

The Reasonableness of Christianity: As Delivered in the Scriptures. New York: Clarendon Press, 1999 [1695].

Lomasky, Loren. "Toward a Liberal Theory of Vice (and Virtue)." In *Civil Society, Democracy and Civic Renewal*, ed. Robert K. Fullinwinder. Lanham, MD: Rowman & Littlefield, 1999.

Lorwin, Val. "Belgium: Religion, Class, and Language in National Politics." In *Political Oppositions in Western Democracies*, ed. Robert A. Dahl. New Haven: Yale University Press, 1966.

"Segmented Pluralism: Ideological Cleavages and Political Cohesion in the Smaller European Democracies." In *Consociational Democracy: Political Accommodation in Segmented Societies*, ed. Kenneth D. McRae. Toronto: McClellan and Stewart, 1974.

Lugo, Luis E., ed. *Religion, Pluralism and Public Life: Abraham Kuyper's Legacy for the Twenty-First Century*. Grand Rapids, MI: Eerdmans Publishing, 2000.

Macedo, Stephen. "Charting Liberal Virtues." In *Virtue*, ed. John William Chapman and William A. Galston. New York: New York University Press, 1992.

"Community, Diversity, and Civic Education: Toward a Liberal Political Science of Group Life." *Social Philosophy and Policy* 13, no. 1 (1996): 240–68.

Diversity and Distrust. Cambridge, MA: Harvard University Press, 2001.

"Liberal Civic Education and Religious Fundamentalism: The Case of God v. John Rawls?" *Ethics* 105, no. 3 (1995): 468–96.

Liberal Virtues. Oxford: Clarendon Press, 1990.

"Transformative Constitutionalism and the Case of Religion: Defending the Moderate Hegemony of Liberalism." *Political Theory* 26, no. 1 (1998): 56–80.

Macedo, Stephen, and Yael Tamir, eds. *Moral and Political Education: Nomos XLIII*. New York: New York University Press, 2002.

MacIntyre, Alasdair C. *After Virtue: A Study in Moral Theory*, 2nd. edn. Notre Dame, IN: University of Notre Dame Press, 1984.

After Virtue: A Study in Moral Theory, 3rd. edn. Notre Dame, IN: University of Notre Dame Press, 2007.

Dependent Rational Animals: Why Human Beings Need the Virtues. Chicago: Open Court, 1999.

Whose Justice? Which Rationality? Notre Dame, IN: University of Notre Dame Press, 1988.

MacMullen, Ian. *Faith in Schools? Autonomy, Citizenship, and Religious Education in the Liberal State.* Princeton, NJ: Princeton University Press, 2007.

Maier, Hans. *Revolution and Church: The Early History of Christian Democracy, 1789–1901.* Notre Dame, IN: University of Notre Dame Press, 1969.

Mainwaring, Scott. "Party Systems in the Third Wave." *Journal of Democracy* 9, no. 3 (1998): 67–80.

Rethinking Parties in the Third Wave of Democratization: The Case of Brazil. Stanford, CA: Stanford University Press, 1999.

Marsden, George M. *Fundamentalism and American Culture*, 2nd. edn. New York: Oxford University Press, 2006.

McCarthy, Rockne, James W. Skillen, and William A. Harper. *Disestablishment a Second Time: Genuine Pluralism for American Schools.* Grand Rapids, MI: Eerdmans Publishing, 1982.

McCarthy, Thomas. "Practical Discourse: On the Relation of Morality to Politics." In *Habermas and the Public Sphere*, ed. Craig J. Calhoun. Cambridge, MA: MIT Press, 1992.

McConnell, Michael W. "Believers as Equal Citizens." In *Obligations of Citizenship and Demands of Faith*, ed. Nancy L. Rosenblum. Princeton, NJ: Princeton University Press, 2000.

"Educational Disestablishment: Why Democratic Values Are Ill-Served by Democratic Control of Schooling." In *Moral and Political Education: Nomos XLIII*, ed. Stephen Macedo and Yael Tamir. New York: New York University Press, 2002.

McGrath, Alister. *Christian Theology: An Introduction.* Cambridge, MA: Blackwell, 1997.

McGreevy, John T. *Catholicism and American Freedom: A History*, 1st edn. New York: W.W. Norton, 2003.

McLeod, Hugh. *Secularisation in Western Europe, 1848–1914.* New York: St. Martin's Press, 2000.

McLeod, Hugh, and Werner Ustorf. *The Decline of Christendom in Western Europe, 1750–2000.* New York: Cambridge University Press, 2003.

McManners, John. *The French Revolution and the Church.* New York: Harper & Row, 1970.

McMillan, James F. "France." In *Political Catholicism in Europe, 1918–1965*, ed. Tom Buchanan and Martin Conway. Oxford: Clarendon Press, 1996.

"'Priest Hits Girl': On the Front Line in the 'War of the Two Frances'." In *Culture Wars: Secular–Catholic Conflict in Nineteenth-Century Europe*, ed. Christopher Clark and Wolfram Kaiser. New York: Cambridge University Press, 2003.

McRae, Kenneth D., ed. *Consociational Democracy: Political Accommodation in Segmented Societies.* Toronto: McClellan and Stewart, 1974.

Mendus, Susan. *Justifying Toleration: Conceptual and Historical Perspectives.* New York: Cambridge University Press, 1988.

"My Brother's Keeper: The Politics of Intolerance." In *The Politics of Toleration: Tolerance and Intolerance in Modern Life,* ed. Susan Mendus. Edinburgh: Edinburgh University Press, 1999.

The Politics of Toleration in Modern Life. Durham, NC: Duke University Press, 2000.

Toleration and the Limits of Liberalism, Issues in Political Theory. Atlantic Highlands, NJ: Humanities Press International, 1989.

Mendus, Susan, ed.. *Justifying Toleration: Conceptual and Historical Perspectives.* Cambridge and New York: Cambridge University Press, 1988.

The Politics of Toleration: Tolerance and Intolerance in Modern Life. Edinburgh: Edinburgh University Press, 1999.

Mendus, Susan, and David Edwards. *On Toleration.* New York: Oxford University Press, 1987.

Milbank, John. *Theology and Social Theory beyond Secular Reason.* Oxford and Cambridge, MA: B. Blackwell, 1991.

Mill, John Stuart. *On Liberty, with the Subjection of Women, and Chapters on Socialism,* ed. Stefan Collini (Cambridge Texts in the History of Political Thought). Cambridge and New York: Cambridge University Press, 1989.

Three Essays on Religion. Amherst, NY: Prometheus Books, 1998.

Miller, W. E., and P.C. Stouthard. "Confessional Attachment and Electoral Behavior." *European Journal of Political Research* 3 (1975): 219–58.

Miller, William Lee. *The First Liberty: America's Foundation in Religious Freedom,* expanded and updated edn. Washington, D.C.: Georgetown University Press, 2003.

Mills, Claudia. "Not a Mere Modus Vivendi." In *The Idea of a Political Liberalism: Essays on Rawls,* ed. Victoria Davion and Clark Wolf. Lanham, MD: Rowman & Littlefield, 2000.

Minkenberg, Michael. "Religion and Public Policy: Institutional, Cultural, and Political Impact on the Shaping of Abortion Policies in Western Europe." *Comparative Political Studies* 35, no. 2 (2002): 221–48.

Monsma, Steven. "Substantive Neutrality as a Basis for Free Exercise–No Establishment Common Ground." *Journal of Church and State* 42, no. 1 (2000): 13–36.

Moore, Barrington. *The Social Origins of Dictatorship and Democracy.* Boston: Beacon Press, 1966.

Morone, James A. *Hellfire Nation: The Politics of Sin in American History.* New Haven: Yale University Press, 2003.

Muirhead, Russell, and Nancy L. Rosenblum. "Political Liberalism vs. 'The Great Game of Politics': The Politics of Political Liberalism." *Perspectives on Politics* 4, no. 1 (2006): 99–108.

Munck, Gerardo L. "The Regime Question: Theory Building in Democracy Studies." *World Politics* 54, no. 1 (2001): 119–44.

Nagel, Thomas. "Moral Conflict and Political Legitimacy." In *Morality, Harm, and the Law,* ed. Gerald Dworkin. Boulder, CO: Westview Press, 1994.

Neuhaus, Richard John. *The Naked Public Square: Religion and Democracy in America*. Grand Rapids, MI: Eerdmans Publishing, 1984.

Newey, Glen. *Virtue, Reason and Toleration: The Place of Toleration in Ethical and Political Philosophy*. Edinburgh: Edinburgh University Press, 1999.

Noll, Mark A. *Religion and American Politics: From the Colonial Period to the 1980s*. New York: Oxford University Press, 1990.

   The Scandal of the Evangelical Mind. Grand Rapids, MI: Eerdmans Publishing, 1994.

O'Donnell, Guillermo, and Phillippe C Schmitter. *Transitions from Authoritarian Rule: Tentative Conclusions about Uncertain Democracies*. Baltimore, MD: Johns Hopkins University Press, 1986.

Oberdiek, Hans. *Tolerance: Between Forbearance and Acceptance*. Lanham, MD: Rowman & Littlefield, 2001.

Okin, Susan Moller. "Comment on Nancy Rosenblum's 'Feminist Perspectives on Civil Society and Government'." In *Civil Society and Government*, ed. Nancy L. Rosenblum and Harry Post. Princeton, NJ: Princeton University Press, 2002.

Ottaway, Marina, and Amr Hamzawy. *Getting to Pluralism: Political Actors in the Arab World*. Washington, D.C.: Carnegie Endowment for International Peace, 2009.

Owen, J. Judd. *Religion and the Demise of Liberal Rationalism: The Foundational Crisis of the Separation of Church and State*. Chicago: University of Chicago Press, 2001.

Parkinson, John. *Deliberating in the Real World*. Oxford: Oxford University Press, 2006.

Paul, Harry W. *The Second Ralliement: The Rapprochement between Church in and State in France in the Twentieth Century*. Washington, D.C.: Catholic University of America Press, 1967.

Perry, Michael J. *Religion in Politics: Constitutional and Moral Perspectives*. New York: Oxford University Press, 1997.

   Toward a Theory of Human Rights: Religion, Law, Courts. Cambridge and New York: Cambridge University Press, 2007.

Pharr, Susan J., and Robert D. Putnam. *Disaffected Democracies: What's Troubling the Trilateral Countries?* Princeton, NJ: Princeton University Press, 2000.

Phillips, David L. *From Bullets to Ballots: Violent Muslim Movements in Transition*. New Brunswick, NJ: Transaction Publishers, 2009.

Phillips, Kevin P. *American Theocracy: The Peril and Politics of Radical Religion, Oil, and Borrowed Money in the 21st Century*. New York: Viking, 2006.

Phillips, Melanie. *Londonistan*. New York: Encounter Books, 2006.

Pocock, J.G.A. *The Machiavellian Moment: Florentine Political Thought and the Atlantic Republican Tradition*. Princeton, NJ: Princeton University Press, 1975.

Prinsterer, Groen van. "Unbelief and Revolution." In *Political Order and the Plural Structure of Society*, ed. James W. Skillen and Rockne McCarthy. Atlanta, GA: Scholars Press, 1991.

   "Unbelief and Revolution." In *Groen Van Prinsterer's Lectures on Unbelief and Revolution*, ed. Harry Van Dyke. Ontario: Wedge Publishing Foundation, 1989 [1847].

Przeworski, Adam. *Democracy and the Market: Political and Economic Reforms in Eastern Europe and Latin America.* Cambridge: Cambridge University Press, 1991.

"Minimalist Conception of Democracy: A Defense." In *Democracy's Value*, ed. Ian Shapiro and Casiano Hacker-Cordon. Cambridge: Cambridge University Press, 1999.

Przeworski, Adam, and Fernando Limongi. "Modernization: Theories and Facts." *World Politics* **49**, no. 2 (1997): 155–83.

Przeworski, Adam, and John Sprague. *Paper Stones: A History of Electoral Socialism.* Chicago: Chicago University Press, 1986.

Putnam, Robert D. *Bowling Alone: The Collapse and Revival of American Community.* New York: Simon & Schuster, 2000.

Making Democracy Work: Civic Traditions in Modern Italy. Princeton, NJ: Princeton University Press, 1993.

Quinn, Philip. "Religious Citizens and the Limits of Public Reason." *Modern Schoolman* **78** (2001): 105–24.

Rath, R. John. "The Deterioration of Democracy in Austria, 1927–1932." *Austrian History Yearbook* **27** (1996): 213–59.

"The Dollfuss Ministry: The Demise of the Nationalrat." *Austrian History Yearbook* **32** (2001): 125–47.

"The Dollfuss Ministry: The Democratic Prelude." *Austrian History Yearbook* **39** (1998): 161–94.

"The Dollfuss Ministry: The Intensification of Animosities and the Drift toward Authoritarianism." *Austrian History Yearbook* **30** (1999): 65–101.

Ravitch, Diane. *The Language Police: How Pressure Groups Restrict What Students Learn.* New York: Vintage Books, 2004.

Rawls, John. *Collected Papers*, ed. Samuel Richard Freeman. Cambridge, MA: Harvard University Press, 1999.

"The Idea of Public Reason Revisited." *University of Chicago Law Review* **64**, no. 3 (1997): 765–807.

"The Idea of Public Reason Revisited." In *The Law of Peoples*, ed. John Rawls. Cambridge: Harvard University Press, 1999.

"Justice as Fairness: Political Not Metaphysical." In *John Rawls: Collected Papers*, ed. Samuel Freeman. Cambridge: Harvard University Press, 1999.

Lectures on the History of Political Philosophy. Cambridge, MA: Harvard University Press, 2007.

"Outline of a Procedure for Ethics." *Philosophical Review* **60** (1951): 177–97.

Political Liberalism, 2nd. edn. New York: Columbia University Press, 1996.

"Political Liberalism: Reply to Habermas." *Journal of Political Philosophy* **92**, no. 3 (1995): 132–80.

A Theory of Justice. Cambridge, MA: Belknap Press of Harvard University Press, 1971.

A Theory of Justice, rev. edn. Cambridge, MA: Harvard University Press, 1999.

Rawls, John, ed. *The Law of Peoples.* Cambridge, MA: Harvard University Press, 1999.

Raz, Joseph. *The Morality of Freedom.* New York: Oxford University Press, 1986.

Rooden, Peter van. "Religious Developments in the Netherlands, *c.* 1750–2000." In *The Decline of Christendom in Western Europe, 1750–2000*, ed. Hugh McLeod and Werner Ustorf. New York: Cambridge University Press, 2003.

Roof, Wade Clark, and William McKinney. *American Mainline Religion.* New Brunswick, NJ: Rutgers University Press, 1994.

Rorty, Richard. "The Moral Purposes of the University: An Exchange." *Hedgehog Review* **2**, no. 3 (2000): 106–15.

——. "Religion as a Conversation-Stopper." In *Philosophy and Social Hope*, ed. Richard Rorty. New York: Penguin Books, 1999.

——. "Religion in the Public Square: A Reconsideration." *Journal of Religious Ethics* **31**, no. 1 (2003): 141–49.

Rosen, Christine. *Preaching Eugenics: Religious Leaders and the American Eugenics Movement.* New York: Oxford University Press, 2004.

Rosenblum, Nancy L. "The Democracy of Everyday Life." In *Liberalism without Illusions: Essays on Liberal Theory and the Political Vision of Judith N. Shklar*, ed. Judith N. Shklar and Bernard Yack. Chicago: University of Chicago Press, 1996.

——. *Membership and Morals: The Personal Uses of Pluralism in America.* Princeton, NJ: Princeton University Press, 1998.

——. *On the Side of the Angels: An Appreciation of Parties and Partisanship.* Princeton, NJ: Princeton University Press, 2008.

——. "Pluralism and Democratic Education: Stopping Short by Stopping with Schools." In *Moral and Political Education: Nomos XLIII*, ed. Stephen Macedo and Yael Tamir. New York: New York University Press, 2002.

——. "Political Parties as Membership Groups." *Columbia Law Review* **100**, no. 3 (2000): 813–44.

——. "Religious Parties, Religious Political Identity, and the Cold Shoulder of Liberal Democratic Thought." *Ethical Theory and Moral Practice: An International Forum* **6**, no. 1 (2003): 23–53.

Rosenblum, Nancy L., ed. *Obligations of Citizenship and the Demands of Faith.* Princeton, NJ: Princeton University Press, 2000.

Ross, Ronald J. *Beleaguered Tower: The Dilemma of Political Catholicism in Wilhelmine Germany.* Notre Dame, IN: University of Notre Dame Press, 1976.

Rousseau, Jean Jacques. *On the Social Contract*, trans. Donald Cress. Indianapolis: Hackett Publishing, 1987 [1762].

Rozell, Mark J., and Clyde Wilcox. *God at the Grass Roots, 1996: The Christian Right in the American Elections.* Lanham, MD: Rowman & Littlefield, 1997.

Rozell, Mark J., and Clyde Wilcox, eds. *God at the Grassroots.* Lanham, MD: Rowman & Littlefield, 1996.

Rueschemeyer, Dietrich, Evelyn Huber, and John D. Stephens. *Capitalist Development and Democracy.* Chicago: Chicago University Press, 1992.

Rustow, Dankart A. "Transitions to Democracy: Toward a Dynamic Model." *Comparative Politics* **2**, no. 3 (1970): 337–63.

Ruud, Kole. "The Societal Position of Christian Democracy in the Netherlands." In *Christian Democracy in the European Union*, ed. Emiel Lamberts. Leuven: Leuven University Press, 1997.

Sandel, Michael J. *Democracy's Discontent: America in Search of a Public Philosophy.* Cambridge, MA: Harvard University Press, 1996.

———. *Liberalism and the Limits of Justice.* Cambridge and New York: Cambridge University Press, 1982.

Scanlon, T.M. "The Difficulty of Tolerance." In *Toleration: An Elusive Virtue,* ed. David Heyd. Princeton, NJ: Princeton University Press, 1996.

———. "Rawls on Justification." In *The Cambridge Companion to Rawls,* ed. Samuel Freeman. Cambridge: Cambridge University Press, 2002.

Schattschneider, Elmer Eric. *The Semi-Sovereign People.* New York: Holt, Rinehart, and Winston, 1960.

Schindler, Jeanne Heffernan. *Christianity and Civil Society: Catholic and Neo-Calvinist Perspectives.* Lanham, MD: Lexington Books, 2008.

Schorske, Carl. "Politics in a New Key: An Austrian Triptych." *Journal of Modern History* **39**, no. 4 (1967): 343–86.

Schumpeter, Joseph A. *Capitalism, Socialism and Democracy.* New York: Harper and Brothers, 1942.

Schwedler, Jillian. *Faith in Moderation: Islamist Parties in Jordan and Yemen.* New York: Cambridge University Press, 2006.

Shapiro, Ian. "Enough of Deliberation: Politics Is About Interests and Power." In *Deliberative Politics: Essays on Democracy and Disagreement,* ed. Stephen Macedo. New York: Oxford University Press, 1999.

———. *The Flight from Reality in the Human Sciences.* Princeton, NJ: Princeton University Press, 2005.

———. "Problems, Methods, and Theories in the Study of Politics, or What's Wrong with Political Science and What to Do About It." *Political Theory* **30**, no. 4 (2002): 596–619.

———. *The State of Democratic Theory.* Princeton, NJ: Princeton University Press, 2003.

Shaw, Brian J. "Habermas and Religious Inclusion." *Political Theory* **27**, no. 5 (1999): 634–66.

Sher, George. *Beyond Neutrality: Perfectionism and Politics.* Cambridge and New York: Cambridge University Press, 1997.

Shields, Jon A. *The Democratic Virtues of the Christian Right.* Princeton, NJ: Princeton University Press, 2009.

Shklar, Judith. *Ordinary Vices.* Cambridge, MA: Harvard University Press, 1984.

Sider, Ronald J. *The Scandal of Evangelical Politics.* Grand Rapids, MI: Baker, 2008.

Skillen, James W. *In Pursuit of Justice: Christian-Democratic Explorations.* Lanham, MD: Rowman & Littlefield, 2004.

Skillen, James W., and Rockne McCarthy, eds. *Political Order and the Plural Structure of Society.* Atlanta, GA: Scholars Press, 1991.

Smith, Christian. *Christian America? What Evangelicals Really Want.* Berkeley: University of California Press, 2000.

———. *Moral, Believing Animals: Human Personhood and Culture.* New York: Oxford University Press, 2003.

Smith, Christian, ed. *Disruptive Religion: The Force of Faith in Social-Movement Activism.* New York: Routledge, 1996.

Smith, Christian. *The Secular Revolution: Power, Interests, and Conflict in the Secularization of American Public Life.* Berkeley: University of California Press, 2003.

Smith, Christian, and Michael Emerson. *American Evangelicalism: Embattled and Thriving.* Chicago: University of Chicago Press, 1998.

Smith, Helmut Walser. *German Nationalism and Religious Conflict: Culture, Ideology, Politics, 1870–1914.* Princeton, NJ: Princeton University Press, 1995.

Smith, Steven D. "The 'Secular,' The 'Religious,' and the 'Moral': What Are We Talking About?" *Wake Forest Law Review* 36 (2001): 487–510.

Sperber, Jonathan. *The Kaiser's Voters: Electors and Elections in Imperial Germany.* Cambridge and New York: Cambridge University Press, 1997.

Popular Catholicism in Nineteenth-Century Germany. Princeton, NJ: Princeton University Press, 1984.

Spinner-Halev, Jeff. "Hinduism, Christianity, and Liberal Religious Toleration." *Political Theory* 33, no. 1 (2005): 28–57.

Surviving Diversity: Religion and Democratic Citizenship. Baltimore, MD: Johns Hopkins University Press, 2000.

Spragens, Thomas A. *Civic Liberalism: Reflections on Our Democratic Ideals.* Lanham, MD: Rowman & Littlefield, 1999.

Stark, Rodney. *Exploring the Religious Life.* Baltimore, MD: Johns Hopkins University Press, 2004.

For the Glory of God: How Monotheism Led to Reformations, Science, Witch-Hunts, and the End of Slavery. Princeton, NJ: Princeton University Press, 2003.

Stark, Rodney, and William Sims Bainbridge. *The Future of Religion: Secularization, Revival, and Cult Formation.* Berkeley: University of California Press, 1985.

Stark, Rodney, and Roger Finke. *Acts of Faith: Explaining the Human Side of Religion.* Berkeley: University of California Press, 2000.

Stepan, Alfred. *Arguing Comparative Politics.* New York: Oxford University Press, 2001.

"Religion, Democracy, and the 'Twin Tolerations'." *Journal of Democracy* 11, no. 4 (2000): 37–58.

Steyn, Mark. *America Alone: The End of the World as We Know It.* Lanham, MD: Regnery, 2006.

Sullivan, Andrew. *The Conservative Soul: How We Lost It, How to Get It Back,* 1st. edn. New York: HarperCollins Publishers, 2006.

Sullivan, Kathleen. "Religion and Liberal Democracy." *University of Chicago Law Review* 59, no. 1 (1992): 195–223.

Sunstein, Cass. "The Law of Group Polarization." *Journal of Political Philosophy* 10 (2002): 175–95.

Suval, Stanley. *Electoral Politics in Wilhelmine Germany.* Chapel Hill: University of North Carolina Press, 1985.

Swaine, Lucas. "Deliberate and Free: Heteronomy in the Public Square." *Philosophy and Social Criticism* 35, no. 1–2 (2009): 183–213.

The Liberal Conscience: Politics and Principle in a World of Religious Pluralism. New York: Columbia University Press, 2006.

Swatos, W.H., and K.J. Christiano. "Secularization Theory: The Course of a Concept." *Sociology of Religion* **60**, no. 20 (2000): 209–28.

Talisse, Robert. "Dilemmas of Public Reason: Pluralism, Polarization, and Instability." In *The Legacy of John Rawls*, ed. Thom Brooks and Fabian Freyenhagen. New York: Continuum, 2005.

Taylor, Charles. *A Secular Age.* Cambridge, MA: Harvard University Press, 2007.

Taylor, Charles, and Amy Gutmann. *Multiculturalism: Examining the Politics of Recognition.* Princeton, NJ: Princeton University Press, 1994.

Tepe, Sultan. *Beyond Sacred and Secular: Politics of Religion in Israel and Turkey.* Stanford, CA: Stanford University Press, 2008.

Thomas, Cal, and Ed Dobson. *Blinded by Might: Why the Religious Right Can't Save America.* Grand Rapids, MI: Zondervan, 2000.

Thompson, Dennis F. *The Democratic Citizen: Social Science and Democratic Theory in the Twentieth Century.* London: Cambridge University Press, 1970.

Thomson, Judith Jarvis. "Abortion." *Boston Review: A Political and Literary Forum* (Summer 2005): 11–15.

Thurlings, J.M.G. "Pluralism and Assimilation in the Netherlands." *International Journal of Comparative Sociology* **20**, no. 1–2 (1979): 82–100.

Tibi, Bassam. "Why They Can't Be Democratic." *Journal of Democracy* **19**, no. 3 (2008): 43–48.

Tocqueville, Alexis de. *Democracy in America*, trans. Harvey C Mansfield and Delba Winthrop. Chicago: University of Chicago Press, 2000.

Tomasi, John. "Civic Education and Ethical Subservience: From *Mozert* to *Santa Fe* and Beyond." In *Moral and Political Education: Nomos XLIII*, ed. Stephen Macedo and Yael Tamir. New York: New York University Press, 2002.

Liberalism beyond Justice. Princeton, NJ: Princeton University Press, 2001.

"Why Political Liberals Should Be Compassionate Conservatives." Paper presented to the American Political Science Association, Washington, D.C., September 2003.

Tuck, Richard. "Scepticism and Toleration in the Seventeenth Century." In *Justifying Toleration: Conceptual and Historical Perspectives*, ed. Susan Mendus. New York: Cambridge University Press, 1988.

Verba, Sidney, Kay Lehman Schlozman, and Henry E. Brady. *Voice and Equality: Civic Voluntarism in American Politics.* Cambridge, MA: Harvard University Press, 1995.

Volokh, Eugene. "The Mechanisms of the Slippery Slope." *Harvard Law Review* **116** (2003): 1026–137.

Wald, Kenneth, Silverman Adam, and Kevin Fridy. "Making Sense of Religion in Public Life." *Annual Review of Political Science* **8** (2005): 121–43.

Waldron, Jeremy. *God, Locke, and Equality: Christian Foundations in Locke's Political Thought.* Cambridge: Cambridge University Press, 2002.

"Toleration and Reasonableness." In *The Culture of Toleration in Diverse Societies: Reasonable Toleration*, ed. Catriona McKinnon and Dario Castiglione. New York: Manchester University Press, 2003.

Walford, Geoffrey. "Building Identity through Communities of Practice: Evangelical Christian Schools in the Netherlands." *International Journal of Education and Religion* **2**, no. 2 (2001): 126–44.

Walker, Graham. "Illusory Pluralism, Inexorable Establishment." In *Obligations of Citizenship and the Demands of Faith*, ed. Nancy L. Rosenblum. Princeton, NJ: Princeton University Press, 2000.

Walzer, Michael. *On Toleration. The Castle Lectures in Ethics, Politics, and Economics*. New Haven: Yale University Press, 1997.

Warner, Carolyn M. "Religion and the Political Organization of Muslims in Europe." *Perspectives on Politics* 4, no. 3 (2006): 457–79.

Warnock, Mary. "The Limits of Toleration." In *On Toleration*, ed. Susan Mendus and David Edwards. Oxford: Clarendon Press, 1987.

Warren, Mark. *Democracy and Association*. Princeton, NJ: Princeton University Press, 2001.

Webster, Richard A. *Christian Democracy in Italy, 1860–1960*. London: Hollis & Carter, 1961.

The Cross and the Fasces: Christian Democracy and Fascism in Italy. Stanford, CA: Stanford University Press, 1960.

Weeks, David L. "The Uneasy Politics of Modern Evangelicalism." *Christian Scholar's Review* 30, no. 4 (2001): 403–18.

Weithman, Paul J. "Deliberative Character." *Journal of Political Philosophy* 13, no. 3 (2005): 263–83.

"Religion and the Liberalism of Reasoned Respect." In *Religion and Contemporary Liberalism*, ed. Paul J. Weithman. Notre Dame, IN: University of Notre Dame Press, 1997.

Religion and the Obligations of Citizenship. Cambridge: Cambridge University Press, 2002.

"Review of George Klosko, *Democratic Procedures and Liberal Consensus*." *Ethics* 112, no. 3 (2002): 621–26.

"Review of Samuel Freeman, *Justice and the Social Contract: Essays on Rawlsian Political Philosophy*." *Notre Dame Philosophical Reviews* (2007), available online at http://ndpr.nd.edu/review.cfm?id=10405.

Weithman, Paul J. ed. *Religion and Contemporary Liberalism*. Notre Dame, IN: University of Notre Dame Press, 1997.

Wenar, Leif. "Political Liberalism: An Internal Critique." *Ethics* 106, no. 1 (1995): 32–62.

Wilcox, Clyde. "Of Movements and Metaphors: The Co-Evolution of the Christian Right and the GOP." In *The Christian Conservative Movement and American Democracy: Evangelicals, the Religious Right, and American Politics*, ed. Steve Brint and Jean Schroedel. New York: Russell Sage Foundation, 2009.

Onward Christian Soldiers? The Religious Right in American Politics. Boulder, CO: Westview Press, 1996.

Williams, Bernard. "Tolerating the Intolerable." In *The Politics of Toleration: Tolerance and Intolerance in Modern Life*, ed. Susan Mendus. Edinburgh: Edinburgh University Press, 1999.

"Toleration: An Impossible Virtue?" In *Toleration: An Elusive Virtue*, ed. David Heyd. Princeton, NJ: Princeton University Press, 1997.

Williams, Melissa. "Tolerable Liberalism." In *Minorities within Minorities: Equality, Rights, and Diversity*, ed. Avigail I. Eisenberg and Jeff Spinner-Halev. Cambridge and New York: Cambridge University Press, 2005.

Wills, Garry. "The Day the Enlightenment Went Out." *The New York Times*, November 4, 2001, 25.

Wolfe, Alan. *Moral Freedom: The Impossible Idea That Defines the Way We Live Now*, 1st. edn. New York: W.W. Norton, 2001.

One Nation, after All: What Middle-Class Americans Really Think about, God, Country, Family, Racism, Welfare, Immigration, Homosexuality, Work, the Right, the Left, and Each Other. New York: Viking, 1998.

The Transformation of American Religion: How We Actually Live Our Faith. New York: Free Press, 2003.

Wolff, R.J., and J.K. Hoensch, eds. *Catholics, the State and the European Radical Right 1919–1945*. Boulder, CO: Westview Press, 1987.

Wolterstorff, Nicholas. "Do Christians Have Good Reasons for Supporting Liberal Democracy?" *Modern Schoolman* **78** (January/March 2001): 229–48.

"Why We Should Reject What Liberalism Tells Us." In *Religion and Contemporary Liberalism*, ed. Paul J. Weithman. Notre Dame, IN: University of Notre Dame Press, 1997.

Wuthnow, Robert. *The Restructuring of American Religion: Society and Faith since World War II*. Princeton, NJ: Princeton University Press, 1988.

"The United States: Bridging the Privileged and the Marginalized." In *Democracies in Flux: The Evolution of Social Capital in Contemporary Society*, ed. Robert D. Putnam. Oxford: Oxford University Press, 2002.

Yamane, David. "Secularization on Trial: In Defense of a Neosecularization Paradigm." *Journal for the Scientific Study of Religion* **36**, no. 1 (1997): 109–23.

Yavuz, M. Hakan. *Secularism and Muslim Democracy in Europe*. Cambridge: Cambridge University Press, 2009.

Zagorin, Perez. *How the Idea of Religious Toleration Came to the West*. Princeton, NJ: Princeton University Press, 2003.

Zimmerman, Ekkart. "Political Breakdown and the Process of National Consensus Formation: On the Collapse of the Weimar Republic in Comparative Perspective." In *Research on Democracy and Society: Democratization in Eastern and Western Europe*, ed. Frederick Weil. Greenwich, CT: JAI Press, 1993.

Zwart, Rutger S. "Christian Democracy and Political Order in the Netherlands." In *Christian Democracy in the European Union*, ed. Emiel Lamberts. Leuven: Leuven University Press, 1997.

Index